MEMORIES

OF

MY LIFE AND TIMES

MEMORIES
OF
MY LIFE AND TIMES

BIPIN CHANDRA PAL

GYAN

Published by

Gyan Publishing House
5, Ansari Road
Daryaganj, New Delhi-110002
Phone: 011-47034999, 9811692060
E-mail: books@gyanbooks.com

Distribution Network
gyanbooks.com
India, USA, Canada, UK, Australia, France

ISBN: 978-81-212-8242-0 (PB)
First Published, 1932

2nd Impression 2023

Printed at: Gyan Press, Delhi.

MEMORIES OF MY LIFE AND TIMES
Author: BIPIN CHANDRA PAL

Memories of My Life and Times

MEMORIES

OF

MY LIFE AND TIMES

BIPIN CHANDRA PAL.

*

CALCUTTA :

MODERN BOOK AGENCY

10, COLLEGE SQUARE

1932

TO MY
SONS, DAUGHTERS, THEIR WIVES AND HUSBANDS
AND THEIR CHILDREN
THESE MEMORIES
OF
MY OWN INFANCY, BOYHOOD AND YOUTH ARE
DEDICATED

PUBLISHERS' NOTE

Mr. Bipinchandra Pal has been an outstanding figure in Bengal for well-nigh half-a-century. His activities have been enormous and many-sided ; and his contribution to the cultural life and thought of the Bengalee people has been profound. As one of the foremost leaders of the Nationalist Movement in India in the first quarter of this century, his influence has been India-wide ; as one of the bravest standard-bearers of the gospel of freedom in social and religious spheres from his very early youth, he has been a most virile force in the protestant Brahmo Samaj ; as an incisive and logical thinker, as a masterly and profound expositor of the deepest problems, political, social, philosophical, religious, as an accomplished stylist in the domain of serious literature, he has hardly had an equal in Modern India. And now in the mellowing years of his maturity when he has retired from the din and bustle of active public life, he has rightly come to be regarded as an embodiment of all that is best in Indian life and culture, in all its simplicity, catholicity and grandeur. In Bipinchandra the man of action has harmonized most wonderfully with the man of contemplation.

It is a source of real gratification to us that we are able to place before the public the memories and reminiscences of this great man from his own pen. And we have no doubt that these memories will be eagerly read and appreciated by all who have any feeling for the life and culture-history of our motherland in all its bearings for the last half-a-century ; for perhaps none is better fitted to write on this period than one of its foremost actors, Mr. Bipinchandra Pal, with all his intimate knowledge of events and acute powers of observation.

We are now laying the first volume of these memories in the hands of the public, and the two succeeding volumes are under preparation, and we hope to be able shortly to publish them. With the publication of the three volumes of Mr. Pal's memories completed, we shall really consider that we have accomplished a worthy task in successfully achieving a work of abiding value to our nation.

ॐ

श्रीश्रीगुरवे नमः।

FOREWORD

The individual is not an isolated unit, but is part of a whole, composed of many other individuals. This whole is called Society. The relation between the individual and the Social Whole of which he is a part, is an organic relation. It means that the individual can fulfil himself only in and through Society, even as this Society can fulfil its collective life only in and through the fulfilment of the individual ends of the numerous humans composing it. The individual and the Society to which he belongs, are, thus, inter-dependent upon one another for their self-fulfilment.

All the things that differentiate Man from the rest of the creation, so far as we know it,—his reason, his emotions, his will, his power of knowing himself and his capacity for love and self-sacrifice,—all these are evolved in and through his social life and relations. The individual finds his highest self-expression and self-realisation in and through his Society, even as his Society finds its highest expression and realisation in and through the life and activities of the individuals composing it. The individual and his Society are like the warp and woof of the social fabric. To truly understand the individual, we must see him in and through his social setting ; and to correctly appraise social values, we must see Society in and through the life and aspirations, the struggles and achievements, of its individual human units.

The value of the life-story of any individual consists, therefore, not in itself, however great or noble that life may be, but only as a revelation, an explanation and interpretation of the hidden currents of social history and evolution that, entering into it, shapes and moulds it to its universal end. That end is the Education of the Race. In this view, biographies of individuals become both the texts and the commentaries of Universal Social Revelations. The real value of the life-story of any individual is, from this point of view, not in itself, but in the elucidation of social life and movements that play around that life.

At one time, History was believed to be nothing more or less than the Biographies of the Great Men that stood on the top-wave of the social movements of their time. That was the view of the old individualism. The organic conception of both individual and social life and evolution had not been fully grasped as yet.

But we now know that though every human is, in himself, a measure of absolute values, these values are discovered not in the life of the individual, considered apart from the general life of the society about him, but always in and through his social environments. The thief, the murderer, the "vilest vermin among humans," men and women who know and understand nothing more than what their primitive instincts and passions reveal, and who really do not understand even their own impulses and movements—all these do not stand by themselves, but are warps and woofs of their social life. No one who does not understand the nature and trend of the Society to which these "waifs and strays" belong, can really understand these "derelicts of humanity." The modern Science of Society or Sociology, has, therefore, called into being modern Realism in Literature. The true obect of this Realism is not to paint the prurient vices of individual life and character in living colours, but really to bring out the universal elements of goodness in our common humanity, from underneath the accumulated debris of social tyranny and injustice which are the real parents of all our personal sins and crimes. Society is reflected in the life of the individual, even as the individual, reacting upon his social environments, contributes to its growth or decay, as the case may be.

The life of an individual, however humble it may be, and howmuchsoever mean may be its value if taken in itself, is, therefore, found to have a worth far transcending its outer qualities, when studied as an expression and illustration of the general social movements about him. From this view-point every biography is a social history, and challenges the attention of all those who desire to study and understand the times of that individual.

The following pages are written in this view only. The personal history is meant only to furnish a concrete and realistic back-ground of the unseen, and oftentimes unappreciated, trends and tendencies of his times.

The period covered by these seventy-two years, 1860—1932, reveals a most important epoch of modern Indian History. These seventy-two years have seen mighty transformations in Indian thought and society. The social life of seventy-two years ago cannot even be conjectured from that of to-day. The social standards, as well as the mental and moral outlook of the present generation of Indians, even in far distant rural areas, among unlettered peasants, have little similarity with those of their fathers and grand-fathers. These seventy-two years have seen first, a violent religious and social revolt, and then, a tremendous political upheaval which would stagger our grand-fathers, if not indeed even our fathers, if they could come back to life to-day.

And the writer of these Memories has had the proud privilege of witnessing, and indeed personally sharing, more or less in his own humble way, the toils and turmoils through which these mighty transformations in Indian thought and life have taken place. And he has tried to use the thread of his personal life only to weave together the history of his times, and not present that life as something of any value, in itself, to the world. He does not hold his personal life to be in any way different from the personal life of thousands of his contemporaries, any one of which might, more or less, furnish as good, if not perhaps in some cases, a much better, structure for sizing and warping the history of these seventy-two years.

KALIGHAT, CALCUTTA,
May 15, 1932.

Bipin Chandra Pal

CONTENTS

Page.

CHAPTER I.

Birth and Parentage 1

CHAPTER II.

Home Influence and Early Education 10

CHAPTER III.

School Days 22

CHAPTER IV.

Domestic Life in Sylhet During My School-Days ... 39

CHAPTER V.

Social Life in Sylhet During My School-Days ... 63

CHAPTER VI.

Village Life During My School-Days 94

CHAPTER VII.

Early Religious Environments and Education ... 119

CHAPTER VIII.

Administration and Officialdom Sixty Years Ago ... 140

CHAPTER IX.

The Closing Years of My School Life 161

CHAPTER X.

Student-Life in Calcutta 180

CHAPTER XI.

The Birth of Our New Nationalism 226

Page.

CHAPTER XII.

The New Stage and National Songs 249

CHAPTER XIII.

Nabagopal Mitra and the Hindu Mela 259

CHAPTER XIV.

Political and Administrative Changes During My College Days 269

CHAPTER XV.

How I Came to the Brahmo Samaj 295

CHAPTER XVI.

Father and Son 324

CHAPTER XVII.

The Sadharana Brahmo Samaj 332

CHAPTER XVIII.

Orissa Fifty Years Ago 351

CHAPTER XIX.

"National" Education and Public Activities in Sylhet 364

CHAPTER XX.

Madras Fifty Years Ago 386

CHAPTER XXI.

Lord Ripon and the New Political Awakening ... 406

CHAPTER XXII.

Hindu Religious Revival and Social Reaction ... 421

CHAPTER XXIII.

The Triumph of Father Love 444

Sylhet town from the other side of the river Surma.

CHAPTER I.

BIRTH AND PARENTAGE

I was born in village Poil, in the District of Sylhet, on Kartik 22, *Shakabda* 1779, (1265 Bengal era) corresponding to November 7, 1858. Sylhet is now a part of the administrative province of Assam; but at the time of my birth, and for many years afterwards during the whole of my boyhood, it was a Bengal District in the Commissionership of Dacca. Assam too was then a part of the Lieutenant-Governorship of Bengal, under a Commissioner. When the Commissionership of Assam was made into a separate Province under a Chief Commissioner in 1874, Sylhet and Cachar were transferred to the new Administration very much against the wishes of the people of these Districts, who are all Bengalees and are still crying out for re-union with Bengal.

Poil is a large-sized village, one of the largest, in the District of Sylhet. It has a large population of Brahmins and Kayasthas, two of the higher castes of the District, with a fair proportion of the other Hindu castes. It has also a large Mahomedan population, headed by a zemindar family, who are connected with almost every aristocratic Mahomedan family of Tippera, Mymensing and Dacca.

It is difficult to say off-hand who were the original or aboriginal natives of this District but the family history of most of the higher caste Hindus, at present resident in the District, clearly shows that their forefathers came and settled here in some long forgotten past from Bengal, particularly from that part of it known to old Bengalee geography as Dakshin Rarh. And it seems that our family was the very first, among the higher class Hindus of Poil, to come and settle here. I read in our family history and genealogical record that one Hiranya Pal came with his wife from a village called Mangalkot in Burdwan District and took up his abode on the "south bank of the river Booriganga" and gave the name of Poil to his new settlement. There is no "Booriganga" now in the neighbourhood of Poil. Perhaps the river "Khoai," which flows by the village at a distance of about a couple of miles from it, was called "Booriganga" at one time; or it may have been mistaken for the river of that name which flows by Dacca and which name must have been familiar to the wanderer from distant Rarh. My father, Ram Chandra Pal, stood twenty-fourth in a direct line from this Hiranya Pal, reputed to be the founder of the clan of Pals of Poil. The village of Mangalkot still exists in the Katwa Sub-Division of the Burdwan District. I made enquiries of my friend Babu Kumudranjan Mullik, the well-known Bengalee poet, who is familiar with Mangalkot and its neighbouring villages, whether there were any Pals of the Batsya Gotra in that village. He wrote to me to say that though there were no Pals now in Mangalkot, a big tank there still goes by their name as "Paler Dighi," from which it appears that at one time there must have been a rich and influential family of Pals in that locality.

My father was educated in Persian and was reputed to be a good Persian scholar according to the standards of those times. Persian was the court-language in Bengal in those days, and his proficiency in it secured for my father, first, the position of a clerk and then of Peshkar or bench-clerk in the court of the Sadar-Ala or Subordinate Judge of Dacca. He was living at Dacca at the time of the Mutiny, and I heard it from him that on the Sunday morning, when the sepoys in the Dacca Fort were betrayed by one of their own men and cut down to pieces by the British, the drains of his house ran in blood.

A story of my father's official life, when he was Peshkar or bench-clerk in the Subordinate Judge's court at Dacca, may be recorded. The Subordinate Judge liked his bench-clerk very much and so entrusted him with a local enquiry in connection with a dispute between two very wealthy zemindars, Babu Kali Narayan Ray of Bhowal and Mr. Wise. Both of these were powerful men and a terror to the people. When my father arrived at the locality, he was approached by the agents of Babu Kali Narayan Ray with a present of a purse of two thousand rupees. My father dared not refuse this. He could not accept it either. So he asked them to send the money to Dacca, as it was not safe to carry so much cash with him, and especially as he would not submit his report before going there. This was done. He put in a true report of the case and refused the present; and was called a fool for it by the Subordinate Judge in open court.

It was not Indian officers only who, like

this Sadar-Ala at Dacca, connived at or even openly encouraged these corruptions, but English officers also sometimes took the same view. A retired English Civilian, who entered Parliament, once declared many years ago that there were few Indian officers who did not accept bribes. A Bengalee gentleman, who had served under this English official, corroborated this. This British officer himself used to distribute the work of assessing values in land-acquisition cases among his Bengalee subordinates, and openly appraised their worth by their capacity to reap the highest financial benefit to themselves from this work.

Examination for the grant of *sanads*, authorising the holders to appear and plead before British courts, was first instituted when my father was still employed as Peshkar in the Subordinate Judge's court at Dacca. He appeared at this examination. Somehow or other all the examination papers from the Dacca centre were lost in transit to Calcutta; and in consequence of it all those who had sat for it were granted diplomas. Armed with it, my father commenced to practise at Dacca. Shortly after, he was offered and accepted the post of Munsif in the District of Jessore. I do not know how long he was stationed at this place. It could not have been very long; because my mother never went there. When I was about three or four years of age, my father was posted to Koterhat, near Nalchiti, in the District of Backerganj. In those days the Munsif was not only a civil judge, but also exercised some measure of criminal jurisdiction as well. At Koterhat my father combined in him the functions of both Munsif and Deputy Magistrate.

My mother was my father's second wife. Her name was Narayanee. She was born in the village Shatiajuri near the present railway station of that name on the Assam-Bengal Railway. My maternal grand-father, Ramkrishna Kar, belonged to the well-known Kars of that village. My father married her, a girl of ten or eleven, during the life-time of his first wife. I heard the story of this marriage from my mother. My step-mother was without any issue and when, humanly speaking, she despaired of getting any, she wanted my father to take a second wife for the preservation of his line. My father would, however, hear nothing of it. What was the use of going against the Divine Will, he urged. This did not satisfy my step-mother; so she commenced to look out for a suitable bride for her own husband. And she herself selected my mother for him. I do not remember how long my step-mother lived after my mother's marriage. My mother told me that she died when I was about two years old. My mother used to tell me that she never tended me herself; my step-mother looked after me as long as she lived. She was quite conscious when death commenced to close upon her; and when she was nearing her end, she took out her jewels and despite the fact that her brothers were then in straitened circumstances placed these in my mother's hands with the request that these should be preserved for my future wife! My mother used to say this also that though sometimes my step-mother had her differences with my father, her treatment of my mother was uniformly most sincerely loving and considerate, and never did an angry look or word escape her towards my mother.

At the time of my birth father was, I think, still employed as bench-clerk or Peshkar in the Subordinate Judge's court at Dacca. But I saw the first light of day not at Dacca but in our village home at Poil. My earliest recollections go back, however, not to my native village but to Dacca, where I must have been taken when I was hardly two years old. I have a faint picture still clinging to my mind of a fairly good-sized brick-built house with a high gate. One of the windows of this house overlooked a mosque; and I remember that I used to sit at this window and holding my ears with my small hands imitated the man who called the Faithful to prayer.

I have, however, more vivid recollections of Koterhat in the Backerganj District. It was a small place, on the bank of a small river, which was infested with crocodiles. Backerganj is in the very heart of the Delta of the Ganges and forms almost a part of the Sunderbans, the notorious habitat of the world-famed Bengal tiger. As the waters about Koterhat were infested with crocodiles, so the land was infested with tigers. We used oftentimes to hear the growl of tigers at dead of night from our beds. Huge beasts were almost every week killed in the neighbourhood and brought and laid out in front of my father's court-house by peasant-folk in the hope of some reward. Reports of people having been carried away by crocodiles or killed by tigers used also to reach us every now and then.

The Munsif's court stood upon somewhat high ground on the bank of the river. It was a thatched bungalow. The Munsif's private quarters consisted of a number of detached huts, covered with thatch, the walls being of mats and bamboos, with mud floor. My father's quarters were surrounded by a cluster of huts, which formed a small colony of our own people from Sylhet, who had gone with my father in search of their fortunes to his new place of work. Some were my father's relations; many were his neighbours and retainers. But my father religiously refused to acknowledge his relationship with them. I still remember how he summarily dismissed a near relation, who was employed under him, because he had inadvertently given it out that he was connected with the Munsif. My father never employed him in his office again, and, if I remember aright, he had to leave Koterhat soon after his dismissal.

One incident of our life at Koterhat has clung to my mind for the last seventy years. I think I was then about four years old. My father used to have me with him during his meals, particularly during his morning meals. One day as we, father and son, sat down to our meals together, my mother served some green, called *kalmi* in our vernacular, that grows wild in tanks and other pools of water. It seems that my father had not seen this particular kind of green in his house at Koterhat; and so he asked my mother wherefrom she had got this green. She said that a *Patuni** woman had brought it from the other side of the river. My father queried, "Did you pay her for it?" My mother said that it was a very common kind of green which grew wild, and no one

* Patunis are boatmen.

either asked nor was paid any price for it. At this my father pushed off the platter set before him and walked out in great anger, severely admonishing my mother for having accepted it from this woman without paying for it. He had this woman immediately sent for and having paid her some coppers as the price of her green, he strictly forbade her his house, threatening her with condign punishment if ever she came near it again. Now, the reason of it was that this *Patuni* woman had a scape-grace of a son who used to be hauled up every now and then before my father for petty thefts and other minor criminal offences. My father could not, therefore, afford to have his mother about his house for any consideration whatever. This incident resulted in my father's, and necessarily in my mother's also, going without breakfast that day; and my mother remembered it as long as she lived.

My mind has very often gone back to my memories of Koterhat, the natural scenery of which impressed me very much. It was a wild place and the play of the tides upon the river and the tanks and other pools of water captured my infant imagination very powerfully. How the waters would overflow the banks, sometimes flooding our courtyard during high tide, was a great wonder and mystery to me, and how I loved to wade through the shallow tidal currents, how I longed to see the tiny fish coming out of their hiding places, as it were for a stroll along the highways of the village,—all these used to fascinate me very much; and I remember the sensation still!

One other incident of our life at Koterhat

has also tenaciously clung to my memory. My younger sister was then about a year and a half or two years old. One morning she was lying asleep on the floor of our bed-room. My mother was engaged in cooking in another hut. Coming to see how she was, in the interval of her cooking, she found two big reptiles, *go-shaps* (iguanas), lying flat and evidently asleep in the vicinity of my sister's bed, one on each side. I had followed my mother into this room; and I seem still to see before my very eyes how she stood petrified by sudden fear at the sight of these monsters lying almost on her child's bed. But with great presence of mind she did not scream or do anything to frighten the beasts. In a few moments the reptiles opened their eyes and, seeing my mother standing near, slowly moved out by a side-door and rushed to the bush in our back-yard which was infested by their tribe.

CHAPTER II.

HOME INFLUENCE AND EARLY EDUCATION

"For five years a son shall be treated with great tenderness. For ten years he shall be subjected to rigorous discipline. When he attains his sixteenth year, the father shall treat his son as a friend." This is a translation of an old Sanskrit couplet attributed to the great Chanakya. The tenets of Chanakya were very much in vogue among the higher classes of Bengalee society seventy years ago. My father shaped his life in many respects by these wise sayings. He followed this injunction of Chanakya almost religiously in my up-bringing. Up to my sixth year I was treated by my father almost as a young divinity. Every whim of mine was satisfied. No one was permitted to lift a hand against me. Though my mother did not observe this law, my father followed it scrupulously and resented its violation even by my mother.

I was not at all a very quiet child. And my parents found it difficult to keep me out of harm's way. Nor did their moral and educational code allow them to leave me in charge of the servants. My father tried, so far as he could, to keep me constantly near him. But he had his work to do. So every morning, while my father was poring over the files of the cases that he would have to try in court, I found myself inside a large bamboo-and-cane *topa* or *polo*, as they are called in our parts, with which the village folks catch fish in shallow waters during the dry months. I still remember the scene how my father used to sit and read his papers or books or write his judgments, and I used to sit and play near him inside that *polo*. At meal-time I used to have a seat placed for me at right angles to my father's and he used to feed me with his own hands. Father and son used to take their food out of the same platter. It was my father who gave me my daily bath at the time he had his own. And every night I slept by him, almost inside his protecting embrace.

Looking back from this long distance upon those early memories, I oftentimes feel tempted to try and realise how my father felt towards me, and ask myself very often, have I the same feelings and mental attitude towards my sons? I cannot say whether my father tried to "spiritualise" and "idealise" the carnal relations of life, as the modern-educated people try sometimes to do with the help of what is called the "religious imagination." I know also this, how we try, but frequently fail, to touch reality with the help of these exercises. But I have a feeling that the way my father tended me in my infancy was part of his real practical religion. He looked upon me—and in later life he plainly said this more than once—not only as an earthly or family asset but as an instrument of his well-being on the other side of the grave also. My father personally never worshipped, that is, tended with his own hands any Idol or Divine Image. The caste to which he belonged has not this privilege, which is exclusively allowed to the Brahmins. But I have an idea that up to the fifth year of my age, my father tended me with the same devotion and almost with the same spirit of holiness and religion with which the devout Brahmin tends the image of the God he worships. My father was a Vaishnava, and I sometimes wonder if in the scheme of his personal religion I did not represent to him, during my innocent infancy, the symbol of Bala-Gopala or the child Shree-Krishna. How I long to know all these things! How I wish I had understood something of the Vaishnavic cult and culture during my father's life-time, so that we could talk these deep things of life together and understand each other more intimately than what was possible in the days of my youth.

My mother, however, did not follow the rule of Chanakya. She was a very strict disciplinarian. I do not remember to have been treated by her, in my early infancy much less in my later boyhood, with outward fondness. In this she differed from most mothers that I knew in my early days. She was remarkably reserved and self-contained. I cannot say if it was part of her original make of mind and soul, or whether it was acquired by self-discipline, which she felt called upon to exercise by the invidious position she came to occupy in my father's house as a co-wife. But in my infancy and boyhood she was so studiously eager to conceal her affection for me that for many many years, indeed until I was quite a young man of fifteen or sixteen, I could never free myself of the idea that she was not my mother, but only my step-mother. I was not very strong as a boy, neither was I as quiet and inoffensive as weak children usually are or ought to be. I had consequently many a quarrel with other boys in our neighbourhood, when we left Koterhat and my father came and settled in the town of Sylhet; and not being very strong physically I frequently got licked. It was my double misfortune. Because whenever the story of these quarrels reached my mother, as it generally did, she never cared to enquire into the cause of the quarrel, and whether that was just or unjust, but used to give me a severe hiding for it. The one question with her was, why should the son of a gentleman quarrel and fight with another person? A gentleman, in her rule of life, never fought or quarrelled or did anything that was mean and selfish. I did not understand these things then, and always inwardly resented the injustice and cruelty of her treatment of me. But now I know and understand how her one aim and intention in briging me up was, to make me a gentleman, a *bhadralok*, as she used to say, according to her ideal. She was indeed, in a way, a very proud woman, proud of her blood and her husband's family, though this pride never sought any obtrusive or offensive manifestation but simply organized itself in her mental aloofness and moral reserve, never in her self-assertion but only in her self-suppression.

But the indulgence and tenderness which I never received from my mother in my infancy and boyhood I had in a superabundant measure from my nurse. It was the custom in those days to send a maidservant from the paternal home of a young bride to her new home in her husband's family. Slavery of a kind was still extant in this province during the early life of my father. Every "respectable" family had a few "slaves" attached to it. They were not labourers like the slaves in the Western Colonies before the system was abolished in the last century but were really members of the family with an inferior social status. This maid-servant, who came to my father's household, was really a member of this class and belonged to my mother's family. She lived with us until I grew up into quite a young man, when my maternal uncle's marriage took her back to his home, as there were no female members in his house at that time who could look after his young wife.

For nearly twenty years she lived in our house, not as a servant but only as a loved and respected member of the family. My mother called her *Didi*, which is the term with which elder sisters are addressed in Bengalee. I used to call her *Mashi*, which is the term for auntie—mother's sister—in our language. My father never addressed her by her proper name, but used to call her "Kanchaneer-Ma" or Kanchanee's mother, Kanchanee being the name of her daughter. To call any elderly person by his or her proper name, whatever be the caste or social rank of that person, was considered very uncivil and a sign of low breeding in those days in Bengalee society. Elder brothers are regarded to rank almost with the father and elder sisters as entitled to about the same respect as mothers in Bengal. Wife's elder sisters are, therefore, entitled to almost the same honour as the mother-in-law herself. And Kanchaneer-Ma was treated in my father's house in every respect as if she was really my mother's elder sister.

In my early infancy my father rarely

talked directly to my mother before others. My grand-mother died when my father was a little boy. My father had no brothers or sisters nor any cousins either as members of the joint family. There were, therefore, no elderly ladies in the house except my step-mother, when he brought his young second wife to him. As long as my step-mother lived she must have been the controller of his household. Upon her death, which took place when my mother was hardly seventeen, Kanchaneer-Ma came to that position. My father always treated her as if she was almost his mother-in-law, and through her he used to consult the wishes of my mother even when she had attained the maturity of a matron. She was literally my mother's, and also to some extent even my father's, friend, philosopher and guide in all matters concerning their family and household. She never hesitated to admonish my mother whenever she went wrong, particularly when she treated me with undue severity. In my boyhood, she used always to stand between me and my angry mother whenever I did anything wrong. I still remember how many a time she threw herself between my back and my mother's birch and took the chastisement upon her own body in going to save my skin. I got therefore, quite naturally, far more attached to her than I ever was in the days of my boyhood to my mother. I still remember how I used to fly at people who teased me by saying that Kanchaneer-Ma was dead; or when they said that they were going to get her re-married according to the new Widow Re-Marriage Act of Pundit Iswar Chandra Vidyasagar, which was then the universal talk of the people. She was much older than my mother. I think she had lost her only child Kanchanee before my mother was born, and had nursed my mother with all the love and longing of a bereaved mother's heart. Her love and affection for me had its root, it seems, in her early love for my mother and grew in strength and volume as it came down from her to me, her first-born. Considering the stern and reserved nature of my mother, my young heart would have been starved of all love and tenderness if it had not been tended with such fondness by my "auntie" or *Mashi*.

At the age of five, after *Sarasvatee*, the Goddess of Learning, had been duly worshipped, I was initiated into the mysteries of the Bengalee alphabet by our family priest, one of the finest specimens of the old race of Brahmins, simple and unostentatious, without the least suspicion of conceit of caste or of sanctity of religion in him. He was not a Pundit, that is, had no title from any *tol* or seat of Sanskrit learning; but he knew Sanskrit sufficiently well to be able to read and understand such spiritual books as the Bhagabad-Geeta and Adhyatma Ramayana, which I heard him recite and expound in my school-days. The first character which I was made to trace, after my initiation, was called "Anzi." It finds no place in either the Sanskrit or the Bengalee alphabet, and the sound or the sign is never found in use anywhere. I wonder what this "Anzi" really stood for. We read in Manu that all learning must begin with the recitation of the mystic syllable "Aum" or "Om." We read in the Upanishads

TOMB OF SHAH JALAL, THE PATRON SAINT OF SYLHET TOWN.

that this "Aum" or "Om" is the Everlasting Reality, that it is Brahman Itself. "This Om is Param or the Highest; this Om is Brahman. Knowing this Om the devotee is glorified in the realm of Brahman." But mediæval Hinduism had interdicted the study of the Vedas, including the Upanishads, to Sudras. In my infant days, the Bengalee Kayasthas had not remembered that they were not Sudras but Bratya Kshatriyas or Kshatriyas who had fallen from their high state as Dvijas or twice-born among Hindu castes, and they had not as yet revived their claim to the rite of initiation or *Upanayana* and the study of the Vedas. We could not then utter the sacred and mystic syllable "Aum" or "Om." Was this "Anzi" a substitute for "Aum" or "Om" for the use of Sudras, I wonder. I do not know if this "Anzi" still figures in the initiation of our people into the mysteries of the Bengalee alphabet and forms part of the ritual of *Vidyarambha* even to-day.

"Shishu-Bodh" was the name of the first printed book placed in my hands. I do not know if it has entirely ceased publication; but though possibly less scientifically arranged and much less nicely got up, I liked this book much better than I did the more modern "Shishu-Shiksha" or "Varna-Parichaya" which I had to read later in the school to which I was sent. These modern primers take the youthful minds, for whose benefit they are written, to be far less mature than they actually are. A boy of five or six knows and feels and understands much more than what is usually taken for granted by the manufacturers of the present-day primers. Their interests in life are very much deeper and wider than what the stories of familiar animals and little boys, which are served out to them through these books, seem to take for granted. "Shishu-Bodh" had, of course, the Bengalee alphabet but instead of placing a number of single words before boys and girls to help them to be familiar with the alphabets, it at once started with nice attractive stories, the subject-matter of which riveted the attention and oftentimes enthralled the imagination of little folks, and thus taught them the use of the alphabets without any serious and conscious effort. Most of the stories in our current school primers of the class to which "Shishu-Shiksha" belonged are commonplace, stale, jejune; these neither excite youthful curiosity nor inspire youthful enthusiasm or idealism. They do not touch any of the deeper emotions, neither of wonder, nor fear, nor any other, which are so common in the psychology of little children. In this respect "Shishu-Bodh" was much better than most of our present-day primers. Another distinguishing feature of "Shishu-Bodh" was the collection of Sanskrit *slokas* which it contained. These were mostly taken from Chanakya or were at least believed to be his. These are in very simple Sanskrit, so that even our peasant folks, innocent of reading and writing, can sometimes understand what they mean. They can be very easily committed to memory. They serve therefore both as moral instruction and as exercises for the memory. When taking my lessons from "Shishu-Bodh" I was never put to the amount of torture to which I was subjected, I very well remember, in learning my lessons from "Varna

Parichaya" or "Shishu-Shiksha"; yet while I soon forgot practically everything that I had been forced to commit to memory from these latter text-books at my school, many of the things that I learnt from the former book still live in my recollection.

Looking back upon these ancient memories, it seems to me that I received my first lessons in democracy, even as a little boy, from the text reproduced in this book from Chanakya. Among the very first stanzas which I was made to read and commit to memory was one which said that of the two, the master of a kingdom and the master of knowledge, the man of culture was superior, because,

स्वदेशे पूज्यते राजा विद्वान् सर्वत्र पूज्यते ।

While the king is honoured only in his own country, the man of learning is honoured everywhere. Of the stories in this book, that of "*Data* Karna," the man who sacrificed his first-born to do his duty as a house-holder by a guest, made the profoundest impression upon my child-mind. I read and re-read it and eagerly committed the whole poem to memory until it became almost a part of my mental life.

I did not go to school until I was about ten years old. The custom of engaging private tutors had not come into vogue in those days. My father was my first tutor. He taught me the alphabets. He made me recite Sanskrit *slokas* from Chanakya and other books, all of these *slokas* having been retained in his own memory, and which, taught by him, formed the whole of my mental repertory in my early boyhood. It was he who taught me my first

Arithmetic through the old addition and multiplication tables which I was made to repeat after him and commit to memory. Every evening, after his court work was over, he used to sit with me and teach me these things until dinner was ready, when father and son went together to our evening or night meal.

When I was about seven years old, the "Chowki" at Koterhat in Backergunj was abolished, and my father was temporarily thrown out of employment. He went home to our native village, Poil. And here an incident happened which showed the strength of my father's character, which has had possibly very great influence in shaping my own also. Upon reaching home, my father heard it that the leaders of the village society had unfairly put a poor Brahmin family out of caste through the spiteful influence of a few powerful people. My father sent for those who could help him to know the whole truth about this matter; and having heard them all, he sent for the head of this ostracised Brahmin family and at once installed him as his family-priest, and asked him to come and perform the Durga Puja, which was near at hand, in his house. In consequence of it, my father was himself put out of communion by the village Bhadraloks, and I was told that for sixteen years he lived in this social isolation because he would not be party to what he believed to be a wrong, and would not submit to the tyranny of the majority. He did not know English and had no idea of this thing which we call conscience in our modern parlance; but his own sense of truth and right always towered above all considerations of material advantage or social expediency. I came to know later in life many other instances of this trait in his character.

My father was, however, not long out of employ. Before the long Puja vacation was over, he was offered, and he accepted, the post of Munsif at Fenchuganj, in his own district of Sylhet. Fenchuganj is a station now on the Sylhet-Kulaura Branch of the Assam Bengal Railway. Before this line was opened, it was a very important station of the Cachar-Sunderbuns Steamer-Service of the India General Steam Navigation Company, which has, since some years past, been amalgamated with the River Steam Navigation Company and a joint service is maintained now by the amalgamated Company between Calcutta and Cachar *via* the Sunderbuns. When my father went to Fenchgunj (about 1864 or '65), it was a small village. I went there with my father. Our house stood upon a hillock, on the bank of the river, and commanded a very long view of land and watercourse. The Munsif's court-house stood upon another. I do not remember if my mother came to live here; it seems that she did not. My one joy here was fishing with the rod in the river below our house. My father also loved this sport very much; and though following the injunction of Chanakya he imposed all sorts of disciplines upon me at this time, and ceased to treat me with the manifest tenderness which marked our life at Koterhat, we found a common object of pleasure in fishing and helped each other very often to catch the poor fishes of the stream flowing by our bungalow.

CHAPTER III.

SCHOOL DAYS

My father did not continue in service for long. I was growing up and it was time that I went to school. But in those days there were no schools except in the district headquarters. The exigencies of his service gave him, however, little chance of being stationed at headquarters. He found, therefore, as he wrote to me many years after, no alternative to his resigning his post as Munsif and returning to his practice as pleader. From Fenchuganj he soon came and joined the Bar at Sylhet. This was in 1865 or 1866.

There were no English-knowing lawyers in Sylhet at that time, and my father found no difficulty in soon getting to the very top of his profession. He had the reputation of being a good Persian scholar,—was especially noted for the quality of his Persian style or *ebarat*, as it was called. Owing to his service on the Bench, his knowledge of law and procedure was also very sound and of a high order. And all these helped him very materially in his profession as lawyer. I have no idea what his actual income was; but I think it stood somewhere between two to three hundred rupees a month, which was quite a high income in those days, when the cost of living was very low, and a man generally counted fairly rich on hundred rupees a month.

Life also was very simple. Even among British officials, the District Judge alone had a carriage which was driven by a single horse. The Magistrate and other high officials maintained their dignity by riding on ponies to and from their offices. Among Bengalee gentlemen, one person only owned a four-wheeler, and he combined with his profession of law the ownership of a big zemindary. Another brother-pleader of my father's had a buggy which he used to drive himself. All the rest of the local gentry walked about their business on foot attended by a servant, who held a huge bamboo umbrella over their head and carried their papers in a big bundle on their back. These umbrellas were between four to six feet in diameter, and were held up with strong and long bamboo poles. To walk under the shade of these state-umbrellas, as they might very properly be called, was considered quite aristocratic in those days.

Good, fine rice sold at about two rupees a maund. Any time a big fresh fish of the best species could be had for from four to six annas. Milk could be had at the rate of twelve to fifteen seers a rupee from the milkmen. In the villages, every peasant household had its "*go-dhan*" or wealth of cattle, and they oftentimes gave away their excess milk for the mere asking, as their dignity as cultivators would not let them sell milk, which might even have led to loss of caste. *Ghee* or clarified butter sold at from eight to twelve annas a pucca seer of eighty tolas. Pure mustard oil was usually sold at about four annas a seer. Wages were correspondingly low, and dometic servants could be had at a monthly wage of from eight to twelve annas, with all found. And in view of it all, it was nothing strange that people passed for rich on forty to fifty rupees a month, and could spend freely on religious and other ceremonials.

Rent was very low even in the towns. My father rented a fairly big building, though not quite in repairs, which he had to do himself, standing by the public road in the very heart of the town, almost at a stone's throw from the District Judge's Court and close to the other courts and the Sudder bazar (called Bandar Bazar), and he paid, if I remember aright, eight rupees a month for it. It stood upon more than four acres of land. In the course of a year or so quite a small colony of officials and lawyers grew on this plot. The central portion with the brick structure was occupied by my father and a friend and very distant relation of his, who was employed as Deputy Inspector of Schools. This gentleman, the late Rai Saheb Nabakishore Sen, was for some time with my father at Dacca in his college days. His sister had been married to a maternal uncle of my father's. He shared the central brick building with us. Babu Deenanath Sen (the father of Babu Priya Nath Sen, the editor and proprietor of the "Herald" of Dacca) who has left his mark upon the history of English education in Dacca, and who rose to the position of Inspector of Schools, was a class-mate and contemporary of Babu Nabakishore Sen. Nabakishore Sen might have risen as high in the service, if he had not been transferred from Bengal to Assam upon the institution of the new Province and the transfer of Sylhet and Cachar, which formed his jurisdiction, to the new Administration. But though deprived of the larger opportunities which the Bengal

Educational Service offered to his colleagues and contemporaries, Babu Nabakishore rose to the highest place in the Subordinate Educational Service of Assam. Sylhet owes the organisaton of her primary and middle vernacular schools and, indeed, that of the entire school system of the district to Babu Nabakishore Sen. A man of very exceptional native intelligence and purity of character, combined with very rare tact and great dignity of deportment, due to his high birth—because his family held a very high position among the Bhadraloks of Sylhet, Tippera and East Mymensing—Babu Nabakishore Sen became the recognised leader of Sylhet society long before his retirement from service with the title of Rai Saheb.

After settling down at Sylhet, my father first sent me to school with a Mahomedan Maulavi. It seems he wanted that I should not be entirely cut off from the culture which claimed him as its own. But I did not stay long with this Maulavi. Having learnt the Arabic alphabet, I started, in about six months' time I think, to read Shah-Nama. But I could not proceed further than the first page, or possibly even less, only the first few sentences of this book, a word or two of which, *Karima babaksha* etc., I still remember. And my father in utter despair took me away from the Maulavi and put me in an English school. Looking back upon my early attempt to learn Persian, it seems to me that not my native intelligence or my capacity for application was really at fault and was in any way responsible for my failure. The system was unsuited to my nature. I was asked to commit to memory things that I did not understand and the meaning of which was not explained to me. The Maulavi evidently wanted to train my ear and memory first, and when I had committed the story to memory, he would take me through its grammar and meaning. That process did not evidently suit my impatient intellect, which was eager to know and understand, before trying to remember things. I found this out when I was put to read English. I had absolutely no interest in this new study until I could essay to express my thoughts in this language. And an English letter which I wrote to Babu Nabakishore Sen, who had gone on his inspection tour to Cochar, when I was just commencing to read and spell "b l a bla" etc., was the talk of the elders for many a year to come. It was the first English letter of mine, which like all primitive language was simply a string of words without or with very little verbs or prepositions. Thinking of it now, it seems to have been an indication of my mental character and constitution. Words without meaning never enter my mind or are retained by my memory. Even to this day I can never keep in my mind non-essentials in the things that I read, while the essential facts or thoughts are retained in a very fair proportion. My memory is like a very faithful record-keeper, who furnishes me with whatever may be wanted for my work, out of its own store-house of facts or thoughts, which, however, for the very life of me, I could not recall at any other time. And this mental constitution of mine is, I think, responsible for my failure to study Persian. I wish, however, Providence had otherwise ordained my early education and that I had been able to get a fair hold upon Persian, before I went to the English school. That would have stood in very good service to-day, and would have been of immense help and profit to me, both intellectually and spiritually, in making a comparative study of our Bengalee Vaishnavic poets and the great Persian poets, among whom there seem to exist so many deep and soulful affinities. But what was to be has been.

There were three English schools and one vernacular school in the town of Sylhet when my father went and joined the Bar there in 1866. Of the three English schools one was a Middle school, owned by a Bengalee gentleman, and the two others taught as far as the Entrance standard of the Calcutta University. The first English school in Sylhet was a Government school. It was established, I think, before the Munity, in pursuance of the new education policy laid down in Sir Charles Wood's historic Despatch of 1854, which is rightly regarded or, more correctly speaking, was regarded before the present reaction set in, as the "great educational charter" of the Indian subjects of Great Britain. This school was, however, abolished during the dark days of the Mutiny, and for some little time Sylhet was without any English school. I have no notion as to what results were achieved by that first English school in Sylhet, but it could not have been much; for when I went to Sylhet I found that one Rev. Mr. W. Pryse was described as the Father of English education in my district.

Mr. Pryse was still living in Sylhet in 1866, though he no longer was a regular teacher in the two missionary schools which had been started by him and were owned by the Mission to which he belonged. Pryse belonged, though in a smaller way, to the type which was represented by Carey, Marshman and David Hare, and latterly, by Duff in the larger history of English education in Bengal. He was educationist and philanthropist combined; and the first generation of English-educated men of Sylhet always cherished his memory with deep love and respect. A library, got up by public subscription and located in the Town Hall of Sylhet, is a small attempt of our people to keep the memory of this good and kind man green among them.

The town of Sylhet stretches from east to west along the bank of the river Surma. And these two schools were located almost at two ends of it. One was situate in the eastern part of the town, known as Nayasharak; while the other was at Sheikh Ghat, on the western boundary of it. Nayasharak was close to my father's residence and I first went to this school. The school at Sheikh Ghat was however reputed to be the better of the two; and in a few days I got my transfer to it. When I went there, the late Babu Jay Govinda Shome, an Indian Christian gentleman from my own District, a student and convert of Dr. Duff, and one of the first graduates of the Calcutta University, the very first to win the distinction of passing his B.A. and M.A. Examinations in the same year,—was the Head Master. Babu Jay Govinda Shome rose subsequently to considerable distinction as a leader of the Bengalee Christian community. He was a life-long friend of Babu Kali Charan Banerjee, the finest specimen of the Bengal school of oratory, who made his mark both at the High Court Bar and at the Calcutta University, of which he was a Syndic for many years and became, towards his closing days, its Registrar. Babu Jay Govinda, with the help of his friend and co-religionist, Babu Kali Charan, founded the weekly newspaper, the "Indian Christian Herald," of which he was the editor. Later in life, he realised the need of organising a truly Indian Christian Church, which would graft the fundamental doctrines and disciplines of Christianity on to the general social and spiritual ideals and traditions of Hinduism. I had talks with him on this highly interesting topic, after I too had settled down in Calcutta and was engaged as a lay preacher of the Brahma Samaj; and Babu Jay Govinda's idea, I found, was to secure recognition of the worshippers of Jesus Christ as a sect of the Hindus.

Babu Jay Govinda Shome did not continue for long in his post as Head Master of the Sheikh Ghat school. He was succeeded by Babu Durgakumar Basu, whose services were subsequently transferrd to the Government school at Sylhet when it replaced the missionary schools, about the year 1869 or '70. Babu Durga Kumar spent his whole official life in Sylhet as Head Master of this school.

The school houses both at Nayasharak and Sheikh Ghat were very simple structures of bamboo and mat, with the roof covered with a kind of straight and smooth grass, very much like the English hay, without the smell of it. It is called *chhon* in our local vernacular. The posts were either of trunks of trees or of a kind of strong and straight bamboos, which grow in abundance in the district, particularly in its hilly tracts. The partitions were of mat. Wooden benches for the boys and chairs, made of split bamboo and cane which grew in the district in large quantities, for the teachers, constituted the principal school furniture. The boys had no desks, and the school library consisted of just a few books, which found place, along with the school registers and other school records, inside an almirah. There was no clock or timepiece in my first school. At Sheikh Ghat we had a sun-dial set upon a brick platform in front of the school house. But it was of no use on cloudy days; so there was another device also to mark time. It consisted of a light metal cup with a very small hole, almost of the size of a very small pin, in the centre. This cup was placed on a vessel of water, and the time it took to get filled and sink marked one hour. The chowkidar or watchman of the school kept watch and ward over this time-marker, and took out the cup as soon as it sank, and rang the gong indicating the hour of the day. The boys played tricks with this time-cup whenever the chowkidar was either absent or was found dozing away; and unless they overdid the thing and tried to steal not minutes but quarter or half hours from the regular school time, they were not detected. During the last period, between three and half past three in the afternoon, which last was the hour for dismissing the classes, there was an almost constant procession of little boys to the room where this precious hour-cup was kept, and many a time they gave a little push to the cup to hasten its sinking. We used to call this device water-clock or *jal-gharee*.

There were eight classes in our school, counted from the first or Entrance class—the class which prepared students for the University Matriculation Examination, called

Entrance Examination in those days—to the last or infant class, where boys commenced to learn the English alphabet. Murray's Spelling Book and Pyaree Charan Sircar's First Book of Reading were the text-books for the lowest class in English schools in Bengal in those days. I read Murray's in preference to Pyaree Charan Sircar's. I do not know why except this that that was the prescribed text in the Sylhet Mission school in my time. Iswar Chandra Vidyasagar's "Varna-Parichaya" Part II, and Madan Mohan Tarkalankar's "Shishu-Shiksha" Part III, were my earliest Bengalee text-books at school. In the lowest class of my school, I read these, and was taught mental arithmetic. English and Bengalee caligraphy or hand-writing formed also an important and compulsory subject in this class. When I got promoted to the next higher, the seventh class, elementary geography, notation, numeration and simple addition and subtraction were added to my curriculum, along with Vidyasagar's "Akhyan Manjaree" for my Bengalee text-book. At the close of my second year at school in 1868, I got what was called a double promotion, that is, I was allowed to pass over the sixth and was taken into the fifth class. I forget what my English text-book was in this class, possibly it was Third Book of Reading. It was in this class that Lennie's English Grammar was first placed in my hand. Akshay Kumar Datta's "Charu-Path" Part I, Vidyasagar's "Charitabali," a collection of biographies of European savants and philanthropists and men of science, with "Padya-Path" Part I, and Loharam Shiromani's Bengalee Grammar were among my text-books in this class. But this double promotion instead of being a help became a very serious handicap to me in my studies; and from this time onward I lost the position which I had secured in my eighth and seventh classes. My growing intelligence could not evidently keep pace with the subjects of my school studies, and I commenced to take a lower place among my class-mates. There was however, one subject in which I fairly maintained my position, and that was English. I remember how the District Judge coming to visit our school at this time, saw my Engilsh exercises, and highly commended me for my English composition. It may have been partly due to the fact that my teacher introduced me to him as the son of my father whom he knew so well and held in great respect. At least this was how the superior boys in my class tried to explain his partiality for me. But I think I really had even then a certain aptitude for languages. I know this much in any case, that I used to write English in utter disregard of the rules of grammar, but yet with some distinction of childish style, and a certain amount of flow; and it seems this was what attracted the notice of the District Judge.

Bat and ball, not the more scientific game of cricket, which came into vogue a few years later, when I was in the third or second class of my school, and *Kabati* or a kind of wrestling, were the principal school games in those days. But I was never an expert in these games, having been rather sickly in my boyhood. Fishing with the rod and line was my principal sport at home; and a small tank in our compound, just in front of our house, which was full of small fish, and a small rivulet which

DURGA KUMAR BOSE.

flowed by the public road and lost itself in a marsh at the back of our quarters, that ran down in fairly strong currents during the rains, carrying a lot of fish from neighbouring tanks, found very good ground for this sport. As at Fenchuganj, so here also, my father used very often, after his return from his work at court, to join me in it. During the Puja vacation, when the courts and schools used to close for about a month, we enjoyed very good fishing in our own tank at Poil which had quite a large stock of big fish.

The present Government school at Sylhet was established when I was in the fifth class of the Missionary school at Sheikh Ghat. It was in 1869, I think. There was trouble between the Missionaries and the local gentry. I forget what was the cause of it, possibly some conflict between Hindu orthodoxy and the teachings of Christianity. The Missionaries either themselves or through their Indian converts, some of whom were employed in their schools, gave some cause of offence to the sentiments of the Hindu community; and the latter became very anxious to boycott their schools. I have a very faint recollection of a new school having been set up in opposition to the Mission schools and I was transferred temporarily to it. An agitation was also set up to secure a Government school in the town, and my father took a fairly active part in this agitation. As a result of all this, a Government school was established about the middle of 1869. An unoccupied bungalow standing on a small hill in the northern part of the town,—just opposite a higher hill known of old as Monaray's Tila (Tila is a hillock in the local vernacualar) which subsequently accommodated the Government school in a big brick building that stood on it,—found the first habitation for the new school; and we all went to it. Babu Durga Kumar Basu also resigned his place as Head Master of the Mission school at Seikh Ghat and assumed charge of it.

It was about this time that a soda-water machine was set up in Sylhet and a Mahommedan from this factory commenced to bring soda-water and lemonade to our school every day to sell to the boys. We used to enjoy this new drink very much and treated one another with it. It so happened that I had a bottle of lemonade from this man the price of which had not been paid at the time. One morning, as my father was just starting for his court, this man appeared at our house. Asked as to who he was and what brought him there, he said that he had sold some lemonade to me and he had come for the price of it. My father called me at once and the debt being admitted and immediately paid, he caught hold of me and gave me a severe hiding the memory of which still sends my flesh creeping into my bones. I was guilty of a double offence, first, of enjoying something which I had not paid for, and second, which was far more serious from my father's point view, outraging the rules of caste by drinking water touched by Mahomedans. All this came through my reading English, he said, and at once took me away from school. For full six months I did not go back to school after this incident.

My mother was not with us at Sylhet at this time, but was staying at our home at Poil. She came back after six months; and seemed to have convinced my father of the futility of keeping me away from school and thus ruining my future in a hopeless fight against the inevitable tendencies of the times. So I went back to school again.

In this connection I remember another anecdote of my school-days and how I tried to pay back my father for the chastisement which I had for drinking lemonade. This happened about a couple of years later. I had an attack of choleraic diarrhœa. My father, though otherwise a man of very strong character, used to get unusually nervous if there was any illness in the family. This illness of mine made him very anxious. He sat by me the whole day. Towards evening a large number of people, his brother pleaders and other officers from the court, came to see me. I was exceedingly thirsty and the doctor in attendance said I might have some lemonade. It was immediately sent for, and my father himself poured out a glass of it for me and held it to my lips. But I nodded my head and refused to touch it, saying that it was unholy, having been manufactured by Mahomedans. I was of course not at all serious. I simply wanted to settle old scores with my father. He insisted upon my drinking it, as there was no harm in taking even forbidden things if prescribed as medicine. "Everything is of Narayana if it came as medicine"—*aushadh rupe Narayana*—he urged. After much coaxing at last I drank the refreshing draught. And I have never forgotten the sense of satisfaction I had as a boy by scoring this point against my father.

In those days I used to read a fair number of outside books. The Calcutta School Book Society was then the chief purveyor of English and Bengalee books. Babu

Nabakishore Sen, my father's friend and co-tenant, was the agent of this Society in Sylhet; and he used to regularly indent all the new Bengalee publications of this Society. These publications mainly consisted of pleasant stories from foreign literature. "Cheenadeshiya Rajkanyar Upakhyan" or the Story of the Princess of China, was one of these Bengalee publications which fascinated me very much. The story of the Weaver of China was another book of this kind. "Gulevakaolee"—translation of some Persian story, and "Kamini-kumar", both of which were rather prurient publications, which modern-educated parents would be sorry, if not very seriously angry, to find in the hands of their children, were two other books that caught my boyish fancy. I read all these, however, before reaching adolescence; and I do not think that they did much harm to my mind or morals.

My father's discipline did not extend to my readings. He rarely took any notice of what I read. He was quite satisfied as long as I did not keep evil company; or did anything revolting to his sense of propriety or piety.

As I gradually advanced towards the Entrance or Matriculation Class, my text-books approached the standards of that University Examination. Bain's English Grammar, Morell's Analysis, Clarke's Physical Geography, Todhunter's Arithmetic, Euclid's Geometry, Barnard Smith's Algebra, Mensuration and Surveying with Field Exercises, Sanskrit Grammar (Vidyasagar's Upakramanika) and Rijupath (selections from Vishnu Sarma's Hitapodesh and the Ramayana and the Mahabharata), Bengalee Charu-path Part III, Hygiene or Shwasthya-raksha, Indian History (Lethbridge's) and English History (Collier's), McMordie's English Composition, Rowe and Webb's Hints on the Study of English, Goldsmith's Vicar of Wakefield, Addison's Spectator, Johnson's Rasselas,—these were the principal text-books which I read at school between the fourth and the First or Entrance Class. Scott's Tales of a Grand-father and Gulliver's Travels, were among my home studies at this time.

Babu Durga Kumar Basu, our Head Master, used to teach us English and History. And I have always felt that I owe whatever aptitude I may have got in handling the English language to the training which I had from him in my school-days. He used to take us to the central concept of every word which we read, by giving its root and the historical developments and the changes in its meaning, wherever there were any. Trench's Study of Words was a favourite book of his, and I read it, at his instance, when I was in the Second or Preparatory Class of the Sylhet Government School. This was a very useful training for me, and I have often wondered if I could use English words with the freedom and facility with which I am credited if Babu Durga Kumar Basu had not led me through this training. He helped me also very materially in this by recommending suitable English books for my private studies, as soon as he found that I was fairly able to read and understand them without the help of a coach. In this way, I read many English books as a school boy, which most Bengalee students read now, if they read them at all, after they have left school and joined the University.

Lamb's Tales from Shakespeare and Thackeray's novels were already more or less familiar to me when I left school for the University.

CHAPTER IV.

DOMESTIC LIFE IN SYLHET DURING MY SCHOOL-DAYS.

Upon his arrival at Sylhet from Fenchuganj my father lived for a few days with a maternal uncle of his, at that time practising in the local Bar. He was much older than my father. I have a very faint recollection of him. There is only one fact in connection with him which still lives in my memory, because it was the talk of the town for some time. Upon his death, which took place at Sylhet, a number of currency notes of higher values were accidentally discovered inside old copies of Bengalee Law Reports belonging to him. I have remembered this incident as a proof of the sense of insecurity in which our people used to live in those days. In rural parts people used to bury their savings underground for safe custody, and when paper currency was introduced, town-folks evidently thought old and useless books and papers as the safest repository for their money.

In a few days, however, we went and took up our quarters in the old and dilapidated building which my father rented and to which reference has already been made in a previous page. My mother was not with us at that time. The house was not yet quite ready to receive her. It was surrounded by jungle, and the building was entirely out of repair. It took some time to put it in order and make it fit for family residence. There were only a couple of rooms which could be used, and we lived in these. But it was somewhat of a wild life. The rooms had no well-fitted doors. As for windows, the whole building had none; windows were not in fashion in those days. The grounds around, and particularly at the back of this building, were infested by wild cats and cobras. And I still remember how difficult it was to keep our milk from the attacks of these unbidden and wild guests. Sometimes it was the wild cat that had its meal on our milk, and sometimes it was some cobra which entered into our room and drank the milk off. Sometimes in the depth of winter even tigers used to pay a visit to the town from the neighbouring hills; and how we children would creep into our quilts at the sound of the fox, called *pheu* in our parts, which is said to always accompany tigers and give warning to the neighbourhood of the approach of this enemy of man and cattle! With the clearing of the jungles, the wild cat left our grounds for more peaceful and safe resorts, but it took many years to get rid of the cobras.

I still remember two or three adventures that we had with huge cobras. One of these happened on a Sunday. It was about 2 o'clock in the afternoon, and my father was taking his *siesta* in his office room. The season was June or July, the very height of summer. The doors of this room were all closed to keep the heat and glare of the mid-day sun out. Our gardener was clearing some jungles in the back-yard, preparing the ground for the planting of summer vegetables and greens. Suddenly there was a frightened cry, and running out to see whence it came, we found the gardener trying to escape from a big cobra which was trying to get at him with its hood extended and its body raised about two or three feet above the ground, and the poor man was moving his hoe in front of it, crying aloud upon the Goddess Bishahari, the deity which is supposed to preside over the snake-world, for protection, moving backward towards the outer yard of the house. The whole household came out at this cry, and seeing us all and frightened by our terrified cry, the enemy glided away, and being pursued, entered the room where my father was sleeping, through an opening in the mat-door. I still remember the extreme fear and nervous tension in which we spent the next few moments, until we saw the snake slowly moving out by another side of the room, and found my father open the door and come out, and enquire what was all this confusion and consternation about.

We lived at this time in such constant fear of these cobras that sometimes we fancied one where it did not really come. An amusing incident of this kind happened one night when we had a number of guests in our house to dinner. The dinner was just finished, when the cry of a huge cobra having appeared in the kitchen-yard was raised. It was a moonlit night; and we all went to see the reptile. The servants came out and ran with big bamboo-sticks to kill it. There, in the shade of a plantain bush, lay the deadly thing curled up in a circle, with its hood slightly raised. Simultaneously two or three blows came down upon it from the servants, and lo and behold, when we all thought with great joy that a big enemy had been laid to rest for ever, it turned out to be nothing more or less than a dry plantain leaf lying in the dim moonlight. And the young lady who had raised the alarm came for a good deal of ridicule from those whose relationship permitted them to cut jokes with her.

In about two years' time our grounds were almost cleared of the jungle with which it was covered when we first came and occupied our new home here. Babu Navakishore Sen came to share the *pucca* building with my father, and thatched houses were constructed on the outer or front yard. Gradually two other gentlemen, one a Munsiff-Court pleader and another a clerk in the Public Works Department, who was a distant cousin of mine by my father's side, came and built their residence on either side of our quarters. We thus formed a small colony.

By this time my father's family also grew to fair proportion. My maternal uncles, both of whom were younger than my mother; two cousins, one of whom was a little older than myself, and another my younger by a couple of years or so, the sons of my only maternal aunt, my mother's sister; a cousin of my mother; a brother of my step-mother; two of my own cousins by my father's side; and a boy who was not at all related to us but whose father finding it difficult to provide an English education for his only son had come and asked my father to give food and lodging for him—these formed our new house-hold at Sylhet. Besides these there were two or three relations, much older than myself, who coming in search of employment to the town, also lived with us at this time, of whom one, a cousin of mine, worked as my father's clerk. Among female members of the family there was an old aunt of mine, the widow of a distant cousin of my father, who having no home or family of her own, came to live with us at Sylhet. My younger sister, the only one that grew up,—all the others, and I had quite a number of them, had died in early infancy,—was about eight years of age at this time. My old "auntie" the maid-servant who had come to us with my mother when my mother was married, was, of course, a member of our family at this time also.

We were about nine or ten boys ranging from the age of ten to fourteen in our house at this time. My father had religious scruples to employ Brahmins as cooks in his house. The cook, whatever his caste, when he worked for wages, became a domestic servant; and my father refused to treat a Brahmin as such. All through his long life he never employed, therefore, a Brahmin cook whether at Sylhet or anywhere else. The duty of cooking for this large family, consisting of about twenty members, including the servants, fell therefore on my mother. But she never grumbled at it, on the contrary, she took not only unfeigned delight but a very real pride in this opportunity of loving service. There was also a special reason for it, because she was a very expert cook, an accomplishment which once almost cost her life a few years later, when I was about the age of fourteen, reading in the Third Class of my School.

It happened in this way. At that time my father used very often to give big dinners to his friends and acquaintances in the town, almost every other Saturday in the month. On these occasions the company used to number nearly a hundred, sometimes running even to a hundred and fifty, including her own household and the servants of her guests, as in those days every respectable guest used to bring a servant with him wherever he went to have his meals. One Saturday my father asked this large company to dinner, which was given in honour of a friend who had come on a short visit to the town from the mufassil. The dinner consisted of about thirty courses,—as was usual in those days in Bengalee society,—of vegetable, fish, and goat's meat and sweets of various kinds. And my mother prepared all these with her own hands, with such little help from the domestics as relieved the purely physical part of her labour. The cooking was so well done that before getting up from his meal Babu Navakishore Sen off-hand invited the whole company to dinner the next evening and sent a request to my mother to take charge of the cooking. My mother agreed; and the next day she cooked for these hundred and fifty people and served them the same number of dishes with some variations. A friend of my father's, employed at that time as Head Clerk in the office of the District Superintendent of Police, invited the same company to our own house the evening following in honour of the same friend from the mufassil and my mother was for the third time asked to take charge of the cooking. She did it all right; but after the cooking was over, and the first batch of guests had finished their meals, she went off in a swoon; and for nearly three months after this she hovered between life and death, owing to this serious nervous break-down. But though she suffered so much and for so long a time for it, she never refused to take the same risks over again and used always to take a genuine pleasure in cooking and feeding people. She never, in all her life, entertained the services of a paid cook in her house.

Though tea had been discovered in Assam some years previously, and tea-gardens were being started in the neighbouring district of Cachar, our people had not as yet taken to drinking it. The elders among the so-called higher classes of Hindus never had anything like an early morning meal. They had only two meals a day, one the mid-day meal at about eleven or twelve, and the other the night-meal at between nine and ten. These were the only meals which my father took, though occasionally, after coming back from court, he drank a glass of cold water with a couple of *batasa*, a preparation of pure sugar. We had neither *sandesh* nor *rasagolla* in those days. But our ladies used to prepare a large variety of sweets with cocoanut and sugar. These were, however, reserved generally for special festive occasions like, for instance, the Pujas. The peasants and the labouring classes usually had three meals a day, one very early in the morning, oftentimes at early dawn, which in the winter consisted of hot rice and a little boiled vegetable or curried fish kept from the previous night's preparations, and during the hot months, of cold rice preserved in water, with some fresh baked or burnt dried fish or only with a little salt and curd or whey. Their next meal-time was in the afternoon, when they came back home after the day's work was practically done, and the other was at night time. These were hot meals, and consisted of two or three courses of fish and *dal* and vegetable.

We boys, however, had four meals a day. Our first or early morning meal consisted of hot, steaming boiled rice, with *ghee* and some boiled vegetable. Sometimes we had a kind of porridge made of the broken particles of rice, which was something like a by-product of the husking of rice, called *khood* in our vernacular. This, served hot and steaming with home-made *ghee*, was one of my most favourite dishes, and I never cared for any other if I could get it. But at Sylhet we purchased rice from the bazars, and we could not get this *khood*, which the peasant folk kept generally for their own consumption. Our next meal was between ten and half-past ten in the forenoon, which we had after our daily bath and just before going to school. This was a full meal, and we had rice and *dal* and fried fish and vegetable, and curried fish and occasionally curdled milk or *dahi*, or whey or *ghol*, called *matha* in the vernacular of the district. We had our next meal after we came back from school, between four and four-thirty in the afternoon. It consisted of boiled rice, *dal*, vegetable dishes from the kitchen of my widow aunt, and what remained of the preparations for the mid-day meal. At night between nine and ten, we took our meals with my father and other elders, and in some respects this was the principal meal of the day, with a larger variety of courses than could be made ready for the somewhat hasty meal in the morning, when most of the elders had to rush to their work in court or office.

But the one meal which we young folk enjoyed most was the afternoon meal. After the fairly long school-hours, and the running and romping that we had during the mid-day recess at school, we were, for one thing, generally ravenously hungry at this time; in the next place, as it combined all the courses of our morning meal cooked in the "fish kitchen," as it was usually called, with the simple but delicious and spicy and hot vegetable dishes prepared in the widows' kitchen, this afternoon meal was about our richest meal in the day. But the greatest attraction of it was my mother. At this meal she used generally to come and sit with us, boys and girls, forming a circle round a fairly big bell-metal plate or bowl or *gamla*, in which she mixed the rice and *dal* and other curries and used to feed us with her own hand. We were not allowed to touch the food but sat frequently with our mouths half-open in eager expectancy of the tender hand that came round with the delicious mouthful of food. Looking back upon this scene, I sometimes picture my mother as a fine hen feeding her loved brood. My mother was a fine, fair, tall woman, one of the most perfect pictures of motherhood that I have seen in all my travels almost over half the world. And sending my mind back to the days of my boyhood, and reviving this scene with my present art-perceptions, I often wonder what a beautiful picture we made at this afternoon meal of ours more than half-a-century ago. That scene has passed away from our life, never perhaps to be revived again. We have become more "civilised," we have larger knowledge of hygiene, and are far more afraid of disease and death, and are perpetually anxious to protect ourselves and our children from all sorts of contagion, even the contagion of their own flesh and blood! The practice of brothers and sisters and cousins and dear friends of boyhood eating out of the same platter or snatching food in loving contest almost from one another's mouth has been condemned as insanitary and unsafe. The fear of the unseen and unknown disease-germs has chilled the natural instincts of our human love and affection to some extent and has made our most endearing caresses more or less self-conscious and calculating!

To me, however, this afternoon meal when my mother used usually to feed us—and we were about ten or twelve—was sometimes a bit trying. Every one of us, quite naturally, wanted to get the first serving and the best of every course, the most delicious portion of the fish or vegetable, before us. But unless there was enough of these to go fully round to all the children, I could never, by any chance, get a helping. I tried all positions in this charmed circle, some day sitting next to my mother, sometimes farthest from her, but wherever I might be I never had the first serving, but always and studiously she would serve me last! She had a special order of precedence, it seems, in her own mind; and in this order, those who had no manner of relationship with her, came first; next came our relations by my father's side; then our relations by her own side; after these came my younger sister; and last of all, almost invariably, came my turn! I remember how bitterly I resented this wrong; and in my bitterness oftentimes I actually believed that my own mother was dead and she was only my step-mother! When I grew up—I think I was then reading in the Second or Preparatory Class and was fifteen years of age,—and

AUTHOR'S FAMILY GROUP (age 30).

she thought that I could understand and appreciate her ways, she one day explained it all to me. It seems that I had resented something that she did to me that day, and must have cried for it. When my anger had calmed down and I went back to her, she asked me to sit by her, as she was peeling and cutting vegetables for the next meal, and said: "You are growing up, won't you understand these things even now? When shall you then? These other boys in *your* house have not got *their* mother here to look after them. If I am not especially careful of their comforts they will be easily neglected; but even if I wish to, I cannot really neglect you, can I?" I replied, "But what about *Kripa* (my younger sister)?" My mother said: "Oh, Kripa, poor girl, she will be with us only for a year or two more, after which she too will go to her own home, among strangers; while whatever is in this house will remain yours for always. Should'nt she have for just these few days a little preference over you?" I do not remember if I understood all that she meant then. I do now when I cannot have her back to me to tell her and bless her for all she did. Would my daughters and sons understand!

I oftentimes feel exceedingly thankful that my father was innocent of our modern education and ways. He was not obsessed with the sense of duty towards his own family as most of us are; and therefore did not feel any hesitation in accepting his poorer relations in his own house and treating them as his own. Of all gifts the gift of knowledge was regarded as the greatest by our fathers. And my father never refused to help any one to receive the best available education so far as his means permitted it. And in those days many people wanted only a little food and shelter for their boys in towns, where there were schools, to qualify them for their life. While he was at Dacca he found food and lodging for some poor but promising students. One of these rose later in life to a fairly high position, became the Dewan of the Tippera Raj, if I remember aright. And my father told me that this gentleman wrote frequently to him to let him have me with him to bring me up. Of course that was out of the question. My father had no need of this help either. But he talked of it frequently with evident satisfaction. I am thankful that my father had these old ideas; because if he had our modern ideas, my early life would have been exceedingly lonely and dreary. I had no brother, and only one younger sister, who coming immediately after me was in our childhood more the object of my jealousy than of my love and affection. And the group of boys and youths who came from different families to live with us at Sylhet found room for the play and exercise of my growing youthful affections.

Besides my uncles, cousins, and one or two boys who though not related to us come and lived with us reading in the school at at Sylhet, there were others also living with their own people in the same compound with us. We thus formed a fairly large company, about twenty in all. And we had the run of the whole compound, and of every house that stood upon it. The ladies' quarters ran in a line at the back of the men's or outer houses; and though every house was separated by walls of split hamboos from its neighbour, there were doors that led from one house to the other. The ladies, though living according to current custom in zenana seclusion, had a certain measure of freedom, could, and always did, meet together and spend a few hours after the morning's work was over, in friendly gossip or play. And during school holidays we boys used to have the time of our life during these hours, freed from the restrictions of our guardians and the supervision of our mothers.

A few days after my father joined the Sylhet Bar, the District Judge, one Mr. Shaw, retired from service and went "home" to England. His furniture, according to the usual practice of those days, were sold by public auction. My father took a fancy, it seems, to the small table, teapoy, chair and easy-chair of Mr. Shaw's boy, who must have been of my age, and bought the whole lot of this furniture for me. It was a very small thing but this had, I fear, a great effect in shaping my character, even long after I had left school and college. Chairs and tables were not in general use among our people in those days. My father sat and worked on a *farash*, that is, a raised platform made up of two or three large and oblong wooden seats raised on fairly high legs, on which a *durree* was spread covered with a bleached sheet, with one or two round and high pillows or cushions to recline on, when wanted. He had a few wooden chairs, office chairs, as they are now generally called, in front of this *farash*, for such clients or other visitors of his who were either Mahommedans or Hindus of those castes, *hookas* or pipes filled inside with water touched by whom could not be used by so-called higher caste people. But they had no tables or easy-chairs even in the house of rich people in Sylhet in those days. In buying the furniture of young Shaw for my use, my father unconsciously introduced a very great innovation in my life, which had, I fear, a far-reaching effect in giving certain impulses to my future life and evolution. In my young days I was very partial to English ways and ideas; and I have often wondered whether the accident that led my father to bring me up, while I was a boy, in the use and enjoyment of the furniture of young Shaw had not something to do with it.

My father evidently bought this furniture so that I might sit at this small table and read and write. But I put these more often to other uses. What was meant to help in my studies was turned by me as instruments of my play. School holidays were then, even as now, more numerous than court holidays. So on many of these holidays, while our guardians were away at their work in court or office, we gave ourselves over to all sorts of frolic and even mischief. In my early boyhood we used to organise imitation schools when my small table and chair rendered excellent service as school furniture. But in those plays, somehow or other, I almost invariably took the part of either the Head Master of the school, or when some one else contended for this honour, I managed to act as School Inspector, and the younger and weaker boys had rather a bad time of this "play." Sometimes we changed the subject, and played at judge, pleader, complainant and defendant etc. And here also, owing perhaps to my closer acquaintance with the ways of courts which I had during the days when my father was Munsiff and I used very often to go and sit by him on a high chair on his *ejlash* or bench, trying to read the Bengalee Gazette the time he was engaged in his judicial work, as frequently happened when we were at Koterhat in Backerganj,—I was almost invariably the presiding judge. And how proud I felt when, dressed in made-up pants and coat, I sat at my small table, other boys standing or sitting as their position entitled them, about me! I say made-up pants, because none of us had any pants then; and what I did was to turn the shirts or coats we had upside down, and putting our legs through the arm of these made them do temporary duty for pants. I remember how while playing at these judicial proceedings I once tried and sentenced a poor dog to be hanged by the neck on a charge of cat-slaughter. The dog was caught hold of and hung by the rope of the *punka* in my father's office room, and the poor thing, though we did not actually kill him, must have had a very bad time of the very few minutes that he had the rope of the punka round his neck!

Sometimes we played at other scenes of the life of our elders also. There was a good deal of drinking in those days in Sylhet among the *bhadralokes.* They were all orthodox people, affecting the Shakta cult. Some of our own relations belonged to this group. We were always hearing stories of their doings in the talk of our elders. One day we took it into our head to play at drinking and getting drunk. Our boyish imagination never failed in its resources on these occasions. So we got a big brazen pot filled with water and putting a good dose of salt into it, made this saline preparation do duty for wine, and we got heavily "drunk" on this not-very-tasty liquid; and acting our parts with great realism, we made a hell of the house for a tumultuous half-hour. Drunken bouts cannot be had without some damage to the furniture of the house. The furniture in my father's house necessarily came to some grief. The whole room was also in woful disorder, when my father suddenly turned up, earlier than usual, from his court. And the servant gave us all away, telling my father how we had got drunk on a free potation of salt water, and done all this mischief. My father, as I have said, was a very strict Vaishnava. Vaishnavic piety and morals enjoin absolute abstinence as a religious duty. He could not tolerate this evil thing even as a play. Why should sons of gentlemen even play at getting drunk? That was how he looked upon the whole thing. And I had a very severe whipping from him for this folly. I think this put a stop to all our attempt to put again on the stage of our youthful play these scenes from the life of our elders. We too were also fast growing up. And cards and chess, among indoor games, and cricket and *kabati* and riding, among out-door games, took the place of these frolics.

When I was in the Third Class of my School, Sir George Campbell became the Lieutenant-Governor of Bengal. Sylhet was still a Bengal District. And the changes that were taking place in Bengal reached us in Sylhet also and influenced our thoughts and aspirations. Competitive examinations for the Subordinate Executive Service were first instituted about this time, if I remember aright. And riding formed one of the compulsory accomplishments of the candidates for appointment to this service. My father evidently had his dreams concerning my future along these lines; so he encouraged me in my desire to ride and manage horses. Babu Navakishore Sen had a couple of ponies and I soon commenced to take my exercise in riding from him. By the time I left school I became a fairly good rider, and could carry a good horse at the rate of ten to twelve miles an hour.

Swimming was also a fairly favourite sport with me in my school-days. My father was my swimming master. When I was about eight or nine he commenced to teach me how to swim. He used to take me to the tank every Sunday and while I screamed and kicked about, he used to push me beyond my depth, and after I had got a few mouthfuls of water into me, he took me up and stretching his fore-arms underneath my body would ask me to use my arms and legs to keep me afloat. And as he held me up very lightly, and threatened to take his arms away every now and then, I had no option but to ply my arms and legs as best as I could, to save myself from getting drowned. Bladders are not used in our country in learning to swim. Trunks of plantain plants are used instead. At least we used these in the earlier stages of our swimming exercises. Sylhet, like the rest of Eastern Bengal, is a riparian district. The greater part of it goes under water during the rains. Tanks are the principal sources of water-supply for the people in those parts that have no rivers. Country-boats were in those days the only means of transportation for six months of the year over by far the greater part of the District. These conditions of their life made swimming a necessity to them; and every child, whatever the sex or the station of life, had to be taught swimming as early in life as possible. When I grew up, swimming and diving became somewhat of a passion with me. My cousins and uncles and the other boys in our house and in the neighbourhood oftentimes competed with one another in this game during the hot summer months, particularly on Sundays and other school-holidays. Sometimes we used to walk down to the river *Surma* that flows by the town of Sylhet to have a swimming competition ; and though I myself do not remember to have ever made the attempt, some of my companions used very often to swim across to the other other bank, sometimes returning on the ferry boat and sometimes, after taking a little rest, swimming back to the landing stage or Ghat.

Though many of our elders, including Babu Nabakishore Sen, of whom the young people in our house stood as much in fear as they did of my father, used to play at cards and chess and dice very often after the day's work was over and especially during Sundays and other holidays, my father never took part in these. But I soon caught the contagion, and by the time I got into the Third Class of my School, I attained considerable proficiency at the particular game of cards called *graboo* in Bengalee, which was very popular in those days. I also learnt a little chess but did not attain much success in it. It called for much greater concentration than what I could stand.

Our life at Sylhet was rather simple. We had enough good things to eat, but few or no luxuries at all. My father kept fewer servants than people of his standing do to-day. We never had more than three, and more often only two servants in our house, one of whom did all outside work, that is cleaning the pots and pans which used to be put for him every noon and night after the meals were over. He was a so-called untouchable, that is, he could not enter our kitchen or the living rooms, because we could not, according to the rules of caste, drink water or take cooked food touched by him, or kept inside the same roof with him. He also carried my father's papers to the court and held the "state umbrella", when required, over him. The others were what is called caste-men now, that is, they could fetch water and clean the kitchen and help in preparing the food though they could not actually cook for my father or other elders. There was no harm in us boys taking cooked food from their hands.

As a rule, these people came from our village, and were either my father's retainers, that is, belonged to the family of our old hereditary servants, whose first parents had most probably been bought for a price, or they were his tenants or even simply neighbours belonging to the caste from which domestic servants used to be drawn in those days. But though of a much lower social status, they were scrupulously treated with consideration and even a certain amount of respect. We boys were never permitted to call them by their proper name or order them about as menials. Here their caste did not count at all. We had to address them as *Dada* or elder brother, or *Kaka* or paternal uncle, or *Mama* or maternal uncle. They also, in their turn, used to refer to my parents in the terms of these relationships, as *Dada* and *Didi* or *Kaka* and *Kaki* or *Mama* and *Mami* and so on and so forth.

I very well remember a servant in our home at Sylhet, who was of a very low caste, indeed, an untouchable, as some people would call him to-day. He could not enter our kitchen or touch our drinking water or go inside the room where there was any cooked food for us. His name was Sadan. I used to call him Sadan Dada. He was by caste a "Mali" as it is called in our parts. The occupation of this caste is very much like that of scavengers in our modern towns. They swept the outer yards of the house and the lanes and roads, constructed privies, but never touched or removed night-soil. He used to address me as "Thakurdhan," the pet name which my mother gave me. He called my father *Mama* or maternal uncle and my mother as *Thakooran Mami.* I have no recollection of his mother, but I have an idea that she was much older than my father and used to address him by his pet name of "Ramdhan." Many of our retainers used to address him as "Ramdhan Mama," which was indicative of the relationship in which my grand-parents stood to their own parents and grand-parents. One day, I remember, in a fit of anger, for having boxed my ears for some mischief that I had done, I called Sadan "Sadan Mali" and raised my hands upon him. As luck would have it, just at this moment my father turned up there, and I got a severe thrashing for my insolence, while Sadan was asked to beat me soundly whenever I was insolent or insubordinate. A few days later, when I had grown up somewhat, Sadan's wife fell ill when we happened to be at home during the Pujas; and my father was by her sick-bed when the end drew near. I think Sadan married again, and my father practically stood host to his guests from his father-in-law's place, and saw to it that his relations could not find any fault with hospitality, which would reflect much less upon Sadan himself than upon our house. Caste-restrictions obtained in those days only in the matter of eating and drinking; but these never interfered with the exchange of neighbourly good offices or with loving service of the lower or untouchable castes by the higher castes during disease, death, or other difficulties. I was told that when my father was at Dacca one day he had a man carried to his home, who was lying by the roadside, ill with small pox, and had him tended there without making any enquiry into his caste.

In fact, in my father's home both at Poil and in Sylhet, the so-called menials were always treated as younger members of the family. His moral code was never outraged by his occasionally inflicting physical chastisement on his servants any more than it was by his giving me a severe hiding when I went wrong. And in my school-days a young servant from our village used to be almost daily beaten by my father for his neglect of duty. But he never took it seriously or felt his dignity and self-respect hurt by this ckastisement. He took the thing in very good humour, and when asked why he was so careless and rendered himself liable to these chastisements, he used to say that he rather rather liked to tease my father and did not mind the mild beating which hurt my father's hands more than his own back!

In my father's home no manner of distinction was permitted to be made between the children and the servants in the matter of food. They had the same quality of rice which we had, and whatever was cooked in the house, or whatever edibles came as presents from friends and relations and my father's clients, used to be served out to them in the same measure as it was to us. I remember very well that at one time, during our stay in Sylhet, my father having purchased a big estate in a public auction, got involved in heavy and costly litigation that very seriously drained his purse. As a result he had to cut down his expenses. He stopped our milk supply. His own health was not so well at this time as it ought to have been. A cousin of mine, seeing my father's growing weakness, insisted upon his having some milk every day. But my father would have none of it; because, as he said, he never had in all his life enjoyed any food himself which he could not share equally with every one in the house, including the servants. That settled the matter and no one dared to reopen the question to him again. Indeed, this was also the rule of life with my mother. If anything, she was even perhaps more particular than my father himself in these matters. When I grew up, and had to look after our poorer guests on festive occasions, she used to tell me always to see to it that they had the very best of everything. "The Bhadralokes do not come to your house for a feed," she used to say. "What can you offer them which they do not have in their own home? But these poor people do not always get fine things to eat. And the Bhadrolokes don't discuss what they eat in your house, whether it is good or bad; but the poor people always talk of it among themselves. The good name of your house is in the keeping of your poor neighbours; remember this always."

We were used to few luxuries in our school-days. Dhoti, or loin-cloth, manufactured by local weavers from thread spun locally, and an upper sheet of the same make and material, was our entire apparel in my early boyhood. Manchester had not yet fully established itself in our markets in these distant country parts. Shirts and coats, of the pattern that had come into fashion during the Moslem *régime*, were used by the elders of the higher classes. My father's court-dress consisted of a loose pyjama and a "chapkan" with a "chadar" or thin cotton rolled almost into a rope, thrown over it. He used varnished shoes, but no socks. At home and in his own society he went about in *dhoti* and *chadar* with a *mirzai* or Persian waist coat, put on occasionally as a protection against cold. His court head-dress was a rimmed *pugree* of plaited muslin, that used to be remade every now and then when it became dirty, by the local tailors. My school dress consisted of *dhoti* and *chadar*, and a shirt (without cuffs) and occasionally a coat of imitation silk or wool. When I was very young, I remember to have been given a pair of pants and a coat for my school-dress. I was allowed only one pair of shoes during the year. It used to be bought during the Pujas, in autumn; and lasted generally three or four months. Sometimes, after I had grown up somewhat, I was found a pair of India-rubber shoes or goloshes, during the rains. For the greater part of the year, however, I had to go about unshod; and I still remember the ugly figure that I made in going to school in pants and coat, but without socks or shoes.

There were neither chemise nor bodice nor jacket in our society in those days. Women of ill-repute only used bodices in our parts, though "kachulis" were in almost universal use among all classes of women in the other Indian provinces. The Bengalee ladies never put on any "sewn" garment. My mother never saw a chemise or bodice in all her life. Yet it would not at all be true to say that our ladies went about in those days in a state of semi-nudity. They used one single piece of *sari*, generally ten cubits long, and about forty-four inches in width (if I remember aright), and they knew to tie it round their person in such a way that no part of it ever remained in any way exposed. Besides they never appeared in public in those days. My mother had, I think, just a pair of silk sarees for use on special occasions. Jewels she had very little, and those were all made of silver, except a string of gold beads which she put around her neck.

CHAPTER V.

SOCIAL LIFE IN SYLHET DURING MY SCHOOL-DAYS.

Society in towns is always of a very mixed character. The majority of the educated people in a town are generally outsiders, gathered together in the pursuit of business or through the call of their office. Sylhet had a very small number of English-educated persons in those days; and the result of it was that most of the offices under Government were held by outsiders, particularly people from Dacca. This gave birth to a kind of parochial or local patriotism among our people and there was a more or less open rivalry and antagonism between the people from Dacca and other districts residing in Sylhet, and the natives of the district. We of Sylhet used to look upon these outsiders as "interlopers."

Society in Sylhet was mainly Hindu; though there were two or three highly respectable and influential Mahommedan families also in the town. The Hindus were broadly divided into two sections; the Brahmins, the Kayesthas and Vaidyas with their dependants and others, water touched by whom could be used by these higher castes, forming one section; and the Shahas, forming the other. The Shahas were a very rich and refined class; but, unfortunately, they were not admitted into the communion of the other high-caste Hindus. They were believed, though we now know very unjustly, to belong to the brewer caste. Recent researches into the ancient history and evolution of the Hindus castes of Bengal have been bringing it to light that more than one Bengalee caste, now condemned to the position of untouchables, were at one time very respectable members of the community. During the Buddhistic period these people held very high position in society. But when Brahminism was established they refused to submit at first to the supremacy of the Brahmins and were, in consequence of their revolt, condemned to a low status in the new and reconstructed Hindu society. This is how the Shahas and the Subarna Baniks who, as their name implies, were rich and influential merchants and traders, and who, in the pride of their wealth and position, dared to defy the authority of the Brahmins, were relegated to a lower social position. But even to this day, the descendants of those brave people, who refused to sacrifice their conscience to secure earthly profit, have held their head as high as the so-called higher castes, and have not proved themselves in any way inferior either in native intelligence or education or in culture and refinement to the so-called higher castes in Bengal. The Shahas of Sylhet were in those days, as they are even to-day, about the richest class in the town of Sylhet. They had a fair percentage of English-educated men among them; and they very naturally resented the inferior social status to which mediæval Hinduism had condemned them. And while they could not interdine with the Kayesthas and the Vaidyas of the District, they used to purchase girls from the poorer members of these so-called higher castes, particularly of

PEARY CHURN SIRCAR.

East Sylhet, for their boys; and to secure, whenever they could, bridegrooms also from these castes for their daughters. Many Kayestha families in East and North Sylhet came, in this way, to be related to the Shahas, though they could not openly interdine with them and otherwise treat them as members of their own family or caste. Daughters of Kayesthas or Vaidyas marrying a Shaha were never taken back into their parents' house or society but remained for life as outcastes. The same thing happened also to the boys who were married into Shaha families.

This desire of Shaha parents to secure bridegrooms for their daughters from the Kayestha and Vaidya families of the District found field for romance to adventurous youths of the Kayestha and Vaidya castes in our school-days. The marriage of Kayestha or Vaidya boys to Shaha girls was oftentimes arranged in secret in those days; and young men from our school used sometimes to be tempted to steal away from their home and form these connections. Our people used to describe the thing as "kidnapping." And sometimes there was a regular scare in the community over these cases of "kidnapping." Whenever any young man did not return home at the usual hour from school, particularly of a Saturday evening, there used to be regular consternation among his family and friends.

The peace of our own household was once disturbed from this cause. I had a young cousin of mine, my mother's sister's son, about three or four years older than myself, living with us and reading in the school at this time. He was a fine-looking youth, supple of limb, and very attractive in both contour and colour, which was of the tint of the young and tender leaves that first commence to shoot out at the kiss of the warm southern breeze of early spring and which gave a sense of exquisite softness to the eyes. He had lost his father a few years before, and was just the kind of young man eagerly sought by the parents of comely Shaha maidens. He did not turn up from school one Saturday evening and was away from home for the whole of that week-end; and there was great trouble in our house over his escapade. I forget where he had spent this time, but he came back safe and whole on Monday morning. And as the guardians of young men of the Kayestha and Vaidya castes were, in those days, very afraid of their wards making these run-away matches, they dared not take any serious notice of their escapades. My cousin's absence from home was not also taken very seriously either by my father, much less by my mother.

There was, and still is, a very respectable Mahomedan zemindar family in the suburbs of Sylhet, who represented the highest Moslem culture and refinement in the District, and lent considerable dignity and grandeur to the society of our town. Theirs was the only house which entertained high English officials and which was furnished in the prevailing Anglo-Indian fashion of those days. The head of this family, in my school-days, was Syedbakt Mazoomdar, who was a very pious man and had made pilgrimages to Mecca and Medina. The ancestors of this Moslem family had been Hindus. Though their present title is Mazoomdar, their Hindu forbears went by the name of Dastidars. Both Mazoomdar and Dastidar are Mahomedan titles; but the Hindu family name of these Dastidars was Das. A branch of this family belonged to our part of the District, and a representative of this family, Babu Haramani Dastidar, was related to us on my mother's side. He was a cousin of my mother and used very often to come and stay with us in Sylhet. The Mazoomdars recognised their relationship with him, and used to receive him as a clansman or kinsman. Another branch of the same family lives in the suburbs of Sylhet. They are Hindus and have retained the title of Dastidar. They are also zemindars and count among the leaders of the local Hindu community.

The Shahas of Sylhet had their own Brahmins. It seems that when they were condemned to a lower social status upon the revival of Brahminism, the Brahmins, who ministered to the religious and sacramental life of the so-called higher castes of Hindus, refused, or were not permitted, to minister to the religious and sacramental life of the Shahas. And these Shahas, when they were forced to come back into the Hindu fold, must have created or ordained a class of Brahmins from among themselves. This has been actually done by some of the excommunicated castes in our time also. And the Brahmins of the Shahas of Sylhet, like the Shahas themselves, used in my school-days to seek matrimonial connections with the Brahmins of the higher class, those who were recognised by the Kayesthas and Vaidyas. The representative of a rich Brahmin zemindar family of the town, in my young days, had thus originally belonged to the higher class of Brahmins, but he or his parents formed matrimonial connection with this Shaha-Brahmin family and became a member of this caste. These connections, however they might be condemned by Hindu orthodoxy and looked down upon by caste-proud Brahmins and Kayesthas and Vaidyas, helped very considerably to liberalise the social outlook of the whole Hindu community of Sylhet and contributed very materially to bring the ways and manners of the Sylhet Shahas into line with those of the other higher castes of Hindus. And as the Shaha girls in these inter-marriages naturally adopted the name and *gotra* of their Kayestha husbands, there are many Shaha families who cannot be distinguished from their Hindu clansmen or kinsmen, either by their name and *gotra* or by their character and culture.

Though social intercourse was still regulated by the rules and restrictions of Hindu castes, all the really higher and more refined and well-to-do castes freely mixed with one another except in the matter of eating and drinking. The Shahas are Vaishnavas of the school of Shree Chaitanya Mahaprabhu or the Gaudeeya School; and they used to have all the Vaishnava worships and ceremonials in their house to which the entire Hindu community was duly invited. My father rarely responded to those invitations himself; but he used always to depute some one from our house to these socio-religious functions. When I grew up this deputation generally came to me.

Of the Vaishnava festivals, *Jhoolan* or the Swinging Festival was the most popular among the Vaishnavas of Sylhet in those days. It was held during the week preceding the full moon in August. This full moon is called in our calendar as the *Jhoolan Poornima*. And the festival commemorates the *leela* or sport of Shree Krishna with Shree Radha, when he swung with her to the tune of heavenly music in Shree Brindaban. Images of Radha and Krishna, either in bronze or silver or stone, were placed on a throne which was made to swing, while devotees or hired musicians sang appropriate songs. There were a number of Vaishnavic temples or *Akharas* in Sylhet in those days; some exist still, though they have lost their old position and prestige. These *Akharas*, most of which had been originally endowed by rich Shaha gentlemen, were in my school-days in charge of holy Vaishnavas from Upper India, Ramayat or other mendicant devotees, who, having renounced the social order, were outside or above all caste-restrictions. We could take our food from their hands, though my father hesitated sometimes to do so. The *Jhoolan* festival used to be performed with great *éclat* by these *Akharas* in our time. We used to visit them during the *Jhoolan* week, when the town became resonant with strains of music and the talk of sight-seers passing to and fro, in the cloud-covered moon-light, all through the night. As soon as the rains set in, we used to look forward with very great eagerness and expectation to this *Jhoolan* week, when we went about from one festive house or *Akhara* to another, seeing the pretty decorations and illuminations of the places of worship, making our homage to the divine images with presents of money, partaking of sweets wherever the rules of caste did not interfere with it, and elsewhere receiving "pan and attar," gossiping all along the way with friends and school-mates. This was the only time of the year when I had the freedom of our moonlit highways and by-ways, and the memory of the youthful abandon with which I used to throw myself into it still sends my old blood rushing through my veins. I did not understand either the music or the words of the exquisite love-lyrics which used to be sung by professionals or more often by devout amateurs on these occasions; but the mere joyousness of the thing, the weird beauty and romance of the moon trying to peep from behind flying banks of cloud, and the company and fellowship of young friends, who clung to each other almost lover-like while walking in this moon-light, all these had a very great fascination for my youthful imagination and emotions.

Though not exactly a social function like the *Jhoolan* festival, *Ratha-Yatra* or the Car Festival, which falls in July, was also a very popular Hindu institution in Sylhet in those days. And the beauty and grandeur of this festival were contributed almost entirely by the Manipuri community of the town. I cannot exactly say when these people first came to Sylhet, whether before or after the first Manipur War. There was a house in the town in our school-days which was known as the palace of the Manipur Raj or Manipur *Rajbatee*. Raja Gambheer Singh was said to have been brought as a prisoner to Sylhet and this house was either built for or given to him as his residence. Gambheer Singh had been dead long before my time, but his name and tradition were still green in the public mind.

A number of Manipuris lived in and about this "palace." There were colonies of this people in other parts of the town and its suburbs also. Originally these Manipuris must have been Buddhists, like the rest of the Mongolian stock from which they came, but they were converted to Hinduism by some disciple of Shree Chaitanya Mahaprabhu about the 16th century of the Christian era. Since then the Manipuris, as a class, follow the Shree Chaitanya cult and look upon Navadvip, the birth-place of Shree Chaitanya Mahaprabhu, and the other localities associated with his life, as sacred places which they visit in large numbers during the various Vaishnava festivals, particularly during the *Holi* festival, which falls on the full-moon day of the Bengalee month of Falgoon, corresponding to February-March of the English calendar.

The Manipuris are a very fine race. Though of undoubted Mongolian origin, with the flat nose and the long-drawn eyes of the Chinese and the Jap, their pigment while still preserving the yellow tint has taken, perhaps owing to our climate and association, a much softer hue than is usually seen in the Yellow races. They have besides a general tenderness of flesh and form which one does not always find in the tougher specimen of this race. And this tenderness is also reflected in their mental character. Bengal Vaishnavism has had perhaps something to do with this special feature of the Manipuri mentality. Though classed as Hindus, the Manipuris, at least in my school-days, were free from some of the popular prejudices and customs of the rest of the Bengalee Hindus. They formed, so far as I can remember, one single caste, and regarded themselves as Kshatriyas, claiming descent, I think, from Arjuna, who had during his exile married a daughter of their race. All the Manipuris, therefore, wear the sacred thread after the manner of the Kshatriyas. Though claiming to be Kshatriyas, they did not necessarily follow the profession of warriors, for which, at any rate in British India, there was in those days little or no scope. The Manipuri community in Sylhet followed many professions; some were weavers, some carpenters; some were agriculturists, while some were engaged in buying and selling, especially food-products. Manipuri women did not observe zenana seclusion; nor had they adopted, with their Vaishnavism, the custom of early marriage from their Bengalee teachers. They have very fine artistic instincts. Lovers by nature of flowers and leaves, with which both men and women beautifully decked themselves, the homestead of these people frequently looked like a picture or a place of divine worship, so clean and so orderly was everything about it. I think these Manipuris are the cleanest of the clean people of Hindoostan, both in their person and their ways and habits. They are strict vegetarians and are the best-washed humans in these parts. They use sandal paste regularly. And all these things contribute to the peculiar loveliness of this race. Their dress also is simple. Unmarried and young girls use a kind of bodice or jacket and a skirt; but the elderly women go about with one single piece of thick cloth, tied with a knot above their chest, that fell down to their ankle, with the arms, head and the upper part of the body bare. The men use, or did use in my school-days, the ordinary *dhoti* and *chadar* affected by the general body of respectable Bengalees. I do not remember to have seen a Manipuri, whatever his social position or economic condition, going about, like our poorer and working classes, with only a narrow loin-cloth tied round the waist. And this seems to have been due to the especially developed art-sense of this people.

The Car Festival was peculiarly a Manipuri institution. The *Akharas* or Vaishnava temples, of course, had their cars on which they used to place the images of their Deities and bring them out into the street. But the private cars came mostly from the Manipuri colonies of the town. And there was a speciality in these cars. The temple-cars were built of wood, were preserved from year to year, being repaired or repainted from time to time. But these Manipuri cars were simple and light structures of bamboo and reed, the roof being uniformly of beautifully woven fresh leaves, generally of the jack-fruit tree, and adorned with flowering creepers, mostly the scented *Madhabi*, so beloved, according to Pauranic traditions, of Shree Krishna, and the gold-tinted *Champaka* or the ever-green *Malancha* wreaths, that looked like live snakes, coiled round pillars or hanging from the eaves of these cars. These cars looked, therefore, more like lover's bowers than the war-chariot of Arjuna in the field of Kurukshetra, which they were meant to represent. But the character of the worshippers always alters the nature of the symbolism through which they seek to worship their Deity.

This *Ratha-Yatra* or the Car Festival attracted large crowds from the villages, and the streets along which these cars used to be drawn, were converted for the day into a big fair where a good deal of business, particularly in fruits and toys for young folk and bamboo and rattan things of household use and sweets of various sorts, was carried on. Every car was preceded by a company of musicians playing on the holy *mridanga* and cymbals, and chanting *keertans* or religious songs describing the career or character of Shree Krishna or simply dilating upon the great virtue of chanting His sacred and salvation-giving name; and the whole country-side rang from afternoon, when the cars commenced to come out into the streets, up to late in the evening with the name of the Lord and the cry of "*Hari-bol.*" But to us, young folk, the thing that found the greatest attraction was the sight of the Manipuri cars and the general crowd of the fair.

Another festival, to which our Manipuri neighbours made the largest contribution, was *Rasha-Yatra*, which falls on the full-moon day of Agrahayana, corresponding to November of the English calendar. This *Rasha-Yatra* commemorates the dance of Shree Krishna in Brindaban with the Gopinees, chief of whom was Shree Radha. It was like a ball such as they have in European society, only with this difference that among "sixteen hundred Gopinees" there was only one male partner in this ball, and he was Shree Krishna; but the Bhagavata, the sacred book which relates these sports of the Lord, says that at one point in this ball when the Gopinees gave themselves up to it with absolute abandon, Shree Krishna multiplied himself and every Gopinee found him dancing with her in this great and charmed circle of dancers as her sole partner. The festival of *Rasha-Yatra* has been ordained to symbolise and commemorate this sport of the Lord. In the Bengalee Hindu home they make images of Radha and Krishna and setting them on a circular plane they worship the Lord with the Gopinees. But the Manipuris performed this festival in a different way. Instead of setting up images of Radha and Krishna, they dressed up the youths and maidens of their own families from the age of seven or eight up to that of fifteen or sixteen or even more as Krishna and Radha and they had this sacred dance or ball with these lovely and pure-minded youths and maidens as partners. These young people decked out in leaves and flowers—the plume of the peacock adorning the crown of the young men, who carried in their hands reed flutes to represent Shree Krishna,—dancing in a wide circle in a large hall covered from floor to ceiling with green leaves and flowers of various sorts and the air resonant with soft and weird music of Saranga and fragrant with the scent of a hundred flowers, presented the loveliest scene that I have witnessed in all my life. Such combination of nature and art, such display of colour and contour, such unstudied expression of the very soul of the music and the dance in the face and eye of the dancers, such unconscious innocence with just a suspicion of budding and conscious romance of an absolutely impersonal character, are things that are not, and I am afraid can never be, found anywhere in our civilisation. No one who has not seen this Manipuri *Rasha* can understand the poetry and purity of the Vaishnavic idylls that have been woven around the Radha-Krishna legend and cult in this country, particularly in Bengal. The whole town used to turn out during this festival that lasted for some days, as it reproduced not only the great ball in Brindaban but many other episodes in the life of Shree Krishna there, including the destruction of the demon called Baka-Asura. This last was, I think, the closing exhibition of the life of Shree Krishna by the Manipuri youths and maidens of Sylhet in our time.

Sylhet was pre-eminently a Vaishnava town, though there were some very influential Shaktas or worshippers of the Shakti cult among the Brahmins and other so-called higer castes in the suburbs, who were notorious for their drinking habits, which formed in those days an element of the worship of the Goddess Kalee. The Shahas were entirely Vaishnavas. The Subarna-Baniks in West Bengal are, I think, of this denomination. And it may possibly be due to the greater liberalism and freedom from Brahminical prejudices of the Vaishnava cult and culture, particularly of the followers of Shree Chaitanya Mahaprabhu, that these remnants of the old Buddhistic communities were brought inside the Hindu fold through Vaishnavic propaganda. Be that however as it may, the Shahas of Sylhet are all Vaishnavas; and consequently many Vaishnavic institutions flourished in the town. Scenes from the story of the life and *leela* or sport of Shree Krishna, like the *Rasha-Leela* or the Ball-Dance, which was yearly represented with such exquisite art and beauty by the Manipuri youths and maidens, were enacted by the community from time to time.

Goshtha-Leela, in which the boy Shree Krishna as cowherd led the calves and cows of his father's place to wild pasture-grounds in the woods, along with those of his neighbours, led by the boys and youths of those families, and in which, having taken the cattle to their pasture, the youthful cowherds enjoyed themselves in all sorts of sports,—forms one of the most touching episodes of the boyhood of Shree Krishna. This *Goshtha-Leela* presents a perfect picture of pastoral life and depicts, with inimitable beauty and tenderness, the romance or *rasa* of *batsalya* or parental affection and *sakhya* or youthful friendship. During my earlier years at school in Sylhet, this episode of Shree Krishna's life and *leela* used to be annually reproduced upon a large and realistic scale, with young boys as cowherds and quite a flock of well-groomed cows and calves, with cotton or silk wrappers thrown over their back, and garlands of various wild flowers on their neck. They used to be collected in a central square of the town, and taken with appropriate hymns and music to the hills outside it, where the company used to spend the day in various sports, mostly representative of the life of Shree Krishna, and have their meals there, and return home with *keertans* and illuminations by nightfall. Practically the whole town joined in this sport, which took place, if I do not forget, on the Gopastami Day, or the eighth day of the moon in the bright quarter of the month of Kartic; and it was really a red-letter day in our local calendar. This *Goshtha-Leela* is the subject of some of the finest lyrics of the Vaishnava poets of Bengal; and these used to be sung with great skill by either professional or amateur singers. And among the latter the very best was one Babu Kunja Behari Sen; and I have an idea that he had learnt his art from the *Keertaniyas* of Burdwan and Nadia. I had no understanding of his art in those days, nor had we, little boys, any perception of the theme of his songs, but there was a charm in the man, in his voice and expression, which captivated our unillumined intelligence also. Looking back upon these simple pleasures of our simple folk sixty years ago, I wonder what a pleasant and pure life they must have lived before the dawn of our present civilisation!

All round the seasons we had something or other to kill the dull monotony of our lives. This *Goshtha-Leela* took place in the month of Kartic, corresponding to October-November of the English calendar. The *Rasha-Leela* took place in Agrahayana or November-December. Then there was Pous or Makar Sankranti in January. It celebrated the winter solstice or the turning back of the sun from his southerly course (Dakshinayana) to his northerly one (Uttarayana). There was very little religious rite connected with this festival. But it was celebrated all over Bengal in those days as what may be best described as a Day of National Sports. The young folk of every village used to build toy-houses of bamboo and straw gathered from the fields the previous evening. Early next morning they used to take their bath in rivers or tanks, as the case might be, and then shivering with the bitter cold of the wintry dawn, they would gather around these toy-houses, and setting fire to them, warm themselves by the fire of these burning houses. This was also the day of what has been called the cake-festival in West Bengal. The ladies used to prepare a large variety of cakes and sweets for this occasion, and there was a general invitation to all friends and neighbours, particularly to the young people of the village, to these cake-feasts. In the afternoon, the whole village, old and young, used to assemble in some open space, generally the village pasture, and there used to be all sorts of sports and manly games here. Thus the whole day was spent in feasting and playing; and though we missed the simplicity of rural life and relations in the towns, the Uttarayana Sankranti was a school holiday, and as our elders had to attend their business in court or office on this day, this not being a holiday observed in the Government offices, we enjoyed it much better. Then in February or early March, there was the Sarasvatee Puja or the annual worship of Sarasvatee, the Goddess of Learning and the Fine Arts in Hindu symbolism. In my father's house we did not set up any image of this Goddess; but the priest performed the *puja* before a new earthen pot, which represented the Presence of the Deity; and we, young people, still in *statu pupillari*, had to repeat certain *mantrams* and make offerings of flowers to the Goddess. We were not permitted to open our books or touch our pens on this day. And we spent it in various games and sports. The whole of the month of Chaitra, the last month of the Bengalee year, was perhaps the gayest part of the year in Sylhet in those days. Kite flying was a very popular sport in the town; and the wealthier towns-people used to spend a lot of time and money over it. They used to make huge kites, and there used to be a keen competition among rival houses or communities over this game. They prepared especial twines of cotton or sometimes even of silk, to which broken glass used to be pasted and dried, to render these twines as sharp as possible, so that the twine of the rival kites might be easily cut. Sundays and other holidays were especially utilised for these kite-flying competitions; and I remember that sometimes the party, who was victorious, went back home at nightfall in procession with torches and music. Sometimes, if there was any foul play, there used to be even free fights between the retainers and friends of the parties. Throughout the month of Chaitra every Sunday there used to be a fair in the outskirts of the town, to which a large concourse of people came from the rural parts near about and, besides the usual buying and selling of all sorts of things, there used to be various kinds of *tamashas* also at these fairs. We had the *Ratha-Yatra* in the month of June or July; *Jhoolan* in August or September, and the great Pujas in October-November. The whole year was passed, thus, in a round of feasts and festivals. And all these contributed very materially to the simple joyousness of the life of our simple people a century ago.

Besides these public or communal or national festivals, we Hindus had an almost perpetual round of private festivities in our homes, to which our friends and neighbours used to be invited, and the general public also had free and welcome access. Travelling *yatra* parties or opera troupes used to visit our town once every year during the dry

80

ANANDA MOHAN BOSE,

season. These generally came from Dacca, and occasionally also from West Bengal. These *yatras* are a peculiarly Bengalee institution. These are kinds of musical dramas, the different parts of which are represented by boys and men only. There is neither stage nor scenery of any kind, the only outer help to these dramatic presentations being the dress and make-up of the principal actors, which too was of the simplest and most primitive kind. It, therefore, left it to the imagination of the audience to picture in their minds the scenes and situations in which the different parts were being acted. And as the theme of these musical plays was generally some well-known episode from the Puranas or our religious stories, which were familiar to everybody, the absence of outer paraphernalia and theatrical properties did not at all interfere with the inner enjoyment of it by the audience, particularly the older and really appreciative part of it. But it provided ample enjoyment also for the unillumined by the introduction of clowns and jesters, whose oftentimes coarse and vulgar ribaldries appealed to the multitude. And we, young people, also belonged to this unenlightened mass in those days, because we had little knowledge and less understanding of the sacred traditions upon which these plays were generally based.

The subject matter of the plays was usually drawn from the story of the Ramayana, or from some episode in the Mahabharata, for instance, the story of King Nala and his consort Damayantee; and sometimes it was built upon the much more modern and historical incidents of the life of Shree

Chaitanya Mahaprabhu. The "Exile of Rama" was a very popular musical drama of my school-days. Another was the Renunciation or *Sannyasa* of Nimai or Shree Chaitanya Mahaprabhu. But neither of these plays could be performed in our house. My mother could not stand these tragedies of mother-love. Other episodes from the Ramayana, as for instance, "Ravana-*Badh*" or the Destruction of Ravana or "*Lakshaner Shakti-Shel*" or the wounding of Lakshana by the deadly lance known as *shakti-shel* from the mortal effects of which he was saved through the good offices of Hanuman, who, not knowing the particular herb that could bring the hero back to life, took up the entire mountain, where it was to be found, and brought it to the physician attending his beloved Master's brother—these could be played in our house. The story of Nala and Damayantee also did not hurt her mother-love, and she could listen to and enjoy it. But she could not stand any tragedy which came from the separation of the son from his mother.

The most popular of these musical plays were those that had the love of Shree Krishna and Shree Radha for their subject. The old Vaishnava poets of Bengal, dating from the 14th century of the Christian era, have dealt with this theme with an art peculiarly their own, of which there exists no parallel, so far as I know, in any other literature of the modern world. These lyrics are still sung by our *Keertaniyas* in the style which came into vogue at the time of Shree Chaitanya Mahaprabhu. But these *yatras* are modern compositions and are played in a modern style, though both the words and the music are very largely drawn from the old source. The most favourite composer of these *yatras* in my young days, in our part of the country, was Pandit Krishna Kamal Goswami, three of whose musical plays—"Swapna-Vilas", "Rai-Unmadinee" and "Vichitra-Vilas"—were the best and used to be most liked by our people. Krishna Kamal Goswami was by caste a Vaidya or physician; but though not Brahmin by birth, he came of a long line of highly respectable and revered spiritual teachers or *gurus* of the Bengal Vaishnava denomination. He was well versed both in the Sanskrit Bhagabata and the Bengalee religious and philosophical and poetical works of the Shree Chaitanya School. His plays breathe, therefore, the exceedingly devout spirit of our Vaishnavic cult and culture, particularly of our Vaishnavic art. All these plays,—"Swapna-Vilas", "Rai-Unmadinee" and "Vichitra-Vilas"—are what may be called psychological plays in the truest sense of the term; but the psychological developments and denouments are worked entirely within the mind and soul of the heroines and other principal actors, and not brought out by delineation of outer events and actions, except so far as these are helpful to the quickening of the inner emotions. "Swapna-Vilas" opened with the recital of a vision of young Krishna, who had gone away from Brindaban, in his mother's dream. It was an exquisite picture of mother-love crying out for the absent son, and it delineated how, in the very anguish of separation, the presence of the beloved is realised in the inner consciousness of the bereaved parents. In "Rai-Unmadinee" the poet describes Rai or Shree Radha in her bereavement due to her desertion by her lover, Shree Krishna; and starting with the recollection and recital of her happier days in the company of her lover, finally ends with a "madness" in which she is possessed with a consciousness of his presence about her, and mistakes whatever she sees or touches or perceives by any of her outer sense-organs as the form or the touch or the fragrance of Shree Krishna. The entire experience is mental or emotional, subjective; and the processes through which these are gained is purely psychological. As "Swapna-Vilas" opened with the recital of a dream of Shree Krishna seen at the dead of night by his mother Yashoda, so "Rai-Unmadini" opened with the memory of Shree Krishna's flute playing in the woods. Whether this was quickened by some chance playing of the flute by some cowherd, or whether it was purely a subjective experience, and had no outer stimulus at its origin, it is difficult to say. Both interpretations might equally hold good. But henceforward, Shree Radha gives herself up with complete abandon to these happy recollections, until, at last, she entirely loses all sense of outer actualities and re-lives, so to say, her old life with her lover, within herself. She is absolutely mad, and is therefore called Rai-Unmadinee or the Mad Rai or Radha. She sees a *Tamala* tree on the top branch of which sits a peacock, with its feathers spread out; and she mistakes it for her lover, and rushes and embraces it; and immediately the cruel actuality forces itself upon her and with return to the outer objective world, she commences to curse her fate, and gradually sinks again into the subjective or trance state and develops the same "madness" over again. In "Vichitra-Vilas" we have more or less the same experiences related in regard to Shree Krishna, who completely obsessed with the presence, within his mind so to say, of his love, Shree Radha, takes whomsoever he meets for her and rushes to embrace her. This gives endless fun to Radha's female companions, who run about with a view to escape Shree Krishna's mistaken embraces, crying out "I am so and so; I am not Radha, your beloved Shree Radha stands yonder." I cannot say that in the days of my youth I understood either the psychology or the art of these operas, but the music and play nonetheless fascinated me very much.

These performances were given by what may possibly be called a kind of public subscription. Some leading gentleman of the town used to be approached by the proprietor of the *yatra* troupe, with a request to arrange for a performance in his house, and invite the local society to it, in his own name. He would not have to pay anything himself but the *yatra* party would be quite satisfied with whatever collections might be taken at the performance from the visitors. The host had a silver or bronze plate, with a few rupees, either two or five or more, whatever his own contributions might be, placed on it, in front of the players, and every guest personally invited to the performance used to put in his mite, from an eight-anna piece to a couple of rupees, on it; and, in this way, a fairly big sum was collected for the players. These offerings were regulated by well-known principles. Whatsoever the host was used to pay on similar occasions to his guests' parties, generally determined the presents of the latter; and an account of these presents used to be set down in black and white and preserved in every family, and returns were made always by a reference to it. This custom obtained in all social functions. No person, however rich, was allowed to give more than what his host paid him on similar occasions. To do so was taken as an insult. No one, indeed, ever dreamt of doing it.

In this way, a pretty large sum of money used to go out of my father's pocket every year as presents, on these festive occasions. The society in Sylhet was very largely composed of outsiders, who rarely or never had marriages and other domestic functions performed in their town houses. These were almost invariably performed in the villages. The Durga Puja was also performed there. So in the town practically the only social amenities were these musical performances and other social functions. These musical parties were also more patronised by the younger than by the older men. My father rarely gave these. There were others like him who did not patronise these troupes. But they had, all the same, to pay for these in their neighbours' houses. They were entitled to a return of these presents as well. And these elders used to invite people to what was called "Purana-Path" or reading of sacred books. As a matter of fact, there were neither sacred books nor any reading of them generally on these occasions. The invitation was to "kindly come and hear the reading of Purana or sacred lore," at such and such hours, at so and so's house. The usual hour was Sunday afternoon; and all the preparations made for the occasion by the host was to clean up his *baitakh-khana* or reception room, spread a clean and bleached sheet on the *farash*, set up a small platform covered with carpet, on which some book (whatever it was mattered really very little), tied up in a piece of clean red-cloth, in the manner in which our sacred manuscripts used to be tied, was placed, with a few flowers on it, and a silver or bronze plate was put in front of it, on which the guests were expected to put in their offerings of silver (for it was always what might be called a "silver collection"). The guests used to come and making their obeisance to the tied-up book gently place their offering on the plate, and spend a little time in conversations with the host or the other guests, *pan* and *attar* being served to them on behalf of the host along with the popular *hookka* or tobacco pipe. This was our "Purana-Path" in those days. It was almost invariably a fiction; and everybody knew it to be so. It was devised to give an occasion to the guests to return what they had been getting from the host during the year as offerings or subscriptions to their own parties and other functions. The monies thus collected from these "Purana-Paths" used to go to the family priest or the *guru* of the host, and sometimes to some learned Brahmin-Pandit deserving of public support. I cannot say if this old social institution still exists in our town; but in my younger days it was, though a fiction—and we, irreverent young men, oftentimes used to make fun of it—a very useful instrument of our social life, which kept up the self-respect of people in many ways.

Sometimes this "Purana-Path" found

occasion for ugly practical jokes to irreverent people. And I remember how on one of these occasions actually a pair of old and cast-away slippers was tied up and wrapped in a piece of red cloth and made to do duty for some sacred book. The secret was given away subsequently and was the talk of the town for some days. But though this was an extreme case, even in our own house, where my father would never tolerate such irreverence, we could not always secure a real Purana for this function, particularly when our family priest was not present in the town at the time. And I have a faint recollection that once or twice we were driven to wrap up one or two of my father's law journals to serve duty for a holy scripture. The sacred books had not yet commenced to be printed and circulated among the general public; and they were to be found in manuscripts only with learned Brahmins and devout people. Most people had, therefore, to do as we did on these occasions.

Though not quite a social function among us, Hindus, the Mohoram was a very popular and exciting institution in our life in Sylhet in those days. Sylhet has a large Mahomedan population. There is a noted Moslem *Darga* or shrine in the town, dedicated to Shaha Jalal, who may be called the Patron Saint of the town, which is one of the great sights of the town, visited both by pilgrims and sight-seers, and where offerings are made by Moslems and Hindus alike. We used to go to Shaha Jalal's *Darga* every now and then during our school-days. There was a large ostrich-egg in this mosque, reputed to have been brought from Arabia, which was one of the curios that attracted considerable notice from visitors.

There was a sacred well, where there were a goodly number of "gold and silver fish", as we used to call them. We now know that these are imported from China and may be had for a few coppers in Calcutta from street hawkers in Dharmtala and the New Market. But in my younger days, particularly in out of the way tracts like Sylhet, these were looked upon as miraculous products, and the "gold and silver fish" in the well inside the shrine of Shaha Jalal were in some way associated in our minds, like the big ostrich-egg, with the holiness and divine powers of the great Moslem saint. In the outer court-yard of the *Darga* there was a big tank, which was full of various kinds of fish; and as no one was permitted to catch or molest these fishes, they used to come up to the surface of the water whenever any food was thrown and even take it from human hands. This too was an object of great wonder and admiration to our boyish imagination; and we used to go, whenever we had a holiday and were not otherwise engaged, to this shrine and enjoy these curiosities.

All over the town there were Moslem populations and every Moslem quarter had its own *Akhara* or place of sword and stick play from which *Tazias* and processions used to be taken out during the Mohoram. For the whole of the period, from the first to the tenth day of the Moslem month of Mohoram, the whole town was resonant with the music of these *Akharas*, while during the last four or five days preceding the final ceremonial, there used to be a great and gorgeous display of *Tazias* in our market place at night, and the whole town practically turned out to witness the processions and the sword and stick play of the men. Processions from neighbouring villages also used to come here and occasionally there used to be free fights between the adherents of rival *Akharas*. Owing to these disturbances, my father did not encourage our going out at night to witness these rowdy processions, though we did manage frequently to steal out at dead of night and see these from a safe distance. On the tenth or last day of the Mohoram, when all the *Tazias* in Sylhet and the neighbouring places used to be brought to a large open space outside the town, called Idga-Maidan or the field of Id, my father used to take us himself to see the show. This Idga is one of finest spots in the vicinity of the Sylhet town; and I have seen few places finer than this. It is an open space surrounded almost on all sides by verdant hills of various altitudes, forming part of the Jayantiya range, which runs along the north of Sylhet up to Shillong, the seat of the present Assam Administration. We used to go up to one of these hills whence we could easily command the whole open space wherein the 'Tazias' and processions used to come and gather in their respective spots assigned to them by the police to avoid needless friction and fight. The whole of the gentry of the town and the suburbs used to take their seats on durries or mats which their men carried from home, and see the show from a safe distance. In my early days, the hills and jungles about Sylhet were infested by tigers; and even when we went and sat on some of these hills amidst all the crowd and noise of the Mohoram show, we could not easily rid ourselves of the nervousness due to these memories of roving beasts on these hill-tops.

My father also would not allow us to tarry here after dark, though we were always very eager to do so, because the most important and gorgeous of the processions from across the river used to arrive by candle light.

The Mohoram was one of the grandest institutions of Sylhet in my school-days. People were far more virile and bubbling over with physical energy and courage then than they are now. Like all people, who live a life of nature more or less in the wild places of the earth, the Sylhet peasantry, especially the Mahomedan peasantry of the suburbs, were very quick to resent any insult, whether real or fancied, and free fights between rival zemindars or social factions were very common. The Mahomedans used to work themselves into a frenzy during the Mohoram. We had no trouble, in those days, during the Id'ul Fatr, or Bakr-Id, as it is usually called. Both the Hindus and the Mahomedans were tolerant of their mutual religious practices. The Mahomedans never objected to the performance of Hindu Pujas, many Mahomedans actually joining these, so far as they could do it within the limits of Hindu ritualism; and the Hindus were equally tolerant of the religious practices of their Mahomedan neighbours, even of the practice of cow-killing, during the Id. But the Mohoram was different. During the Mohoram processions and plays, different sections or *Akharas* frequently came into collision and there were more or less serious breaches of the public peace in consequence of it. The Mahomedans of the town proper were more peaceful than their co-religionists from the villages round about. The townspeople were numerically weaker, and being divided into rival groups, representing the different wards so to say, they were less consolidated than their rivals from across the river Surma and particularly from a large Mahomedan village called Khitta. The procession from Khitta was the biggest that came to the Idga on the last day of the Mohoram. It was frequently about a mile long and six to eight deep, who rushed with their long sticks of dark and seasoned bamboo, like a large and invading host, making the air resound with the cry of 'Allah' 'Allah,' 'Din' 'Din'; and the very sight of it used to send our hearts throbbing with fear. Sometimes we met this procession on our way back in the dreamy moon-light; and as the procession covered the entire width of the public street, we had to run down to the ditches for fear of being crushed or carried away by this avalanche of maddened humanity. And what a time the local officials had with these processions! The District Magistrate, the Police Superintendent and a good number of Police Inspectors and Constables had to be constantly on the run between the ferry-stage and Idga, trying to regulate these processions, while the Assistant and Deputy Magistrates had to stand guard over the gathering at Idga to see to it that there was no bloody fracas between the different groups. But these memories have faded from the public mind with the passing away of the generation to which I belong.

I heard it from my father and other elderly people in my boyhood that, at one time, in the early days even of John Company, the Mohoram used to be signalised by real tournaments and fights between rival *Akharas*, not with blunt swords or bamboo sticks only, such as we saw, but with a kind of firearms, called *tota*, made of thick bamboo barrels filled with gun-powder, and used as a mortal missile by the people. At the close of the Mohoram, the Idga used to have not a few broken heads and jaws, and one or two dead bodies also, as a result of this wild play. But the manufacture of gun-powder and the bullets and their use were prohibited by the Government sometime before my school-days.

CHAPTER VI.

VILLAGE-LIFE DURING MY SCHOOL-DAYS

I spent only a small part of my early life in our village. I do not remember to have lived in our country house, which has been the home of my ancestors for many generations past, continually for three months during my conscious existence. My earliest days, as I have said, were lived in Koterhat in the District of Backerganj. After leaving Koterhat I came with my father to the town of Sylhet, where I lived from my sixth to my sixteenth year. During these years I rarely went home to Poil except during the annual Durga Puja holidays, when the whole family went to our home for the celebration of the Pujas. The Puja vacation extended then, as now, for a little over a month, from the new-moon day of the Bengalee month of Aswin to the new-moon day of Kartick, both days inclusive. This was the annual vacation for our civil courts; and in my school-days the schools in Bengal also closed with these courts. We had no summer vacation at that time, and only a couple of days for Christmas and another day for the English new year. Even the Mahomedan holidays were much fewer than now. Most of our holidays, whether for the courts or for the schools, were Hindu holidays and of these the Durga Puja holidays were the longest and most important.

And my father paid his annual visit to his village home during the Puja holidays. His court used to close then, as this is closed even now, on the last day of what is known among Bengalee Hindus as the *Pitri-Paksha*, or the fortnight dedicated to the recollection of the *pitris* or the ancestors. Throughout this fortnight every Hindu householder takes a ceremonial bath in tanks or rivers, as the case may be, early in the morning and standing breast-deep in the water, offers oblations of water with both of his hands to his forbears, naming each one and remembering his relationship to him or her. This is done from the first day of the dark quarter of the month of *Aswin* to the following new-moon day, when he performs a *shradh* and makes regular offerings of cakes to the dead and of food and clothes and cash to the presiding priest and other Brahmins. This closes the *Pitri-Paksha*. And the *Debi-Paksha* or the fortnight dedicated to the Debi or the Goddess Durga starts with the next morning. On the sixth day of this bright moon the real *puja* of Durga begins and is continued for the next three days, closing on the fourth with the immersion of the image or the symbolic earthen water-pot in the afternoon or evening of that day.

We had, like most well-to-do Hindu families, the Durga Puja in our house. It was the most joyous time of the year to us all. And we boys used to look forward to the Puja season with great and gladdening expectancy. The first rays of the autumn sun, after Nature had been washed by the continuous downpour of the previous two or three months, had a peculiar brightness and softness in it. Every morning, from the middle of September, and sometimes from even earlier than this, used to bring to our boyish fancy some sign of beauty or some secret tiding of great hope and joy. The sky was getting more and more cloudless; the heavens brightening up with its hosts of glittering stars, shining like diamond out of the azure vault; the nights commencing to be brighter and brighter, and the mornings cool and fragrant with the scent of the autumn flowers; the land looking fresh and purer; the waters throbbing with the fullness of life; rivers running up to the very brim; vast expanses of watery wastes, in which our District abounds, dancing sometimes in subdued passion in ripples and sometimes rising in fairly high waves at the lash of the autumn gale;—whole Nature carried to our boyish imagination a new sense of joy and a new perception of beauty in land and water, on earth and sky. This was the Durga Puja season in our boyish days, when to our boyish imagination Nature seemed to beat in joyous harmony with our own hearts, beating with joyous expectation of the great Pujas.

Sometimes we used to go home a day or two before the holidays commenced, so that my father might perform the new-moon day rites in memory of his ancestors in our village home; but more often we used to start for our home the day after the holidays commenced. But whenever we left for home, the previous week, if not the previous fortnight, used to be spent by us in feverish excitement, making purchases for the Pujas. This was the time of the year when I was allowed out shopping with my elders. My father never did any shopping himself. Shopping was not considered quite respectable and dignified in his time. Some of my cousins, particularly my cousin who acted as my father's clerk, used to do all the shopping for our house. In my

Surendranath Banerjea.

Keshab Chandra Sen.

early school-days I was not allowed to go to the bazar on any account whatsoever. Whatever I required, whether it was a pen or a pencil or paper or slate or books or clothes, used to be bought for me by one of my older cousins. My father never let me touch a copper, much less go to the bazar for anything, until I was sixteen years of age. But I could go out with my cousins once in the year to the bazar when they went to make the purchases for the Pujas.

There were no railroads in those days in Sylhet, nor was there any steamer communication between our village and the town of Sylhet. There is railway communication now, but no steamer communication between Sylhet and Poil even to-day. Our only means of transportation during the rainy season was the country boat. We could get a fairly large-sized boat with three men to drive it for between three to five rupees for the whole trip from the town to our village. It took usually from twenty-four to thirty hours, including stoppages for our meals on the way. The roofs of these boats were cut into two parts with an awning or opening in the middle that had a removable cover. This helped to divide the length of the boat into two parts or compartments, the front serving as an outer room for the men and the back, curtained off from it, served as a zenana, with bath and w. c. improvised by a bamboo platform abutting out through the opening in the middle of the boat. Generally we got into the boat after an early dinner in the evening, and got home some time the following night.

We have no large and tumultuous rivers

in Sylhet. Our waterways, during the dry winter months, are narrow streams that rise in the Cachar, the Manipur, the Tippera or Jayantia Hills and flow into some branch or tributary of the Meghna or the Padma, the great river-courses of lower East Bengal. During the rainy season and the autumn months, the entire low-land of the District lies under water, and there is free boat transportation from one place to another across flooded wastes or paddy fields that always leave some margin of unsown land along the boundaries of the sown fields. Then there are small channels or *khals* that serve as drainage canals, which though dried up in the winter and spring, are filled during the rains and provide free passage for country boats. It was a pleasant experience to me passing through growing paddy fields, rich with the promise of the coming harvest, along the vast and weedless expanse of water that gave to my unillumined imagination the idea of the sea, through shallower water-courses smelling the cool scent of water hyacynths and other water weeds, or by villages half-submerged in water, resounding with the vesper hymns of the devout, or with the ribald songs of the gayer folk late in the night: and all these rendered our annual journey from Sylhet to Poil one of the happiest experiences of my young days.

But the most exciting part of the journey was when we approached our village. It is a rather large village; and as it stands on very low land, it lies practically under water during the rains and throughout the autumn months. It is divided into a number of *pallis*, or *paras* as we call them, containing a group of dwelling houses. These *paras* are converted into islands during these months. These *paras* are named after the principal families occupying them. Our quarter is known as *Pal-para* or the *para* of the Pals. There was *Sen-para* or the *para* of the Sens. The Pals and the Sens were the oldest among the *Bhadraloks* of the village to come and settle here, and were, therefore, counted in those days as the most respectable, taking precedence over the others (except, of course, the Brahmins, who did not come really within the order of precedence among the Kayesthas and Vaidyas) in all social functions. There was a *Deb-para* named after the Debs, another Kayestha family. The Brahmins lived in what was called the *Paschim-para* or the West-*para*, and there were in this *para* in those days, and are still, two families, who are not Brahmins, the Guptas and the Endas, who came and settled in our village long after the Sens and Pals and had not sufficiently multiplied to people a whole *palli* and give it their name. On the outskirts of the village there were the fishermen's quarters, called *Machooa-hatee* and the *Vedia-hatee* or the Gipsy quarters, and the Mussalman-*para* which held the home of a very respectable family of Mahomedan zemindars. In the centre there were also *Teli-hatee* or the oilmen's quarters and the *Bania-hatee* or the quarters of the goldsmiths. The other castes lived mixed up with the rest in these *paras*. These *paras* were divided from one another by ditches or narrow canals that formed, during the rains, the main waterways of the village. Our boat had to steer its course along these waterways that intersected one another; and it was no easy thing for boatmen, not very familiar with these, to direct their boat to its destination, particularly in the darkness of the night.

As we approached our village, the boatmen oftentimes got confused by the intersecting waterways in it, and commenced to cry out for guidance to our landing stage or *ghat*. Our own people were not more familiar with these as they frequently changed from one year to the other. The directions and counter-directions given to the boatmen then commenced to create confusion and mutual protests and even abuse, causing considerable disturbance in the sleeping village, breaking the slumber of the people, who cried out from their beds, where the boat wanted to go and who was the passenger; and then there were cries of recognition and rushing out of beds and exchange of greetings and of friendly enquiries about health and clear directions to the boatmen; all these created a joyful excitement in us all. And when the boat stopped at our *ghat*, there was the auspicious cry of *ulu* from the women, and rushing out with light of the servants and maids, the greetings, the salutations, the questions and answers, and the hurry and bustle of getting on land, and the removal of the luggage. All these still linger in my mind, after seventy years, as landmarks of a period of life which was among the sweetest I have lived.

My father had no brothers nor any first cousins, except on his mother's side, who, of course, did not belong to his family, but had their own home in their own village, though they used to live with us at Sylhet. And as my father practically lived in the town, our home in Poil was in charge of a dependent who formed, with his old mother and his wife and a daughter or two, a part of our own household. His mother was much older than my father and used to call him by his pet-name of Ramdhan. My father called her *Didi* or elder sister, and her son, Dagoo by name, used to call my father *Mama* or maternal uncle, my mother *Mamee* or maternal aunt. I used to address him as *Dada* or elder brother, and his wife as *Bau-di* or *Dada's Bau*. Slavery of a kind existed in Bengal at the time of my grand-father, and was not altogether unknown even in my father's earlier days. I think Dagoo's mother had been bought by my grandfather for a small sum; or it may be that she was herself the daughter of some bond-slave of my ancestors. But though not of our flesh and blood, Dagoo was as much a rightful member of my father's family as myself. He was the master of our house in Poil during ten to eleven months in the year, and employed and worked the labourers and domestics required for the upkeep of the house. He responded to all the social invitations of the village as well as those from our friends and relations in the country-side on my father's behalf and as his representative. The tenants looked upon my father as their nominal landlord, while they regarded Dagoo as their real master, and uniformly treated him with the consideration due to his position as such. He collected all the rents and spent whatever was necessary for the upkeep of the house or for other purposes himself, with as much freedom as if he was the master of the house and all its property, rendering a rough account of his stewardship to my father when he went home for the Pujas.

How my father's tenantry looked upon this "retainer" of my father was brought home to me once when I was passing through his estate on my way from Poil to Sylhet in the summer of 1875, after I had left school and had joined the University in Calcutta. It was my summer vacation, and hearing that my parents were staying in Poil, I went from Calcutta to our village to meet them. But they had left Poil for Sylhet before I arrived; and I was going by boat to Sylhet with Dagoo (whom I always called *Dada*), a servant and a couple of Mahomedan *payiks* or peons employed in my father's zemindary. There was a large dairy farm on the bank of the river in my father's estate; and as it is usual for these tenants to make presents of their best dairy produce to the landlord if he happens to pass by, one of our Mahomedan peons went up to the owner of the dairy and asked for some cream and curd for me. The man wanted to be paid for his things; but as this was refused, he also refused to part with them. The peon came and reported it to us; and then *Dada* went up to the river bank, and called out to the milk-man in an angry tone. He came at once with due humility and, when asked why he had refused to give the things wanted, he replied: "How could I know, Dagoo *Dada*, that you had sent for the things? The *payik* came and told me that these were wanted for Bipin Babu, I did not know they were for you." At this *Dada* introduced me to the dairy-man, and the dispute was settled to the satisfaction of all parties. But this revealed to me the position that *Dada*, though a mere retainer or the son of a slave girl, had acquired in our household and among my father's tenants.

Dagoo was for a few days with us at Koterhat, when I was a little child of four or five. And I remember that he had a bad attack of cholera and was in a state of collapse for many hours, hovering between life and death, and how my father nursed him almost day and night, and how I was taken to have what they then thought was my last look of him, and how my mother, prevented by cruel custom from going out to attend his sick-bed which was in the outer or men's quarters, wept incessantly throughout the time he was ill, as if he was her own flesh and blood! His wife was treated by my parents almost as a daughter-in-law and had everything almost that my younger sister had. When *Dada* had children, two daughters, they were tended and brought up almost as my sister, and my father looked upon them as his own, and could not rest contended until they were duly married. Dagoo came to Calcutta in 1883 with my sister on his way to Gaya. I was then a disinherited and excommunicated son of my father. Dagoo walked about the vast wilderness of this city in search of me, longing to see me once again. But he found no trace of me, and going to Gaya died there of cholera. My sister on her way back managed to discover my whereabouts, and coming to see my wife and child, told me the story of *Dada's* fruitless search of me, and how he died with my name on his lips, saying that there was one unfulfilled wish with which he was leaving this side, and that was that he could not see me once before he died!

Our home at Poil was a group of huts,

built of bamboo and wooden posts with the walls of a kind of straight reed called *shar* in our vernacular, that grows in abundance in our parts, and the roof made of meadow grass supported by bamboo rafters. It stood upon two or three acres of land, including the two tanks or water reservoirs of a fairly large size, one in front of the house and the other at the back, reserved for the use of the ladies and protected from the public eye by high bamboo walls, and the houses of retainers and tenants stood on the bank of the outer tank. It was divided into two parts, the outer and the inner. The outer part consisted of a *Chandi-Mandap* or the house of the Goddess Chandi, which is another name for Durga, where the image of the Goddess used to be set up every year during the Durga Puja, and where the other Pujas also used to be performed. In front of this *Chandi-Mandap* there was a big shed, with eight triangular roofs, and therefore called an *at-chala*, which could accommodate from two to three hundred people, all squatting on the floor. It had no wall, and was used as the music hall during the Pujas and as general reception hall on other festive occasions. To the east of this shed stood a long hut divided into two or three rooms, that combined both kitchen and dining room for our Brahmin guests, when we had any, and where sometimes such of our friends or relations before whom my mother and other ladies of the house could not or would not freely move about used to be accommodated when they came to visit us. To the south of the open hall was another hut, that opened on the north to the outer or men's quarters and on the south to the inner court-yard where the ladies reigned. This was the living and bed-room of the younger folk; for me, when I grew up and was assigned a separate bed and bed-room for myself; and my cousins and uncles used to occupy it whenever we were at home in Poil. The inner or the ladies' part of the house also had three or four huts, besides kitchen and cowshed. At the back of the ladies' quarters was the ladies' tank, and a fairly big compound on which vegetables used to be grown for the kitchen. A public road, or lane strictly speaking, ran between the *Chandi-Mandap* and the outer tank which had a brick bathing *ghat* or platform. Some tenants were settled on the northern and western banks of the tank, and another lived inside our own compound, who belonged to the class to which Dagoo belonged and were related to him. The other branches of our family lived in this *para*, which was therefore called *Pal-para*. And they too had their own retainers living about them. There were also one or two families who, though belonging to the servant class, called "Singhs" in our parts, occupied a higher social status than our retainers, and who never inter-married with them. There were a few families of *Malis* or so-called untouchables of the scavenger group in this *para*, who were our dependents and had their land and homestead free of rent in consideration of the service which they were expected to render us in sweeping our yards and compounds and generally keeping the *para* clean. The other *paras* were also of this type.

And looking back upon the social life of our village, as it was sixty years ago, it is borne in upon me that in spite of our caste exclusiveness and the restrictions that obtained in the matter of eating and drinking between the touchables and the so-called untouchables, and the honour that used to be paid to so-called higher or *Bhadralok* classes by the so-called lower or common people, there was a far more real and powerful spirit of democracy of a kind in our rural life than what strikes the eye to-day. There was a clear distinction between the obligations of caste and the obligations of the social life. For instance, no one in the village, however low his place in the scale of caste, would come and take his food in the house of the highest caste people, Brahmin or Kayestha or Vaidya, unless he was properly invited and porperly received and served. He did not want to dine under the same roof or in the same line with the so-called caste people, but he claimed—and enforced this claim when occasion called for it—in other respects the same honour which was due from a host to his guest. He had to be served by the host or some one of his family, or some near relation who could legitimately represent him. In the house of a *Bhadralok*, no untouchable *Mali* would accept food served by another *Mali* or by a servant of the host, but it had to served by a *Bhadralok*. This was a point of honour with them. The so-called Singhs or the servant-caste equally stood upon their own rights and dignities and would not touch food in our house on any ceremonial occasion or at any social function, unless it was served by us. And, I think, the same rule obtained in the houses of Brahmins also. Every class or caste had their own seats assigned on all ceremonial gatherings, and were equally served with *pan* or betel leaves and areca nuts and the tobacco-pipe or the *hookka*, the different castes having their own *hookkas*.

Indeed, our caste prejudices did not seem, in those days, particularly in our village life, to interfere in any way with the freedom of our social intercourse. Our old ideas of this social intercourse were different. It did not mean what is called inter-dining among members of the different castes. The non-Brahmin never felt hurt because the Brahmin could not take his food out of his hands; nor the Brahmin looked upon this thing as in any way a proof and sign of his social superiority. People used to take these restrictions as matters of course, which did not indicate any real personal superiority or inferiority. In Bengal, at least, we have no memories of any time in our social history when the Brahmin and the so-called untouchables did not freely mix with each other except only in the matter of eating and drinking. The untouchable Chandala used to address the highest Brahmin as brother or uncle and was similarly addressed by the Brahmin himself. These social honours used to go neither by birth nor by riches nor rank, but uniformly by age alone. And as no one could claim any credit for himself for having come to the world earlier than others, the order of social precedence or regard based upon age seemed to preserve the spirit of equality and democracy in the midst of the inevitable differences in learning or wealth or rank or even birth and parentage.

Our poorest and most untouchable neighbours were never excluded from any social functions in our house. They used to come and sit on mats reserved for them in my father's house alongside of the so-called higher castes, and used to freely take part in their conversation. And my father also used to go to their house every now and then, particularly if there was any illness or function there, only he was given a separate seat from the people of their own caste. The very wide intellectual and moral chasm that our modern English education has created between the classes and the masses was absolutely unknown in my young days, particularly in our villages.

We had a *Tol* or Sanskrit Seminary in our village in those days presided over by a learned Pandit who had received the title of Vidyalankara. He was in some sense the leader of our village society. He interpreted the ceremonial law of the Hindus to our people, Brahmin or Kayestha or Vaidya. His house was open to all classes and conditions of people of the village, including those that are called untouchables. People used to go there at all times of the day, even when he was engaged in teaching his pupils. And in the interval of his discussions or expositions of the subtle points of grammar or logic or complex questions of Hindu ceremonial law, the amiable Vidyalankara could make time to exchange a few kindly words with these people, who oftentimes simply sat and listened to his talk to his pupils which, of course, they could not really follow; but all the same they spent some part of their time in an atmosphere of refinement and culture. And it is this subtle atmosphere of good manners and noble thoughts and pure sentiments, in which our ignorant and unlettered people lived in our villages, which contributed to their higher humanity. All our liberal education notwithstanding, I am afraid, we have not been able to create or keep up this helpful atmosphere in the presnt social environments of our people! The most orthodox of our Brahmins were rigidly sanctimonious and exclusive in their religious rites and practices and in their eating and drinking only; but in the other affairs of their life they were generally as free from exclusiveness as those of the most democratic among us, English-educated people.

The community in our village was, as has already been said, a very mixed one. We had not only almost every important Hindu caste but a fairly large Mahomedan population also. And the intercourse between the Hindus and the Mahomedans was almost as free and friendly as that among the different Hindu castes themselves. In my father's house we used to invite our Mahomedan neighbour, the zemindar, to all our domestic functions, except the Pujas, which they could not attend, though there was regular exchange of presents between us during the Mahomedan festival of Id as well as on occasions of marriage or death. This Mahomedan neighbour, I still remember, used to send a piece of cloth and a couple of rupees whenever there was any *shradh* or after death ceremony in our house; and we used to return these to them on similar occasions. We were permitted to catch fish from their tanks on every festive occasion in our house as they were permitted to freely use our fish preserve for their own use on festive occasions in their own house. In these matters no manner of distinction was made between our Hindu and our Mahomedan neighbours. And the general Moslem population of the village were treated similarly and practically on the same footing of social equality, within the limitations that caste and religion imposed, as the Hindu peasantry used to be treated. Our differences in religious faiths and practices made not the slightest difference in these social amenities and relations. There was perfect toleration of one another among members of both the communities.

There were neither carriages nor even bullock carts in our parts in my school-days. Everybody, including the ladies, therefore, had generally to walk from house to house on festive occasions, whether religious or social, unless occasionally palanquins or the lighter *doolies* were requisitioned for going from one part of the village to another somewhat distant part. Boat was used for this purpose in our village during the rains when the country was under water. But in our own *para* my mother and other ladies of our family and class used to go about freely, just standing by the roadside with their back turned to any stranger, who might by chance be met on the road, to let him pass. And though there was some sort of zenana seclusion, it did not materially affect the freedom of movement or social intercourse between the sexes.

We had a Vaishnava temple or *Akhara* in our village. It stood very close to our home and was originally endowed, I think, by our family. It was not a very old institution. I heard that at one time we had our own family Deity or the symbol of *Narayana* in our own house and our family priest used to come and attend to his worship twice every day. But when there was no one living from year's end to year's end in our village home, the worship of the God came to be neglected; and it was thought advisable to transfer the image or symbol of the Deity to some shrine and to place it in charge of some people whose vocation it would be to tend and worship it. There were other images and symbols in other homes also belonging to our clan, and these also went to this *Akhara* to be tended by the Vaishnava Mohanta there who must have brought his own images also. For, in my early days, there was quite a goodly collection of these in this *Akhara.* And I remember to have heard it from elders that this *Akhara* was endowed by our people with lands sufficient in those days to pay for the upkeep of the institution.

An old Mohanta was the head of this *Akhara* in my young days; and he had at that time, I think, about a couple of assistants or disciples and two or three females of the Vaishnava mendicant class. There are two kinds of Vaishnavas, the householder and the mendicant. The householders, again, are of two classes. One class follow the rules of the Hindu Smritis, like those, for instance, of Manu and Parasara; while the other class follow the social law as given out by Shree Chaitanya or his friend and premier apostle, Nityananda. These latter Vaishnavas, though householders, do not really observe the rules of caste but form a new caste by themselves. The mendicant Vaishnavas take the vow of celibacy and poverty like the other religious mendicants of India and take up the staff and the bowl and affect the loin cloth or *kaupin* of the general body of our Sannyasins; and though they do not take forbidden food or things cooked by low caste householders, and frequently even by Brahmin householders, they do not acknowledge their birth or caste or family or home. I cannot say to what caste the old Mohanta in our village *Akhara* originally belonged; and as these Vaishnava mendicants, unlike those of the other orthodox Hindu Sannyasins, generally come from the lower castes of Bengalee society, and as the female mendicants were too often the mistresses of the Mohantas or other Vaishnavas, these people did not receive that social honour to which their order and vocation fairly entitled them. And it sounds curious, but nonetheless it is true, that though our family Deity, *Narayana*, used to be brought to our house from this *Akhara* for every domestic function as well as during the Durga Puja, the men who performed the daily worship of the Deity had no share in these ceremonial worships in our own house. Our family priest had to fetch the *Narayana* from the *Akhara*, and had to purify it by administering the sacramental compound known as *panchagavya* or the five products of the cow, and then worship it in due form. Indeed, my father never took food cooked or touched by the Mohanta or his assistants; nor would my mother receive the Vaishaveens of our *Akhara* into her living room, but she used always to receive them in the outer verandah.

This *Akhara* was a very useful centre of the social life of our village in those days. It combined the functions of both poor house and rest-house of the village. Whoever had nothing to eat or a hole to lay his head in at night, had simply to walk to this *Akhara* during the mid-day *puja* and offering of cooked food to the Deities here, to have a free meal, and any decent person could find shelter in the open shed or the music hall of the temple, that stood just in front of the thrones

PANDIT SHIVANATH SASTRI.

of the images, for as many nights as he wanted to stay there. All the Vaishnava feasts and festivals, *Dol-Yatra*, *Jhoolan-Yatra*, *Ratha-Yatra*, *Rash-Yatra*,—all these used to be held here with due pomp and circumstance, with feastings and music parties and other amusements, in which the whole village took part. Besides these, there used to be *keertans* every evening bfore the Gods, and not only the devout elders but even youngsters, to whom the mere sound of *mridanga* and cymbals and conch-shell made a powerful appeal, used to gather here to pass a pleasant hour of the evening. Sometimes the Mohanta used to read of an afternoon from some Vaishnavic scripture, the Bhagabata or the Chaitanya Charitamrita, which was in Bengalee; and people, with nothing else doing or going in the village, used to assemble here to listen to these readings. More frequently the gossips of the village gathered here to spend their idle hours in the afternoon in idle talk or in dealing out local scandals. We had neither public houses nor many people, perhaps not a single person, given to drinking spirituous liquors; but the social purposes, which 'Pubs' perform in England and America, used to be more than fully met by this *Akhara* in our village. It had very little real religious value to the generality of our village population but it had an undoubted social value.

The present system of primary education was introduced in Bengal in the seventies of the last century. Before this, however, we had our own elementary schools both for the Mahomedans and Hindus of the higher or literary classes. We had, I think, some of these schools in our village also. There was a teacher or *Guru-Mahashaya* in our *para*, who held his classes, in my early boyhood, in our own house, and little boys came here every morning and afternoon to learn their alphabet and elementary arithmetic and mensuration and practise Bengalee caligraphy under him. They used to squat on the ground and having learnt to trace the alphabets on the ground, used first to write words and sentences on fresh banana leaves; and after they had sufficiently advanced in this art, and when they could be trusted to write out things with a certain measure of accuracy and their hand had become steady, they wrote out their lessons on dry palmyra leaves. Every boy when he was allowed to write on palmyra leaves considered himself quite learned and carried himself with a certain degree of conscious superiority over his fellows. No regular fees were charged by the *Guru-Mahashaya* but he received a little cash either monthly or annually from the more well-to-do people of the village, while the boys themselves made some payments in kind, in the form of rice from their home or the vegetables of the season from their gardens every now and then. There was a Moulavi also to whom the boys of the higher classes of Mahomedans used to go for elementary lessons in Arabic and Persian. Before my time, when my father was a boy, boys of many a respectable Hindu family, who looked forward to employment under the Government, also went to the Moulavi and had their training and education there. This Moslem school used to be held in the house of the Mahomedan zemindar in our village and, I think, the Moulavi was attached to their family mosque also.

Though copper and silver coins had already come into vogue in my young days even in our villages, cowrie shells were still current, to some extent, as token values among our people. Barter was still the general practice in local trade. There were cotton plants in almost every homestead, and the spinning wheel was found in almost every house. The widows, particularly of the so-called *Bhadrolok* classes, used to ply these wheels in their leisure hours, and the yarns thus produced by them were exchanged for cloth by the weavers in the neighbourhood. Family was the unit of our social system. Almost every family had its own culturable land, either owned and held by them as free-hold or on lease from the zemindar of the village; and agriculture was the universal occupation of the rural populations. They drew their main subsistence from land with the labour of their own hands and plied whatever other professions they pursued, more or less, during their leisure hours. This gave the artizans an amount of freedom which contributed both to the perfection of their art and the preservation of the basal elements of their humanity. And in the disposal of their art-produce they frequently followed the method of barter. Not only artisans but others who produced the necessaries of our village life usually followed this practice. The oil-man pressed oil for his neighbours, in exchange for the mustard seed, grown by them on their fields. The carpenter exchanged the contrivance used for pressing oil for oil from the oil-man. The milk-man exchanged *ghee* and curd for the produce of his neighbours. So on and so forth. The ordinary economic life of the village was conducted upon barter in those days. Even the land-lord not infrequently received his rent in kind instead of, as now, in cash. And though people had few luxuries and had little cash in their house, life was much easier and pleasanter, with much less of storm and stress and the inevitable wear and tear of a competitive economic system than it is to-day.

Much less money was in circulation in our villages, indeed in the whole country, then—sixty or seventy years ago—than now. But though judged by cash or money accumulations, people were much poorer than they seem to be to-day, they had enough to eat and enjoyed their simple life much more than we are able to do. A lakh of rupees seemed to our boyish imagination sixty years back as quite a fabulous sum; while to-day one hears accounts, almost at every turn of trade or land, of transactions covering many lakhs. And this very scarcity of huge cash kept down the value of money to its natural level in my younger days. Money could buy land or horses and build palaces and secure gold and diamond ornaments or fine household furniture; but it could not buy social distinction in the way and to the extent that it does at the present time. Wealth was, no doubt, a power of a kind then as it is now. But its power and potency depended entirely upon how it was used and not at all simply upon its existence in the hands of its owner. No one was permitted to gain any social advantage over those who were otherwise his equals or superiors, simply because he could command large cash or credit.

In fact, money had little social value in those days, particularly in our villages.

Social honour went generally by caste; and in those rare instances where caste considerations did not enter, as in the case of men with saintly character and reputation, it used to be regulated by what may be called moral and spiritual values. Wealth made no difference among men of the same castes; and the poor man with greater family prestige or higher social connections, within the caste rules, had precedence always of the richest man in the community. Indeed, people openly resented any display of wealth by the richer members of their caste, especially outside those who are called *Bhadraloks*.

A very significant story in elucidation of this fact was current in our neighbourhood during my young days. We had a very rich zemindar or land-lord in a neighbouring village who came of a lower caste. Once he had invited his caste-people to a feast in his house. He made great preparations for the dinner and brought out all his bell-metal platters and cups and glasses, such as are usually ueed in the house of Brahmins, Kayesthas and Vaidyas, or the so-called *Bhadraloks*, for his guests. His idea was, of course, to honour them in this way. But when his guests saw all these things, they refused to sit down to their meals. The host was very much perplexed by their attitude. They went and stood silently at the door of the dining room, where cushions had been arranged for their seats, and plates and glasses had been set for their use. After repeated questions, the oldest among them, who had led his fellows, said in ill-concealed anger: "Have you invited us to your house to insult us?" The host fell from the skies at this charge and humbly begged their pardon, if unwittingly he had done anything wrong, and wanted to know what his offence was. "Your offence?" cried the old man,—"Don't you know that we cannot entertain you in this way when we ask you to our house. We are poor, we have neither plates nor glasses nor carpet in our house. Have you invited us to insult us by this display of your riches? We won't touch food in your house unless you can serve us exactly in the same way as we are able to entertain you when you come to us." At this all the plates and glasses and cushions had to be removed, plain banana leaves had to be brought and set, and it was then that these poor people would agree to accept the hospitality of their rich caste-man.

CHAPTER VII.

EARLY RELIGIOUS ENVIRONMENTS AND EDUCATION

The cry of "religious instruction," as an essential element in the education of the young, had not been raised in the days of my early youth. My father never received any "instruction" in religion, such as is wanted and, in some instances, being actually attempted to be imparted to-day in some of our schools. Teaching of doctrine or dogma and inculcation of ethical ideas and principles are the objects of "religious instruction." But our people never troubled themselves over questions of doctrines or dogmas; nor learnt their ethics from the Decalogue. They usually accepted their beliefs from their forbears and followed the rule of life to which they had been used from generation to generation. Yet, it would not be fair to think that their children received no manner of religious or ethical training at all. To do so would be to ignore the fact that there may be very superior and effective religious and moral training without the help of church catechisms and school text-books.

I have no knowledge of the inner history and psychology of the evolution of my father's personal faith. He had received his education in Persian; and though I do not think that the theological speculations of Islamic culture were studied by him, yet it is hardly possible that he did not come across, in the course of his readings in Persian, Moslem religious books, inculcating the severe monotheism of Islam and condemning the worship of "stocks and stones." But the Hindu too is a monotheist. He never believes in a multiplicity of gods. There is only One God, the One Brahman "without-a-second." The various Gods and Goddesses of popular Hindu ceremonialism are really not so many different and independent Supreme Beings, but only powers and instruments of the One Supreme Deity for the governance of His world. I used sometimes to hear all these from my father, in course of his talks with his friends or visitors. And this faith did not necessarily contradict the monotheism of Islam, which he found inculcated in Moslem literature. Indeed, my father was something of a rationalist himself; and I heard him openly refusing to accept many a popular Hindu belief as true. For instance, he never accepted the Pauranic theory of earth-quakes. He frankly declared many a time to pious Brahmins, that he did not believe that this earth of ours was supported on the hood of a serpent, that rested on the back of a tortoise, floating on the waters of the ocean whence this world has come to being.

I have no idea of the psychology of the child-mind in Christendom in regard to religion. But I remember that, as a child, I became conscious of religion as something that stood somewhat apart from my ordinary life. This consciousness must have come to me from the rites and rituals in our house. In the first place, though I was not taught or called upon to worship or pray, I saw this that I was not permitted to touch my father when he sat down to his *puja*, nor the things that were used by him for his daily worship. I could not go near the priest when he came to perform any religious ceremony in our house, though at other times he used to take me even on his lap as he smoked his *hookka*. Even my mother, on her fast days, would keep herself aloof from us and would not touch food or drink until the *puja* was finished; and even then she would not take her usual food, but live for the day, only on fruits or sweets and milk or home-made curd. During the Durga Pujas in our home at Poil we were allowed to enter the Puja-house before the ritual commenced and sit by the artist who was moulding the figures of the Gods and Goddesses and touch them. But from the morning of the Puja-day, when the priest came and started the ceremonial, we were not allowed to cross the threshold of the Puja-house. This prohibition was extended also to our elders, and even to Brahmins not engaged for the worship of the Goddess. And the priest himself had to live during the three Puja-days according to certain rules that prohibited the pursuit of his usual mode of life, enjoining vegetarian food and other rules of personal holiness. And all these things created an impression upon my child-mind that religion was essentially something "apart" from our ordinary, natural life. It stood aside from the usual work and enjoyment of life. And in this way, I think, there grew up in me, quite unconsciously to myself and without any teaching or instruction, some sort of an impression that there was a world beyond this world of ours, a world that we could not see with our eyes nor reach with any of the other senses, which was peopled by unseen beings very much like ourselves but infinitely more powerful, who controlled our life and happiness and held power of life and death over humans. I did not reason and analyse the thing in this way, but looking back upon my early memories I feel that this must have been the way that my boyish faith grew up quite unconsciously to myself.

But though I never had any regular instructions in religion in my young days, I had some religious training through what may be called "playing at religion." When I was hardly five, my father bought for me a toy set of the copper things,—water-vessel and spoon, lamp-stand tripod and plate, and a small cup for sandal paste,—which were used by him in his daily *puja.* And I remember how I used to sit quietly near him with these things pretending to worship, like him, a Nameless and Invisible Being. When I grew up, and particularly when I was at home in Poil, I used to join the village boys in organising imitation Pujas among ourselves, building toy Puja *Mandaps* for the purpose, setting up small images, oftentimes made out of soft clay, gathered from our tanks with our own hands, making offerings of soaked rice and fruits and other things to these Gods, and invariably sacrificing plantain stalks, made to represent the sacrificial goats, before these images. Sometimes we used to set up a whole trunk of banana plant with four bamboo legs as a buffalo and sacrifice it to the accompaniment of sacred music made by beating bell-metal plates with a stick. And all these things helped to quicken and develop the religious sense in us, because during these mock Pujas we used to scrupulously observe the ways of our elders and follow the rules of personal purification enjoined upon the worshippers. Looking back upon these things, it seems that our forefathers followed, without knowing anything about it, the methods of Froebel in building up the religious life of their children.

When I grew up, and reached the age of discretion in some sense, that is, from the age of twelve or so, I was allowed some active participation in the duties of these Pujas, and particularly of the Durga Puja. Flowers and the leaves of the *Bael* tree are used in very great profusion in this Puja; and the duty of gathering flowers and cleaning the leaves of the *Bael* tree was entrusted to the grown-up boys of the house. And there used to be keen competition among the boys of the different houses, where they had the Durga Puja, in the matter of collecting flowers. In most Hindu homesteads they had a few flowering trees or bushes or creepers. The most popular among the flower-trees or bushes were those of the China rose, of various colours—dark red, cream white, and light blue. The China rose has no scent, but it is believed to be, particularly the dark red variety, a great favourite of the Goddess; the blue *Aparajita*, a thin but sturdy creeper, the flower of which was also favoured by the Goddess; then there was what is known as *Sthala-Padma* or "land-lotus" in Bengalee, with white or pink flowers somewhat of the shape and size of the lotus; the *Atasee*, the soft yellow tint of which reflected the colour of the Goddess herself; water-lilies of white and the rarer red variety; and lotuses from far afield, that used to be collected and brought by my father's Hindu tenants;—these were the flowers used in the worship of the Goddess. And we used to collect these from our neighbours' homesteads. In my early days, five or six families in our village had the Durga Puja in full form; that is, they set up the image of the Goddess and her companions, and worshipped her for three days with due pomp and circumstance. And there used to be quite a feverish rivalry between us and the boys of these other families in regard to the collection of these flowers. We kept almost half the night awake for this purpose. Stealing flowers from people's gardens or back or front yards was not viewed as wrong. And we took a peculiar pride in despoiling the flower plants and bushes of these houses where they had the great Puja themselves. So a double task devolved upon us during the three Puja nights, namely, of protecting our own trees and bushes from our rivals, and despoiling their flowers. We used to get up quietly in the small hours of the morning and taking a lantern went out collecting these flowers, sometimes causing considerable nervousness to our parents, because some of these bushes were said to be visited by venomous snakes during the cool hours of the night, and disturbing the people of the house where we went in their sleep by our movements in their back-yards or along the eaves of their huts.

Early in the morning we had to take our bath and change our clothes, and putting on a fresh-washed *dhoti*, we boys were put to washing the *Bael* leaves, quite a heap of which was used in the worship of the Goddess. This had to be done with great care, so that every leaf was washed and cleansed of all dust and other obnoxious things, particularly cob-webs that generally covered them. We were not permitted to talk aloud, lest particles of saliva should fall on the leaves, much less to sneeze or cough, while engaged in this holy work. Nor were we allowed to leave our place until the work was finished, and if ever we did so, we could not come back and resume the work again unless duly purified. All these things gave us some training in self-denial and discipline, which are essential to the truly religious or ethical life and culture.

Then, the music of the Puja, the chanting of the *mantrams*, the sonorous recitations from the Chandee, the chapters of the Markandeya Purana which describe the exploits of the Goddess and how she killed the demons Shoombha and Nishoombha, and particularly, the *stotra* or hymn in her praise, —all these had a weird effect upon the youthful mind. I did not understand the meaning of most of the *mantrams*; nor was I able to follow fully the recitations from the Chandee; but this did not seriously interfere with my enjoyment of these. It was something like the enjoyment of wordless tune, such as is sung on some musical instrument, like the violin, for instance, or the flute. And, then, the intense excitement of the sacrifices! Goats only were sacrificed in our house, as a rule. I had then no sense of the cruelty of the thing. No tender feelings for the poor dumb animal that, when forced down into the sacrificial halter, used to look up to its tormentors with such pitiful gaze, with tears trickling down from the corners of its eyes,—touched me then. The one thought that possessed my whole being, body and soul, was how to get through the function without a hitch; for I had heard it that if the head of the animal was not severed at one stroke of the big knife, it meant that there was some flaw in the Puja, some unpardonable offence had been committed against the dignity of the great Divinity, for which she was offended, and therefore refused to accept the sacrifice. This portended serious calamity to the family of the worshipper. And this fear so possessed our souls during these sacrifices that there was literally no room whatever at the time for any other thought or sentiment in us. And as the music of the sacrifice started simultaneously from drums and *kansis* and conch-shells and *kansars* and bells, and the assembled people cried out—"*Ma*!" "*Ma*!", with great fear and devotion, tears flowing from their eyes and their throats half-choked with emotion, a kind of exhilaration, running even to ecstasy, possessed us all. Looking back upon these early experiences, I cannot help feeling that though the outer occasion and material environments were different, the mental afflatus of some of our refined and intellectually purer forms of religious exercises, the *keertans* during the Brahmo Samaj or Arya Samaj *Utsabas* or the so-called "revival meetings" of the Christian denominations, is more or less the same as that of the Hindu sacrifices. And I am not at all sure that these early experiences did not help me very materially, later in life, to understand and enjoy the deeper and more rational emotional exercises and experiences of the worship of God "in spirit."

And the images of the Gods and Goddesses too had a profound influence upon me. The colour and contour of these images appealed powerfully to my dawning art-sense. I did not analyse the feeling. I was too young and unenlightened to understand the realism and romance of the ten-handed, full-breasted, three-eyed figure of clay that was worshipped by my people as the Mother; but I loved it all the same with a secret love, and longed to look at it for hours and hours without weariness or satiation. To my young imagination it was really no lifeless figure of clay, but something made, for the time that it was being worshipped, of real flesh and blood. To me during the three days of the Puja, this image was a live thing, and the well-shaped face of the Goddess seemed to beam with love and joy, as at eventide we lighted rows of lamps in front of her shrine, the glow of which, dancing before the evening breeze, threw a weird glare upon her form and face, which, seen through the haze of the incense that went up in white clouds from the huge censers in front of her, seemed to play with all the tender pity and sympathy of Mother-Love. And on the eve of the fourth-day, the *Bijaya*-Day, when the Goddess is bidden farewell with the prayer that she may return at the end of the year to her devotee's home, I actually believed that all the gladness that brightened the face of the *Devi* during the previous three days, had gone out of it, and she was weeping unseen tears at the coming separation from her children. These were not fancies, but stern realities to my young mind. It was, I now know, only the projection of my own sentiments upon the face of the image. The experience was entirely subjective. But all the same it offered a very helpful ground for the quickening and exercise of that imagination which constitutes the soul of the difference between theology or philosophy and religion. Looking back upon these early experiences, I realise it that the soul of our so-called image-worship is, seen through the prism of rational analysis and judgment, really worship of the Nameless and Formless Ultimate Reality through the art-sense of man. And I cannot ignore the help that these so-called superstitious forms and ceremonies rendered to whatever religious life it has been my good fortune to have. Without these early exercises and training I might have got more or less theology or philosophy, and perhaps some moral principles also, but very little real religion.

Our Pujas are, however, a good deal more than either ritualism or religion or even art; they are, or were in the days of my youth, great social institutions. The Durga Puja specially was a great social event. For four days there was continuous feeding of guests of all classes and ranks. Even Mahomedans were invited to these feasts. They would not take cooked food in our house, particularly during these Pujas; but came in hundreds from my father's estate, with presents of vegetables and banana leaves on which the guests were served, and were treated to parched rice and curd and jaggery and sweets, served in earthen bowls, called *malsha* in our vernacular. The lower castes of Hindus, the so-called untouchables, had to be personally invited by a representative of my father, and they were treated to cooked food,—rice and *dal* and vegetable and fish and curd and sweets. And when I grew up, I had oftentimes to serve them myself, while my father

Durga Mohan Das.

Bhuban Mohan Das.

came and stood by the place, personally supervising this hospitality, with almost the same sense of sanctity and humility with which he used to look to his Brahmin guests. In his social philosophy a guest was the very personification of the Deity, whatever might be his caste or social standing.

But while I enjoyed these great festivals from various points of view, I commenced to lose my fear of the displeasure of the Gods from my young days. There were some festival or other, the worship of some God or Goddess, almost every week in every Hindu household in those days. In the month of *Vaishakh*, the first month of the Bengalee year, my mother used to have Puja every week. In the month of *Magh*, corresponding to January—February of the English calendar, the ladies of our house used to dedicate every Sunday to the Sun. They bathed before dawn, and used to stand the whole day in the Sun, and the rule was that they must keep their faces turned towards this great God all day long, as the sun-flowers are reputed to do. They could not touch food or drink the whole day through. At the end of the month, on the last day of it, there was a regular Puja performed by the priest, when we used to have a small feast. This Puja was meant for the especial benefit of my sister, who had to join in all the rites and disciplines of it, and the prayer sent up to the great Sun-God throughout whole of these Sundays, was for a good and noble husband for her.

Then, there was the worship of the Goddess Mangal-Chandee, which was performed by my mother during certain Tuesdays, and the prayer to this Goddess was for the well-being of her children and all others who were the objects of her mother-love. Packets of green leaves of grass in their stalks and grains of paddy, with a little vermillion, covered by the leaves of the jack-fruit, folded in the shape of a triangle, pinned up by means of a thin bamboo piece, were a favourite offering made to this Goddess; and these packets used to be preserved with great care, and one of these used to be tied up in a corner of our cloth or sash, as a talisman, whenever we left our home on some long journey.

My father, like all Hindus of his generation, was a believer in astrology. And faith in astrology to the Hindu meant in those days not merely acceptance of the truth of the calculations which astrologers are credited with making regarding a man's past or future from an examination of the position and movements of the planets, but in the personality of these planets, who can, therefore, be propitiated by prayers and offerings according to prescribed formulas and rituals. The worship of the planets was, therefore, part of the old and orthodox Hindu belief in astrology. We had every Saturday the worship of Shani or Saturn. A Brahmin used to come every Saturday evening to perform this Puja. The offerings to Shani consisted of soaked raw rice, milk, sugar, ripe bananas and other luscious fruits of the season. Sometimes, instead of raw rice, wheat or corn-flour also was used as the basis, so to say, of this offering. And we boys used to relish the "leavings" of Shani very much.

An incident in connection with this weekly worship of the planet Shani or Saturn still lives very vivid in my mind. My mother was not then with my father at Sylhet. We were living by ourselves, my father and my cousins and other boys and the male servants, in the house at Sylhet. Now Mondays and Fridays were the two great marketting days in Sylhet at that time as they are perhaps even to-day. On these days people from distant villages used to bring their produce, rice and vegetable and fruits and fuels also, besides fish and animals for food or sacrifice, to the town in large quantities; and the residents of the town used to buy their necessaries on these days and store them for use until the next market-day. Fruits, specially plantains, of which Sylhet produces a large and delicious variety, came in large quantities to the town on these two market-days; and it was the usual practice in our house to buy these for next day's worship of the planet Saturn or Shani from the market on Fridays. It so happened that one Friday's stock of ripe and juicy plantains, meant for the worship of Shani, could not be found when required the next evening, when the Brahmin came for the Puja. It was the usual practice with my father to personally supervise these preparations, unless some unavoidably pressing business kept him away. He was present when the Brahmin came and set about his preparations for the Puja; and when he called for the plantains they could not be found. The servant was called and asked to explain where had these fruits gone, or whether he forgot to get these from the market; or what else had become of these, if he had them. After a good deal of fencing under my father's angry cross-examination, he finally blurted out that I must have had them. I was at once sent for. Hardly knowing the fate that awaited me I went to my father. He asked me if I had taken the plantains meant for the worship of Shani; and so far as I remember, without giving me any chance either to confess or deny the charge, he came for me in a violent fit of anger. At this I bolted right off. My father ran after me. Father and son had a race of the whole compound; and at last finding escape impossible, I rushed to the inner or ladies' quarters in a cousin's house and took shelter in the place where his wife, my sister-in-law, was sitting. Now, according to our social custom, husband's maternal uncle must not see the face of the wife of his nephew. My father was the maternal uncle of this cousin; so he could not enter the inner appartments of his house. He had, therefore, to give up the pursuit, when he found that I had ran to this sanctum. I have no recollection whether I had actually despoiled the fearful God Shani of what had been ear-marked for him. But I might have done it, because at the time when this incident occurred I was sufficiently grown up, reading perhaps in the third class of the Government School, and before then I had already lost my faith in these restrictions as to eating and drinking.

But this does not mean that I had really lost my belief in Hinduism. I still believed, in a way, in our old Gods and Goddesses. I had not commenced as yet to reason about these things. But whenever I was in any difficulty I used to pray to Durga and Kali for help and protection. Every morning, I still got up from my bed by reciting a Sanskrit text which rendered into English meant that whoever every morning remembers the two letters, *Dur-ga*, all his dangers disappear like darkness before the rising sun. When going to school, particularly if I had not properly learnt my lessons and feared unpleasant consequences due to this neglect, I used to take my first steps with uttering mentally the name of the Goddess. I used to do the same thing whenever there was any illness in the family. I still remember how, during a long spell of very serious illness of my mother, when her life seemed to hang as if by a slender thread for three or four weeks, I used to go to every nook and corner of the house, with this unbearable anguish in my heart, and offer up fervent prayers to Durga and Kali for her recovery. This was when I was about the age of fourteen, reading in the third class of the Sylhet Government School.

But even at this time, I had already commenced to rebel against the current social laws and restrictions of Hinduism. I had already lost my faith in caste; and felt no manner of compunction in taking forbidden foods and drinks, whenever any opportunity offered of doing it. So far as I remember, my first inspiration of this heterodoxy came from a Brahmin from Navadvipa. He was a Goswami, traced his descent to one or other of the two great friends and coadjutors of Shree Chaitanya Mahaprabhu, Nityananda and Advaita. He was, therefore, a spiritual teacher of the Vaishnava denomination. He went to Sylhet, if I remember aright, as a reader of Bhagabata Purana and singer of Vaishnava *keertans* or religious lyrics. In this last art he had very considerable proficiency. He happened to put up with a near neighbour of my father's, who was also related to us. My older cousins became exceedingly friendly with him, and he used to take his food frequently with them. He did not mind whether the food was cooked by a Brahmin or a non-Brahmin and would take anything that was good. Though the rules of his caste and order did not allow eating of fish or meat, this fair-looking and genial Vaishnava Brahmin never refused either, whether cooked by his own caste or by our people. Sylhet abounded in those days with wild boars; and the meat of wild boar, though avoided by decent people, was not strictly forbidden. No body lost caste through eating it. I remember how one day a cousin of mine procured a loin of this animal and secretly gave it to my mother to cook. My father never touched nor tolerated indulgence in these kinds of meat of doubtful virtue. My mother cooked the meat; but when my cousin wanted a plate of it for this Goswami, she refused to be a party to the destruction of the caste of a Brahmin. And I know that my cousin had considerable difficulty in getting a portion of this delicious meat for his Brahmin friend! He was the first person to disobey the rules of caste within my knowledge during my school-days. And his example had a great effect upon my own decadent orthodoxy in social matters.

About this time, or more correctly speaking, about a year later, when I was in the second or preparatory class of the Sylhet Government School, a distant relation—some sort of a nephew of mine—came to live with us. He had been to Calcutta and had imbibed the freer thoughts and habits of the Metropolis. At Calcutta he was used to taking loaf and biscuits prepared by Mahomedans. And he initiated me and other young boys in our house in his unorthodox ways. There were only two ovens in the town of Sylhet in those days where they baked loaves and biscuits. These were also the only places where they made flour. We could not go to these shops without rousing ugly suspicions. So we struck upon a clever ruse. We wanted paste to bind our books. And we used to go to these shops ostensibly to buy a copper's worth of flour to make paste with, but really to get hot loaves and biscuits, which we managed to secrete inside our shirts or our sashes, and bringing the forbidden things home, we used to go out to the garden after dark, and enjoy these with very mixed feelings indeed.

These secret enjoyments once gave me an exceedingly bad quarter of an hour. It was just before the Pujas. I had an attack of fever; and had been put on liquid diet for about a week. Though I was then free from fever, my father would not let me have solid food yet. And I was ravenously hungry. I appealed to my nephew from Calcutta to get something from the baker's. At night-fall he went out quietly and brought some hot and crisp biscuits, the very smell and touch of which made my mouth water profusely. But I dared not take these immediately, lest I should be discovered in the act by my father, who was very inquisitive about what we took, especially when we were unwell. So I put these away on the top of the mosquito-curtain over my bed, and waited for the time when my father would retire to bed and I would find the coast clear for my dinner. Now, my bed was set by a door facing the pond in our outer yard. It was rather a close evening; and my father after taking his meals, took up his huble-buble and sat on my bed, and gradually moved up to its very centre, and reclining on my pillow, commenced to enjoy his after-dinner smoke. At the sight of my father in this position, all my wits seemed to leave me. I was in a terrible funk. What would be my fate, if when he had finished his smoking and wanted to go to bed, he should stand up and discover my stock of hot biscuits over his head! I was not hopelessly lacking in mental resources; and taking off my shirt and throwing it on the top of the mosquito-curtain from the other side of the partition that separated my bed from my father's *farash*, I commenced to complain of a feeling of chill and called out to the servants to fetch my shirt. But where could those poor people find it? So I commenced to search for it myself; and after looking a bit here and there, at last went up to my bed at the back of my father, and saying that I had found it on the top of the mosquito-net, rolled up the incriminating things in it and ran out with the bundle to another room, and lay low there until my father had retired, when we had our own little forbidden feast.

I do not remember when the wave of religious revolt and reform, started under the leadership of Keshub Chunder Sen, reached our little town. I have a faint recollection of a lecture on Raja Ram Mohan Roy in the Mission School Hall at Nayasharak by a Brahmo missionary from Calcutta which I went to hear. I think this missionary gentleman was Upadhyaya Gour Govinda Ray, known at that time as simple Babu Gour Govinda Roy. But the address did not interest me at all. I had heard of Raja Ram Mohan Roy from my father, who spoke of him as a great Moulavi. But I was too young to understand anything of his mission and work. This lecture also did not help me to know or understand the Raja better. A few days later, when, I think, I was reading in the fourth class of the Sylhet Government School, Sita Nath Datta, who has since made his mark as a religious thinker and writer and is well-known among the members and sympathisers of the Brahmo Samaj and others interested in liberal religious thought as Pandit Sita Nath Tattvabhusan, came and joined our class. He belongs to our own District. But as his uncle was living in Calcutta and had a shop of hardware things in Burrabazar, Sita Nath had his early education in the Metropolis. One of his cousins, Babu Sree Nath Datta, an old and well-known member of the Church of the New Dispensation, had already come under the influence of Keshub Chunder Sen and had publicly joined the Brahmo Samaj. Young Sita Nath was already something of a Brahmo when he came and took his admission in our class in the Sylhet Government School. He became the centre of a Brahmo propaganda among the older students of our school. Sundari Mohan Das, the well-known medical practitioner of Calcutta and Principal of the new National Medical College, was a classmate of mine; and he was among the very first to join this new Brahmo movement in Sylhet. Nabin Chandra Shome, who became a leading Mukteer or criminal lawyer in Sylhet subsequently, was another prominent member of this young Brahmo Samaj. It created some little stir in our small community; especially because of the practical protest which was entered about this time by Sundari Mohan against Hindu ritualism. Sundari Mohan's father held a very high position in Sylhet society. He was the Sheristadar or head of the Collector's office, which was, in some respects, a very important post in those days, and was regarded as one of the leaders of the Hindu society of the town. Soon after Sundari Mohan joined the Brahmo Samaj in Sylhet, his father died; and the young reformer refused to perform his *shradh* ceremony according to Hindu rites. It was, however, not absolutely incumbent upon him; for he had an elder brother, and the real duty of performing the *shradh* fell upon him. So the matter was somehow quietly settled, and though Sundari Mohan did not take any part in the rites, neither he nor his people were put out of caste for his revolt. Only the event created some talk in the community.

I was not drawn to this Brahmo Samaj; but rather took up a somewhat unfriendly attitude towards it. I cannot recall or state my reasons. I do not think I had any reasons at all for this antagonism except that I did not like it. Looking back upon those old recollections, it seems to me that the superior airs which these young reformers gave themselves, the sanctimonious ways which some of them affected, the natural exuberance of youth, characterised by more or less reckless abandon and pursuit of the normally pleasant in preference to that which was said to be good, and which was too much the product of an artificial habit of mind that scented harm and sin in everything or almost everything, which this new moralism openly discouraged and frowningly condemned;—all these perhaps set my back up against this new Brahmo Samaj movement in our midst. It was too morose and serious for me. I remember to have attended only one of its prayer meetings; and that finished all chances of my going there again. From that time forward some of us commenced to ridicule the whole business.

But yet we did not stand up in defence of popular and current Hinduism. We had lost our faith completely in it; and our youthful candour did not allow us to defend that which we had actually discarded ourselves. I remember to have taken up not a reactionary, but onlv a more conservative attitude. I had heard already of Maharshi Debendra Nath Tagore. I had heard that he did not entirely discard Hinduism, but only wanted to reform and revive it. I had heard that Debendra Nath wanted to revive the religion of the ancient Vedas. And I took up this idea of his to fight this new Brahmoism of my comrades. But all this time, though pleading for the ideals of Debendra Nath Tagore, which, truth to say, I knew little and understood still less in those days, as against the more violent reforms of Keshub Chunder Sen, in my talks and arguments with my class fellows, I participated as before in all the popular rituals and ceremonies in our house, and used sometimes to be moved to send up honest and fervent prayers to Durga and Kali for relief and safety, as well as fully enjoyed the emotional and artistic exercises of the Durga Puja.

CHAPTER VIII.

ADMINISTRATION AND OFFICIALDOM SIXTY YEARS AGO

Like the rest of British India, Sylhet has a highly organised and centralised administration now. It was not so during my early school-days there. The District is divided today into five Sub-Divisions, each a district in itself, with its civil and criminal courts and its army of subordinate officials. These Sub-Divisions are again divided into a number of Thanas or police stations holding jurisdiction for, what is called, the preservation of peace and order over a number of villages. In the villages themselves we have the Panchayets or representatives of the executive authority in the Sub-Division, who control the village police and otherwise operate as the eyes and ears of the District Officer in their localities. Any one with a grievance against his neighbour has ready and easy access to the courts of justice. Distances have been very much shortened by roads and railways, and litigation has inevitably enormously increased.

Things were, however, very different in my boyhood. The present Sub-Divisions had not yet come into being. There were a few Chowkies, literally seats or stations, with an officer empowered to administer justice in the rural parts. And at each Chowkie there was a Thana or police station. But though the Munsif or Judicial Officer in charge of the Civil Court at the Chowkies could try petty civil disputes, all criminal cases, from the most trivial to the most serious, had to be taken before the courts in the head-quarters of the District. And the difficulties of transportation, the time and cost it involved in going from distant rural parts to the town, which had to be done in the rains, generally, by boat, and on foot during the dry season, the want of sufficient accommodation for chance visitors there;—all these effectively discouraged people from going to the British Courts with petty complaints. These were generally settled either by the elders of the village or by the zemindar, if both parties happened to be tenants of the same person.

In my maternal uncle's village, one of my mother's relations was a big zemindar according to the estimates of those days. Theirs was an old house, commanding an annual rental of about ten thousand rupees. During my visits to my mother's people, I spent practically the whole of my time in this house, and saw how either my grand-uncle (my mother's uncle) or some of my uncles (my mother's cousins) belonging to that family administered justice among their tenants. And calling those early recollections to my mind and comparing the present system of administration of criminal justice with those "primitive" methods of our own old village life, I cannot say that, generally speaking, the latter suffers in comparison with the former either in impartiality or in efficiency. This family not only had their court but also all the accessories of judicial administration. They had their *payiks* or peons to fetch offenders to the zemindar and enforce payment of the penalties imposed. They had even a small room that served for a house of detention, which never extended beyond a few hours or a day or two at the utmost. It was both a criminal and a civil prison; and not only people guilty of offence against their neighbours had to suffer detention here, but recalcitrant and defaulting tenants also used to be locked up here until they agreed to pay up their dues or swear complete obedience to the zemindar. The new foreign political Power in the country commenced, naturally, to look upon these privileges and prerogatives of the "natural leaders" of the people with jealousy and suspicion; and the exercise of these simple rights was soon classed as a crime, and the British law courts gradually killed those old instruments of the administration of simple and "primitive" justice among our people. The passing away of this old order took place before the very eyes of the generation to which I belonged.

Apart from the big zemindars, the elders of the village also settled most of the smaller civil and practically all petty criminal disputes in the village. The zemindar had no jurisdiction over men of his own class and social status, the so-called *Bhadraloks*. And petty disputes among these used frequently to be settled by the intervention or arbitration of the elders of the village. During the Puja vacation, when my father went home on his annual holiday, he used to be called upon sometimes to settle long-standing disputes among his friends and neighbours. There were, however, two or three elderly people in the village, who were held in universal respect by their neighbours and who used to help in the settlement of most of the differences that arose from time to time among their co-villagers. I still remember one or two of these good people. One of them was the oldest living representative of the Sens who, along with the Pals, as the earliest settlers in these parts, took precedence in all social functions of the other *Bhadraloks* of the village. He was a lean and lanky person with grizzled hair and thin face, that seemed to have been emaciated by life-long ethical and psycho-physical disciplines, and that lent, with his keen and piercing yet pleasant eyes, overhung with bushy eye-brows, an impression of deep spirituality. He was much older than my father; and I called him *Jetha* or old uncle. He was a man of very few words; and never mixed himself up with, nor let his own family to be entangled in, the rivalries or quarrels of the village. And I remember how people eagerly sought his intervention to settle their differences with their relations or neighbours. And rarely was his verdict resented, much less repudiated, by any party, whether it went for or against him. Sometimes he would be asked to settle these disputes himself; sometimes he would be invited to join a committee of elders to arbitrate between rival peoples or families. In this way justice used to be administered and peace and order preserved in our rural society before the growth, into its present proportions, of the system of British law courts and other foreign instruments of peace and order in the country.

And there was very great difference between the ways of the administration of justice among our people and of those established by the British. The British system may be more scientific, as it is sought to be absolutely impersonal. But even science and impersonality have their disadvantages. The so-called science of justice in modern Western civilisation is built upon the hypothesis that the instinct of the man who comes to a court of justice is to try to cheat it by every possible means; and of the man who comes to bear witness to anything before a judge, is to try to conceal the truth or tell a lie. The entire Law of Evidence in civilisation is built clearly upon these hypotheses. The tendency so far of the entire system of so-called Civilised Justice has been to go more by the light of abstract logical formulas than by actual insight into the psychology of the parties concerned or of those who help in its administration. Simple statements of honest truth, *as honestly perceived* by a witness, are twisted and turned on the screw of formal logic, to be made to appear as falsehood in so-called cross-examination. Our people instinctively saw these dangers and pitfalls of the British system of administration of justice and they tried religiously to avoid these courts, so far as they could, in those days. People who went to a British court of justice ran the risk of losing their souls,—that was a very real fear in the mind of our orthodox people in the days of my youth. People with the fear of religion in their heart, would never agree to go to the witness box in a British court of law. They were mortally afraid of telling a falsehood, however, unwittingly it might be, upon their oath. And the oaths in those days used oftentimes to be administered to the Hindus in orthodox Hindu fashion, that is, the witness had to swear with the sacred leaf of the *Tulsee* plant and a copper-cup containing

Nagendra Nath Chatterjee.

Dwarka Nath Ganguly.

Ganges water in his hand—materials that are universally used in all Hindu rituals—that he would tell the truth, the whole truth, and nothing but the truth. But there might be confusion of thought, many things beyond the control of the individual deponent might happen to mislead him and make him bear false witness against his neighbour. All these thoughts and sentiments very powerfully disuaded good people, in those days, from going to a British court of justice. The vast majority of our people preferred the rough and simple justice of the local zemindar or the village elders to the complex and confusing methods of the new law courts. These courts were established and ruinously multiplied in British India not really to supply but to create the demand for this so-called British Justice. It was done not in malice but in ignorance and conceit.

Murder, grievous hurt during some faction fight, cattle-lifting and serious cases of theft or burglary; these practically finished the catalogue of crimes that were investigated by the police or went to a court in my early days. Occasionally theft of boats also brought the red-turban to the village. Cases of arson also occurred sometimes. But except for these, people did not take any serious notice of the misdeeds of their neighbours. The more serious crimes were committed in connection with disputes over land or prestige among rival zemindars. The general population was, on the whole, very quiet, inoffensive, respectful of each other's rights and honour, and rarely disturbed the public peace. I do not remember to have heard of a single case of murder or any other serious crime in our village or in that of my maternal uncle's, the two villages with which I was most intimately acquainted, during the whole of my life in Sylhet. Neither do I remember any one among the Hindus of these villages, who had ever had to suffer imprisonment. Sometimes a Mahomedan was said to have been sent to, or returned from, prison; and his offence was oftentimes either common or serious assault committed in a fit of anger, or provoked by sex-rivalry or more often still in revenge for some wrong committed at the instance of the zemindar against a recalcitrant tenant or a rival zemindar.

A good many of the murder cases in Sylhet in those days had a woman in the case. The story of one of these I remember still. There was an element of horrid romance in it which could not be easily forgotten. The late Mr. Sambhu Chandra Mookherjea, the Editor and Proprietor of the "Mookherjea's Magazine," and later of the well-known English weekly, the "Reis and Ryot," was so profoundly impressed by this case that he wove something like a romance out of the materials of it which was published in his magazine. I do not remember to have read it, but when I came to know Mr. Mookherjea personally in the eighties, he asked me if I had any knowledge of the actors in this brutal drama. Of course I had. Indeed the memory of it was kept green for a long time among the rural population of Sylhet by a pathetic ballad, sung by cowherds and boatmen and indeed all classes of our rural populations. Part of this ballad ran:

"For Titu Mian, the life of the life of his
mother, cries her soul,

On water cries the water-fowl, on land cries the camel
On his bed crieth his double-barrelled gun."

Titu Mian was a young Mahomedan landlord. He was a keen *shikari* or sportsman. He was liked by his peasantry. He was cruelly murdered one night in his own bedroom by three men, who were incited to take his life by his own wife. She was the common paramour of all these three. She invited them to her house to kill her husband, and thus free her from his lordship. The men dragged their victim from his bed and strangled him to death, while his wife used a beetle-nut cracker to draw out the eyes of the dying man. All these things came out in the trial, on the admission of the accused themselves. They were sentenced to death. When the time for their execution came, the woman expressed a last desire to be hung from the same gallows by the side of the man who seems to have been her special favourite. The whole town turned out to see the execution. I remember to have gone in the company of a number of fellow students to witness the ghastly scene. The woman had wonderful nerves. Death seemed to have no terrors for her. She walked with firm steps to the gallows and seemed apparently very pleased that her last prayer had been granted. All this lent a strange but cruel element of romance to the story of her crime, which became the theme of many a rustic ballad, to one of which I have already referred.

There were about half a dozen English officials in Sylhet in my early school-days, namely the District Judge, the District Magistrate and Collector, a Joint Magistrate, an Assistant Magistrate, the District Superintendent of Police and the Civil Surgeon. The Judge was regarded as the highest official; and the etiquette of the District Bar, at least in Sylhet in my father's time, prevented any lawyer from the Judge's Court appearing to plead any case before the Magistrate. Practice in the criminal courts was therefore confined to the Mukteers and Revenue Agents only. The District Court pleaders appeared only in sessions cases before the District and Sessions Judge, but refused to take up any other criminal case, however important or whatever might be the fees offered. Nor did the District Court pleaders pay any ceremonial visit to any official except the District Judge. All this tended to keep up some distance between these two officials of the District, that was rather helpful to the purity and integrity of criminal justice and the independence of the Bench from executive influence.

There were two or three Deputy Magistrates in Sylhet, in those days. They were all from outside our District. One was from Calcutta, another a Mahomedan gentleman with the highest University Degrees, was from Tippera. There was an ugly case concerning the latter, in which a young and clever lawyer of the new English educated school had a hand, and which created great sensation in the town at the time. It resulted in the enforced retirement of the young Deputy Magistrate. My father tried to help him in his troubles; and this gentleman remembered it years after when I met him in our public life. I never met the Hindu lawyer who was the cause of this gentleman's official ruin; but he too had, I think, to retire from Sylhet; and I cannot call to mind if he attained any success in his profession elsewhere or had to spend his days in obscurity. My father always believed in the innocence of the young Moslem Deputy.

This case had some historic significance also, as indicative of the kind of official and moral atmosphere in which young Surendra Nath Banerjea found himself upon his first appointment as a member of the Indian Civil Service. Surendra Nath came to Sylhet, I think, either towards the end of 1871 or beginning of 1872. I was reading then in the second or preparatory class of the Government School. Our old School house, on the top of the hill known as Mona Rai's Tila, was undergoing thorough repairs at this time; and the classes were being temporarily held in the house of Babu Loknath Sarma, one of the biggest zemindars of the town. I remember how one afternoon in April or May, the young Bengalee Civilian came to see our School and in course of this visit came to our class room and "inspected" our work for a few minutes. I cannot call to my mind what kind of a figure he made then; but this much I know that he was dressed up as a *pucca Saheb* and talked to us in English. I have, however, more vivid mental pictures of Mrs. Banerjea, who, riding, after the fashion of those days, on a high pony, with flowing skirts and veil that covered her hat, was the wonder of the town. There was an Armenian Deputy Magistrate in Sylhet in those days, whose clothes, though not his blood or colour, lent him something of the dignity of the ruling caste in the country. He was on very friendly terms with the

Banerjeas; and he used to accompany Mrs. Banerjea in her rides through the town.

We were too young, and stood too far away from the English or official society of the town, to have any correct and intimate knowledge of the social relation between the young "brown" Civilian and the "white" officialdom in the place. I forget who was the Joint Magistrate of Sylhet at this time. Was it Mr. Anderson, who in his retirement was for many years the Bengalee Reader at Cambridge? I seem to have a very faint idea that Mr. Anderson was either a Joint or an Assistant Magistrate at this time in Sylhet. I very well remember that a Mr. Posford was one of the high officials of this period in Sylhet. He was the Secretary of the District School Committee; and we knew him, therefore, somewhat intimately. But whoever might have been the younger English officials in Sylhet at this time, they did not freely accept the young Bengalee and his wife, who had forced himself into their preserve, into their society.

I think Mr. Muspratt was our District Judge at this time. One Mr. Sutherland was the District Magistrate. No one, young or old, who once had a vision of the spacious and heavy form of this gentleman, could forget him all through his natural life. I have no idea as to how many stones he weighed in his *pyjamas;* or what was the exact measure of his girth; but I know this much that he was the fattest specimen of human flesh that our people had seen upto that time. In all my roving round the world, I do not remember to have seen a fatter man than Mr. Sutherland; and I doubt it very much if I saw any one even as fat as he was. It was the talk of the town that Mr. Sutherland took one big and ripe sweet pumpkin, common to our parts, during his dinner; and considering his bulk everybody believed it. Local gossip said that when young Surendra Nath first came to Sylhet, Mr. Sutherland tried to befriend him. But at the same time he refused to admit him upon terms of equality with the European officials into society. Surendra Nath naturally resented this. And that was the real root and origin of the misfortune that befell him in his official life. Mr. Mackertich, though not a Civilian, was also ambitious of being accepted into the society of local English officials, but was treated with ill-concealed rebuff. Naturally enough, the two Asiatics, suffering under the same sense of racial or the same colour disability, fell into each other's company and formed a small but defiant set between them. Those who have no knowledge of these things can never correctly understand or appraise the circumstances that led to Mr. Surendra Nath's enforced retirement from the Indian Civil Service.

In the first place, the official atmosphere, that is, the ways and habits of the ministerial officers of the courts, and particularly of the criminal courts, was not at all what one could have wished. This came to light a few days previously in the case which involved the young Mahomedan Deputy Magistrate to which I have already referred. In the next place, there was something like an unspoken desire in the coterie of English executive officials to let the young Bengalee Civilian find out his limitations and realise it that there were many other things than passing a competitive examination that went to the making of a true Civilian; and that these other things were not easy to acquire by one not born to the station, so to say. Thirdly, there were "native" officers in the lower ranks, who had easy access to the Magistrate, and were easily tempted to carry tales to him; and who were shrewd enough to know what kind of tales would be likely to be acceptable to their master. And all these things conspired to make an easy victim of the foolish, and rather easy-going young Bengalee Civilian, whose unique position as a *Saheb* had somewhat turned his head.

Though I was a young school boy then, I had glimpses of all these things at the time from the gossip of our elders. Subsequently, when I came to Calcutta and joined the University, I had something like an inside view of the case from my talks with Babu Kailas Chandra Deb, Surendra Nath's Bench Clerk in Sylhet, who too was dismissed for complicity with the offence for which his master was tried and punished.

It is very difficult to say, if and how far, any active conspiracy was hatched against Surendra Nath by his English colleagues in the administration of Sylhet. But it was the general impression among the people that Mr. Sutherland actively worked for the dismissal of young Surendra Nath from the Civil Service. I cannot say how far, if at all, he had any active share in the conspiracy against Surendra Nath. But calling to my mind the things that were talked about in the town I cannot get rid of the conviction that but for him this young Indian Civilian would have never come to grief for an offence which was really not so unusual among young officials in those days. Mr. Sutherland encouraged spies to carry tales about Surendra Nath to him. We knew this at least to be a fact at the time.

The enemies of Surendra Nath have tried to make so much political capital out of the "crime" for which he was dismissed from the Civil Service, and so few people really know the actual facts of this case, that I make no apology for giving all the details of it from the letter of the District Judge of Sylhet to the Hon'ble the High Court at Calcutta.

> "Jaykrishna lost a boat and some twenty days after found it in the possession of Judhistir. In reply to a charge of theft to the police Judhistir said that the boat had been bought by his brother Gadadhar from Sarat. On July 15th the Assistant Magistrate (Mr. Surendra Nath Banerjea) examined the witnesses sent in by the police. Gadadhar and two other witnesses deposed that the former had bought the boat of Sarat. On that both the accused (Judhistir and Sarat) were released on bail, and a charge of theft and knowingly receiving stolen property was preferred only against Judhistir. On 24th August, witnesses on behalf of Judhistir were summoned by the Assistant Magistrate and examined; there was no proof against Judhistir and he should have been acquitted. The Assistant Magistrate ought to have asked Sarat if he could get witnesses to prove his innocence and if he could adduce reasons for suspecting that Judhistir and Gadadhar had falsely accused him of selling the boat, before drawing up charges against Judhistir............
> It is evident that Mr. Banerjea after the 24th August forgot all about the case and did not draw up any charge against Sarat till 30th October (1872), when certain witnesses on behalf of Sarat appeared in his court. On September 2, Sarat petitioned the Assistant Magistrate to summon witnesses to prove his defence; but even then the Assistant Magistrate was not awakened to the fact that there was no charge against Sarat; on the 10th, 20th and 30th September also orders of some kind or other were passed; yet Mr. Banerjea did not notice that there was no charge against Sarat. On the 30th October when a charge

was drawn up against Sarat, no orders were passed regarding Judhistir. On the 30th one of Sarat's witnesses, who had been arrested was in attendance, but Sarat refused to examine him saying that he had been tampered by Judhistir. On this date also no orders were passed regarding Judhistir, but 28th of December was fixed for causing the attendance of other witnesses of Sarat by arresting them. On the 28th December no witnesses appeared for Sarat, and so far as I can learn from the record the case was not before the court at all on that day. On the last day of the year, although there was no cause for bringing up the case, yet a report is made by the Court Head Constable that the accused were called but were not in attendance. The Mohurrer records the order that they be entered up as a "Ferari" in the monthly statement and that warrant be issued for their arrest. This warrant bears Mr. Banerjea's signature. The warrant for the arrest of Sarat was sent to the Magistrate on 7th January (1873) to be forwarded to the Magistrate of Tipperah for execution.

"But as regards Judhistir, it appears he was produced by his surety on 31st December and by a petition permission was asked by his surety to be released of his suretyship. An order was passed thereon that he was to be brought up on the next court day, but nothing further was done in the matter.

"Mr. Banerjea says he did not know what a "Ferar" register was and that he never gave the order to place the accused on that register. Did he know nothing of the warrant sent to the Magistrate on the 7th January or of the order on the Lashkerpur Police to use every exertion to arrest Sarat and send him up in order that the case might be disposed of during the month of January?..............Mr. Banerjea also should have observed before signing the return for December that this case regarding which he had furnished explanation for two previous months had vanished from the December return.

"The shifting of onus on to the shoulders of his subordinates cannot exempt Mr. Banerjea from the effects of his own carelessness or his ignorance when there were so many opportunities which should have brought the case to his remembrance. It is also to be observed that no order was passed calling on Sarat's surety to pay up nor was Sarat examined, when he of his own accord made his re-appearance in Mr. Banerjea's cutchery.

"On 27th January one more witness on behalf of Sarat was examined in presence of both the accused ....The *finale* of the case was that both the accused were acquitted on the 30th January, (1873).

"The above facts speak for themselves, and I am reluctantly compelled to record my opinion that the explanations given by Mr. Banerjea are most unsatisfactory and fail in every way to clear him from the charge of keeping the case against Judhistir pending for months after completion and of allowing an incorrect and improper return to be submitted to the Magistrate. I therefore accede to the request of the Magistrate that this case should be laid before the Honourable Court in order that they may determine whether Mr. Banerjea should, for the present, be allowed to exercise the power of a Magistrate of the first class. In coming to this opinion I have not overlooked the fact that Mr. Banerjea has had a great deal of work to do.............."

We did not know all these details at the time. I was too young, for one thing, to enter into them; and there were no popular Vernacular newspapers at the time, like those we have now, that published and discussed these. All that we knew then was that Mr. Banerjea had falsely entered some persons as *ferar* or absent when they were really present in his court. This thing has come down to posterity, through popular gossip, as "falsification of records," and has lent to his "carelessness", as the District Judge himself called it, the colour of serious and deliberate crime. But no one, who reads the Judge's letter to the High Court, can possibly take the thing so seriously. Indeed, the thing for which poor Surendra Nath had been sought to be pilloried throughout his public life, is not at all uncommon in our courts; and there are very few Civilians, fresh from "home," who could not, if their early records were carefully searched, be convicted of the kind of carelessness, for which such indignities were heaped upon this young Bengalee Civilian. And we all knew it at the time, as it was the universal belief among our people, that the crime of young Surendra Nath was really his colour and race and not any grave misconduct in regard to his official duties.

Looking back upon Surendra Nath's case in the light of the general spirit and policy of the then Government of Bengal, if not of India, one finds the real reason of Surendra Nath's disgrace in the almost open hostility of the British Bureaucracy in Bengal (the word was unknown to us in those days) towards the English-educated Bengalees. Sir George Campbell was the Lieutenant-Governor of Bengal and Lord Northbrook the Viceroy and Governor-General of India at that time. Sir George had declared an open crusade against higher English education in his Province. In carrying out the educational policy enunciated in Sir John Wood's Education Despatch of 1854, the Government of Bengal had opened a number of colleges for high English education in the Province. Burdwan, Hooghly, Krishnagar, Dacca, Berhampore, all these Districts had thus each a high grade college of its own. These had been turning out hundreds of English-educated young men, who commenced to crowd the higher offices under the Government and the learned professions, particularly of law. These young men were also the pioneers of a great freedom movement in the country. Already four Bengalee young men,

Satyendra Nath Tagore, Beharee Lal Gupta, Romesh Chandra Datta and Surendra Nath Banerjea, had gone to England and passed into the Indian Civil Service with distinction. The British-born members of this Service, naturally, did not very much like all these new developments in the subject populations. So this higher English education had to be curbed. And Sir George Campbell started his crusade against it. Krishnagar College was abolished. The other colleges in the Mafassil were also threatened with the same fate. Even in far away Sylhet we learnt of these things from the two most popular and powerful Bengalee weeklies, the "Somprakas" and the "Amrita Bazar Patrika," particularly the latter, whose trenchent criticism and vitriolic satire fascinated the people very much. The "Patrika" described Sir George as the great Destroyer, the Mahesvara of the Hindu triad. Mr. Woodrow, who was the Director of Public Instruction in Bengal at the time, was described as the old Bull—"the Booda Brisha"—on which Siva rides, and with the help of this old bull, Siva was destroying the educational world of Bengal. Looking back upon all these things, I feel that the popular view that found expression through the Bengalee press at the time of Babu Surendra Nath's case, namely, that he was a victim to jealousy and colour hatred, was not really without reason or justification.

No one can read the letter of the District Judge of Sylhet even to-day without having the same feeling. The offence revealed in this letter amounts to nothing more than grave carelessness and laxity of due supervision of the acts of his subordinates. But what young Magistrate, belonging to the Civil Service, is there who has not been guilty of these offences in his early official life? Even the District Judge did not take a very serious view of Mr. Banerjea's lapses.

> "I therefore accede to the request of the Magistrate (he wrote) that this case should be laid before the Hon'ble Court in order that they may determine whether Mr. Banerjea should for the present be allowed to exercise the power of a Magistrate of the First Class."

And as if to extenuate Mr. Banerjea's carelessness, he added,—

> "I have not overlooked the fact that Mr. Banerjea had a great deal of work to do."

I do not remember if there were any other charges against Mr. Banerjea. At least this *ferari* business was all that we had heard of at the time. I have not before me any report of the proceedings of the special court of enquiry that sat to examine this matter, nor the final Resolution of the Government or the Secretary of State upon it. But public opinion at the time saw no justification for the measures taken upon such a small and very common thing. The District Judge, at the instance of the District Magistrate, who was no friend of Mr. Banerjea, asked only for the withdrawal of his powers as a First Class Magistrate. It is inconceivable, considering all that was the common talk of the town at the time regarding the relations between Mr. Sutherland and Mr. Banerjea, that if the latter were guilty of anything more serious, action would not be asked for to be taken against him.

Inspite of it all, we find that a special court is constituted to enquire into this trivial matter. Mr. Prinsep, who subsequently became a Judge of the Calcutta High Court, and who was then District Judge at Hooghly, was appointed President of this special court. Mr. Reynolds, Magistrate of Mymensing, and Major Lamb, Deputy Commissioner of Nowgong, were appointed members of this court. But it is curious that Major Lamb refused to sit on the commission; and I do not remember, and have not been able to find out from such materials as are within my reach, who was appointed to take the gallant Major's place.

But the most curious and significant thing about it is that Mr. O'Kinealy, the Civilian Remembrancer of Legal Affairs in Bengal, who had been in charge of the celebrated Wahabi case on behalf of the Government, was placed in charge of the prosecution in Surendra Nath's case also. And Mr. O'Kinealy acted not only as Counsel for the prosecution but also practically as the Government Attorney, for he examined witnesses for the prosecution in his bungalow before the trial commenced and behind the back of the accused! Surendra Nath applied to Government to have the trial in Calcutta instead of at Sylhet. It was by no means an unreasonable prayer. The attitude of the Sylhet officials was notoriously unfriendly to him. All the witnesses for the prosecution were practically under the influence of these officials, many of them were ministerial officers under the Magistrate, Mr. Sutherland. But the Government refused to make this fair concession, though they generously offered him assistance of Counsel or any other officer in the service of the State, to help him in his defence. Surendra Nath, in reply, asked for the services of the Advocate-General or the Standing Counsel. The Government replied that these law officers were not available. So Surendra Nath engaged Mr. Montriou for his defence. All these facts leave little doubt in the mind regarding the spirit that moved the Government in first directing Surendra Nath's trial before a special court, under Act XXXVII of 1850, and then conducting the whole prosecution, as if it was a great State trial involving important issues affecting the very existence of the Raj!

SUNDARI MOHAN DAS.

JAY GOVINDA SHOME.

CHAPTER IX.

THE CLOSING YEARS OF MY SCHOOL LIFE

By the time I was in the second or preparatory class of the Government School at Sylhet, I reached my fifteenth year. This was in 1872. And my father, following the old injunction of Chanakya, that when a boy attains his sixteenth year the father should treat him as a friend, commenced to relax the rigorous discipline to which I had hitherto been subjected. I was now permitted to go out shopping by myself sometimes. I was no longer subjected to any physical chastisement for my lapses; but my father commenced only to remonstrate with me, or admonish me verbally for my misconduct. I was also allowed to handle small sums of money for my personal expenses. During the Durga Puja this year (1872), I remember how I had a share in making the purchases for the Puja, and for the first time introduced Hinks' double-wick kerosene wall-lamps into our house at Poil for lighting the big "Dancing Hall" or *Nat-Mandir* during the festivities of the Puja, which had till then been lighted by chandelliers and wax candles. This was quite an unorthodox innovation; and though I was allowed to fix up these kerosene oil-lamps in the *Nat-Mandir* and on the verandah of the *Chandi-Mandap*, inside that holy room, where the image of the Goddess was set up, nothing except wax candles and cocoanut oil lamps were admitted. In short, from this time forward I was treated as a responsible member of the family and duly consulted upon every important matter by my father, who never discharged his duties as the head of the family without due and indeed respectful consultations with every member of his household. The *Pater Familius* in the old Hindu household, as I saw him in my boyhood in my own home and among my friends and relations, was by no means the autocrat he is generally painted to have been by ignorant foreigners. I do not know anything of the position of this *Pater Familius* in the law and social constitution of the ancient Roman people, except what can be generally gathered from popular books. It may be that the Roman *Pater Familius* was an autocrat and held absolute authority over the members of his household. But our family life and structure do not seem to support this idea of the position of the Hindu *Pater Familius.* At least the saying of Chanakya, which enjoins that as soon as a son attains the age of sixteen he should be treated as "a friend" by the father, lends support to the contrary idea that the ideal and structure of the Hindu family, like that of the Hindu society and State, was constitutional and democratic and by no means military and despotic. As soon as the son comes of age, he becomes a responsible member of the family-republic, and has a voice, along with his elders, including his father, in the direction of the affairs of the joint family, even as he has an equal share, with the rest, in the property of the family. I did not know or understand these things in this way in the days of my youth, but looking back upon my experiences of my early relations with my father I can find no other reasonable interpretation of it than this. From my fifteenth year onward, though I was too young and immature to render any real help in decisions regarding our family affairs, my father commenced to consult me on every important matter. And this is how at the age of fifteen I became a party to the settlement of my sister's marriage that caused for some time very great trouble in our family.

My mother had many children, nearly a dozen I think, but of these we two, myself and my sister Kripa, were the only ones living at this time, the rest had died after a few days' life here and some only after a few hours of birth. My sister Kripa was about three years younger to me. But as I had no brothers or sisters between us, she had frequently a bad time in my hands. With the instincts of the housewife in her, she could not put up with my wasteful ways and used often to call mother whenever I was up to any mischief. One of my mortal sins in those days was to steal sweets and other edibles from my mother's store, whenever she was taking her afternoon rest or went to see the ladies in the neighbouring houses, and enjoy these in company with other boys. And my sister used very often to keep watch over my movements when mother was not in sight, and call out to her that I was doing this, that or the other thing, particularly running away with the sweets in her store. And as often as she did this police duty, she had more or less severe beating from me, as after having taken the things that I wanted, I would always punish the police officer for her gratuitous interference with my predatory excursions. In justice to myself I must say this, however, that I invariably tried to bribe her and give her a share of my booty before trying to punish her. But as she invariably refused with ill-concealed scorn my incriminating offers, I had no option but to try to silence her by physical means.

Kripa was still unmarried when I attained my fifteenth year. She was over twelve then. That was a rather rare age for girls of respectable families among us to remain unmarried. But my father held somewhat liberal views in these matters; and he was evidently not anxious to secure a place for himself in heaven by giving his daughter in marriage at the age of eight or even ten, according to the law of Parasara; nor did he refuse to give her some little literary education either. My mother never knew to read or write. It was considered an evil thing in those days for respectable ladies to learn to read or write. It was not because the men were jealous of their women and did not wish them to be as educated and cultured as they themselves were, but because education had then no intrinsic value in itself, except in the case of the high caste Brahmins, who had to read the Law to be able to interpret it to their *yajmanas;* and by whom, therefore, the study of these holy books was regarded as of some intrinsic virtue and value. But Sanskrit was a very difficult language to learn and it took quite a long time to master. Those whose professional duties did not require a knowledge of this sacred and difficult language, therefore, rarely or never cared to waste so much time over it. Even the Brahmins themselves rarely studied Sanskrit seriously; most of them, even among those who officiated at sacred rituals, wherein holy texts had to be recited, hardly understood the meaning of their own *mantrams* or of the texts they recited during their daily prayers. Persian was the language of the court; and those who wanted to enter the service of the Government learnt Persian just as the present generation of office-hunters learn English. Our vernacular was in a most neglected condition, and few people had any serious call to learn it. Under these circumstances, it was nothing strange that our ladies did not, in those days, receive any literary education.

But all the same, it will be a great mistake to think that Bengalee Hindu ladies did not know to read or write before the British came to our country. One Mr. Lushington was deputed by the Government of the East India Company in the early years of the last century to make a survey of the indigenous education of the people of Bengal, and he found that there were two classes of Bengalee women who knew very well their own language and literature— who were very well educated in the vernacular of their country. These were women of the Vaishnava denomination, who considered it a religious duty to read the scriptures of their sect; and as all, or almost all, the sacred books of the followers of Shree Chaitanya Mahaprabhu were in Bengalee, every devout Vaishnava of this denomination, male or female, had to learn to read their own vernacular as part of their religious duty. Thus it was that Vaishnava ladies, as a rule, were all literate as far back as the beginning of the last century; and they must have been literate from generation to generation, almost ever since the days of the Mahaprabhu, to be able to furnish such a large class of literate women during Mr. Lushington's investigations. I had it from

Pandit Bijoy Krishna Goswami that he himself saw about the seventies of the last century learned Vaishnava women in Brindaban, and he noticed one in particular, who was a recognised and popular interpreter of the Bhagabata lore, and who used to draw large audiences to her exposition of this sacred book. She was a Bengalee lady. And she must have got her education both in Bengalee and Sanskrit long before girls' schools were started in Bengal under British auspices.

There was another class of Bengalee ladies, whom also Mr. Lushington found in his survey, who were fairly well educated. These ladies were found among the higher classes of Hindus of North Bengal. And unlike the Vaishnava ladies these ladies were prompted to educate themselves or be educated by their parents and guardians by secular motives. These families were generally connected with the big zemindar families of North Bengal; and the girls of those castes and families, who could be married to these zemindar families, were taught to read and write and understand accounts as a provision against the unhappy contingency of their premature widowhood, that would leave charge of big estates in their hands, and in that case it would be of very great help to them, in discharging the heavy responsibilities of their position, if they knew how to read, write and cast accounts. This is how among the Brahmins and Kayesthas of North Bengal there grew up a class of ladies who were literate and who were systematically taught the three R's by their parents.

And as this education was given to meet the unfortunate exigencies of widowhood, it seems that the idea got abroad and took possession of the popular mind that if a girl learnt to read and write she called down the miseries of premature widowhood upon her. This prejudice was very strong in our community in my young days. I am not sure that my mother was herself absolutely free from it. But my father was a confirmed fatalist, like most people of his time and class; and his one incontrovertible argument was that if it was fated that his daughter should be cursed with early widowhood, nothing could prevent it; nor could her learning to read and write any way be instrumental in bringing about that calamity. Besides, my father's Islamic education must have proved the fallacy of the popular notion in this matter, because his Persian studies must have acquainted him with the stories of Moslem ladies of the higher classes, who were not only literate but some of them highly educated in Persian and Arabic. My father, therefore, did not at all object to my sister's receiving some literary education. And Babu Nava Kishore Sen, my father's friend and co-lodger, took upon himself the work of teaching my sister. He had already taught his young wife to read and write; and he now most willingly took up the duty of teacher to my sister. Indeed, but for him and if he were not our neighbour and had not such great influence over my father, I doubt it very much if she would have received even the little education which she did.

Considering my father's position, proposals for my sister's marriage commenced to come to him, I know, from the time when she was hardly ten; however, neither my father nor my mother paid any heed to these. But when she had passed her twelvth year, my father became a little nervous about her marriage. There was a young man, who was then reading in the Government High School at Sylhet; my father had an eye on him as a possible bridegroom for my sister. And when he passed the Entrance Examination, the marriage was settled. My father went home to Pôil with us all for the celebration. A couple of days before the formal settlement of the marriage, a messenger arrived from the bridegroom's father demanding a couple of hundred more as the bride's dowry than had been previously settled. This very much upset my father. He saw in this an attempt at extortion. He said if they had asked for five hundred rupees more instead of only a couple of hundred, when the arrangements were being made, he would have gladly paid that sum. But this was an attempt to extort money by placing him in an awkward position. He had come home for the marriage, all arrangements had been made for the ceremony on a day fixed in consultation with the boy's father; indeed, friends and relations had been already apprised of it. My father point-blank refused to accede to this preposterous demand. He wrote to him to say that the marriage was definitely broken off.

Having broken off this marriage my father resolved, however, not to return to his work in Sylhet without finishing my sister's marriage. There had been other proposals also for her hand. My father, like the rest of his generation, believed in an overruling Providence or Fate that ordered the affairs of men. Marital relations, they believed, were specially pre-ordained. No proposal for marriage was therefore definitely rejected by any respectable and pious Hindu. To all the proposals that had come for my sister's marriage, my father had simply replied that he could not give a definite answer immediately, as it all rested upon the will of God. After this arrangement was broken off, he commenced to look into these other proposals and took up one of these seriously. The party was very respectable. The bridegroom was fairly educated. His uncle, the head of the family, was well-known to my father and had personally asked for my sister's hand for his nephew. My father now thought of him and made up his mind to accept this offer.

Though he was the head of the family and could exercise absolute authority in these matters, he did not like to shoulder the entire responsibility himself. So he came and asked, first, my mother, whether she was willing to accept this proposal. My mother replied, "If you think it right, do so." My maternal uncle had come to our house for my sister's marriage as previously arranged. Having consulted my mother, my father went and asked him, whether he should immediately accept that other offer. He also made a similar reply. My father next asked a cousin of mine, who was his clerk and general assistant. He too accepted the suggestion. I was then in my sixteenth year and, following the injunction of old Chanakya that as soon as the son attains the sixteenth year of his age, his father should regard him as an equal and a friend, my father next called me and asked my opinion about this proposal which he wanted to accept. I too gave my consent. Last of all, there was our old retainer or serf, who too was a member of our family, though not of our caste, and as a member of the family he also had a right to be consulted in a serious matter like this. My father called him and explaining the situation to him asked him whether this proposal might be accepted, and he also made a similar reply to that given by all of us. So my father at once wrote to the uncle of the bridegroom, saying that if he could arrange to have the marriage celebrated within a fortnight he was agreeable to accept his old offer. Thus my father committed himself definitely to this proposal. This letter was sent by a special messenger to avoid preventible delay in its delivery and getting a reply to it. The reply came almost post haste. My father's condition that the marriage must take place on a particular day mentioned by him was accepted by the bridegroom's party, and so there was no getting out of it.

Though all of us gave our consent to it, we did not really approve of this selection. The bridegroom, while eligible in every other way, was known to be addicted to strong drinks, which was the curse of young Bengal of that generation. My father's family, as I have already said, belonged to the Vaishnava denomination, with whom drinking spirituous liquor was counted as a mortal sin. We had, all of us, therefore, a strong aversion against those who indulged in it. My mother was furious with herself for having given her consent to this proposal. Her opposition increased through a casual remark made within her hearing by a mason then working in our house, who had been to Silchar, where the prospective bridegroom was employed, and who said that though in every respect he was a very fine and esteemable young man, he was rarely sober for even a couple of hours during the day. My maternal uncle, my cousin, my *Dada* Dagoo, and myself,—we were all strongly opposed to this marriage. But having given our assent to it, when my father asked us before accepting it finally and formally, we commenced to bitterly repent of our folly now. But what could we do? How could we prevent it? We put our heads together, and saw that the only chance of escape lay in the bridegroom's inability to come home from Silchar, his place of employment, in time for the ceremony to be performed on the day fixed by my father, for he had set that down as an absolute condition of the marriage. So we decided to send a telegram in the name of the uncle of the bridegroom to the latter at Silchar, asking him, at the last moment, not to come home until he heard again from him. We had, if I remember correctly, this telegram sent to Sylhet, through a special messenger, for in those days there were no telegraph offices except in the head-quarters of the Districts; but whether it was actually sent or not, I do not remember, most probably it was not sent. In any case, the young man left for his home in due time, and all chance of our preventing the marriage was destroyed.

On the day when the ceremoney of *pan-patra*, called *pane-khili* in the patois of our District, when the marriage is finally and formally settled and presents are exchanged between the bride's and the bridge-groom's families, was to be celebrated and our house was filled with friends and neighbours, and the musicians came and started to play, my mother took up an openly hostile attitude. She commenced to cry aloud, taking my sister's name, as if she was dead and threatened to first kill her and then kill herself before she would agree to such a match. My father was in a fix. He commenced to walk up and down between the inner or the ladies' quarters and the outer or the men's quarters like one distracted. I also began to alternately go to my mother trying to pacify her, and coming out to consult my maternal uncle and cousin as to what must be done in the circumstance. The one idea that obsessed my mind was that if in a serious matter like this my father failed to keep his word, whose word was universally accepted by the people as a bond, it would so hurt his self-respect, that he would not perhaps survive the shock for long. So, though I was myself strongly opposed to this marriage, I felt impelled to sacrifice my sister's future happiness to my father's reputation for veracity and reliability. My maternal uncle and my cousin and my *Dada* Dagoo also took the same view. After about two hours' hesitancy and struggle, I at last made up my mind to make a final appeal to my mother; and going to her explained my reasons for allowing this marriage to take place to save my father's character, and possibly even his very life. This somewhat quieted my mother's opposition; and she told my father that since the matter had advanced so far and he could not honourably go back upon his word, the marriage could not be broken off; so let the will of the Lord have its course. Having thus given her consent to the final ceremony, she commenced to weep bitterly thinking of her dear daughter's future.

At first I was in mortal anguish thinking of my father, and whether, if the proposal broke through at that stage, he would survive the indignity of it. Now when my mother gave her consent and the preliminary ceremonies were over, I became equally frightened at the thought of my mother, whether she would survive this shock to her mother-love. So I bethought myself of her own people, and without a moment's delay, as soon as the formalities were over, I had a pony fetched from our friend, the Mahomedan zemindar, who kept a fairly good stable, and rode to my maternal uncle's place, which was about twenty miles off, to invite my mother's relations and, indeed, bring them to our house immediately. This was done, and it was only after her own people came that my mother became a little quiet and applied herself to the usual preparations of the marriage.

In the meantime, however, a letter from Babu Nava Kishore Sen very much upset my father also. Babu Nava Kishore was touring in the Mafassil, and, as luck would have it, he chanced to meet my sister's future bridegroom on his way home from Silchar, riding furiously with a couple of bottles of strong spirits bulging out of his coat-pockets. He must have been more or less tipsy, as he took little notice of Babu Nava Kishore, who was very well known to him. Babu Nava Kishore asked my father to break off the engagement at any cost. My father held Babu Nava Kishore in such deep affection and high regard that he never did anything without consulting him. Such a letter coming from such a source, very naturally, upset him. He showed this letter to us; and asked us as to what was to be done. But the thing had advanced too far. This letter was received only two days before the marriage. Our house was full of friends and relations, who had come for the marriage from all parts of the District. The Brahmins were being fed in honour of the occasion at the very time when a special messenger brought this letter. To break off the marriage after all this would cause a very grave scandal in the community. So there was nothing left to us but to resign ourselves to the hands of Fate. But the thing so rankled in my father's heart that when the bridegroom came, and the ritual was being arranged, he sternly forbade any display of the presents intended for the bridegroom, saying, that it was enough that he was sacrificing his daughter, why should he add to it the sacrifice of so much valuable furniture and other household goods as well? Thus it happened that during the marriage ritual, my father gave away his daughter, like a very poor man, simply with the things that she had on her, and without those things which it was customary in those days, as it is even now, to give to the bridegroom, as part of his presents. My father relented somewhat the next day, and yielded to our request to let him have the things that had been bought for him, when he was leaving our house with his bride.

My sister's husband, Iswar Chandra Nag, was, however, soon found to be by no means a bad character at all. He very much improved upon closer acquaintance. He was fairly well-educated and highly intelligent, and was one of the most genial of men I have ever come across. He had a very fine presence, was an exceedingly handsome man, both in colour and cut. And it seems to me that these very fine physical and mental qualities were the cause of the fatal habit which he contracted. And after his marriage, though he did not or could not give up this habit, he always stood in great fear of my sister, and would never come home in a state of intoxication. Generally he gave himself up to it when he went out of town in course of his official work as a police officer investigating some crime in the Mafassil. Once when he was travelling by boat and my sister was with him, she discovered about half a dozen bottles of brandy among his kit and threw the whole lot into the water; and it is worthy of note that my brother-in-law never uttered a word of protest or expressed any anger against her act, but took it quietly, like a school boy discovered in some wrong-doing. But this drink killed him; and my poor sister became a widow within three years of her marriage, when she was just sixteen! She had only one daughter, born after her father's death.

My acquaintance with modern Bengalee literature commenced about this time, when I was about fourteen or fifteen years of age, reading n the second class of our School. Iswar Chandra Vidyasagar's "Seetar Banabas" or "Exile of Seeta", which was a free adaptation of Bhabhabhuti's immortal Sanskrit drama, the "Uttara-Rama-Charita," as well as the works of Akshay Kumar Datta, which were free translations from standard English books on popular science and morals, were our school text-books; and we had to read them in our class. But about this time I came to know Bankim Chandra Chatterjee through his earlier novels, "Doorgesh-Nandinee" or "The Chieftain's Daughter" as it has been christened in its English translation by Mrs. Knight, and "Kapalakundala." Babu Nava Kishore Sen became a great admirer, I think, of Bankim Chandra, as whatever he wrote used to be bought by Babu Nava Kishore; and thus it was that I was able to see and read them. My father never took any notice of what I read, and I found no difficulty in securing whatever books Babu Nava Kishore bought, through his wife, who exerted a great influence ever the evolution of my early youth. She was about four or five years older than myself, but except my sister Kripa, who was three years my younger, and could not be treated upon terms of equality and frank friendship, there were no other ladies among my acquaintances, who could treat me upon terms of more or less equality. I was also the only youth in our compound before whom she could freely come, and with whom she could mix freely, as the others were either about her own age or older than herself. So it happened that we two became like brother and sister, and she treated me all through her life with sincere love and affection. And she was my medium in getting whatever Bengalee books Babu Nava Kishore Sen bought at this time.

When I was reading in the first class of our School, Bankim Chandra's "Banga-Darshan" made its appearance. And I still remember how eagerly I read it. The skit headed *Byaghracharya Brihallangool*, which painted a gathering of learned tigers and how

Umesh Chandra Dutta.

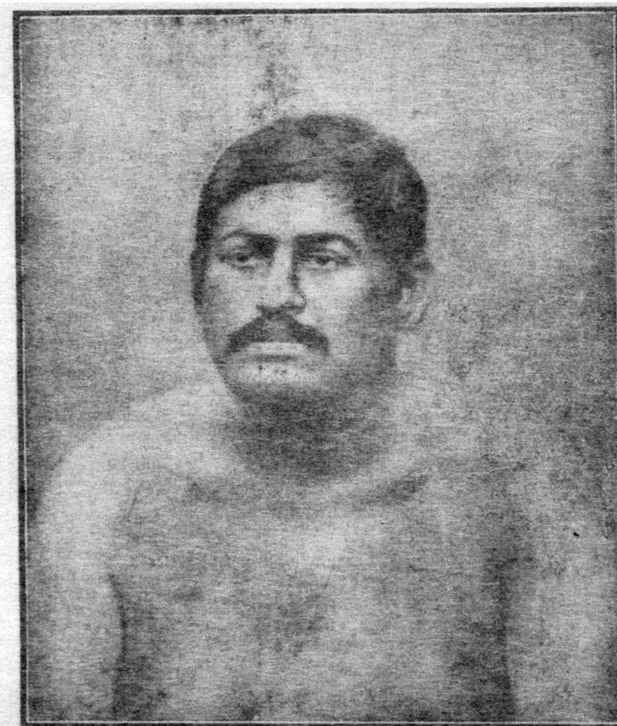

Kalinath Dutta.

they discussed various burning topics of the day, made the profoundest impression upon my young mind. Of course, I did not understand its reference or import. I cannot recall these even to-day. But the story by itself was exceedingly fascinating. The opening chapters of "Bisha-Briksha" or the "Poison Tree" also left a lasting mark upon my mind. I have never been able to forget the thrill which I had as I read the vision or dream of poor Kundanandinee; and the picture of the dark and stormy night and Nagendra's boat and his appearance to the girl, whom fate had ordained to be entwined with his own life; all these things, read more than fifty years ago, live still as things of yesterday in my memory.

In the ordinary course, I should have sat for the Entrance Examination of the Calcutta University, as the Matriculation Examination was called in those days, in November 1873, but I did not pass in all subjects in the Test Examination. And Babu Durga Kumar Basu, though allowing other boys of my standing to appear at the examination, came and spoke to my father and kept me back, in the hope that I would be able to pass in a higher class, with better preparation, next year. And as my father agreed with him, I could not sit for my final school examination with my other class-fellows. I felt slightly hurt, specially as I did not like being left behind some of my class-mates

The next year, however, did not find me more diligent in my studies. But my father engaged a private tutor for me to coach me in mathematics, a subject in which I was woefully defficient. The Second Master in the Government School, Babu Gobinda Chandra

Das, was our mathematical teacher; and my father engaged him as my coach. This was of great help to me; and I still believe that but for his help I could never have got through my mathematical papers, particularly the Algebra paper, in the next year's Entrance Examination also.

But, generally speaking, I was not more diligent in my school work in 1874 than I was in 1873. But I read more outside books, and indulged in dreams of literary eminence all through this year. I commenced now to write Bengalee poems and send occasional contributions to the "Dacca Prakash" and the "Hindu-Hitaishinee," the two Bengalee weeklies of Dacca in those days. I remember a few verses sent by me to the latter paper in memory of Justice Anukul Chandra Mukerjee found a place in its columns, and it raised me somewhat in the eyes of my fellow students. There was really no worth in these essays in versification; but I have held it ever since as an article of my literary creed, that a man, who does not write "poetry" before he is eighteen is not human, and he who writes it after that age, is either a true poet or a great fool.

These literary ambitions and efforts, however worthless in themselves, were the psychological origin of a youthful friendship which has had a profound influence upon my moral and spiritual evolution. Sundari Mohan Das had been a class-mate of mine ever since the establishment of the Government School in Sylhet in 1868 or '69; but there was hardly any special intimacy between us. In 1873 he passed the Entrance Examination with some distinction, and left Sylhet for Calcutta early in 1874. He came back during the Summer Vacation, and hearing of my literary ambitions and efforts, he came to see me one hot and steaming June day in our School. Having seen the old teachers he sent word to me, and I was proud of this especial recognition from one who, having passed out of School and joined the Presidency College in Calcutta, had attained a position far above us all old boys in the School. And what was my wonder when I saw the great transformation that a few months in Calcutta had worked in him! The glow of youth and health in his ruddy cheeks, the sudden development, at the touch of the spring-tide of life, of his youthful figure, the clean and well-arranged *dhoti* and sash or *chadar*, his smiling face and genial greeting, all these made a very profound impression upon me. And how proud I felt of myself, when he asked me, if it was true that I had commenced to write poetry and send articles to the press. And at that moment, on the top of the high hill, where our School stood, in the southern veranda, swept by the cool southern breeze, first germinated a friendship that has, by the blessing of God, lasted our whole life-time.

CHAPTER X.

STUDENT-LIFE IN CALCUTTA.

The examinations of the Calcutta University used to be held in my time during the winter. So far as I remember, the Entrance and the First Examination in Arts, which is now called the Intermediate Examination, were held about the first week of November; and the college session used to begin in January, after the Christmas holidays, which we knew then as the "Winter Vacation."

I sat for my Entrance Examination in November, 1874. For the first time in that year prescribed text-books in the English language were abolished, and we had to prove our proficiency in this language by our general knowledge of English grammar and literature, and by our ability in original English composition and re-translation, as it was called. About this time Sir George Campbell's new system of recruitment for the Subordinate Executive Service, that is, for appointments as Deputy Collectors and Deputy Magistrates and Canoongo's or lower settlement officers, was introduced; and in consequence of it, Surveying and Mensuration were made optional subjects in the Entrance Examination, because these were compulsory subjects in the new examination for Deputy Magistrateship. These innovations were introduced in 1872, when we had a Survey Master from the Engineering Department of the Calcutta Presidency College appointed to our School in Sylhet.

In 1874 Sylhet was separated from Bengal, upon the institution of the province of Assam under a Chief Commissioner. Assam was regarded as a very backward province, and the Government thought it necessary to offer special encouragement to the people by allotting a large number of scholarships to students passing the University Entrance Examination from the Assam schools. This is how, though I passed the Entrance Examination without any manner of distinction at all, I secured a monthly scholarship of rupees ten and came and took my admission in the Presidency College at Calcutta as a "scholar" or scholarship-holder.

Facilities of railway and steamer communications have brought Calcutta much nearer to Sylhet now than it was when I first left my home to join the University in Calcutta. Goalundo was, as now, the farthest limit of our Eastern Bengal Railway system. Two or three years previously, about 1869 or '70, Sylhet saw, for the first time, a steam-boat. And I still remember what a stir of wonder and admiration the sight of such a huge boat, floating on our river and making all sorts of sounds, evoked in our minds. We approached the thing with great awe, and relying upon our knowledge of the English language, some of us, school boys, approached the commander of the vessel, an Englishman, praying for permission to have a look at the machineries. This permission was readily given, and we went into the boat with great eagerness, and had a look at the huge iron rollers and other parts of the machinery. It was however not merely a feast to our eyes. The smell of roasting chicken and curried mutton also made our mouths water. We had never any experience of these before; and all these things made our first visit to a steamer a memorable incident in our life.

It was a cargo steamer, belonging, I think, to the India General Steam Navigation Company. Subsequently an irregular service, which was called on paper a "fortnightly service", was opened between Sylhet and Calcutta. The steamers went up to Sylhet during the rains only, when the river Surma was navigable by such big boats up to the town. During the rest of the year Chhatak, about twenty miles down from Sylhet, was the terminal steamer station of this line.

Towards the end of December 1874, I left Sylhet for Calcutta. It was rather a far cry from Sylhet to Calcutta in those days. And Calcutta was not quite the kind of sanatorium that it is regarded to be by our Mafassil friends today. People from our parts rarely came to Calcutta except when they were upon a pilgrimage to Benares or Gaya, or when on some specially auspicious occasion they wanted to have a dip in the sacred Ganges. And the whole journey was looked upon as so risky that their friends and family used to look upon it almost as the commencement of their travel to the "other side." My father had been on these pilgrimages more than once, and on every occasion he had left a few of his fellow pilgrims behind, victims of cholera and malignant fevers. It can, therefore, be easily imagined with what feelings my parents, and specially my mother, permitted me to take these risks. But not only my father, but even my mother as well, were determined to give me the best education available, so that I might keep up, and indeed enhance, the position of their family, and add lustre to their name. This was quite natural to my father. But such sacrifices of personal sentiments for the future good of the son were not very common in those days among Bengalee mothers. My father had secured a fairly good competence for his family. He was the owner of a fairly big estate with an annual rental of about 2500 rupees, and with every prospect of further increase, in course of time, with the expansion of the cultivated area and better management. He had, besides this estate, other smaller landed properties that also brought in a fairly good income, according to the standards of those days. I might very well, therefore, spend my days as a respectable village landlord and hold a fairly good position in society, without any University education. But my father had higher ambitions for me. He wanted me to succeed him in his profession also and some day become the leader of the Bar of which he had been in his time a leading member. He felt bitterly the handicap under which he had to work owing to his ignorance of the English language. He was anxious that I should never suffer this disadvantage. My mother was always anxious that I should not be a "dunce", as she would oftentimes say. Whenever I was lazy or neglectful of my studies, particularly when, as a boy, I refused to leave her and come to school to Sylhet, she always declared that it would be a hundred times better that I, her only son, should die in my boyhood rather than I should grow up as a "dunce" and a "boor." Many a Bengalee mother of her time and class would have opposed her son's sojourn to Calcutta for completing his education. But my mother not only did not oppose, but, on the contrary, positively encouraged my leaving home for the University in Calcutta.

It was thus that on an auspicious day, selected by careful examination of the calendar and the position of the planets at the different signs of the zodiac by a learned Brahmin, I left home for Calcutta after the usual rituals prescribed for these occasions. Having dressed for the journey, I was made to sit on a carpet, facing eastward, just on the threshhold of our living room in the inner or ladies' appartment. Ripe paddy, some flowers, a few sheaves of green grass, called *durba* in our language, and sandal-paste, a cup of fresh curd, a silver coin and some other auspicious things, were placed on a plate and set before me. I was made to touch and smell these, as I recited the usual *mantram* or text after the priest. I still remember part of this *mantram*. It means that if a man, desirous of going on a journey, should see or hear or read of *dvijas* or Brahmins, and kings, and courtezans, and garlands of flowers, and flags, and fresh meat, and ghee, and curd, and honey, and silver, and ripe paddy, he shall surely attain his object. After this, I stood up, and noticing by which nostril, the right or the left, I was breathing at the time, I was made to put forward the corresponding foot first, and repeating the name "Durga" walked out of the house.

My mother was standing a few paces away, on my way to the outer courtyard, with the packet of the Mangal Chandi's talisman, described in a previous page, in her hand.

She tied this in a corner of my sash, and after I had bent low to the ground, and taken the dust of her feet, she first spat on the ground, and making a paste by rubbing it with the small toe of her left foot, she took up this paste with the small finger of her left hand, and marking my forehead with it, smelt the crown of my head, and bade me God-speed on my journey, with a calm, and indeed, smiling face. There was not a trace of anguish or even the slightest shade of concern in her face. But when I went back home from college, six months later, during my first summer vacation, I heard that as soon as I had passed out of our compound, my mother took to her bed, so overcome with grief at my separation, that for three days she could not get out of it or take her food. I wonder if I could have left my home with such unconcern, if not, indeed, with positive joy, if I had an inkling of what was eating my mother's heart out in such a way all the time she was making preparations for my departure and particularly when she blessed me with a smiling face as I stepped out of her room.

From Sylhet I rode to Chhatak, (the winter terminus of the steamer service between Narayanganj and Sylhet), a distance of about fifteen or twenty miles. Babu Sundari Mohan Das had been to his home, which was on my way to Chhatak, for the winter vacation, and it had been arranged that he should "chaperon" me during this first journey to Calcutta, and we two should travel together by the same boat. I met him at Chhatak, and as the steamer did not leave till about eight o'clock next morning we had to spend the night in the Bazar, in a shop, which provided accommodation for travellers. It was a tumble-down sort of hut, and though we had excellent food, good rice and pure *ghee* such as the people of the present generation rarely find even in rural Bengal, and fresh fish from the river, which were cooked by Sundari Mohan's uncle, who had come to see him off, the sleeping accommodation was simply execrable. A creaking and uneven bamboo-bed, supported by shaky posts fixed on the ground, covered with two bamboo mats, one placed over the other, did duty for a cot. We spread our scanty beddings over it, and lay down to sleep. To add to our discomforts, down came a heavy rain during the small hours of the night, and we woke up shivering with cold. Chhatak stands almost on the foot of the Cherapoonjee Hills, and cold here during the winter months is naturally severer than even in Sylhet, which is fairly cold during December, January and February. Neither Sundari Mohan nor myself was provided with heavy quilts for our journey; and we tried to keep off this shivering cold by pooling together, so to say, the natural warmth of our youthful bodies.

The inland steamer which we boarded at Chhatak was a big cargo boat. It had two huge flats, one attached to either side of it. There were gangways from the steamer to the flats; and we had practically the run of the entire lower decks of the three boats. There was little or no accommodation for upper class passengers, of whom there were really very few in those days. Indian gentlemen generally travelled by country boats from one place to another. These boats plied sometimes from Sylhet to Calcutta, and even further up, as far as Benares. My father had made pilgrimages to these holy places in these boats. As for the Europeans, they too oftentimes travelled in a better class of country boats, called pinnaces, which used to be rowed by six and sometimes even by eight or ten men. I still remember one of these pinnaces on the river Surma between Sylhet and Silchar, early in the seventies of the last century, which was rowed by about ten people, singing a boat-song the refrain of which was: The *Shaheb* is going out on a journey, the *Shaheb* is going out on a journey: he has a *topee* of gold on his head, and tiny bells tingle at his ankles. Dr. C. B. Clarke of the Bengal Educational Service, who was Inspector of Schools, Dacca Division, in my young days in Sylhet, and who was the simplest Englishman that I had seen till then, created quite a sensation among English educated Bengalees of those days by publishing an ignorant criticism of Indian music, the best specimen of which he found in these boat-songs of our tea-garden coolies. The very few European passengers who travelled by these steamers plying between Sylhet and Narayanganj or Goalundo, were accommodated by the captain, who was a European, either in his own cabin, or on the upper deck, where stretchers used to be put up for them at night. The engineer was also a European, who had a small cabin on the lower deck.

The flats were loaded with tea-boxes, and packages of bay-leaves, which grew in large quantities in the Sylhet hills, and with open boxes or baskets containing orchids in which a new and profitable business was just growing then. Messrs Englis and Co. were the collectors of these orchids from the Cherapoonjee Hills in those days. We made our bed between the tea-boxes, which gave us protection from the wintry wind.

I enjoyed my first steamer journey from Sylhet very much. I had travelled a good part of this river-way in country boats with my father when very young, and he was stationed as Munsif at Koterhat. But those memories had almost completely faded away; and everything seemed so new and romantic to my eyes. Though this steamer service between Sylhet and Narayanganj had been opened two or three years previously, the people of the villages on the banks of the river along its route had not as yet become sufficiently familiar with it to treat the sight of these huge things, moving on the water without human hands, with indifference. As soon as we passed close to a village, the whole population, men, women and children, especially the women and the children, came out in full force to the river-side, and literally rendered *puja* or worship to the boat. The women cried out *ulu*, *ulu*, the cry which is made by them on all auspicious occasions, and prostrated themselves devoutly on the ground, taking the apparently self-moving boat to be some sort of a manifestation of the Deity. Sometimes they would bring flowers and vermillion and other materials of worship, and throw these in the direction of the boat to the intense amusement of the European captain and his crew.

The clerk of this steamer was a Bengalee gentleman from the Dacca District. Hari Mohan Babu, if my memory does not betray me, was his name. I think he was a Vaidya by caste. He had his food prepared on a "jolly boat", something like a life-boat, which was tied to the tail of the steamer with a stout rope and danced along on the top of the waves produced by the paddles. Hari Mohan Babu was a nice and generous man, and he offered hospitality to the *Bhadralok* passengers who travelled by his boat. Sometimes when the steamer made a long halt at any port, we had our food cooked on land. In this way, we were able to "keep our caste" on my first steamer journey from Sylhet to Narayanganj.

Our boat took about six or seven days to reach Narayanganj from Chhatak. We made a fairly long halt at Soonamganj, which was an important centre of the trade in lime-stone in those days, as I believe it is even today. After Soonamganj, we made a very long halt at Bhairab. Bhairab is now a station on the Mymensing section of the Assam Bengal Railway system, and joins the main line *via* Ashuganj, which is situated on the other side of the river Meghna, on which Bhairab stands. Bhairab had however been a very important centre of trade in East Bengal long before either steamer or railway communication was established with it. Its position on the Meghna, the high waterway in Eastern Bengal, made it the centre of our inland communication. It tapped the resources of the three Districts of Sylhet, Mymensing and Tippera, all very rich in agricultural and mineral products. When jute was first discovered as an important article of foreign trade, and the East Bengal peasantry took greedily to its cultivation upon a commercial scale, Bhairab became, within a very few years, the most important centre of this industry, after Narayanganj, long, long before Serajganj had dreams of its present premier position as a jute mart in our province. Our boat stopped, I think, for nearly two days in this port, much to the disgust and impatience of passengers like ourselves, two young men, eager to reach Calcutta as quickly as possible.

We left this boat at Narayanganj. Narayanganj has grown into a very big town today. In those days it was merely an old and fairly large market. There were only two or three brick-built houses then in the whole of the Bengalee section of the Bazar. Some European firms had already established their offices and godowns here, and they had one or two fine buildings, but the rest of the port was covered with ordinary huts. There were no hotels for outsiders; though a few Vaishnava *Akharas* or places of worship found both food and accommodation for *Bhadralok* travellers. We went from board our steamer to one of these places. It was a nice and clean place, and the priest in charge was a very genial soul, who gave us good value for the money he charged for the *prasad* or the holy "leavings" of the food served to the Gods in the temple. Neither fish nor meat was permitted to be cooked or served in this holy place; but the vegetable courses were very good. He gave us good *ghee* and curd and whey, and even milk or cream, if we asked for these and were willing to pay extra for these delicacies. We slept in the open *Nat Mandir* or Dancing Hall of the temple at night, and spent the day roving about the Bazar, and particularly in going to and fro between our lodging and the steamer station on the river-side, looking out for the vessel that was to take us from Narayanganj to Goalundo. These steamers ran in those days only twice a week; and were very irregular in their service. The names of these two steamers, if I remember aright, were the "Prince of Wales" and "Prince Alice." The latter, I think, was regarded as the swifter of the two; and we were naturally eager to catch this boat in preference to its rival.

These steamers of the Dacca-Goalundo service were fitted out more as passenger boats than as cargo boats, though they did carry a lot of cargo also. It took nearly two days to reach Goalundo from Narayanganj. We had no friend on board these steamers between Narayanganj and Goalundo, like Hari Mohan Babu, to help us to preserve our orthodoxy. Here it was that I was initiated into taking food cooked by Mahomedans for the first time in life. But the materials were not repugnant to Hindu orthodoxy, for we had only fish and mutton from the "Khalasis" or lascars of this boat.

I have no memories of the feelings with which I first saw Calcutta. It was, in any case, nothing like what the British provincial is said usually to feel when he first sees "the lights of London." Sylhet students reading in the Calcutta colleges had in those days a "mess" of their own. It was in Nimoo Khansama's Lane, that joined College Street to the south of the Medical College, and Medical College Street, which ran to the west of this institution. The extension of the Medical College and the construction of the present Eden Hospital and the buildings attached to it, have obliterated all traces of that old lane now. It was here in the Sylhet students' mess on this lane that I first commenced my life in Calcutta. It was a small establishment. Though known as the Sylhet Mess, all the members were not from Sylhet. There were three members of this mess who belonged to Kumarkhali in the Nadia District. One of them, Babu Navadvip Chandra Pal, having passed his L. M. S. Examination from the Medical College, went and took up private practice in his own village. Two other members, both of them medical students, came, one from Dacca, and another from North Bengal. The former Babu Manomohan Das took service under the Government after taking his M. B. degree, and years after he passed out of college, I met him stationed as Civil Surgeon at Muttra, where he held a high position in the Indian society. The other friend was the well-known Homeopathic practitioner of Calcutta, Dr. Chandra Sekhar Kali. The other members of this mess came from Sylhet, and were about ten or twelve in number. One of them came from a very respectable Brahmin family of Soonamganj, and it so happened that they were my father's clients; I was specially recommended by him to the care of this gentleman, the oldest member of our mess, who, having already taken his B. A. degree, was then reading for his Law Examination. His name was Babu Nabin Chandra Sarma. Having passed the B. L. Examination he went and joined the District Bar at Sylhet, where he attained a fairly high position.

Thus for the first time in my life I found myself among strangers, and I shall never be able to get over the feelings with which I sat down to my first meal in this mess, and found different kinds of special delicacies which some had specially provided for themselves. In my father's house, whether at Poil or in Sylhet, everybody, whether master or servant, had the same kind of food. But here, for the first time, I saw that my neighbour had fried eggs which were not served to me. Another gentleman had ghee with his *dal*, which he did not share with anybody else; and some one had curd which was not given to the others. And all this created an intense repulsion in me. In course of time I understood that these special things were provided by individual members at their own expense, while the common fund of the mess found everybody the common food, consisting of rice, *dal*, fried vegetables, curried fish and an acid preparation. I too gradually lost the sense of delicacy, which I had brought with me from my home, and commenced to order special things for myself, or, more accurately speaking, for Sundari Mohan and myself, as we had, generally speaking, a common purse almost from the very day I arrived in Calcutta.

Students' messes in Calcutta, in my college days, fifty-six years ago, were like small republics and were managed on strictly democratic lines. Everything was decided by the voice of the majority of the members of the mess. At the end of every month a manager was elected by the whole "House", so to say, and he was charged with the collection of the dues of the members, and the general supervision of the food and establishment of the mess. Generally an estimate of the probable cost of the messing and other charges was made and the manager was voted this amount for carrying out his duties. If the actual fell below the estimate, the manager, on the last day of his office, arranged for a big feast in which he spent all his saving; if his expenses for the month exceeded the estimates, the deficit was, of course, met by the members, but the manager had to face the unkind criticism of his executive abilities by his colleagues and, in extreme cases, which were however rare, even their frank censure. A successful manager was frequently begged to accept re-election; while the more careless and lazy members, who had often to pay out of their own pockets for their mismanagement, tried to avoid this honour.

But not merely in these financial matters, but almost in every thing that concerned the common life of the mess, the members had a supreme voice. If a seat was vacant, applications for it came before the whole "House", and no one was admitted into the mess unless he was known to or certified by responsible people to be a decent and respectable fellow. Strict discipline was maintained, by the opinion of his own peers, over every young man who belonged to a mess. Disputes between one member and another were settled by a "Court" of the whole "House"; and we sat night after night, I remember, in examining these cases; and never was the decision of this "Court" questioned or disobeyed by any member. Nor were the members of the mess at all helpless in the matter of duly enforcing their verdict upon an offending colleague. For they could always threaten the recalcitrant member either with expulsion from the mess, or if he refused to go, with the entire responsibility of the rent being thrown on him. And this had a powerful appeal to the good sense of the offending member who always submitted to the verdict of his peers on all matters.

We were by no means prurient purists in our youthful days. The Calcutta theatres, which had just introduced female artistes in our stage, were very largely patronised by us. At home we gave ourselves up oftentimes to all sorts of amusements with an abandon, that would shock the puritans of our community. During our leisure moments we sang, we danced, we indulged in all sorts of satire and mimicry, all of which were by no means within the confines of what is called delicacy or decency in certain circles. But for all that, a really pure moral atmosphere pervaded our life in these messes. No manner of vice was tolerated; and the least suspicion of loose morals in a member would make him liable to very serious displeasure of his friends and, in extreme cases, to expulsion from the mess. And such was the force of public opinion in these small republics that I have known of cases of this punishment of offending members, which so worked upon them that after a week of their expulsion from a mess, they looked as if they had just come out of some prolonged or serious spell of sickness.

We made from time to time laws and regulations for the proper administration of our little republics. I remember that a few months after I came to Calcutta, a set of laws were made for the conduct of the members of our mess. We were rather a mixed lot. Some were orthodox Hindus, though their orthodoxy did not go so far as to prohibit association or inter-dining, provided the food was cooked by a Brahmin, with those who did not observe the rules of caste. Others were absolutely heterodox and openly violated all the rules of Hinduism in regard to eating and drinking. One or two were honest and professed Brahmos. Babu Nabin Chandra Sarma, who was the oldest member of our little republic, and as the most advanced University student among us who was held in sincere respect by every one, though not quite orthodox in his opinions, was yet exceedingly scrupulous in the matter of his way of life. He used to frankly tell us that personally he had absolutely no objection to take cooked food out of a non-Brahmin's hands, but he did not like to get cut off from his family on the one hand, nor to tell lies about his ways and habits when questioned by his people. So he thought the most honourable thing to do was to avoid everything that might create trouble or force him to a denial. He would not, therefore, take cooked rice out of the hands of us, Kayesthas and Vaidyas, but had no objection to our cooking curries and *dal* and other things for him. And the reason why he made this distinction, he would tell us, was that nobody would ever ask him if he took curries or *dal* cooked by non-Brahmins; the only question, if ever any were raised, would be if he had taken *bhat* or cooked rice out of their hands. The Bengalee idiom never used curries or *dal* as the name for cooked food, *bhat* or cooked rice was the only term used in this context.

The composition of our mess called for some sort of a compromise between the so-called orthodox and the Brahmo and other heterodox members of our republic. So a rule was passed by the unanimous vote of the whole "House", that no member should bring any food to the house (except, of course, loaves and biscuits that had commenced to be tolerated by the orthodoxy of the Metropolis) which outraged the feelings of Hindu orthodoxy. It was, however, clearly understood that the members of the mess, as a body or even individually, would not interfere with what any one took outside the house. So we were free to go and have all sorts of forbidden food either at the Great Eastern Hotel, which some of us commenced to occasionally patronise later on, or anywhere else.

This law put us sometimes to very great inconvenience. One such incident has lived in my mind all these years. We had left Nimoo Khansama's Lane, and had taken a house in Madan Baral's Lane, off Wellington Square, at this time. One day our Brahmin cook was absent; and there was no dinner at home. So Sundari Mohan and myself, we two, went in search of food in Bow Bazar, where we had seen cooked meat and crabs and prawns and hot flour-cakes, fried in ghee or butter, called *pooris* in Northern India and *loochis* in our own vernacular, put out for sale. We went to one of these shops and having bought a good quantity of curried mutton and *pooris* or *loochis*, asked the shop-keeper if there was any room where his customers could have their meals. He showed us a door leading to a hall where we could safely enjoy our meal. So we eagerly went in, and found a table and a few chairs in that hall, which was lighted rather dimly by a kerosene lamp hanging from the ceiling. The place was by no means inviting, but we made ready to use it gladly on the principle of any port in storm; because though our own house was very close to this place, the laws of our republic forbade the introduction of any cooked food into it from outside. We had just set our things down on the bare table and were going to sit down to our dinner, when there entered a stranger with rather unsteady steps and a blue bottle peeping out of his armpit. This gave us such a fright that we really did not know what to do. The new-comer noticed our nervousness and in a very kindly way, but with a broken voice, stammered out: "What is there to be ashamed of, my friends? I have come for the same object as yourselves." And as with these words he brought out a small glass from his pocket and set the bottle from his arm-pit on the table, we gathered up our precious food and ran out of the room like thieves, trembling all over. Coming out into the street, we commenced to cast about for some place where we might go and sit and have our dinner. There was a small platform, just opposite the small lane which led to our house, in front of a neighbour's residence, which was never used by the inmates of that house, but where the Municipal officers, whose rank had better not be disclosed, used to rest early in the morning, and which had rather unappetising associations about it. In our extremity, we went to this place and finished the *pooris* and curries standing there in the dim light of the lamp that lighted our lane. And as soon as the prohibited things passed out of our hands into our gullets, we ran to our house and there gulped the food down with the water from the house tap.

I had my first truly forbidden food in the house of a friend, a class-mate of Sundari

Mohan, and a near relation of a leading lawyer of the city, a well-known and wealthy member of the Calcutta Kayestha community. He invited Sundari Mohan, Tara Kishore Chaudhuri and myself to dinner at his house, which was not very far from our mess. It was here that both Tara Kishore Chaudhuri and myself had chicken curry for the first time in our life. And the incident is specially remembered by me, because early next morning Tara Kishore came out of bed and standing in the morning light, stretched out his arms and commenced to examine what strength and flesh he had gained through the forbidden meat taken overnight! Tara Kishore Chaudhuri rose to considerable eminence in the Calcutta High Court Bar. A few years ago he gave up a very profitable practice and retired to Brindaban, where he has since been elected to be the head of an important temple, with the title Braja-Videhi, the highest spiritual recognition that one can get among the Vaishnavas of Shree Brindaban, reputed to be the scene of the life and *leela* or sport of Shree Krishna in the Hindu legends.

Talking of Tara Kishore Chaudhuri I am reminded of another anecdote of his student-life in Calcutta, which found us considerable fun for many days. There was illness in our mess. I think Sundari Mohan was ill, and the doctor prescribed chicken soup for him. Tara Kishore Chaudhuri was sent to the Great Eastern Hotel for it. When asked if he had brought any vessel to carry the soup in, he innocently took out a copy of the "Statesman" newspaper that he had with him, and asked the man, who came out to serve him, to put the soup in it!

The story of my first lunch at "Wilson's", as the Great Eastern was called in those days, also deserves recording. It was typical of our educated classes in those days (1875-'76). Sundari Mohan, myself, and three or four others went to have our "tiffin" in this place. We had a private room to ourselves. But none of us had any experience of European food, and our first difficulty, when the menu was placed before us, was how to make our selection. We avoided this by leaving it to the Mahomedan *khansama* to get us the very best there was in the Hotel. None of us had any practice in handling knives and forks. That was our next difficulty. And we tried to solve it by just trying to play with these as long as the waiter was present, but sending him out on all sorts of errands, we commenced to attack the victuals on our plate vigorously with hand and teeth. It was a very miserable experience after all. We did not like to hurt our dignity by honestly eating with our hands the things that we had to pay for so much; nor could we really eat in the unfamiliar way the Europeans do. That experience was so unpleasant that as long as I was a student, and not until I had become absolutely familiar with the foreign ways, did I ever again cross the threshold of the Great Eastern or any other hotels in India. The story of that first fight with knives and forks and spoons used to be frequently repeated among our friends in those days to their intense merriment.

These students' messes were, naturally, only of Mafassil young men reading in the University. They were generally grouped according to the Districts from which they came. We had thus a Tippera mess; a Barisal mess; a Sylhet mess. Dacca had more than one mess; there was the Bikrampur mess and, if I do not forget, another, the Manikganj mess. Of these, somehow the Bikrampur, the Tippera and the Sylhet messes were most prominent in all kinds of public activities of those days among the student population of the Metropolis. Towards the close of my life in the University, 33 Mussalmanpara Lane, the Bikrampur mess; 28 Mechuabazar Street, the Tippera mess; 14 College Street, the Sylhet mess;—these became something like landmarks in the life of the East Bengal students in Calcutta. 33 Mussalmanpara Lane came to receive the highest distinction because of its association, first, with some of the most brilliant students of the University, and, next, for its liberal social and religious views. Babu Ananda Mohan Bose, who subsequently went to Cambridge and was the first Indian Wrangler, passed his M. A. Examination and Roychand Premchand Studentship, which carried a prize of 10,000 rupees in those days, while he was an inmate of this mess. Babu Rajani Nath Roy, who subsequently rose to the position of Deputy Accountant General, was also a member of this mess; and his success in the University Examinations, in most of which he topped the list of successful students, shed considerable distinction on it. Babu Shasi Bhushan Datta was another brilliant student of the Calcutta University, who took his degree while he was a member of this mess. Dr. Prasanna Kumar Roy, Babu Shreenath Datta, Sir Krisna Govinda Gupta, all of them distinguished students of the University, had intimate associations with the mess at 33

Mussalmanpara Lane. And their name and fame secured for it the distinction of being the premier students' mess in Calcutta in our time. 33 Mussalmanpara Lane was also a very prominent centre of social and religious revolt associated with Babu Keshub Chandra Sen and his Brahmo Samaj of India in the seventies of the last century. It was from this mess that Ananda Mohan Bose, Prasanna Kumar Roy, Shreenath Datta, Rajani Nath Roy and Aghore Nath Chattopadhyaya went to be publicly initiated into Brahmoism by Keshub Chandra Sen, a few days previous to his departure for England in 1871. Babu Dwaraka Nath Ganguly, the pioneer of liberal female education in Bengal, and the Editor of "Abala-Bandhaba" or the "Friend of the Weaker Sex", who was later the Assistant Secretary of the Indian Association, also lived during the first few years of his life in Calcutta, in 33 Mussalmanpara Lane. It turned out a larger number of distinguished graduates, many of whom made their mark in the public life of their province, and some, indeed, in that of the whole of India, than any other students' mess of our time. 33 Mussalmanpara Lane became thus almost a sign and symbol of culture and progress in our community in those days. The Tippera mess at 28 Mechuabazar Street and the Sylhet mess at 14 College Street came to considerable prominence after 1874, and particularly after the great schism in the Brahmo Samaj, due to the marriage of the eldest daughter of Keshub Chandra Sen to the minor Maharaja of Cooch Behar, on account of the intimate association of some of us with the new Brahmo movement under Sivanath Sastri.

The Presidency College was the premier college affiliated to the Calcutta University in my time. There were also a few private, that is, non-Government colleges in the city. Three of these, the General Assembly's Institution, situate in Cornwallis Square or Hedua, as it was and is still known among our people; the Free Church Institution, which was situate in Nimtola Street, called also Duff College, having been established by Dr. Duff; and the Cathedral Mission College, which stood in Mirzapur Street and occupied the building that still stands on the south-eastern corner of College Square and is occupied by the Calcutta Corporation as a District office—belonged to Protestant Christian Missions; the first two, as their name indicated, belonged to the Free Church of Scotland, and the third to the Church of England Mission. Then, there was the St. Xavier's College, owned and conducted by the Jesuit Fathers. Doveton and La Martinere were meant exclusively for the European boys, and, as a rule, no Bengalee was admitted to these institutions; though I think, young Surendra Nath had his early education, preparatory to his going to England for the Indian Civil Service, in the former college, from which he passed his B. A. Pandit Iswar Chandra Vidyasagar had established the Metropolitan Institution a few years before I came to Calcutta; and this was the only college affiliated to the Calcutta University which was owned and managed by private individuals. When Sir George Campbell opened his campaign against higher English education and laid down the policy of gradually withdrawing from the field of this education, on the plea of releasing the funds of the State available for the promotion of education among the people, from collegiate education which benefited only a small section of the community, with a view to its employment in the cause of mass education, the opening of the Metropolitan Institution showed the way in which the new menace to higher education in the province might be fought and removed. Pandit Vidyasagar was not a very rich man. But he did not seek public help in this new educational venture. He had no faith in corporate action so far as his people were concerned. So he dedicated whatever he owned to the cause of higher English education, and practically staked his fortune and his position upon this enterprise. The fees charged in his Metropolitan Institution were much lower than those of the Presidency College, these were even less than what was charged by the Missionary Colleges. Poor students were helped with freeships and half-freeships as their condition justified. When I came to Calcutta, the Metropolitan Institution had already secured a high place among the Calcutta colleges. Tara Kishore Chaudhuri, who took a high position in the Entrance Examination from my school in Sylhet in my year (1874), and got a scholarship of rupees fifteen a month, went and joined the Metropolitan Institution, though I took my admission in the more expensive Presidency College.

Mr. Sutcliffe was the Principal of the Presidency College at that time. In the early years of our University, the Principal of the Presidency College was, almost ex-officio, the Registrar of the Calcutta University. The most brilliant students in the province, therefore, sought admission in this college if their means allowed it. Mr. Sutcliffe's dual position, as Principal and University Registrar, offered certain advantages to the students of the Presidency College, which the students of the other colleges did not enjoy. Students who passed with distinction from the Presidency College, stood greater chances of securing superior appointments under the Government owing to Mr. Sutcliffe's dual position than their brethren from the other colleges. Though the institution of special examinations for selecting candidates for the Subordinate Executive Service under the administration of Sir George Campbell somewhat restricted the field of Mr. Sutcliffe's patronage, there were other appointments, notably in the newly organised Financial Department, that were practically in his gift. All these offered great temptations to ambitious young men to prefer the Presidency College to others. Though I had no such definite ambitions and was really not likely to succeed even if I had any, because I had passed the Entrance Examination in the Third Division, and was exceedingly ill-equipped for successful competition with the brilliant students of the University who flocked to this College, as a scholarship-holder I fancied it would be profitable and convenient for me to join it. So at the beginning of 1875 I found myself in this College.

Mr. Tawney, who after his retirement from the Bengal Education Service was for many years in charge of the India Office Library in London, was the senior Professor of English in the Presidency College at that time. But he was in charge of the B. A. and M. A. classes. Mr. Bellet and Mr. Hand, a Indo-European gentleman, and Babu Pyari

Charan Sarkar, were Assistant Professors of English. They were in charge of the Intermediate classes. Mr. Bellet had the typical Anglo-Saxon features. He was a rather short man with a red face. He had, however, the reputation of being a good English scholar; and his teaching was very popular among the students. But he had rather a short temper, which brought some troubles to us all when I was reading in the First Year Class. He had abused some students of the Second Year Class, and had, indeed, gone so far as to order one of them to stand up like a school-boy. This gave very serious offence to the whole class. The next day the Second Year students refused to attend his class. There was great uproar towards the last period; and almost all the students came out and stood at the foot of the stairs in an ugly angry mood. Mr. Bellet, finding the situation rather more serious than what he had thought it was ever likely to be, took selter in the Professors' Common Room, on one of the upper floors, and waited there for the College to be dismissed and the boys to go to their messes or homes. But he was disappointed. The College was dismissed at the usual hour, but the boys of the First and Second Year Classes, and they were a large number, refused to disperse but waited in angry groups at the portico and the veranda through which the offending Professor would have to pass out. After about an hour and a half's waiting, Mr. Bellet came down the stairs with another English Professor who was, I think, Mr. Parry, who taught us Logic. As soon as Mr. Bellet stepped down to the veranda, he was struck on the head by one of his enemies. His hat went rolling out into the portico, but his head was safe and sound. He tried to catch the youth who struck him, but as the whole body, gathered at the foot of the stairs, went to the help of this young man, he had to give up the pursuit as risky and hopeless. Here the matter ended for that day. Mr. Sutcliffe took up the enquiry next morning, and called a few students of the Second Year Class to have the whole story from them. He was a very tactful person, and took an almost fatherly interest in the young men of his college. Though he did not openly show it, we all knew it, that the sympathies of the Principal were entirely with the boys; and it was even believed that he did not conceal from Mr. Bellet his view of the indiscretion that he had been guilty of, in dealing with grown-up University students as if they were mere school boys. One young man, however, who had struck Mr. Bellet, was punished with rustication; and the matter was allowed to rest here. Would any Principal of the Presidency College deal with an assault of this kind on a European Professor in this way today? How have the times changed since I was a student in the Presidency College sixty years ago!

Mr. Sutcliffe was, indeed, exceedingly jealous of the prestige of the College and the honour of his boys. I heard it that one of his students got involved in a police case of some sort and the police officer in charge of the investigation went to his college to identify the youth and investigate into the complaint. As soon as the information of the presence of the, police in his premises reached Mr. Sutcliffe he came out and ordered the policemen off, declaring that he was the sole authority within the walls of his college, and neither a policeman nor a Magistrate had any right to come here without his permission. This permission he sternly refused in the present case, and the officer was sent about his business, without any opportunity of holding any inquiry into the case in the College, and as the matter was not very serious, the whole case was discreetly dropped. All this was in full consonance with the traditions of the British Universities where Mr. Sutcliffe had been brought up; and even the Government dared not question the authority of the Principal in a matter of this kind. The prevailing idea in my young days among British officers of our Government Education Department was to build up our University after the model of the British Universities, and hence they were always exceedingly jealous of their independence in all matters affecting the training and discipline of the youths committed to their charge.

Mr. Bellet and Babu Pyari Charan Sircar were my English Professors in the Presidency College. Mr. Hand taught us History. And, oh, the history that we read! Taylor's "Ancient History" was our text-book. The first half of it was full of the so-called history of the Jews, collated from the Old Testament legend. The discoveries of modern scholars regarding the history of the Semitic peoples were then beyond the boldest imagination of the most diligent and imaginative historians of the ancient world. Taylor, if placed in the hands of our sons, would be thrown away as dry and incredible fancies dressed up as history! We were, however, on firmer and much pleasanter ground when reading the history of ancient Greece and

Rome. I have no recollection of the abilities or the methods of Mr. Hand. He stands out in my mind as a quiet and inoffensive gentleman, who was always kind to us. Mr. Sutcliffe, the Principal, taught us Mathematics. He knew every scholarship-holder by his name and face; and we had to be particularly diligent, or at least appear to be so, during his period; as otherwise we ran the risk of being called to his room, and we knew what that meant. Not that he was ever harsh or rude, but still we stood in fear of being called to see him in private. It always meant some admonition. Mr. Bellet was a very good teacher; and, on the whole, a good man. But he was exceedingly reserved. He came to the class just as the hour struck, and without saying a word or casting a glance about him he would open his book and start his lecture. And though he rarely called for the Register, very few students wanted to be absent from his class, so well did every one like his way of teaching. Pandit Nilmani Mukhopadhyaya, who subsequently became a Mahamahopadhyaya, was one of our Sanskrit Professors. He was a very strict disciplinarian, and used every day to call for the Register to see which of the boys were present and who were playing the truant. But he was a very able teacher all the same, and we liked him for it. The other Sanskrit Professor was Pandit Raj Krishna Banerjee, who was a very great friend of Pandit Iswar Chandra Vidyasagar. He was a very genial sort of person, and indulged in all sorts of witticisms during his lectures.

But the one man, who had the greatest influence over forming my mind and character, was Babu Pyari Charan Sircar, who was

Assistant Professor of English in the Presidency College during my first year there. His was a magnetic personality. I cannot say how his personality affected my fellow-students, but it exerted a very great influence on me. He was a man of few words and I do not remember to have exchanged even half-a-dozen words with him during the five or six months that he taught us. But these few words were so gentle, and his whole being seemed to breathe such a sweet gentleness and sympathy for everybody that when he died after a brief spell of illness, I felt that I had lost an old and personal friend or dear relation. That was the first time in my life when the death of one who was not connected with me by blood or marriage or long association, touched me so deeply and drew out tears from my eyes. I had, though in a much lesser degree, the same sense of personal loss, when, years after, the news of Mr. Sutcliffe's death reached us from England. But I had closer acquaintance with him than I had the good fortune of having with Babu Pyari Charan Sircar.

Babu Pyari Charan Sircar belonged to the first generation of English-educated Bengalees. He was about sixty at the time of his death in 1875. The Hindu College, which first offered opportunities of systematic education in English language and literature and modern sciences and European histories and humanities to our people, was established in 1820, when Pyari Charan must have been a boy of eight or nine years. He was a pre-University man, and he passed what was known as the Senior Scholarship Examination with great distinction. Though he might have easily become a Deputy

Magistrate, he chose the humbler but more sacred and responsible vocation of the school-master, and dedicated all his culture and intelligence to the promotion of this new education among his people. His school primers, called the "First Book of Reading", the "Second Book of Reading", the "Third Book of Reading" and the "Fourth Book of Reading", were the most approved text-books in my school days; I do not know why had "Murray's English Spelling Book" been placed in my hands at the Missionary School at Sylhet in preference to Mr. Sircar's primer. But Pyari Charan was not only an ardent educationist, but a very enthusiastic social reformer also, though of the more conservative school. It is said that he spent as much as nearly 70,000 rupees, practically the entire savings of the life-time of a poor school-master and an author, in promoting the cause of widow remarriage among higher caste Hindus, to which his friend Pandit Iswar Chandra Vidyasagar had consecrated his life. He was a very enthusiastic advocate of female education, and established a Girls' School at Chorebagan, the part of the city of Calcutta where he lived and which contained his family homestead, and maintained it at his own expense. This School was continued after Babu Pyari Charan's death, by his cousin, Dr. Bhuban Mohan Sircar, who was a well-known citizen of the metropolis and a prominent member of the Calcutta Corporation up to the closing years of the last century. But Pyari Charan Sircar stood apart from the earlier generation of his English-educated countrymen in his complete freedom from the drink habit that worked such havoc in their life. He was, in my young days, the leader of a movement against this drink evil, to which Young Bengal had taken with as much avidity as they took to the study of Shakespeare and Milton. His advocacy of total abstinence found expression even through popular Bengali songs, one of which was current in and about Calcutta sixty years ago, and used to be sung by the masses. It declared: "Don't drink wines or spirits; Pyari Charan has asked you not to. The inside which is used only to pulses and vegetables, if it runs to excess in the matter of strong drinks, will not take long to land you at the home of Pluto." It was a comic song, supposed to have been composed by one who was addicted to the hemp-drug; and so the last line declared that "though it was dangerous to go by water (i.e. indulge in drink), there was no prohibition against travelling by land (i.e. smoking hemp or ganja)."

A typical anecdote revealing the personality of the man has come to my knowledge recently and may very profitably be recorded here. Dr. Ganga Prasad Mukherjee, the well-known physician of Bhowanipur, father of Justice Sir Ashutosh Mukherjee, was a pupil of Pyari Charan Sircar while at school. Ganga Prasad had to pursue his studies under very great difficulties. His parents were not sufficiently well-off to be able to pay for the expenses of his education. When Ganga Prasad was sent up for the Entrance Examination he had not the wherewithal to pay his Examination fees. He asked his elder brother, who was living in their village home, for these. He disposed of some of the household utensils to procure the amount and sent it to him. Unfortunately poor Ganga Prasad lost the solitary ten-rupee note, and did not know what to do. A friend suggested that he might approach Dr. Duff, who was known to help indigent boys in such matters; and Ganga Prasad went and saw him. Dr. Duff was very much impressed with the honest and intelligent look of the young man and readily agreed to meet his want, but asked him to get a note from his Head Master. Ganga Prasad next came to Babu Pyari Charan and told him everything. Pyari Babu felt hurt at the fact that Ganga Prasad had never told him of all this before. "Could'nt I find rupees ten for you, Ganga Prasad, that you had to go to Dr. Duff for it? But since you have been to him, I cannot deprive him of the pleasure of helping you now; but please, whenever you are in difficulties in future, do not hesitate to come to me."

Over two hundred boys, I think, came and joined the Presidency College in my year; and so we had two sections in the First Year Class. Among my class-mates here were Babu Bhutnath Chatterjee, who had stood first in the University Entrance Examination in 1874. Bhutnath went to the Engineering College, which was then a part of the Presidency College and was located in the same building in College Street, after passing his First Examination in Arts. He entered Government Service. Amulya Charan Basu, who stood second, was also a class-mate of mine in the Presidency College. He took his Law Degree and joined the Bar, but his health gave way and he has been living practically in retirement. Krishna Lal Datta, who, after taking his M.A. Degree, found employment in the Financial Department, rose to the distinguished position of Assistant Controller and was a trusted officer in that Department; Pankaj Kumar Chatterjee, who rose to be a District and Sessions Judge; Parvati Nath Datta, who secured a Gilchrist Scholarship, went to England, took his B.Sc. Degree in London, and got a post in the Geological Survey of India; Babu Bhupendra Nath Basu, though of the same year, was not in our section. Babu Heramba Chandra Maitra, Principal, City College, was also in that section.

I do not know how things are now; but in my young days, students in the Calcutta colleges, who came from East Bengal Districts, and particularly in the Presidency College, which was patronised by the sons of the aristocracy of Calcutta, had a rather bad time of it, specially if they were very sensitive. Their local patois was the object of open ridicule by their more refined metropolitan fellow-students. Many of these Mafassil boys were very shy and of a far more serious mood than the Calcutta boys; and they failed oftentimes to freely mix with the latter or throw themselves into the playfulness of their Calcutta friends. The Calcutta boys made fun of their Professors behind their back. Some of them, including the very best indeed, wrote horrid satires on their teachers, and others, instead of listening to their lectures, drew caricatures of them on their exercise books. Ganga Govinda Gupta, a younger brother of Sir Krishna Govinda Gupta, was specially distinguished in this art and he had quite a collection of caricatures in his exercise book. All these things seemed to hurt the more serious-minded East Bengal boys, and stood somewhat in the way of their freely mixing with the metropolitan boys. But there were, of course, exceptions. Ganga Govinda was himself one, for he too was a *Bangal*, as his native District was Dacca. So was Krishna Lal, who came from Jessore. But generally the East Bengal or *Bangal* boys found it rather hard to put up with the ridicule of the Calcutta boys. Dacca boys were too proud of their own District and of their old traditions as one-time capital of Bengal to accommodate themselves to the new conditions; so while we Sylhet boys put forth strenuous efforts to give up our local patois as soon as we came to Calcutta, and learn the idiom and intonations of the metropolis, our Dacca friends kept up the habit of talking in their District patois as a matter of parochial pride and patriotism; and this tended to keep them away somewhat from the general life of the Calcutta students. This was, however, helpful to them, because they were able, owing to their aloofness, to devote themselves with greater diligence to their studies and thereby oftentimes to beat their rivals belonging to the metropolis in the University Examinations. As these students from East Bengal had fewer interests beside their studies, they were looked down upon by the Calcutta boys as "book worms."

My first summer vacation took me back home to Sylhet in May 1875. That was, however, the saddest period of my young life. The morning after I reached Sylhet, my youngest sister, a lovely little child, about two years and a half old, the only one of my many brothers and sisters who survived the early weeks of their lives and who therefore created a great hope in our mind that she would live and grow into youth and age, died on my arms! This so upset my poor mother, who was then in a delicate condition, that she wished to kill herself by madly striking her limbs with a pestle. We snatched it away from her hands, but not before serious harm had been done. Fever and what was taken to be dysentry followed. She was ill of it for nearly two months. This detained me at home even after the recess in my College was over. When, however, she was confined without any mishap, both the doctor and the Kaviraj, who were attending her, declared that her life was now safe; and the next evening freed from all further anxiety on her account, I got out of our house, after nearly two months, to enquire about the date of the next steamer for Narayanganj. On my return, I found my mother in a state of semi-collapse, due, as I understood afterwards, when I had gathered some knowledge of midwifery and female diseases, to internal hœmorhage, to which she succumbed in an hour or so.

Ever since I was a boy, I had oftentimes tried to mentally realise what my condition would be in case I lost my mother; and ever during her last illness, when her life was hanging as it were by a slender thread, I had always felt that I would not be able to live without her. But the extreme anguish with which I had thought of her death during her lifetime, did not overcome me when she actually died, and that so unexpectedly! I was as calm as a block of cold stone. I went about coolly making preparations for the funeral. Not a drop of tear escaped my eyes. Not a sigh escaped my lips. Looking back upon all this

I am amazed at my insensibility; and even sometimes question if I really had so little love for my mother. But though I set fire to the funeral pyre on which was placed her body, without any hesitation or pain, I completely broke down the next morning when I woke and saw my father shedding silent tears by my bed-side.

My father was visibly upset by this bereavement; and the sight of his desolation made me suppress my own grief. In the usual course my mother's *sradh* or the first monthly death service, should have taken place at Poil, or, in any case, in Sylhet. Considering my father's position, it would have to be performed upon a more or less grand scale, marked by larger presents to the Brahmins all over the District, feeding of hundreds of these people as well as of friends, relations and neighbours, and numberless unbidden guests, who gather from far and near at the news of a big *sradh*. My father felt that he could not stand all this in his present mood and was also unwilling to spend such a large sum of money upon so sad an occasion. So he decided to send me back to Calcutta with our family priest, and have the ceremony performed on the banks of the Ganges, which was considered far more meritorious from the ritualistic point of view than the most costly ceremony elsewhere. So within about ten days of my mother's death, I left for Calcutta in a country boat, with my *Dada* Dagoo, another retainer of my father's, a cousin of mine and our family priest. I left this boat at Dacca and took another which brought me to Goalundo. It was the first week of July, and the monsoon was in full swing ; and the Padma was in her worst mood. But in those days our people were used to travelling by country boats, and nobody thought anything of crossing the boisterous Padma or the angry Meghna in country rafts. The Meghna near Bhairab was very bad when we came near it; and we had to wait for two days, in a small canal on the other side, until the weather had become calm. That was all the inconvenience we suffered. A few hours or sometimes even two or three days' wait was all that people travelling by country boats had to put up with in those days. But they had steadier nerves too!

I was at that time in that psychological state which can only be described as a queer mixture of belief and un-belief. I still appealed to Durga in my extremity, as when my mother was in her last sick-bed. It was really an appeal to the Unseen to which the primitive mind always turns when the seen fails it. But I had absolutely no faith in the virtue of the disciplines to which I was made to submit on the death of my mother during the period of mourning, which was, in our case, full one month or thirty days. I had to live on one cooked-meal a day. It consisted of boiled rice, cooked by myself, and ghee without any salt or other accompaniments as of *dal* or vegetables. I could take milk either by itself, which I did at night, or with boiled rice in the morning, but without sugar. I could not cook my rice in metallic pots or pans but use only earthen pots, and it was to be cooked with one single bundle of fuel, and I had to pour this food out on small *dongas* or boat-shaped vessels made of the bark of fresh-cut plantain or banana trees. This took away whatever natural taste there was in hot or steaming rice and ghee. Then, having poured out my food on this *donga* I had to carry a portion in another *donga* and give it to the crows; and I could not touch my food until some crow had come and taken this *bali* or offering made to its kind. If through any chance no crow came and ate my offering, I had to go without my own food for that day. I had to sleep on the ground, on a piece of mat, and could not change my clothes, but had to use the same loin-cloth in which I had my bath, allowing it to dry on my body. At night I could not lay my head on a pillow, though I could have blanket of pure wool as a protection against cold or draught. I could not play or engage in any sort of merriment, even so much as witnessing it. For the first four days, I had to perform some kind of minor *sradh*, making offerings of rice-cakes to the dead. This had to be repeated on the tenth day. All these seemed to my sceptic mind to be meaningless magic and not deserving of being honoured by reasonable and educated people!

My father felt the hardship to which these mourning rites and disciplines subjected my young flesh; and one day, as he sat chatting in our Sylhet house with a Brahmin, who though not quite a Pandit, that is, a title-holder or proprietor of a *tol* or Sanskrit school, was yet considered a bit learned in Brahminical laws, and was held, therefore, in considerable respect by our elders, he incidentally said, in my presence, that if I found it difficult to take my rice and milk without sugar, there was no harm in my taking ripe plantains of the purer variety, which was offered to the Gods. To this without actually being asked, this revered Brahmin readily assented. That was a way of my father's with these Brahmins. He would himself make some decision on points of ceremonial conduct, and then express it in the presence of some of these Brahmins, who, he knew fairly well, would not care to contradict it. So from that day forward, I was allowed to take plantains, and this considerably relieved the austerities of my mourning.

Personally I did not attach any value at all to these austerities. My grief for my mother was a thing too intimate and sacred to be paraded in this way: this is how, like so many of my rationalist friends, I looked upon the whole business. What put me up particularly against these was that instead of being a spontaneous expression of my grief, these were super-imposed upon me by an outside authority, which hurt my conceit of personal liberty. Years after when I lost my father, I followed these same hardships freely and of my own will and pleasure, as a mark of respect, not as an expression though of my grief, for him. I know, or think I know, much better to-day. The entire meaning of these has changed to me with the revelation of a new philosophy of Man, which I may, if it pleases God, discuss another day, when and if I am permitted to write of my later years. But as a young man of seventeen, I had no appreciation of these old disciplines; and though through fear of offending my father, I submitted to them outwardly, my reason revolted all the same against this meaningless interference with my personal freedom.

So, when I found myself in Calcutta, out of my father's ken, with only our old family priest and my *Dada* and a cousin to look after me, I commenced to disregard these rules altogether. I could not come and take up my quarters in our mess with all these people. So we went to a place in Belliaghata, where a few merchants and traders from our parts lived, as they do even to-day, and found a couple of rooms there. Here I used to have my morning meal of boiled rice and ghee and milk and ripe plantains; but in the afternoon, I used to walk daily to our mess in Madan Baral's Lane, and as I passed along Bow Bazar Street, I provided myself with boiled eggs and crabs and *poories*, on which I had my evening meal. I do not know if I ought to feel sorry for it. But if my mother lived to now, and if I lost her to-day, though I would not certainly call in the Brahmin to perform the *sradh*, I would scrupulously observe the old rules prescribed for the month of mourning for my people by orthodox Hinduism. That would be an act of free choice on my part; and I would do it, because I seem to understand the inwardness of these disciplines now more than I did then.

I performed my mother's *sradh* on the banks of the Ganges in strict accordance with Hindu rites; and for nearly a year after I regularly performed the monthly *sradh* also, under the direction of a priest, who belonged to our District and who was living in Calcutta at that time ministering to the Hindu residents from our parts. Towards the close of the year, and before the day of the first anniversary of my mother's death came, I had openly rebelled against the old faith and society, and thus gave it up. That was the first cause of open rupture between father and son.

In due course, I would have to sit for my First Examination in Arts in 1876; but towards the close of that academic year, a couple of months before the examination, I had an attack of chicken pox. Sundari Mohan nursed me through it, utterly regardless of the consequences; for chicken pox, though generally not dangerous, is exceedingly catching. So he had it in a much severer form than what I had. It was now my turn to nurse him. Thus I missed my examination. Sundari Mohan had at that time left the Presidency College, and having passed the F. A. had taken his admission into the Medical College. Medical College students had no winter vacation, like those reading in the General or Arts Department of the University. So even after he got well, and though I had nothing to do in Calcutta until the opening of the next session after Christmas, I wanted to spend the vacation here. But news of my illness had made my father very nervous and as he insisted upon my going home, I left Sundari Mohan as soon as he was able to take care of himself, and went home.

It was rather a sacrifice. Because that was the time when the Prince of Wales (the late King Edward VII) was timed to come to Calcutta. The whole city was busy with preparations for the royal reception. Triumphal arches were being put up at every important crossing along the streets which he was expected to pass during his visit to the metropolis. The entire population was excited with the coming *tamasha*. Naturally enough, I did not quite like leaving all this and go to our small town at this time. But my father's wishes had to be respected, specially since my mother's death, six months previously, he had really no one except myself and my sister, who was, however, living with her husband at Silchar. But though I did not participate in the festivities of the Prince's visit to Calcutta, it led to certain events that had a far-reaching influence upon my life and character. But I must defer that story to another chapter, in which I shall, God willing, relate the story of how I came to join the Brahmo Samaj.

That I could not sit for my First Examination in Arts in 1876, was not at all a very unwelcome thing to me personally, though my father was naturally disappointed at it. The fact is, I had done little or nothing, in the way of my College studies, during the two years that I was in the Presidency College. As a scholarship-holder, I had to regularly attend Mr. Sutcliffe's lectures. He was very particular about us, and noticed whenever any one of his scholarship-holders were absent from the class. Therefore, though not for love of Mathematics, which was his subject, but for fear of losing his good opinion, if not the scholarship, I had perforce to be in my place during his period. I attended Mr. Bellet's class and Babu Pyari Charan Sircar's for love of the things they taught. Pandit Nilmani Nyayalankara used invariably to have a roll call every day he came to our class, and I could not escape him without losing my stipend for the day. Thus about a couple of hours every day, and some days only an hour, I used to be in my class. The rest of the time I played truant, and as there were no railings round the compound of the

Presidency College like they have now, I used to run out and spend my time in a book-shop that stood just a few paces off, somewhere near the place where the Harrison Road cuts the College Street on the opposite side of that street, and devote the hours when I should have been in my class, in miscellaneous reading, both Bengali and English. The name of that book-shop was Canning Library. It was owned by Babu Yogesh Chandra Bannerjee, who was a very genial sort of man, and was somehow very friendly towards me, and let me have the run of his whole stock of books among which I freely rummaged for hours and hours together. I was consequently very ill-prepared for my examination, and the attack of chicken pox was a veritable God-send to me; for it saved me from my father's angry remonstrance at wasting my time and his money in this way in Calcutta.

Next year I went and joined the Cathedral Mission College, as the allowance from my father was not sufficient, now that I had no scholarship, to pay the heavier fees of the premier College of the University. I appeared at the First Examination in Arts in 1877 from this College but got plucked in Mathematics. I tried another chance the next year; but owing to differences with my father over religious and social convictions, he had stopped my remittance, and I was in difficulties financially for more than six months. Though he did, after all, send all the arrears towards the close of the year, that enabled me to appear once more at the examination, but that did not help me to make up lost time. And this time also I got plucked.

This was the end of my career in the

University. The breach between father and son had become by this time too wide to hope for an early reconciliation. I could no longer depend upon him for my expenses. I had, therefore, no option but to look out for some employment. A friend who knew me well, and had confidence in my general knowledge of English language and literature, recommended me for the post of head master and teacher of English in an Entrance School at Cuttack, owned by a local Brahmo gentleman. He agreed to take me on trust, and by the beginning of the year 1879, I found myself in the responsible position of the Head Master of this school, called the Cuttack Academy.

CHAPTER XI.

THE BIRTH OF OUR NEW NATIONALISM.

The years 1875—1878, which synchronised with my life in the University in Calcutta, saw the birth of our new Nationalism. This new Nationalism had its origin in a renaissance in Bengalee literature brought about by our contact with modern European thought. Bankim Chandra was, in a special sense, the prophet of this renaissance. The "Bangadarshan" started in 1873-74, was the organ of it. Bankim Chandra gathered around him a group of intellectuals, who were the finest flowers of the Calcutta University. Hem Chandra Banerjee was the poet of this renaissance. Raj Krishna Banerjee was its historian. Akshay Chandra Sarkar, Taraprasad Chatterjee and Chandra Nath Basu were its essayists. While Bankim Chandra, combining in himself the novelist, the historian, the essayist, and the critic, was the centre and organising genius of this renaissance. The "Bangadarshan" School did for contemporary Bengalee thought and literature what the French Encyclopædiests did for 18th century European thought and French literature. Of course, the "Bangadarshan" had been preceded by the "Tattabodhini Patrika" on the one side, and the Rev. Dr. K. M. Banerjee's researches in and translations from ancient Hindu philosophy on the other. The "Tattabodhini" represented the Brahmo Samaj movement, revived under the leadership of Devendra Nath Tagore. Practically, all the leading Bengalee men of letters of the period were associated with the "Tattabodhini." Iswar Chandra Vidyasagar and Bhudeb Mukherjee were both on the editorial board of this paper. Its chief writers were Akshay Kumar Datta, who was the editor, Rajnarain Bose and Ram Chandra Vidyabagish. While Akshay Kumar's studies and writings were mainly inspired by the scientific spirit and investigations of middle-19th-century European culture, Rajnarain Bose, Ram Chandra Vidyabagish and the other regular contributors of the "Tattabodhini" were more interested in theological speculations and the revival of the ancient wisdom of the Upanishads and the higher Hinduism of the Vedanta.

The generation of Bengalee youths to which I belonged came, however, in more direct contact with the "Bangadarshan" than with the "Tattabodhini" School. The "Tattabodhini" was a bit too serious and learned for our youthful minds; while the "Bangadarshan", with its fictions and poetry and satire as well as historical and social essays, appealed more powerfully to us. I had, if I remember aright, read Bankim Chandra's "Durgesnandini" and "Mrinalini" even before I came to Calcutta. "Durgesnandini" quickened my earliest patriotic sentiments. Our sympathies were all entirely with Birendra Singha, the Hindu chief of Gad-Mandaran; and the court scene, wherein the Moslem invader was stabbed through his heart by Bimala, one of the wives of the chief of Gad-Mandaran, made a profound impression upon my youthful imagination. Among English novelists Sir Walter Scott was a favourite of our generation. We read his poems, "Marmion" and "Lady of the Lake," in our college curriculum. Outside, we devoured literally many of his Waverly Novels. His "Ivanhoe" was most popular with us. And in Bankim Chandra's "Durgesnandini" we found a strange similitude with Ivanhoe. Bankim Chandra at once rose in our estimation as Sir Walter Scott of Bengal.

Michael Madhusudan had preceded the "Bangadarshan" in the history of the new Bengalee literature. He had liberated Bengalee poetry from the old fetters of Sanskrit prosody, or more correctly speaking, of ancient Bengalee epics and lyrics. He was the first to introduce blank verse in our literature. The wealth of imagination and the almost immeasurable store of words in Madhusudan's "Meghanad-Badha" created a new pride in our hearts, the pride of race, and we commenced to compare him with Milton.

Hem Chandra, however, was our special favourite. The intense patriotic passion that breathed through his poems captured our youthful minds in a way which no other Bengalee poems had done. The new generation of English-educated Bengalees had already commenced to advance themselves to positions of trust and responsibility in the new Administration. In the learned professions of law and medicine also, they were gradually asserting themselves as against the British members. A new spirit of independence and self-assertion was increasingly manifesting itself in the conduct and conversations of the English-educated

Bengalee. All these had already commenced to provoke a racial conflict in the country. Hem Chandra was, in a special sense, the poet of this new conflict and of the new racial self-respect and sensitive patriotism, born of it.

Side by side with all these, the Brahmo Samaj, under Keshub Chunder Sen, had proclaimed a new gospel of personal freedom and social equality, which reacted very powerfully upon this infant national consciousness and the new political life and aspirations of young Bengal. Keshub's controversies with the Christian missionaries were widely read and greatly enjoyed not only by his own followers and co-religionists but by the entire body of our English-educated countrymen. In his victories over the Christian missionaries in these controversies, Keshub's countrymen, even outside his church and community, felt a genuine pride, which powerfully fed their national conceit. Keshub's English visit and the way he was lionised by the British public and the British press also reacted very powerfully upon the mind of his people in India. The old paralysing sense of superiority of their new political masters over them was visibly replaced by a new self-confidence in our educated countrymen in consequence of Keshub's successful missionary propaganda in England. All these had worked together to create a new mental and moral atmosphere in Calcutta, if indeed, not all over Bengal, when I arrived from my distant native District of Sylhet and entered the Presidency College.

I came to Calcutta, as already stated, at the beginning of 1875. The latter end of 1874

Ananda Mohan Bose had come back from England, having taken honours in mathematics at Cambridge and having been classed as one of the Wranglers of his year, standing, if I remember aright, ninth in the list. Ananda Mohan's success at Cambridge had also contributed materially to our new pride of race. The very first public act of Ananda Mohan was the establishment of the Calcutta Students' Association. Surendra Nath, after his compulsory retirement from the Indian Civil Service, had gone to England in the hope that the justice, which had been denied to him by the British Government in India, would be granted by the higher authorities in England. In this he was, however, sorely disappointed. Not only did the Secretary of State for India refuse to review the decision of the Government of India and reinstate Surendra Nath in his position in the Indian Civil Service but even the Benchers of the Inn at which he kept his terms and whose law examinations he had successfully passed, refused to call him to the Bar. Thus disappointed Surendra Nath came back home to Calcutta in the middle of 1875, not knowing really how to obtain a living, and yet, as he puts it in his autobiography, "do some useful work for the country."

Sir George Campbell was Lieutenant-Governor of Bengal during the early seventies. He was not friendly to the new English-educated middle class in the province. He thought that they were gradually becoming a menace to the British authority in the country. He initiated, therefore, a new education policy or, more correctly speaking, tried to emphasise a neglected principle enunciated in the Education Despatch of 1854, popularly known as Sir John Wood's Despatch, in which the Directors of the British East India Company had laid down the education policy of their Administration in India. This Despatch, which was at one time regarded by our people as their educational "Magna Charta", had urged upon the Government that instead of directly taking charge of higher education, they should encourage leaders of Indian society to increasingly take it in their own hands and invite private enterprise to establish and manage these new schools and colleges. In fact, the earliest initiative in introducing English education among the people of this Province had been taken, not by the Government of the East India Company, but by the leaders of the Indian community themselves. The first English College in Bengal, the Hindu College, was, thus, established not by the Government but by the Hindu leaders of Calcutta, including the most orthodox among them. Gradually, however, the Government commenced directly to take the higher education of the people into their own hands. They required a body of administrators from among the natives of the country, who would be able to assist the English officers in their work, both judicial and executive. In pursuance of this policy, a number of colleges came into existence in Bengal. Sir George Campbell realised the menace which the yearly increasing out-turn of English-educated young men from these colleges offered to the undisputed authority of the British rulers of the country. The time had come, he thought, when this higher education must be restricted. Sir George, therefore, proposed to abolish some of the Mafassil colleges and divert the funds spent on them to the promotion of primary education among the masses. This new educational policy naturally roused fierce opposition from the leaders of the English-educated community in Bengal. While, however, the politicians and publicists indulged in protests and abuses, Pandit Iswar Chandra Vidyasagar, realising the practical futility of these, resolved to establish and maintain out of his own resources, a college in Calcutta, under the name of the Metropolitan Institution. Its object was to find means of higher collegiate education to the youths of Bengal at such cost as was within their means. The Metropolitan Institution commenced, from the very beginning, to attract large numbers of students. Pandit Vidyasagar had been an intimate friend of Surendra Nath's father, Dr. Durga Charan Banerjee. Naturally enough, therefore, he took almost a parental interest in young Surendra Nath and had been largely instrumental in sending him to England to compete for the Indian Civil Service. When Surendra Nath returned from England in 1875, after his unsuccessful attempt to get reinstated in the Indian Civil Service, Pandit Vidyasagar, seeing him stranded in Calcutta, invited him to the chair of English in the Metropolitan Institution. It was here that Surendra Nath first came into close association with the students of Calcutta and at once became the most favourite leader of the youth of Bengal.

On his way from England Ananda Mohan had spent a few days in Bombay to study the educational and social reform institutions of the Western capital. In Bombay he found an association of youthful students, which was practically leading a new movement of female education among the middle classes of the Hindu community. From Bombay he brought the idea of organising a similar movement among the students of his own University. Within a few days of his return to Calcutta Ananda Mohan established the Calcutta Students' Association. Surendra Nath almost immediately after his appointment as Professor in the Metropolitan Institution, joined Ananda Mohan in the leadership of this Students' Association and became at once the very life and soul of it. Ananda Mohan continued to be the President of the Association, but Surendra Nath's eloquence and burning patriotism lent to it a new strength and inspiration. Surendra Nath's first appearance on the platform of the Students' Association at once established his claims to the leadership of our new youth movement.

Keshub Chunder and the Brahmo Samaj had, no doubt, preceded Surendra Nath in the leadership of young Bengal. Keshub Chunder's appeal was exclusively to the religious and moral sensibilities of the rising generation of his English-educated countrymen. But the education which they received in their schools and colleges had very seriously unsettled their faith not only in the traditional religion of their own people but, more or less, in all religion. The Brahmo leader was able, therefore, to touch a comparatively small section of the rising youths of his country. They might be the most serious-minded among them, but they were never a very large class; and though they exerted very considerable moral influence over their fellow countrymen, and set a very high standard of personal character and social service to their generation, a very large section of the educated intelligentsia of their time was left more or less cold by the Brahmo propaganda. In fact, Keshub Chunder had almost as many detractors among young Bengal of his day as he had admirers. The acceptance of the Brahmo ideals of life involved very serious sacrifices. It led to separation from home and family, excommunication from society and, in many cases, loss of patrimony. There was as yet hardly any Brahmo community, and those who joined the Samaj found themselves in more or less complete social isolation. All these inevitably deterred many people, who had the fullest intellectual sympathy with the new movement of religious and social reform, from openly throwing their lot into it. Their very inability to be true to their convictions, gradually led them to set up a kind of moral defence of their inner weakness, by openly repudiating the Brahmo ideals and holding up the conduct and conversations of those, who were loyal to these ideals at such sacrifice, to public ridicule. For all these reasons, Keshub Chunder's preachings affected a comparatively small section of the youthful intellectuals of his time.

Surendra Nath, however, brought a new message and inspiration of freedom. His appeal was predominantly political. He did, no doubt, specially in the earlier years of his political leadership, combine social with political idealism and sought to draw the inspiration of both from religion. But the emphasis of his teachings was, all the same, far more on political freedom than on personal and social freedom. Politics did not involve in those days any sufferings or sacrifices. The political authorities in the country did not take our infant political freedom movement seriously. They saw no menace to their authority in it. The whole thing was, more or less, as a pastime, though certainly the more serious minded of our youthful intellectuals did not consciously pursue it as such. Our new politics was on the plane of intellection only. The political ideal possessed our mind, its contemplation satisfied our emotions; but there was as yet no call for any strenuous practical political action such as might bring us into open conflict with the Government and lead to those personal consequences that follow every movement of revolt against constituted and organised political authority. For all these reasons, Surendra Nath's political propaganda gathered a much larger following than that of the religious and social revolt of Keshub Chunder Sen and the Brahmo Samaj.

In fact, by the time when Surendra Nath entered upon his life's mission, the Brahmo Samaj had already commenced to lose popular sympathies owing to the new doctrinal developments of it. The educated mind in Bengal was still under the influence of 19th century rationalistic thought of Europe. Scepticism and materialism were the loudest notes in the intellectual life of young Bengal. Hume and Spencer and Comte were, more or less, the leaders of thought of the new English-educated classes of the province. Keshub, and before him Devendra Nath, had to fight this spirit of European scepticism and rationalism, that denied sometimes the existence of God, and even when it did not do so, openly repudiated the duty of worship and the necessity of prayer. The intellectual movement outside the Brahmo Samaj in those days was completely without any religious inspiration or reference. Devendra Nath, and, after him Keshub, both tried to fight this new spirit of irreligion by filiating their movements to the new Intuitionalist School of middle 19th century European thought. The implications of this Intuition had not as yet been fully realised. These came out subsequently, mainly through the teachings of M'Cosh and Flint. The earlier Intuitionalism in our country, as also perhaps to a very large extent even in Europe, was intensely subjective. It set up individual reason and intuition as the ultimate and absolute standard of judgment in the determination of what was true and what was right. The opponents of the Brahmo Samaj tried to expose the logic of this subjective intuitionalism and present the religion of the Brahmos as "a conjugation of the verb to think". Dr. Dyson was one of the most powerful Christian protagonists against the propaganda of the Brahmo Samaj and its leader Keshub Chunder Sen. And in a criticism of the Brahmo doctrine he described the religion of the Brahmos as a conjugation of the verb to think. "I think, we think, you think, he thinks, they think," this, declared Professor Dyson, was Brahmoism. This parody of the religion of the Brahmo Samaj was enjoyed very much by the Hindu opponents of Keshub Chunder Sen, and particularly by that large and increasing body of our youthful intellectuals who, though they had no faith in the religion of their fathers, yet found it impossible, as much from intellectual objections as from considerations of personal interests and social expediency, to accept the teachings of the Brahmo Samaj. The Brahmo Samaj was the butt of ridicule of this large class of our people. When Keshub developed a new theology, built partly upon the Intuitionalist School of European philosophy and partly upon Carlyle's Hero Worship and Emerson's Representative Men, and indirectly commenced to claim for himself and the Brahmo missionaries associated with him, some sort of special, if not supernatural, authority, as the ordained messengers of a New Dispensation, the old unpopularity of the Brahmo Samaj was considerably increased. These doctrinal developments in the theology and church government of Keshub Chunder Sen naturally commenced to turn the bowels of the educated Bengalee youths, fed upon prevailing European rationalism and scepticism, against the Brahmo Samaj. This was the general intellectual and moral atmosphere and environments in the midst of which Surendra Nath opened his new political propaganda.

The spirit of freedom, quickened by contact with modern European thought and history, throbbing under the new impulses imparted by the idealism of the French Revolution, was abroad. It was first organised among us in the movement of religious and social revolt led by the Brahmo Samaj. Though the influence of the Brahmo Samaj had commenced to wane, for the various reasons already indicated, this spirit of freedom was still dominating the educated intelligentsia of Bengal. Surendra Nath found a new and larger scope for its fulfilment in the political propaganda which he initiated. Surendra Nath had studied, while in England, the history of the movements of national emancipation in modern Europe. These studies had revealed to him the very important place which the educated youths of these countries held in the freedom movement of their own land. He had been particularly impressed by the movement of "Young Italy" led by Joseph Mazzini. Surendra Nath started upon his public career by trying to follow in the steps of Mazzini and organised a youth movement in his own province. He had come back from his second visit to England as an outcaste among the older and respectable members of his own people. In those days men who were in the black books of the Government were shunned by the leaders of their own community. The existing political and other public organisations in Calcutta would not touch Surendra Nath even with a pair of tongs. But for Pandit Vidyasagar, who was all his life a man of sturdy independence, who never burnt incense as much to the political masters of his country as to the idols of the market place among his own people, Surendra Nath would have to live all his life as a political outcaste. By appointing Surendra Nath to be a Professor in the Metropolitan Institution, Pandit Vidyasagar not only found him a congenial occupation but also opened the way to his future by bringing him into living contact with the student propulation of Calcutta. Surendra Nath found in the Students' Association, established a few months previous to his return home from England, his first public platform.

This Students' Association had already

drawn to itself the most prominent graduates and under-graduates of those days. The first Secretary of it was Babu Nanda Krishna Bose, who had topped the list of successful candidates at the previous B. A. examination. Nanda Krishna Bsoe, after taking his final degree, entered the public service. When as a result of the agitation started by the Indian Association against the lowering of the age-limit from 21 to 19 of the Indian Civil Service Examination, the Secretary of State for India sought to make a compromise with this growing feeling against his new regulation and opened a way for qualified Indian youths to appointments in the higher executive and judicial services hitherto exclusively held by Covenanted Civilians, Nanda Krishna Bose was the very first to be appointed to this new Statutory Civil Service. He gradually rose to the position of a District and Sessions Judge, and though drawing a smaller salary, exercised all the rights and held all the powers of his office just as the British Covenanted Civilian. Mr. Surya Kumar Agasti was also one of the most brilliant students of the University in the middle seventies of the last century. Entering the University in 1874 he took the first place in all the examinations. If I remember aright, he succeeded Nanda Krishna Bose as Secretary of the Students' Association, and passing out of the University he too found a place in the Statutory Civil Service, and gradually rose to the position of a District Magistrate. Mr. Byomkesh Chakravarty, another of the most brilliant products of the University, was also at one time associated with the Students' Association as its Secretary. Mr. Chakravarty entered the

Educational Service, and held for some time the chair of Mathematics in the Ravenshaw College, Cuttack. When Government provided for higher scientific education in agriculture for qualified Indian young men, by founding a few State scholarships tenable at the College of Agriculture at Cirenchester in England, Mr. Byomkesh Chakravarty was in the first batch of these agricultural scholars. He availed himself, however, of this opportunity not only to study at Cirenchester but at the same time also to keep his terms at one of the Inns of Court in London; and, before returning home, he had himself called to the Bar. Mr. Girish Chandra Bose, Mr. Ambica Charan Sen and Mr. Dwijadas Datta were contemporaries of Mr. Chakravarty at Cirenchester. The Government, while founding these scholarships for advanced and scientific agricultural studies in England, did not make any definite provision for finding adequate opportunities for these trained agriculturists in their own service. It was, I think, some years later that the present Agricultural Department was organised under a Director of Agriculture. The first batch of these agricultural State-scholars returned home from Cirenchester without any covenant with the Government. The Government was under no obligation to provide adequate places for them in the Administration. They were also under no obligation to serve Government. It was, therefore, easy and natural for Mr. Chakravarty, who saw he had better prospects in the Bar than in the Education Department of the Government, where he had been previously serving, to join the Bar. He gradually rose to be one of the leading members of his profession. Mr. Girish Chandra Bose also did not return to his place in the Education Department, on coming home from Cirenchester, but found a more congenial occupation as proprietor and principal of the present Bangabasi College in Calcutta. Mr. Ambica Charan Sen, on his return from Cirenchester, was appointed to the Statutory Civil Service and rose to be a District and Sessions Judge. Mr. Dwijadas Datta was found a place in the Subordinate Executive Service and was for some little time a Deputy Magistrate, but the duties of this office did not fit in quite with his mental constitution and moral temperament, and he soon reverted to the educational service, and after serving in some of our Mafassil colleges, he was finally posted to the chair of agriculture when it was founded in the Government Engineering College at Shibpur. All these, with the exception of Mr. Ambica Charan Sen who took his degree from Dacca, were directly or indirectly brought up under the new influence created by the Calcutta Students' Association. Mr. Ambica Charan Sen had, however, received his baptism in the new Freedom Movement in the country in the Brahmo Samaj of which he had been a most enthusiastic and loyal adherent from his early youth. In fact, the inspiration of freedom was then in the air and as the Brahmo Samaj on the one side organised this inspiration in a movement of religious and social reform and reconstruction, so our Students' Association organised it in another way, among a wider class of the rising youths of the province.

Indeed, in Surendra Nath's early propaganda there was an unmistakable undercurrent of religious and social idealism also. His first lecture from the platform of the Students' Association was "On the Rise of the Sikh Power in the Punjab." It was held in the Hindu School Theatre. This Hindu School Theatre was in those days practically our only public hall. There was also the Medical College Theatre. The Medical College Theatre was, it seems to me, not open to everybody. It drew a more select and even aristocratic audience. Keshub Chunder Sen's earlier public addresses were all delivered there. The Students' Association was a more democratic body. The Medical College Theatre somehow or other seems to have been not as freely opened to its meetings as the Hindu School Theatre. Indeed, many of the more popular public lectures in those days used to be delivered here. Babu Rajnarain Bose's lecture in Bengalee on "*E Kal O Se Kal*" as well as Pandit Ramgati Nyayaratna's address on the History of Bengalee Literature was delivered in this Theatre. Surendra Nath's first public appearance was also on this platform under the auspices of the Students' Association. The materials for his lecture on the "Rise of the Sikh Power" were, no doubt, drawn from English sources, particularly from Malcolm's History of the Sikhs. But the Sikh movement was practically unknown to us. Our school text-books on Indian history did, no doubt, notice the story of the Sikhs in connection with Ranjit Singh. But these references had no inspiration for us. Surendra Nath for the first time presented the Sikh movment as really a movement of freedom, first, against the current ceremonialism and Brahminical domination of the Hindu community; second, against the oppression of the Moguls, who tried to crush a movement of religious and spiritual freedom by the organised brute force of an alien Government; and lastly, against British aggression. British historians of the Sikhs had glossed over the wonderful military skill and valour of the Sikh army, describing signal defeats of the British as draws, and what were really draws as defeats of the Sikhs. Surendra Nath in his address on the "Rise of the Sikh Power in the Punjab" exposed the unreliable character of British historians and painted in burning words the justice of the Sikh cause, the deathless devotion of the Sikh people to their *Khalsa* or Commonwealth and the signal defeats which they inflicted on the British at Chilianwala and Gujerat. Our school histories never confessed frankly these defeats. This revelation of the history of the Sikhs made a very powerful appeal to our infant patriotism and lent new strength and even bitterness to the anti-British feeling that had already commenced to possess our youthful minds. I was not present at this first lecture of Surendra Nath's, but those who were carried with them from this meeting a new patriotic fervour. A friend characterised this lecture of Surendra Nath's as creating, by deafening rounds of applause that followed in quick succession his rapidly flowing periods, almost a literal storm about College Square. Surendra Nath's position as the most powerful orator of his generation was at once established by this performance. His next appearance on the public platform was at Bhowanipore in the hall of the London Missionary Society's Institution. The subject of this lecture was "Chaitanya."

As in his first lecture Surendra Nath brought to us the inspiration of the freedom movement among the Sikhs, so in this lecture he brought to us the message of the great socio-religious reform movement of Shree Chaitanya, which more or less revolutionised Bengalee thought and society of the 16th century. The Vaishnavic movement in Bengal was then under a cloud. Brahminism had literally devoured the Vaishnavic cult and culture. People had little knowledge and less appreciation of the lofty social idealism and humanism of the message of the Mahaprabhu. The literature of Bengal Vaishnavism was more or less inaccessible to the newly educated intelligentsia of our people. To them Vaishnavism presented only a highly emotional cult with an excessive sensual and erotic emphasis in its devotional culture. Even Bankim Chandra held it responsible for the loss of manhood of the Bengalee people. It had reduced piety to erotic excitement and materially contributed to the physical and moral deterioration of the race. The Brahmo Samaj under the leadership of Keshub Chunder Sen and particularly through the inspiration of Bijoy Krishna Goswami had been slowly recovering the higher Vaishnavic ideals of *bhakti* from the debris that had been thrown over it by generations of unlettered and unspiritual Vaishnavas. The life and teachings of Shree Chaitanya were being presented by Brahmo writers in a new light. But even this revived interest in the movement of Shree Chaitanya created by the Brahmo Samaj was more or less narrow, theological and religious only. Even the Brahmo Samaj had not clearly brought out the message of social uplift and emancipation of Shree Chaitanya and Bengal Vaishnavism. Surendra Nath was practically the first to do so in this lecture at Bhowanipore. He presented Shree Chaitanya as the prophet of a new social freedom, and emphasised his revolt against the domination of the Brahmins and the caste system. This social message of Bengal Vaishnavism has been subsequently revived with greater force by the late Babu Sishir Kumar Ghose and the neo-Vaishnavic movement led by him and the late Babu Kedar Nath Dutt Bhaktivinode. Early in the seventies of the last century educated Bengalees were practically ignorant of this social and humanitarian message of Shree Chaitanya's Vaishnavic movement in Bengal. And it was Surendra Nath who brought a knowledge of it to the generation to which I belong.

But the greatest and the most inspiring message of Surendra Nath's early propaganda was delivered through his lectures on Joseph Mazzini and the Young Italy movement organised by him. Mazzini's life and particularly his extremely sensitive patriotism which so worked upon his youthful imagination that even as a school boy he refused to join in any form of gaity of his family and his community, in the face of the bondage in which his country lay under Austrian domination, drew out all the latent passion for national freedom in us. The tyrannies of the Austrian army of occupation in Italy, who showed scant regard for the ordinary rights and liberties of the Italian people and treated even the Italian intellectuals of the middle class as members of an inferior race, indeed literally as helots and slaves, made a profound impression upon our sensitive minds. Neither the person nor the property of the Italian in the neighbourhood of the Austrian military camps, nor even the honour of their women, were safe from the wanton insults and outrages of Austrian officers and soldiers. We saw or imagined a great similitude between the position of the Italians under Austrian domination and our own position under British rule. In the outlying districts in cases between Europeans and Indians the latter could hope to receive practically no justice. The differential treatment accorded to Indians and Europeans even when they happened to be members of the same Covenanted Civil Service wrankled in our heart. The .plight of the indentured labourers in the tea gardens of Assam had already commenced to be agitated in our vernacular press. The "Amrita Bazar Patrika" was circulating broadcast tales of magisterial highhandedness all over the province. All these things working upon our youthful imagination created a profound sympathy in us with the struggle for national freedom in Italy led by Mazzini, when the story was presented to us by Surendra Nath. We commenced to read the writings of Mazzini and the history of the Young Italy movement. Here we saw also the earlier organisations for Italian freedom, particularly those of the Carbonari, with which Mazzini had himself been associated at the beginning of his patriotic career. The Carbonari were secret societies. They hoped to win their national freedom by covering the whole country with a net-work of secret revolutionary organisations, whose idea was to free their fatherland from the Austrian yoke by striking at the

Austrian rulers. Secret assassinations were the main objective of these Carbonari organisations. Mazzini's intense moral consciousness gradually rebelled against these cowardly methods, and he soon broke away from his earlier Carbonari associates. Secret organisations, Mazzini discovered, paid a premium to moral cowardice; and in his diagnosis of the national disease he found that lack of moral courage and the strength of character to boldly stand up for one's ideals regardless of whatever cost or consequences it might involve, were the real roots of Italy's servitude and national degradation. The policy and methods of the Carbonari could not possibly find an effective remedy to this moral disease. Mazzini, therefore, left the Carbonari and boldly faced the persecutions of the Austrian Government. But though without any real revolutionary motive or any plan of secret assassinations as the way to national emancipation, the new inspiration imparted to Young Bengal by Surendra Nath's presentation of the life of Mazzini and the Italian freedom movement led many of us to form secret organisations. Calcutta student community was at that time almost honeycombed with these organisations. Secrecy has a strange fascination for youthful minds. And this was the real psychology of our *penchant* for these secret societies. Surendra Nath was himself, I think, the President of quite a number of these secret societies, and I clearly remember how he used oftentimes to cite the great popularity of a Russian politician (whose name I cannot call to mind) by the fact that he was the President of as many as more than half a hundred secret societies in Russia. These societies were not affiliated to one another. The members of one society did not know the members of the other society. Each society tried to religiously protect its own secrets from all outsiders, and yet this Russian patriot and politician was the head of so large a number of independent secret societies. Surendra Nath's connection with quite a number of the new secret societies among the youthful intellectuals of Calcutta proved similarly the unique confidence which he enjoyed of his young followers. Though without any serious plan or policy of political action aiming at the liberation of their people from the British yoke, these societies were, however, not lacking in seriousness. Their patriotism was serious, and how seriously they took it was seen in the vows and rituals of many of these societies. I knew of one such society, though I was not myself a member of it, whose initiatory rites were almost Masonic in some aspects. Every member of this society had to sign the pledge of membership with his own blood drawn at the point of a sword from his breast. They were dreamers of wild dreams, but harmless dreamers so far, whose thought and imagination alone were of a revolutionary character, but who never seriously meant to rise in physical revolt against the British authority in the country, or who hoped to secure the emancipation of their people by a campaign of political assassinations.

CHAPTER XII.

THE NEW STAGE & NATIONAL SONGS.

The Calcutta Students' Association, started by Ananda Mohan Bose and Surendra Nath Banerjee, was not, however, the only instrument that helped to call into being our new nationalism. The entire decade, 1870 to 1880, worked in various directions in our national life to produce this result. Not the least among the forces that worked towards it, was the Bengalee stage. With the revival of learning, following upon the introduction of English education, every department of our life found a rejuvenescence. A new literature was born, and along with it a new drama and a new stage came into being. We had, of course, Sanskrit dramas that challenged comparison with the best Greek drama. But Sanskrit had ceased to be the spoken language of the people, if indeed it had ever been so. Even the Sanskrit dramas presented not Sanskrit but a dialect of it, called Prakrit, as the language of the masses. It was the learned only and the aristocracy of the land who spoke in Sanskrit. Even their womenfolk did not speak in Sanskrit. They too conversed in Prakrit. The provincial dialects had, therefore, offered little or no room for keeping up the ancient traditions of the Sanskrit drama.

Before the birth of our new stage, the only form of dramatic literature that we had in Bengal was the *yatra*. The *yatras* were a combination of songs and conversations. They had no stage, no scenes, no make-ups, no properties such as constitute essential elements of the stage. These *yatras* in Bengal were mostly based upon the *Vaishnava* lyrics, depicting the love-sport of Shree Krishna and Shree Radha, which were sung as *keertans*. These *keertans* were the special creation of the movement of Shree Chaitanya. The music of these *keertans* was very different from the orthodox Hindu music, though it was a new adaptation of it. The chief object of our Vaishnava *keertans* was to free the new religious hymnology of the Chaitanya cult from the trammels of classical music, which was not accessible to the mass-mind and rarely imitable by the untrained vocal organ or discernible by the untrained ear of the man in the street. Though the leader was trained in all the intricacies of classical Hindu music, those who formed what may be called his chorus could generally follow him without any such special training. The Vaishnava *keertans* are an exquisite combination of drama and opera. They need no sceneries or properties, because the hymns themselves contain perfect pictures of the natural settings and the ideal make-up of the actors in this sacred drama. Our *yatras* were really built upon these Vaishnavic lyrics. But these lyrics had been practically lost except among professional singers. The general population had no or very little knowledge of the lyrics of Vidyapati, Chandidas and the the later Vaishnava poets who received their inspiration from the realisations of Shree Chaitanya Mahaprabhu and his associates. Early in the seventies of the last century the educated Bengalee first came into touch with these Vaishnava lyrics through a new edition of the ancient lyrics of Bengal or "Pracheen

Kabya-Sangraha" edited by Akshay Chandra Sarkar and Sarada Charan Mitra. The most popular *yatras* of that period were, at least in Eastern Bengal, those of Krishna Kamal Goswami of Dacca. I have already mentioned these in a previous chapter. But we did not know then that Krishna Kamal Goswami's operas were practically adaptations of the ancient Vaishnavic *keertans*.

Our new dramas were, however, of a very different class. The Bengalee stage was organised in the early seventies of the last century with the opening of two theatres in northern Calcutta,—the Bengal Theatre and the National Theatre. In the earlier stages female parts were represented by males as in our *yatras*. Gradually, however, actresses were introduced. There was, of course, considerable opposition to this new development at first on moral grounds. This opposition came almost exclusively from the Brahmo Samaj, which represented a powerful puritan movement in those days. But its numerous defects notwithstanding, the Bengalee stage helped very materially to prepare the ground for Surendra Nath's political propaganda. In the early years of the seventies of the last century before Surendra Nath and Ananda Mohan had organised their new platform, it was the Bengalee stage which had found expression to the new spirit of patriotism among our rising generation of educated intellectuals. It was this stage that first proclaimed the gospel of the religion of the motherland in an opera, now completely forgotten, called "Bharata-Mata" or "Mother India". I forget the details of the play, but the name indicates the nature of the theme and the religious idealisation which must have inspired it. Those were the days when a new passion for freedom, personal, social and political, had possessed the educated Bengalee mind. Our youthful intellectuals were not only anxious to acquire political freedom, but also equally, if not more, anxious to break through every shackle that interfered with their freedom of thought and action. Social reform was even more popular than political reform. The desire for freedom is universally born of the sense of bondage. And in those early days consciousness of sacerdotal and social bondage was far keener than the consciousness of political bondage. The conflict between us and our foreign political masters had not as yet come out into the open. And therefore our earlier dramas were all social dramas written in support of widow re-marriage and in condemnation of polygamy by the higher classes of Bengalee Hindus, particularly the Brahmins.

But political dramas were not long in coming. Already Hem Chandrá Banerjee had voiced in his national lyrics the sense of impotence of his people to assert their legitimate rights and self-respect against their British masters. Gradually this political spirit became directly vocal, though it had long been expressed indirectly through the new Bengalee poetry and fiction. "Neela-Darpana" was the first political drama in Bengal. It presented the story of the indigo riots in Nadia and the unspeakable tyrannies on the peasants by the English indigo factors. It opened with a rustic song which lamented the untimely death of Harish Chandra Mukherjee, the Editor of the "Hindoo Patriot", who had courageously espoused the cause of the oppressed tenants, and the imprisonment of the Rev. Mr. Long for publishing the story of these tyrannies in the press. And the refrain was, "It is difficult for the peasant to live." When it was put upon the board of the new Bengalee theatres, the audience got wild with passion against the White planters; and sometimes they so far forgot themselves that they threw their shoes at the poor actor on the stage. The next political dramas were the two productions of the late Babu Upendra Nath Das, the eldest son of Babu Sri Nath Das, who was at that time one of the leaders at the Calcutta High Court Bar,—"Sarat-Sarojini" and "Surendra-Binodinee." In 1876 the then Prince of Wales, Albert Edward, came on a visit to India. In Calcutta Babu Jagadananda Mukherjee of the High Court Bar, who was at that time the Government Pleader, organised a "*purdah* party" to welcome the royal visitor. It convulsed Hindu society to its very foundations. The *purdah* was still an almost religious institution. Hindu women of the upper classes never appeared before strangers, not even when they were male friends of their own families, unless they were closely related to them either by blood or by marriage. To bring these ladies to meet the Prince of Wales was incredible. Nobody believed that the ladies who met the Prince of Wales could have been drawn from the Hindu aristocracy of Calcutta. Hindu society rose up in arms against what they believed to be a wanton outrage on the sanctity of their womanhood. The incident found material for a farce, which was put on the stage of the Bengal Theatre.

The Government of the day, already irritated by what it believed to be the excesses of the Bengalee press, could not tolerate this open libel against the royal visitor, and an Ordinance was immediately issued against the authorities of the stage prohibiting a repetition of its performance, and generally establishing police censorship over our new stage.

From the birth of our new literature, inspired by the ideal which we had imbibed from our new education and contact with European thought and culture, particularly that which was the creation itself of the French Revolution, Bengalee poetry and drama had been finding expression to our new love of freedom, though these expressions were somewhat veiled by fanciful allusions to the conflicts of the Hindu with their erstwhile Moslem political masters. Some referred to Rajput history depicting their conflict with the Moslem invaders. The poems of Rangalal Mukherjee, his story of Padmini, were admittedly based upon the history of the sack of Chitore by Alauddin. There were others, however, which were pure fancy pictures presenting the spoliation of the country by alien rulers.

Towards the beginning of the last quarter of the last century or more accurately in the sixth and seventh decades of it, a number of "National Songs" had given expression to our new love of country. The most popular of them all was

कत काल परे बल भारत रे,
दुःख सागर सांतारि पार हवे?
अवसाद हिमे डुबिये डुबिये

शोकि शेष निविष्ट रसातल रे?
पर जाति दिये धन रत्न सुखे,
वह लौह-विनिर्म्मित हार बुके।
पर दीपमाला नगरे नगरे
तुमि ये तिमिरे, तुमि से तिमिरे।

Freely rendered into English it said:

"How long will it take, thee, Oh Bharata, to swim across this ocean of misery?
Or, sinking and sinking in depression, wilt thou enter the nether regions for ever?
Having gladly offered thy jewels to the stranger, thou carriest now only an iron chain on thy breast.
There are rows of light in thy cities (owned by the stranger)
But thou art in darkness all the same."

Babu Govinda Chandra Roy, who was a Bengalee resident of Agra, was the author. Another song of his was addressed to the river Yamuna:

निर्म्मल सलिले वहिछ सदा
तटशालिनी सुन्दर यमुने ओ।
युग युग वाहि प्रवाह तोमारि
देखिल कत शत घटना ओ।

"Thou, Oh Yamuna, art ever flowing in pure currents between thy banks,
Thou ever beautiful stream!
From age to age thy currents have seen hundreds and hundreds of events."

And starting with this refrain the poet recounts in exquisite pathetic touches the ancient glories of India and the rise and fall of ancient kingdoms and empires.

In another national song the author bursts forth in tears crying

मलिन मुखचन्द्रमा भारत तोमारि
रात्रि दिवा पड़िछे लोचन वारि ।

"O India, gloomy is thy face, beautiful
that was as the moon;
Day and night tears flow from thy eyes."

This was from the opera "Bharat-Mata."

Another national song was an almost open condemnation of foreign economic exploitation. The burthen of it was that India was becoming poorer and poorer every day owing to the loss of her national freedom. It was from a novel by Babu Manomohan Bose, "Bangadheep-Parajaya", depicting the conquest of Bengal by a foreign people who came from a high island on the sea called Tungadweep. "The weaver and the blacksmith are crying day and night. They cannot find their food by plying their trade. Even threads and needles come from distant shores. Even match-sticks are not produced in the country. Whether in dressing themselves or producing their domestic utensils or even in lighting their oil-lamps,—in nothing are the people independent of their foreign masters. . . . . . Swarms of locusts from a distant island coming to these shores have eaten up all its solid grains leaving only the chaff for the starving children of the soil." The reference to the economic exploitation of the country by our present British masters was practically open in this national song.

Hem Chandra Banerjee's "Bharat-Sangeet" or the "Song of India" opened with the words :

बाजरे शिङ्गा बाज एइ रवे

सबाइ स्वाधीन ए विपुल भवे

सबाइ जाग्रत ज्ञानेर गौरवे

भारत शुधुइ घुमाये रय ।

"Sing, O my clarionet! Sing to these words:
Every one is free in this wide wide world,
Everyone is awake in the glory of science,
India alone lieth asleep!"

And the poet continuing in this strain says:

चीन ब्रह्मदेश असभ्य जापान

ताराओ स्वाधीन ताराओ प्रधान

भारत शुधुइ घुमाये रय ।

"China and Burma and barbarous Japan,
Even they are independent, they are superior,
India alone knoweth no waking!"

Another national song sounded a heart-rending note:

यतदिन तोर कलङ्कित परमाणुराशि

सिन्धुजले ना याइबे भासि

ततदिन तुइ कांदरे, ततदिन तुइ कांदरे!

"O India, weep, weep thou,
As long as thy polluted atoms have not been washed away into the waters of the ocean,
So long weep thou, so long weep!"

These were some of our earlier national songs. They were the first outpourings of the new inspiration of freedom that had come to our people with their contact with modern European thought and culture through their English education. When

Surendra Nath and Ananda Mohan returned from England in 1875-76, their political propaganda found the ground ready, owing to the new renaissance in Bengalee literature, the Bengalee stage and the birth of the new hymnology of our patriotism. These new national songs were very popular at that time among the youthful intellectuals of our people. And they contributed as much as the "Bangadarshan" and the new Bengalee stage to the birth and early development of our new nationalism.

CHAPTER XIII.

NABAGOPAL MITRA AND THE HINDU MELA.

The story of the early years of the new nationalism in Bengal would be incomplete without a full and grateful notice of the contribution of the late Babu Nabagopal Mitra and the Hindu Mela started by him early in the seventies of the last century to it. Babu Nabagopal was a prominent member of the Adi Brahmo Samaj. It was here evidently that he came into somewhat close contact with the family of Maharshi Devendra Nath Tagore, and Babu Rajnarain Bose. We find Babu Nabagopal taking a prominent part on the side of Maharshi Devendra Nath and the conservative section of his Brahmo Samaj congregation in their controversy with young Keshub Chunder and his associates representing the progressive elements in the Samaj. Babu Rajnarain Bose was also a prominent and powerful protagonist on the side of Devendra Nath. Rajnarain was personally a progressive Brahmo. He did not believe in current Hindu orthodoxy, particularly in regard to its irksome restraint on personal freedom in the matter of eating and drinking. But he was a born lover of his own country, and his love of country was organised in the very make and constitution of his mind and morals through his deep and deathless devotion to the ideals of Indian and more particularly Hindu culture.

When Keshub and his progressive Brahmos developed unmistakable tendencies towards the modern European or Christian ethics and rationalism, Rajnarain, who had drunk deep of the new knowledge or illumination brought to us by our British masters, stood up boldly to proclaim the superiority of Hindu religion and culture over European and Christian theology and civilisation. His lecture in Bengalee on *Hindu Dharmer Shresthata* or the "Superiority of Hinduism" was really the first challenge of the ancient spirit of India to the aggressive thought and civilisation of Europe.

English education had been more or less destroying the faith of the educated intelligentsia in the religion of their fathers. It was the challenge of 19th century European rationalism to the inherited beliefs of our people. This rationalism, while repudiating Christian orthodoxy, was yet the child of European and Christian thought and culture. It captured the mind and imagination of our newly-educated intelligentsia essentially for European and Christian ideals, even though these were divested completely of the unreason and superstition of popular Christianity. The Hindus had forgotten their own history and culture. They had lost recollection of how in their own cultural history there had been similar movements of reason and similar protests in the name of personal freedom. The first protest of reason in Hinduism or the Vedic religion was raised in the early Upanishads which proclaimed the Unity of the Godhead as against the multiplicity of the old Vedic gods and goddesses. These Upanishads protested against the sacrifices and rituals of the early Vedas; they worked up a rational synthesis between nature-worship and ancestor-worship, the two lines of early Vedic evolution, in first the conception of Brahman, recognised as the unity of all the nature deities, and second, of Prajapati representing the head and source of ancestor worship. Brahman and Prajapati represented the ultimate synthesis of the two parallel lines of Vedic religion called the *devayana* and the *pitriyana* or the way of the gods and the way of the fathers or manes. This duality was also subsequently cancelled by the realisation of the Ultimate Reality or the First Cause as Brahman from whom all objects coming into being continue to be, towards whom all objects move through processes of cosmic evolution, and into whom all objects enter at the final dissolution. This was the final revelation or realisation of the thought and theology of the Upanishads. Here we find a rational basis of the most advanced and complete form of monism or monotheism as yet realised by man. Here in the teachings of the Upanishads we find a real formula of the worship of the Lord who is Spirit in spirit and in truth, as has been inculcated by Jesus Christ himself in the New Testament.

And Rajnarain Rose took up this philosophical monism of the Upanishads which represented not merely the highest generalisation of Hindu speculation but also the deepest and the most direct realisation of the Infinite by the Hindu religious and spiritual culture. Not only have we the most perfect system of theism or monotheism in our ancient theology and religion, but side by side with these religious and spiritual ideals Hinduism presented also a much higher social idealism, all its outer distinctions of caste notwithstanding, than has as yet been reached by Christendom. This was briefly and in the main the substance of Rajnarain Bose's essay on the "Superiority of Hinduism." It was really the first public protest of the age-long Nation-Spirit of India against the threatened domination of our thought and life by the aggressive and colour-proud civilisation of Europe. It was enough that the British had secured the control of our Government and Administration. They could not be allowed to be the masters of our mind and manners, of our social, religious and spiritual life. The spirit of this new nationalism came out particularly into the open early in the seventies of the last century when Keshub Chunder Sen prayed for a new marriage law from the foreign political authority in the country, to legalise inter-caste marriages and other marriages performed without the presence of the *Salgram* as witness, and over which no Brahmin presided. This was opposed not only by representatives of orthodox Hindu opinion on the ground that it would encourage and bring about the gradual disruption of the old Hindu society but also by the members of the Adi Brahmo Samaj who had already been celebrating marriages without observing any idolatrous ceremony or introducing the sacred symbol of *Salgram* as a witness to the marriage-bond, on the ground that by seeking this new law the Brahmos were by implication proclaiming the illegality of the previous Brahmo marriages. In the controversy over Keshub's Brahmo Marriage Bill Babu Nabagopal Mitra took a prominent part in opposing it.

Babu Nabagopal's as well as Rajnarain Bose's nationalism was inspired, however, by a much wider outlook than that of mere theology or religion or social conservatism. Rajnarain Bose could indeed hardly be called a conservative, or if he was a conservative at all, his conservatism was not due to any unreasonable attachment to current customs and institutions of Hindu society, but predominantly, if indeed not exclusively, it was due to his intense opposition to the imitation of European ideals and institutions by his countrymen. His conservatism was, in fact, inspired far more by political than by social motives. As under the Moslem domination Hindu society developed a most dogmatic conservatism with a view to prevent being overwhelmed by the aggressive civilisation of Islam, so Rajnarain Bose and others were opposed to the more radical social reformers of their time because they were afraid that unless this imitative social reform movement was checked very definitely, it would strengthen the hold of the alien political authority established in the country by adding to it the moral and spiritual hold which the introduction of European customs and institutions in our society would inevitably bring about. Rajnarain Bose, though one of the most prominent products of the new English education in the country, was among the very first to initiate a movement for the preservation and purification of our national vernacular and in his loyalty to it he organised a small association of his educated contemporaries who pledged themselves never to use the medium of the English language in their personal conversation and correspondence with their own people. He was the first to use the medium of Bengalee in his public addresses to his own people, at a time when English lectures were almost universally in vogue. Rajnarain was also among the very first to encourage the use of indigenous clothes and other articles to the exclusion of foreign products. He was moved by a complete ideal of national freedom, which would be realised in every department of the nation's life, religious and social no less than economic industrial and political. Nabagopal must have imbibed his own nationalism to a very large extent from Rajnarain Bose, and the Hindu Mela which he organised early in the seventies of the last century was really the joint child of these two early representatives of modern Indian nationalism.

Babu Nabagopal was known among his contemporaries as "National" Mitra. He was the editor and proprietor also, I believe, of an English weekly, called the "National Paper". It was written in almost school-boy English. Nabagopal Babu was proud even of his ungrammatical and unidiomatic English. 'English,' he would say, 'is not my mother tongue, and though I may use the vehicle of this foreign language under practical compulsion, I feel no call to waste my time and energy in trying to master the senseless idioms of it.' His hobby, however, was the development of the physique of the rising generation of his countrymen. Sir George Campbell, Lieut.-Governor of Bengal, in the sixties of the last century had introduced physical culture as part of school training in Bengal. Gymnastic classes were opened in the Government schools all over the province in pursuance of the new education policy of the Government. Babu Nabagopal Mitra threw himself enthusiastically into this physical training of our boys. He had a physical training or gymnastic school run by himself at 1, Sankar Ghosh's Lane, which a fairly large number of University young men, particularly those coming from the Mafassil districts regularly attended. Here we had not only the full paraphernalia of gymnastic exercises of the British schools, horizontal, parallel bars etc., but Nabagopal Babu added to these our national exercises of wrestling, *lathi*, dagger and sword play. These premises were not suited to rifle practice, but that was also in Nabagopal Babu's programme. That was before the passing of Lord Lytton's Arms Act. The younger members of Maharshi Devendra Nath's family, particularly Babu Jyotirindra Nath Tagore, were very much interested in the movement of Nabagopal Babu, and it received, I think, substantial financial support from them. Nabagopal Babu's family residence was in Cornwallis Street at the junction of that Street with Sankar Ghosh's Lane. When I first made his acquaintance he was living as an independent gentleman, devoting not only his time and energy but also practically the whole of his financial resources to the promotion of the cause of physical education of his people, and the revival of national arts and industries. He seems to have come very soon to the end of his personal resources and was compelled to take service in the Calcutta Corporation as License Officer. But he continued to run his hobby and finally organised the first Bengalee circus in which he lost his all, and passed away in the eighties of the last century almost a penniless man.

In 1876 I joined his gymnastic class at 1, Sankar Ghosh's Lane. Early in the spring of this year, the Hindu Mela was held in the garden house of Raja Badan Chand at Tala. I cannot say if that garden house stands still. It was here at this Mela that I first came into conflict with Anglo-Indian arrogance and police aggression. There was a row over a small incident with which I was directly concerned. I was sitting on a chair, waiting for some gymnastic performances which were advertised to be demonstrated at the Mela. A European or Eurasian came from behind, and tried to shove me off my chair, as he wanted it, I subsequently heard, for a lady companion of his. If he had politely asked me to accommodate his lady friend, I would without the least hesitation have given my chair to her. Instead of this he came and rudely asked me to get up and let him have the chair. I naturally refused and then he tried to force me out of it. That was the origin of the row. The youthful students among the assembled crowd soon came up and fell into the fray. The police immediately followed and took sides with the European or Eurasian who had started the quarrel. A general melee between the students and the police followed. Police reinforcements were immediately called up from the Cossipore Thana. The students, however, took their stand upon a heap of brickbats lying in the garden and from there for a considerable time kept the police at bay. Surendra Nath's younger brother, Jitendra Nath, now Captain Banerjee, played a very prominent part in this drama. He was a famous athlete of our time, and rendered an excellent account of himself in this fight. Struck, however, by one of the police brick-bats, he saw blood running from his head. Finding that with this blood on his clothes it would be impossible for him to escape arrest, he jumped over the wall of the garden and laying a policeman who went to catch him flat on the ground by a kick, he walked home quietly via Dum Dum. And when some friends of mine went to Mr. Surendra Nath Banerjea at about dusk or after an interval of about a couple of hours, to inform him of my arrest and that of some other friends, they found young Jitendra Nath, who was, I think, reading in the second year class at that time, pouring over, of all books, Taylor's Ancient History, and asking them what was all this row about.

The whole thing ended in a police case. I was one of the accused. The charge was rioting and obstructing a public servant in the discharge of his duties. Both these charges were as false as false could be. None of us created the riot, and we did not obstruct any public servant in the discharge of his duties. Considering, however, the seriousness of the charge, my father was informed by wire about it, and asked to send sufficient funds to arrange for my defence. My father was very much put out by this information. He could not imagine that unless I had gone absolutely to evil ways there could be any clash between myself and the police, and so he refused to help me. But my father's friends in Sylhet sent the required amount, Rs. 800, counsel's fee for my defence, to the late Babu Jai Govinda Shome, the well-known leader of the Indian Christian community in Calcutta, who came from my own native district of Sylhet and had for a time, after taking his law degree, practised in the District Judge's Court at Sylhet. The case was tried by the Police Magistrate of Sealdah, Raja Harendra Krishna Bahadur, who convicted me and sentenced me to pay a fine of Rs. 20. Mr. Piffard, my Counsel, after the court had delivered its verdict and sentence, came up to me and said, "Well, young man, you need not be ashamed of this conviction. No other court would convict you. You acted as a gentleman." At the end of the trial, Mr. Shome sent the whole record of the case to my father, who had it translated, and after going through it he is reported to have said that I acted as a gentleman, which was expected of a son of his, and he would spend ten times the amount that had been sent for my defence to defend such gentlemanly conduct, should the call come to him again in the future. Though there was loss of some money, it involved no dishonour, and in his values of things honour stood immeasurably higher than money.

This was before I came in contact with Pandit Shivanath. And the inspiration of Surendra Nath's new patriotic and political propaganda on the one side, and Nabagopal's national propaganda on the other, both contributed very materially to the motives and the ideals that drew me to Shivanath and moved me to throw myself unreservedly into the larger idealism of the Brahmo Samaj.

CHAPTER XIV.

POLITICAL AND ADMINISTRATIVE CHANGES DURING MY COLLEGE DAYS.

During my college life in Calcutta (1875—'79) the country was passing through great political changes that had a lasting effect upon our social and political evolution. During the closing years of my school days Lord Mayo was the Indian Viceroy. His brief Viceroyalty was noted for the deportation of the Wahabi leader, Amir Khan. The British Government in those days, specially in Northern India, stood more or less in fear of a possible Mahomedan awakening. The Hindus had taken more kindly to the new education introduced by their British masters. This education, as those who helped to introduce it expected, won the intellectual and moral allegiance of the new educated classes of their subjects to the British Power in the country. But the Mahomedans stood out of this education. The upper classes of the Mahomedans still nursed the natural sense of wrong against those who had wrested the hegemony of India from their hands. The Wahabis were a sect of Mahomedans, who had started a powerful propaganda, religious on the face of it, but not without political possibilities. It had its centre in Patna. The Government, however, did not accept the Wahabi Movement on its face value as a purely religious movement, but scented deep political motives behind it. Those were the days when the Mahomedans were suspect in the eye of our British masters. The leader of the Wahabis, Amir Khan, was arrested, and detained under Regulation III of 1818. An application was made for a writ of *habeas corpus* to the Calcutta High Court which was heard by Chief Justice Norman. That application was rejected: Mr. Annesty of the Bombay High Court Bar was engaged on behalf of Amir Khan. Mr. Annesty's speech in which he hauled Lord Mayo over the coals for what was described as his tyranny over the helpless subjects of Her Majesty in India was published in pamphlet forms along with the proceedings of this case. These pamphlets were for many years something like the scripture of our new patriotism. Chief Justice Norman was stabbed and killed on the steps of the Calcutta High Court by a Mahomedan believed to have been a member of the Wahabi sect. Caught red-handed he was justly sentenced to death. So great, however, was the indignation caused by this assassination among the ruling race, including members of the Government, that the man was refused a Moslem burial and was burnt like the Hindus. The assassination of Justice Norman was followed by that of Lord Mayo in the Andamans by a prisoner, named Sher Ali. These two assassinations were believed to be the reprisals of the adherents of the Wahabi leader for his life-imprisonment. The Wahabi trial, however, helped to strengthen our infant patriotic sentiment by a new sense of wrong against our British masters.

Lord Mayo was succeeded by Lord Northbrook. Lord Northbrook's administration made itself responsible for the trial and deposition of the Gaikwad of Baroda on a charge of complicity with the attempted murder of the British Resident, Col. Fayre. This was the first time when the Chief of an Indian State was tried by a court appointed by the British Power and was deprived of his royal status and privileges in violation of what were believed to be his treaty rights. It created considerable nervousness among the Princes and Chiefs of the Indian States. But they were without much education, and the country had not as yet an organised and powerful public press to give effective expression to the widespread discontent caused by the trial of the Gaikwad. It was the Bengalee press only, led by the "Hindoo Patriot", which was at that time in charge of Babu Kristodas Pal, that found courage to voice this simmering discontent. Of our vernacular newspapers, the "Amrita Bazar Patrika" was the most outspoken in its criticisms of public policy, while the "Somprokas" was the prototype of the "Hindoo Patriot"; and though it did not lack courage, its tone was more sober than that of the "Patrika"; and both these frankly condemned the action of the Government in this matter.

Lord Mayo's brief Viceroyalty, marked by the Wahabi trial, and Lord Northbrook's by the trial and deposition of the Gaikwad, gave birth to a new political consciousness among the rising intelligentsia of the country. In Bengal this consciousness was perhaps the strongest. This consciousness, particularly the anti-British feeling of it, possessed the rising generation of Bengalee students, which was fed by our new Bengalee literature and the new Bengalee press, particularly the "Amrita Bazar Patrika" and the new Bengalee stage. Lord Lytton's Viceroyalty brought fresh fuel to this new patriotic passion among us by bringing home to the Indian subjects of Her Majesty the impossibility of realising their dreams of a new and free India under British rule, and with the help of their new political masters.

Educated India had thought that with Dalhousie's administration, which was very largely responsible for the Sepoy Mutiny, the era of annexations in India had definitely closed, and when the Government was taken over from the East India Company by the Crown, India had entered upon a new course of peace and progress that would lead finally to a free constitution like that of the British themselves in their own country. That hope received a rude shock under the Viceroyalty of Lord Lytton. Lord Lytton came as the nominee of the Conservative Government in England under Lord Beaconsfield. India's foreign policy was at that time dominated by fear of Russia's advance in Central Asia and towards the Persian and Afghanistan borders. Russia was then Britain's rival. The Crimean war had been provoked by the suspicion of the British of their European rival. Turkey was the objective of Russia's advance in Europe, even as India was believed to be her final objective in her advance in Central Asia. Russia was territorially the largest kingdom in Europe. She had enormous natural resources. Her dream from the days of Peter the Great had been to build up a navy that would rival the British navy. But she had no sea-port, and unless she could have free access to the Mediterranean, her dreams would remain eternally unrealised. She wanted, therefore, to push her way through the Black Sea and the Bosphorous into the Mediterranean. Turkey stood in the way, and the Russo-Turkish wars owed their origin to this Russian policy. Great Britain was naturally opposed to this expansion of Russia. And she found in Turkey a helpful instrument in her opposition to Russian ambitions. This was the psychology of the Crimean War. That was also the psychology of the next Russo-Turkish war, wherein the British sided, not openly though, with the Ottoman. When Russia practically won that war, the European Powers combined to deprive her of the fruits of that victory. By the Peace of Berlin (1878) Russia's European ambition was practically strangled. The credit of it was shared by two European statesmen, the British Premier, Lord Beaconsfield, and the Prussian Chancellor, Prince Bismarck. After the Treaty of Berlin, Russia quite naturally, turned to Asia in the hope of satisfying her ancient ambition of building up a world-empire that would enter the lists with the British Empire. She commenced to spread her hegemony into Central and Eastern Asia. Central Asia rapidly came under Russian domination. From Central Asia Russia put forward her foot towards Persia and Afghanistan. Herat became the strategic objective of this new Russian expansion. Herat was believed to be the key to both Persia and Afghanistan. If Russia could get a firm footing in Herat, both Persia and Afghanistan would lie at her feet. And then Great Britain's Empire in India would have to face this new menace. This was how our North-Western Frontier policy was born.

It was admittedly not an absolutely safe frontier. Afghanistan offered the first difficulty. Between Afghanistan and the settled districts of British India there lay an extensive territory inhabited by undependable tribes who could neither be completely subdued and converted into peaceful and loyal citizens of the British Empire nor be trusted to act as faithful allies in the event of a foreign invasion. The same was true also of Afghanistan. The whole of the North-Western Frontier of India was thus a great danger point to British India. These considerations led Lord Beaconsfield to search for what he called a "scientific frontier" for British India towards the North-West. Lord Lytton was appointed to the Indian Viceroyalty to carry out this mission. In search of this "scientific frontier" the Indian Viceroy provoked a new Afghan war. Educated public opinion in India was against this costly quest of Lord Beaconsfield's mare's nest. It did not favour this aggressive war on the Afghans. It hurt, in the first place, their new-born love of freedom. That was by no means a narrow national sentiment. The Indian intelligentsia wanted freedom not only for themselves but for every other country in the world. Another reason of their opposition was the inevitable financial waste which this military enterprise would involve, increasing thereby the burden of Indian taxation. This last fear did not take long to be realised. Simultaneously with the progress of Lord Lytton's Kabul War two things happened in the fiscal history of British India. One was the misappropriation, as our people took it, of the Famine Fund by the drain of this war; the second was the imposition of a new tax to meet its expenses. The Kabul War roused considerable opposition among the intellectuals in India. It brought forth very bitter criticism of the policy of the Government. This criticism was most outspoken in the vernacular press, particularly of Bengal. Lord Lytton was moved to pass a new Press Act with a view to crush the freedom of the vernacular press.

Though Lord Lytton's Vernacular Press Act applied to all India, the real cause of offence came from the Bengalee press. The "Sadharanee," edited by Babu Akshay Chandra Sarkar and published from Chinsurah, was at that time the most powerful organ of educated public opinion in Bengal. I still remember a remarkable article on Lord Lytton's speech at the Delhi Durbar of January 1877 headed "*Bhik nehi mangtehe ham, ehi dushman bolai le*," meaning "Call back this malicious brute, I do not want any alms." It was a reply to the grant of honours and titles and promise of concessions to the people of India on the occasion of the assumption of the title of Queen Empress by Her Majesty Queen Victoria. The awakened political consciousness of educated India did not appreciate this new title of their British sovereign. She was the Queen of England, a constitutional monarch, but as the head of the Indian Administration she was henceforth to be designated as the Empress of India,—not a constitutional monarch but something like an "Oriental" despot. The fertile brain of Benjamin Disraeli (Lord Beaconsfield) had invented this new title in the hope that the intimate relation, which this title sought to suggest between Her Majesty and her Indian subjects, would strengthen the foundation of India's loyalty to the British Crown. But the Indian intellectuals did not appreciate this idea. This new title practically repudiated their claim to rights of equal citizenship with Her Majesty's British subjects. It was an open reversal of the fundamental principles and ideals of the Proclamation of 1858. The spirit of the Disraeli-Lytton policy provoked this remarkable reply from the "Sadharanee."

The papers submitted to the Legislature in justification of the proposed Press legislation contained mostly translations from the Bengalee Press; and of these the "Sadharanee" came in for the largest notice. The first extract was from a violently Turkophile article extending over four and a quarter columns of the paper, discussing the fall of Plevna during the Russo-Turkish war. The fall of Plevna touched our new patriotism, which had a universal outlook. The "Sadharanee" said that it had been deeply moved by the fall of Plevna because—"We Hindus have borne and still bear the hardships and misery which follow the downfall of the prestige of a nation. In every bone, vein and pore of our bodies this sense of national degradation works as a slow consuming fire. God forbid that even our deadliest enemies should suffer as we do." The next extract from the "Sadharanee" was from a fairly long article headed (in its English rendering) "Spurious Loyalty," and ran as follows:—

> "The study of the very alphabet of politics has taught us this, that the performance of pledges forms no part of politics. When the Russian Emperor,

setting aside an old treaty, resolved to station men of war in the waters of the Black Sea, Mr. Mill was asked by the English Minister (of the day) to express his views on the subject. Mr. Mill then frankly declared that there was no connection between 'politics and the performance of pledges.' To-day finding myself in a dangerous position, I agree to pay you a tribute of a million sterling. But ten years hence, becoming conscious of my own strength, I find that if I do not pay you the promised million, you will be powerless to enforce your demands. I accordingly break my promise.

"If you and I were to do anything of this kind, it would be considered a grievous crime. But kings frequently act in this way. The science of politics is in no way concerned with morality or immorality.

"The British Government is continually breaking its promises. Thus it first engaged to pay an annual sum of 53 lakhs to the Nawab Nazim of Moorshidabad. This was reduced to 32 lakhs after some time, which again has been ultimately cut down to half this sum. The Fortress of Gwalior, belonging to the Scindia, and the Berars to the Nizam, once taken as securities, have not been restored. These are common occurrences. A history of the non-fulfilment of promises by the British Government would be the whole history of the last hundred and fifty years. We are not so foolish as to believe that the British Government should now, after a period of profound peace for over eighteen years, redeem the promises which they made on the 1st of November, 1858, soon after the crisis of the Indian mutiny. During that critical period there were dark clouds in the political sky ; bright flashed the lightnings afar and European hearts were chilled with an icy fear. But now the gentle breeze of peace is blowing, the sun of prosperity shines on high. Where is the wonder then that the English should now throw aside the heavy clothes with which they protected their bodies against cold, wind and rain? Who ever uses winter clothes in spring?

"It is the general belief that the Viceroy's speech on the 1st of January, 1877, nullified to a considerable extent the Queen's Proclamation of 1858. Babu Surendra Nath Banerjee, because he gave expression to this belief at a meeting of the Calcutta Municipality, brought down upon himself the wrath of the *Sahibs* (Europeans), who charged him with being disloyal. He who attempted to mar the spirit of the Queen's Proclamation by a cloud of vague phrases, is regarded as a loyal politician, but if you understand the thing and venture to speak out plainly, you are looked upon as disloyal. Do the *Sahibs* take us for such idiots as to think that we can be hushed to silence, because they bring against us some bitter and unfounded accusations?

"We know very well when it behoves us to show our loyalty; we tore our bosoms and poured out our heart's blood to welcome the two Royal Princes who visited India. But what definition of loyalty are we to accept when we are frankly criticising the measures of Government? The Viceroy spoke against the Queen's Proclamation and shall we say, "No, the Viceroy said nothing against it." Such insincere flattery is not loyalty.

"The proclamation of 1858 declared that 'Our subjects, of whatever race or creed, shall, so far as practicable, be admitted to all offices under our Government the duties of which they may be fitted to perform, by their ability, education and integrity.'

"Now, Her Majesty's Representative has declared that in the present state of the Empire, and for its permanent welfare, all political and high executive duties should be entrusted to Europeans only.

"It was declared in 1858 that if the natives of this country proved themselves equal, all appointments, so far as practicable, would be given to them. But now we are told that all high executive offices are to be given to Englishmen only. If these two declarations are not contradictory, then henceforth there will be no difference in colour between black and white. If it amounts to disloyalty to point out this contradiction, and if for this, the Government chooses to punish us, then we with tens of millions of Her Majesty's subjects, are prepared to be punished along with Surendra Nath."

The third extract from the "Sadharanee" was from an article headed "The Final Decision in the Fenuah Cases."

"It neither bespeaks a cultivated taste, nor is it agreeable to have constantly to write against Government. But in view of the arbitrary acts which have become common in these days, we should be wanting in our duty if we passed them over without any protest. The people were hitherto proud of the justice administered in the High Court. In seeking to shield a rash, oppressive and unprincipled European Civilian, Government has now brought that Court into contempt, and struck a blow at the root of British justice. Government has thus worked its own ruin and yet, if after this, the people are found to express discontent, the Anglo-Indian editors will brand the Bengalees with such epithets as ungrateful, disloyal, scurrilous, and what not.

"Long ago we wrote about the Fenuah case. Our readers may remember that the *Sahibs* of the factory wanted to have an embankment opened by force. The ryots resisted and they stretched themselves upon the *bund*. In order to frighten them, the *Sahibs* fired blank cartridges, but this proving of no effect, bullets were regularly used. In the Court the ryots deposed that they saw a gun in the hand of the *Burra Sahib*. The *Burra Sahib*, however, in his deposition said that he had no gun with him, but the *Chota Sahib* had one. A great confusion ensued. Those who said that the *Burra Sahib* had a gun with him were charged with perjury. At first the case was heard by Mr. Badcock, then it was transferred to the Court of Mr. Sarson. After the deposition of seven witnesses had been taken, the case was again transferred to the Court of Mr. Vassey. It was not found necessary to transfer it again in as much as Mr. Vassey sentenced the helpless ryots to six months' imprisonment. All this was the work of the well-known Mr. Kirkwood. An appeal was preferred in the High Court against these partial and illegal proceedings. In the appeal the Government, whatever object it might have had in view, took up the cause of one party.

"The Counsel for the Government made too much of this matter. After this, the Government Counsel, with the sanction of the High Court, appeared in the case not because he had any legal right to do so, but because he was actuated by self-interest, and he frankly declared that his principal object was to exonerate a Government officer from unfounded accusations. However, for many days the discussion went on regarding the legality of Mr. Kirkwood's proceedings. At last the High Court decided that it was of no use to discuss this question. They took it for granted that the proceedings had been all along quite legal, and that there was no legal objection against the judgment of the lower Court. The Judges of the High Court took all this for granted, and found the helpless ryots to be guilty of the charge, but they were of opinion that the punishment they had already undergone was sufficient, for the Counsel for the Government had expressed an opinion, that he had no objection to such a finding.

"As to the final judgment of the High Court in the case, it is observed that perhaps a decision so strange was never passed in even the most barbarous country in the world. It is first taken for granted that there has been no illegality in the proceedings, and then punishment is inflicted on a number of innocent persons on this supposition. There is not a doubt that the fame of British justice is gone for ever.

"But it will not do for us to remain unconcerned any longer. There is no justice in the country. Now for some time we must create an agitation in England. We hope the Associations of Calcutta will join and create an agitation on this subject in the Parliament of Great Britain and Ireland."

The "Bharat-Mihir," edited by the late Babu Anath Bandhu Guha and published from Mymensingh, was another powerful organ of educated Bengalee opinion that commanded universal respect. In an article published on the 20th of September, 1877, under the heading "Our Grief" it wrote:

"The *Samaj Darpana* has taken leave for good. It was published for the last time on the 23rd *Bhadra*. It will not be published any more. We make a few extracts below from what the Editor said when he bade farewell to his readers:

'If to teach loyalty to the public be the object of the Native newspapers then they may as well not exist all, for people are already sufficiently loyal.

'We cannot say how far with a pure heart Mr. Eden or the *Englishman* demand loyalty from us. We know only this much that the English Government has been exceedingly beneficial to us. Never did there exist (in the country) under any other Government such justice, such education, such tranquillity. Nay, even in the times of the Hindu monarchs, there was not such justice, such education, such tranquillity throughout the country. But then we know this also that although the country is sufficiently educated, its tranquillity is complete, yet its administration of justice is not perfect. We have many benefits yet to obtain from the English. We have said so plainly, and have advised the natives of the country to agitate about this subject. It is for giving such advice that Mr. Eden and the English editors call us slanderers or enemies of the Government, and threaten to gag our mouths.'

'If anybody says, there is not the slightest dissatisfaction in the country, not a single man's face is sad, all are satisfied, all are happy, there is nothing to be said against the past acts of the Government, nothing against the present acts, then it will be our duty to reprobate such a man as a liar, as one who has not given a faithful representation of the actual state of things. And such a man is no friend of the English. What is the use of newspapers if they observe a certain state of feelings in the community and represent quite a different state of feelings before the Government or the public at large. Would it not be a misnomer to call newspapers, the organs of the public, if the journalist could not represent the grievances of the people in a free and unfettered manner? Is it necessary to repeat *ad nauseam* that the English are our benefactors? How often shall we abuse loyalty by reiterating on every occasion when we discuss (public questions) that we are loyal? Let Mr. Eden reform his own house before taking upon himself to reprove us. What heart will not be pained to see the spectacle of educated natives crying for want of food, while every month batches of Englishmen, fresh from England, are taking possession of all the appointments in the public service? Or what political economy is this that would sanction the retention in the service of highly paid Europeans, while famine and destitution raged in the land and people groaned under the burden of taxation? Why should Mowla Bux be hanged for an offence for which Heeman receives only 18 months' imprisonment? Why should Surendra Nath be dismissed for a fault for which a Jack or a John receives promotion? That you should despise me as a worthless thing not to be touched, while I should worship you with flowers and sandal wood, is a thing which nature never heard before. We are no boors though we may be worthless in many respects. We can well appreciate the benefits we have received from Englishmen. Perhaps no conqueror race have ever been so generous to a conquered people as have the English rulers been to the people of this country. But is that a reason why we should hold that they are impartial; that what they promise they always fulfil? Are we not to lay our representations before the public when the interests of justice are interfered with? We give publicity to all this, in the hope that Government, on being informed of our grievances, will redress them. If it were not that we are a subject race, such expression of our grievances would never have been considered as amounting to disloyalty. Having worshipped so long in the depths of our hearts the virtuous Victoria, we are at last told that we are disloyal. Mr. Eden has not done a meritorious act by causing pain to the hearts of so many and by reproving a whole country.'

"We are sorry that the *Samaj Darpana* has ceased to exist, because of the threat of Mr. Eden or of the *Englishman* newspaper. We are sorry also because we loved the *Samaj Darpana*. When some one stops our utterance by force, then we may cease to exist under compulsion, though it may be with reluctance. But why should we abandon our sphere of action beforehand? We did not undertake the task of vernacular journalism in the hope of acquiring wealth or fame. Nor will it be a new source of grief to us, if, in consequence of any disaster overwhelming the vernacular press, this country should once again be enveloped in its pristine darkness.

"We could have appreciated Mr. Eden's nobleness (of disposition) if after reproving the vernacular newspapers he had done something for their improvement. If he only chooses he can by various means secure the improvement of the vernacular newspapers. On the other hand, his glory would not be greatly increased if he aimed at the suppression of the vernacular newspapers by insulting them and holding out threats to them. If he destroys one of the chief means for the improvement of the country, whose welfare has been placed in his keeping, history will record the fact in characters of black."

The *Somprokash* was in those days the premier Bengalee weekly. In its issue of 24th December, 1877 it published an article under the heading "The Way to Gag the Native Press", which ran as follows and from which the Government made a fairly long extract to justify the proposed Press Act:

"Many cannot understand why Mr. Eden should have thought fit to abuse the native editors before a number of gentlemen who had been invited to Belvedere. But others think that His Honour has resolved to gag the Vernacular newspapers and this is but a prelude to that act. We cannot, however, understand the meaning of this. How will he do this unless indeed he takes away the freedom of the whole newspaper press which is by no means an easy task under the British administration. We can clearly perceive that if Mr. Eden were to issue any order restricting, even partially, the freedom of the Press, the editors of the Anglo-Indian papers would not tamely submit to such an order. Hence there would be necessity to divide that order into two parts. By one the liberty of the Anglo-Indian journals would remain intact ; by the other the liberty of the Vernacular journals would be taken away. We do not, however, believe that the British Government has really so much degraded that it would enact such an one-sided law. And if such a law is asked for, they would, certainly, we believe, question its necessity. If the Vernacular Press is seditious, there is already a law to repress sedition ; there are courts of law.

Let complaints be lodged against them in the regularly constituted courts of the land, and let their mouths be gagged here. If the British Government hold these views, it will be rather difficult for Mr. Eden to be successful in his efforts to gag the press: and he will be placed in a very awkward position. But in order to relieve Mr. Eden from all anxiety on this score we propose pointing out to him an easy and beautiful means to gag the mouth of the Vernacular press. Let him with other officers of Government follow it, and he will attain his object without any difficulty. He will not expose himself to obloquy or ridicule, and he will secure that upon which he has set his heart. When there is such a means why should he have recourse to more difficult methods? An author has remarked that if a disease which can be cured by bitter medicine can also be cured by crystal sugar, what patient is there that would not prefer the sugar to the bitter medicine? The easy means to which we have alluded are as follows:—

"The authorities should cease to make any distinction between black and white, the native and foreigner, the conqueror and the conquered, and whether in the court, durbar, or the council, should seek to regard all classes of the community with equal impartiality, enact equal laws, give them appointments of equal value, according to merit and ability, award condign punishments to high-handed Europeans, whether official or non-official. If these measures be adopted, Mr. Eden will see that the mouth of the Native press will of itself be stopped. Heenan was at night-time seen prowling about the house of another man. The servants, according to the order of the master of the house, went in pursuit of him. He shot one of the men dead. It was not the case that Heenan was not aware that a pistol-shot would kill the man. Nor was it necessary for Heenan to shoot down the man in self-defence, for the servant did not go to kill but to seize him. If they meant to kill him they would have gone armed, and Govinda (the man who was murdered) would never have caught Heenan by his legs to prevent him from running away. It was not that Heenan did not understand all this (and kill the man in sheer ignorance of his intentions). There was another serious charge against him, namely, that he always walked about armed with a pistol. Govinda was surely not like a beast or a bird, an object of the chase, and yet Heenan felt no hesitation in killing him. For this serious crime he received only 18 months' imprisonment, while Janoki Nath Roy was sentenced to three months' imprisonment and fined Rs. 20,000 for giving false evidence, whether inadvertently or intentionally. In both cases the jury recommended the accused to mercy. We ask Mr. Eden to weigh the sentences in the scales of justice, and say if they are right.

"Natives were occasionally led to expect that they would be appointed District Judges. The subject has been allowed to drop since Mr. Eden became Lieutenant Governor. A Magistrate, the other day, assaulted an unoffending native, whose only fault was that he was washing his mouth when the officer passed by, and did not make his *salam*. If the person assaulted had sufficient strength and courage he too would have turned round and assaulted his assailant. And the spectators would no doubt have felt their curiosity amply satisfied. What punishment was even awarded to this Magistrate, and how is it that he has been left in charge of a district? So long as the authorities do not redress these wrongs, their utmost efforts to gag the Native Press will never be successful. Should they do this illegally and by force, another mouth will forthwith be opened. In conclusion we respectfully ask Mr. Eden not to be angry with us. We have but given him a bit of salutary advice, which however, according to the poet, is scarcely agreeable."

Another extract was from the *Hindu Hitaishinee* of Dacca, dated 10th March, 1877, from an article under the heading "Evil Effects of Drinking":

It chills one's blood (literally dries one's blood) to contemplate the terrible evils which drink is creating in our midst. Even immediately after the first arrival of the English in this country, there were hardly more than one or two gentlemen in any village who used to drink, and amongst the lower orders there was perhaps an individual here and there who would smoke *ganja*. But they had a very bad repute in society. After this, when Government found that there was a very good means of gain in it, it began to encourage the liquor traffic. If we are now to compare the past with the present, it would seem as if a *yuga* has intervened, so completely are times altered. We have heard, and Dr. Wilson has clearly shown in his report, that whereas there was only one liquor shop in Dacca before, there are a hundred now. Good Mussalmans and the Krishna-Mantri Hindus considered it a sin even to touch wine; their descendants are now founders and protectors of grog-shops. Persons of respectable families never owned any grog-shops, and if they were in any way connected with such an establishment, they were exposed to obloquy and not unoften excommunicated. Now-a-days wine is considered as one of the principal articles of trade, and it has become the guardian divinity of almost every household. The Salgram Chakra (symbol of Vishnu) is not now so much honoured as wine. This wine is the index of the modern civilisation of the West. A person will not be honoured in the society of our educated men unless he has learnt to drink. The number of drunkards is gradually increasing, both among Hindus and Mussalmans. Christians have been mainly instrumental in propagating a taste for wine. They themselves have not been ruined by it, but are encompassing the ruin of others. Once on a time a rich man of Nabobpore had a certain disease in his thigh and legs. A doctor advised him to rub brandy over those places. The patient did not at first consent to the proposal, but, being quite helpless, he at last agreed to it, which however made him very uneasy. In a separate room he would have his body rubbed over with spirituous liquors. The servant who performed this duty was never allowed to touch his food, or the things connected with the performance of his devotional duties. He would change his dress at once, and would not enter any other room without having had his bath. Now, if you enquire, you will find his descendants are the slaves of intoxicating drinks; they do not consider their mouth or their homes purified without such drink.

"A few days ago a mukhtear became so excited with drink in the house of a prostitute that while he was coming down the steps from the upper to the ground floor, he lost his footing and rolled down to the floor below. He received such terrible injuries on the head and other parts of the body that he became quite insensible. He is now under medical treatment, but his life is said to be in a precarious state. On another occasion a doctor who was rolling in a drain close by a street, was about to fall under a carriage, but was saved through the kindness of a gentleman. At another time a Deputy Magistrate who came to Dacca for an examination, could not appear on the second day of the examination as he was quite drunk. Moreover, if anybody were to note all the horrible things that have occurred at Dacca in consequence of drinking, it would form a work as bulky as the Bengal Administration Report. At the corner of almost every lane, and by the sides of streets and in bazars, there are shops selling *ganja* or opium or intoxicating liquors. All classes of people resort to these places in large number. The vendors cheat them out of their money in various ways. Although the Government has increased the excise duty and license fee, still the number of drunkards and taste for intoxicating drinks instead of decreasing have been increasing. The profits of Government have, no doubt increased ten-fold, but then a great number of people of this country are being ruined. Drink does greater injury to the people than gambling. There is nothing else but drink which can do all sorts of injury, pecuniary, physical and mental. We have some very influential men who died at a very premature age from the effects of drinking ; some others have become completely useless ; and there are others who through the same cause are on the high road to ruin. Who will not feel grieved at seeing the country in such a wretched state ? The Government cannot do anything to prevent the evil until it consents to forego the profits it obtains from spirituous liquors.

"It does not become the ruling power to gain money by a means so detrimental to the interest of its subjects, and so opposed to humane principles of government."

These extracts were certainly a very fair indication of the tone and temper of the politically-minded Bengal of those days. Whether they justified Lord Lytton's Press Act was another question. The Indian Press had been set free from all manner of official restraint except what could be used through the ordinary criminal law of the country, in the interest of the foreign Government itself. It helped the British rulers of the people to get at least a glimpse of the mind of their subjects. To deprive it of this freedom was to deprive the Government itself of a medium of knowing what passed in the mind of their subjects. The popular slogan was that to interfere with the freedom of the press in India was like sitting on a safety valve. Lord Lytton's Government, however, took another view. The Press might inform the Government of the state of public feeling in the country but at the same time it was also an effective agent for the creation of that feeling itself. It was to provide against this last contingency that Lord Lytton's Press Act was framed.

The Indian Association convened a public meeting of the inhabitants of Calcutta at the Town Hall. The Lytton Administration had commenced to demoralise the aristocratic sections of the community. The British Indian Association, representing the Bengal zemindars, refused to join this meeting. But the educated middle class not only of Calcutta and Bengal but practically of the other provinces also fully supported this protest of the Indian Association. Mr. Ananda Mohan Bose, as Secretary of the Indian Association and convener of this public meeting read a large number of communications received from, among others, the Bombay Association, the Cawnpore Association, the Allahabad Indian Association, the Seetavaldee Native Club,

(Nagpur), as also the resolution of a public meeting held to protest against the new Act at Nagpur. The new political life in Bengal created by the Indian Association and Babu Surendra Nath Banerjee had already organised itself in numerous political associations in the Bengal districts, namely, the Barisal People's Association, the Bogra People's Association, the Mymensingh Association, the Senhati People's Association, the Bhajanghata Indian Association, the Meherpore Indian Association, the Chittagong Association, the Rajshahi Association, the Contai Association, and the Dacca People's Association. All these were evidences of the birth of a new political consciousness and patriotic endeavour in the country.

The Sheriff of Calcutta was asked to convene this public meeting, but he refused to do so. This refusal created considerable nervousness in many people, who were afraid to join it. Indeed, it was felt at one time that it would not be safe to join this demonstration, and the leaders of it ran the risk of being clapped into prison. But neither Surendra Nath nor Ananda Mohan were deterred from doing what was an obvious public duty by fear of its political consequences. Rev. Dr. K. M. Banerjee, the President of the Indian Association, also was not afraid to take the chair at this meeting. In opening the proceedings he said: "When the object was the consideration of a petition on a certain measure of the Indian Government, it could not be unconstitutional in any sense of the term; and the Sheriff's refusal to give to the inhabitants of Calcutta an opportunity of meeting in the most regular and constitutional way in their own city, was deeply to be regretted." Discussing the business before the meeting he summarised it in four questions:

(1) Whether, assuming the possibility of objectional matter in a few Vernacular papers, they were sufficient to exhibit an absolute necessity for an Act which no one denies is opposed to the general principles of the English constitution?

(2) Whether the necessity was so urgent and pressing that the safety of the public required the new Press Bill to be rapidly passed into Law at one sitting without publication, by the suspension of the standing rules of the Legislature.

(3) Whether or not, the Act so passed is fraught with any actual injury or mischief, as regards social improvement and the good government of the country?

(4) Whether, in any case, the present movement for a petition to the Imperial Legislature in England can result in any good?

This Press Act was really a piece of panic legislation. True it is that recent events, particularly the deposition of the Gaikwad and the Wahabi case, and the revival of an obsolete Regulation to arrest and detain without trial the leader of the Wahabis, and in Bengal the retrograde educational policy of Sir George Campbell aiming at the practical abolition of higher English education, had created considerable unrest in the educated community, who had been led to hope that their intellectual, moral and political regeneration would come from British rule. This unrest found outspoken expression in our vernacular press. The writings of this vernacular press frightened the British officials in the country, and even created considerable nervousness in Great Britain. The British people and Parliament had not as yet been able to completely forget the lessons of the Sepoy Mutiny. Twenty years was not really a sufficiently long period to work out the dark fear caused by the Mutiny. Dr. K. M. Banerjee in his speech from the chair referred to this panic. "India", he said, "is at present under a dark suspicion of being given to disloyalty, treason, and 'all sedition,' 'privy conspiracy and rebellion'. It was this suspicion which prompted some of the English papers to laud the Act; it was the same suspicion for which the members of Parliament were afraid to touch the subject." And the Chairman urged that this Act was bound to encourage the enemies of the Queen and damn the spirit of India's friends. Concluding he said:

> "The meeting, by disavowing and repudiating the remotest idea of such disloyalty and manifesting its confidence in Parliament, will reassure friends as well as stop the mouths and confound the hopes of the Queen's enemies, hopes which may be supposed to be fostered by the gratuitous suspicion of India's loyalty at this critical moment."

The nervousness displayed in this apology for holding this meeting was however not merely a diplomatic move on the part of the promoters to save their skin. Educated Indian opinion in those days sincerely wanted the continuance of British rule. The generation to which they belonged had not completely forgotten the state of their country from which the British had recovered it. The last days of the Mogul Empire were marked by universal anarchy and disorder. Almost every man's hand was against his neighbour. Neither person nor property, and not infrequently even the honour of their women, were safe from the attacks of the turbulent elements of society. The British had replaced that reign of terror by a new reign of law. In the sixties of the last century even village urchins in distant and out of the way places used to cry out for protection from the British "Company" when attacked by their playmates. "*Dohai Company Bahadur*" was a familiar cry in our rural parts in those days. Our educated people still remembered these traditions. Their professions of loyalty to the British Queen and the British Government were therefore absolutely sincere notwithstanding their criticism of the acts and policies of the Indian Government. A feature of this protest meeting was the association of representative Britishers with it. The first resolution was moved by Dr. K. S. Macdonald, the head of the Scottish Churches Mission in Calcutta. Dr. Macdonald belonged to the earlier generation of Christian missionaries who always studied to make friends with the people of this country. Alexander Duff, the founder of this Scottish Mission in Calcutta, had completely identified himself with every progressive movement in his country of adoption. Duff was a friend of Ram Mohan Roy, and was equally intimate with Sir Radhakanta Dev, the representative of Hindu orthodoxy. Dr. Macdonald followed the traditions of Dr. Duff in his relations with the leaders of the Bengalee community.

Though the members of the British Indian Association refused to join this protest, the Committee appointed at this meeting to draw up the petition to the Parliament was as representative of the culture and wealth of Calcutta as any Committee could possibly be. Ananda Mohan Bose was appointed its Secretary, and the members were:

Rev. K. M. Banerjee, L.L.D.
T. Palit, Esq.,
Babu Chunder Madhab Ghosh,
Revd. K. S. Macdonald,
Babu Dwijendra Nath Tagore,
Babu Jogesh Chandra Dutt,
Babu Rash Behary Ghosh,
Babu Bhairab Chunder Banerjee,
Babu Probodh Chunder Mullik,
Babu Nitto Lal Mullik,
Babu Jagannath Khanna,
Dr. Gurudas Banerjee,
Babu Nabagopal Mitter,
Babu Kalinath Mitter,
Babu Gonesh Chunder Chunder.

This Act was passed as a "preventive" measure. It was believed by the Government that the passing of this Act would prevent the dissemination of sedition in the community. But the leading Bengalee journals stopped publication the very day this Act was passed. And this practical protest against it roused far more feeling in the community than what the so-called seditious preachings of these papers had been able to do. The "Somprokash", the "Navavibhakar", the "Sadharanee", and other leading Bengalee papers refused to continue their work under the humiliating conditions of the new Press Act. The "Amrita Bazar Patrika", however, converted itself into an English weekly almost overnight and thus went outside the jurisdiction of this Act.

The Vernacular Press Act was not the only retrograde and unpopular measure of Lord Lytton's Government. Next year, 1878, the Arms Act was passed aiming at the wholesale emasculation of the Indian subjects of the British Queen. Like the Vernacular Press Act, the Arms Act was also a discriminating measure. Not only the British subjects in India but the subjects of every foreign State temporarily or permanently residing in India were exempted from the operation of this Act. The Hottentot and the Zulu could carry arms while walking along the streets of Calcutta or Bombay, but the native Indian subject of the British Government could not do so. Even more than the Vernacular Press Act this Arms Act wounded our national self-respect. And the feeling of resentment against it was, though not so vocal, much wider than that aroused by the Vernacular Press Act. By these measures Lord Lytton instead of reconciling the new political consciousness in the country to British rule, which was certainly not difficult at that early stage, helped to create and strengthen a new anti-British feeling among our people.

CHAPTER XV.

HOW I CAME TO THE BRAHMO SAMAJ

It is a queer story which reveals at once my personal character and the character of the times to which I belonged. Freedom in the sense of revolt against restraint was an inherited instinct in me. My father as well as my mother were both endowed with very strong wills. This developed in me almost into wilfulness. I always resented all manner of compulsion. I was too proud to accept the law of my life from anybody else. This is why though we had a Brahmo Samaj in Sylhet and some of my class-mates organised a Students' Prayer Meeting in connection with the Samaj there, I stood out of it. When I came to Calcutta the same "cussedness" led me to take up a more or less openly hostile attitude towards the Brahmo Samaj, at that time almost at the very zenith of its glory. A relation of my sister's, her husband's younger brother, had come to Calcutta and entered the University about two years before me. He had openly joined the Brahmo Samaj and was an inmate of the Brahmo Students' Home, called the Brahmo Niketan at 13 Mirzapore Street. This Home was a centre of Brahmo propaganda. It was overlooked by a missionary of Keshub, and they had regular daily worships as well as weekly conversational meetings in this Home. This Niketan was in those days a prominent Brahmo institution in Calcutta. This relation of my sister's was a zealous propagandist. As soon as I came to

Calcutta he commenced to preach to me and tried his best to induce me to join the Brahmo Samaj. All this had, however, a different effect upon my mind. Instead of drawing me to the Brahmo Samaj it repelled me from it. I not only stood out of the movement but joined the large body of scoffers of it.

A few days previous to my arrival in Calcutta the Brahmo Samaj had suffered a serious set-back through the ugly revelations regarding the management of the Bharat Ashram which was started as a home for Brahmo families run by Keshub and his missionaries. Keshub had his old family dwelling house in Colootola and he maintained his connections with it and continued to live there, though he spent the greater part of his day in the Bharat Ashram. His wife also regularly attended Divine Service in the Ashram. Missionaries of the Brahmo Samaj who had no family dwelling house in Calcutta all resided in the Ashram with their wives and children. Many leading members of the Brahmo laity also took up their residence with their families in this Home. The ideal of those days was to build up a communistic organisation, so far as might be, of the adherents of the Brahmo Samaj. They were to be a "family" tied together by sincere love and affection, having no private or personal interests and owning God Himself as the Father or Pater Familias of this community. The Bharat Ashram tried to give material shape and organised constitution to this ideal. The materials, however, with which Keshub tried to build up this "Family of Love" were not ripe for it. The inheritances of the decadent Hindu joint family, that had commenced to breed intense selfishness and jealousy between the members and unseemly scramble over petty things, were brought to this new Home by the ladies of the Brahmo converts. Nor can it be justly said that the male members of the Ashram were absolutely free from the influences of their womenfolk. Differences and disputes between the inmates became thus inevitable. These grew to such an extent that the story of these quarrels soon found publication in the Bengalee press. Side by side with these unfortunate revelations of the life of the Brahmo families in the Ashram, there arose a dispute over the proprietory rights in the Calcutta School (which subsequently became the Albert School and developed later into the Albert College, of which Babu Krishna Behari Sen, Keshub's younger brother, was the Rector) between Keshub and one of his Brahmo followers, Babu Haranath Bose. Ugly rumours also commenced to be circulated regarding some of the inmates of the Ashram. In a letter to the press a most violent attack was made on Keshub and his Ashram. This convulsed not only the Brahmos but more or less the whole of the educated community of Bengal. The scandal became so serious that the matter had to be taken to court on a charge of defamation. It was, if I remember aright, subsequently settled out of court. But the evil odour of it clung for many years to Keshub and the Brahmo Samaj generally. The Ashram was broken up.

When I came to Calcutta the Niketan or the Students' Home was the only public institution connected with the Brahmo Samaj with which I came to be acquainted through the relation mentioned above. The Niketan made no appeal to me. The inmates of the Niketan were, almost all of them, more religious than human. In fact, the natural humanity of the general body of Brahmo young men of my generation was almost completely overwhelmed by their religiosity. They were almost always talking of sin and salvation, of prayer and Divine worship. All these fortunately or unfortunately had as yet no living reference to my life and ideals. In the Brahmo Samaj itself there were dissentients from this excessive and abnormal religiosity which was being sought to be cultivated by Keshub Chunder Sen. Babu Jyotirindra Nath Tagore had about this time brought out (I think anonymously) a vitriolic satire on the unrealities of current Brahmo ideals and practices. It was named *Yatkinchit Jalayoga*. One of the characters in this farce, a Brahmo leader, was presented as constantly sinning and repenting of his sins. All these unrealities of the current ideals and practices of the Samaj seriously influenced the generation of youthful students to which I belonged. I had, therefore, not only no attraction for the Brahmo Samaj when I first came to Calcutta, but even felt an increasing repulsion towards it. In the Sylhet students' mess the general atmosphere was certainly anti-Brahmo. The only Brahmo member of our mess was Sundari Mohan Das. But his Brahmoism was not of an aggressive type. His loyalty to his religious principles in no way overwhelmed his natural human instincts or made him a sour and sullen young man constantly afraid of being contaminated with sin. Sundari Mohan was a normal young man who freely entered into all the frolics of our youthful nature and never permitted his Brahmoism to interfere with the innocent enjoyments of life. Indeed, he even shared with us the current satires on Brahmo ideals and life. But for the sweetness of his personality and the absolute non-aggressiveness of his Brahmoism, I fear I should never have joined the Brahmo Samaj.

From the very day when Sundari Mohan going home to Sylhet during his first summer vacation called me out of my class and congratulated me upon my early journalistic enterprises a new romance had been born in our youthful friendship. This rapidly grew upon my arrival in Calcutta and the constant companionship in which I lived outside our college hours with him. In the Sylhet mess we shared the same room and gradually had a common purse. Our mess-mates even made our romantic attachment the subject of little ballads. But these intimacies notwithstanding, Sundari Mohan never tried to convert me to his religious views.

The new Bengalee stage had at this time very great influence upon my mind. About a couple of years previously women had been first introduced into our national stage. They were inevitably outside the social pale. The Brahmo Samaj in the name of public morals entered a strong protest against this new development in the Bengalee stage. The Brahmos, as a class, considered it sinful to attend the performances of these public women. Sundari Mohan, however, did not accept this Brahmic interdiction. He freely went to the two theatres that we had then in Calcutta, the Bengal Theatre and the National Theatre, both of which were situate in Beadon Street. Instead of condemning this new development in the Bengalee stage as immoral we really welcomed it as opening an honourable occupation for the class of women from whom our actresses were being drawn. A few months previous to my arrival in Calcutta one of the leading actresses, Shreematee Sukumaree, had been married under Act II of 1872 to an actor, Babu Haridas Datta, both of the Bengal Theatre. A leading Brahmo, Babu Nagendra Nath Chatterjee, officiated as Minister in this marriage. It created a great sensation in Calcutta society, both in and outside the Brahmo Samaj. When I came to Calcutta, these two were prominent personalities, particularly the actress, in our theatre. Though the example of these prominent members of the Bengalee stage was not followed by others, as was expected at the time, yet it did to some extent indicate a healthy line of evolution, and the very possibility of such unions somewhat removed the moral ban against our stage.

But whatever might be the private character of the actors and actresses, the plays generally put on the board of these theatres were exceptionally pure and inspiring. Dinabandhu Mitra was in those days one of the most favourite of our dramatists. Dinabandhu's dramas were instinct with both a lofty social idealism and a high standard of ethical conduct. His *Nabin Tapasvini* really presented the Brahmo ideal of social and domestic life in fascinating colours. His *Sadhabar Ekadashee* was a glowing picture of the evils of intemperance that had attacked the new generation of our English-educated countrymen. His *Jamai Barik* or the Son-in-Laws' Barrack was a burning satire on the practice of some of the richer families in Calcutta, who refused to allow their daughters to go to their husbands' homes and families but had their sons-in-law domesticated in their own homes as more or less dependents on their wives. Those were the days of social reform and political freedom, and the stage fully represented these intellectual and moral currents flowing over the educated Bengalee community. It was indirectly doing the very work to which the Brahmo Samaj had consecrated itself. The members of our mess, including Sundari Mohan, were frequent visitors to the Bengal and the National Theatres.

The *Bangadarshan* on the one side, and the Bengalee theatres on the other, exerted very considerable influence upon me, and quickened very forcibly my literary endeavours and aspirations. This passion for literary culture possessed me to such an extent that I neglected my University studies and spent most of my time in reading Bengalee books and English dramas and novels. And this passion for Bengalee literature was an indirect cause of my coming to the Brahmo Samaj.

Sundari Mohan and myself were, as has already been mentioned, constant companions outside our College hours. But on Sunday evenings he used regularly to go to the Brahmo Samaj in Mechua Bazar Street. These Sunday evenings hang, therefore, heavily upon my mind. I felt exceedingly lonely. After a while instead of staying by myself at home I commenced to go to the Samaj with Sundari Mohan. But while he went to pray I went to sit by him and doze or sleep. After some time one day in course of conversation Sundari Mohan suggested that if I really wanted to be a Bengalee writer and speaker I could not do better than listen attentively to the Service of Keshub Chunder Sen in the Brahmo Mandir as Keshub was universally recognised as a master of Bengalee diction and oratory. This found me a new incentive and a new employment for my mind during Sunday evenings. I no longer went to the Samaj to sleep, but brought all my intelligence and thought to the Service conducted by the Brahmo leader. In this way I felt unconsciously drawn to the Brahmo Samaj.

But I was all the same a mere worshipper at the gate. My interest in the Services of the Brahmo Samaj was merely intellectual and literary. I really had no lot or part in the religious and spiritual exercises of these weekly Services. All my early religion was prompted by fear. I prayed to Kalee and Durga during the serious illnesses of those whom I loved, asking their intervention for the cure and the life of my dear ones. Though I had certainly advanced considerably intellectually from that earliest stage, spiritually I still occupied the same plane. The general body of Brahmos prayed for salvation from sin. There was no sense of sin in me, and consequently there was no call to me for praying for salvation. The God to whom the Brahmos prayed was still to me what St. Paul called an Unknown God. I had commenced no doubt to speculate regarding the Godhead or what I would now call the Ultimate Reality. I did believe instinctively in a First Cause. But when I commenced to reason about it, I was forced to posit not one but two First Causes, one Spirit and the other Matter. God was the fashioner of the universe. He was, as I subsequently came to know, the Efficient Cause of this creation. But He was not, and could not possibly be, I thought, the Material Cause of it. God and Matter were equally eternal and infinite and they co-existed with each other. This was my crude theology, and not, of course, the theology of the Brahmo Samaj. But it was really not the theology of the Samaj that gradually drew me to it. The God of the Brahmo Samaj was to me as much an unknown God as the numerous deities of the Hindu pantheon. All that I felt in my helplessness, when brought face to face with disease and death, was that like the old Hindu Gods and Goddesses, this Brahmo God stood for that unknown and supernatural Power which directed the weal or woe of men and women. And in my helplessness in the face of disease and apprehension of death my heart or my soul, whatever it may be called, went up in supplication to this Brahmo God as it had done in my boyhood to the Hindu Gods and Goddesses.

In 1876 having passed the First Examination in Arts Sundari Mohan entered the Medical College. In the summer of that year he went home to Sylhet. We had, as already mentioned, to pass through Dacca and Naraingunj on our way from Calcutta to Sylhet. The steamer service between Dacca, Naraingunj and Sylhet was very irregular. Sundari Mohan had to stay at Dacca on his way home to Sylhet for a few days. News reached me at this time that an epidemic of cholera had broken out at Dacca. This made me exceedingly nervous about Sundari Mohan, and I commenced to pray to God after the manner of the Brahmo Samaj for the safety of my friend. Twice or thrice every day I commenced to sit by myself in the solitude of my bed-room and send up my supplications to God to protect Sundari Mohan in the perilous position in which he must have found himself at Dacca in the midst of a virulent cholera epidemic. This habit continued for some time even after Sundari Mohan had safely reached his home, and led ultimately to the organisation of a weekly prayer meeting in our mess to which we commenced now and then to invite one of the missionaries of the Brahmo Samaj of India.

But it is very doubtful if even these spiritual or religious exercises would have forced me into the Brahmo fold. Another incident of a very far-reaching character had happened already in the winter of 1876. On the occasion of the Prince's visit a Sanskrit address from the Pandits of Sylhet had been sent to the Royal visitor. The full text of it was published in the local weekly, the *Sreehatta Prakash*. Babu Peary Mohan Das, who had in the winter of 1874 been accused of murdering a Eurasian in Wellington Square and had been convicted of culpable homicide not amounting to murder and sentenced to three months' imprisonment, had on his release from prison gone home to Sylhet and started this paper. The story of that case attracted very wide publicity at the time. It was regarded as what would now be called a *Swadeshi* case. Peary Mohan was employed at that time in a Government office in Calcutta, and was living in a mess somewhere in the neighbourhood of Wellington Square. On his way home from office he saw a Eurasian young man committing nuisance in the Square. He stared at him at which this young man came and picked up a quarrel with him. In course of this altercation, Peary Mohan brought out a steel eraser from his pocket and stabbed this young man, from which he died. Peary Mohan was arrested and accused on this charge and put up for his trial before the sessions at the Calcutta High Court. This case evoked almost universal sympathy for him. It roused considerable racial feeling on both sides. After serving his sentence out Peary Mohan, who had lost his place in consequence of it, retired to his native district and set up a press and started this weekly newspaper. In 1876 Babu Manohar Ghosh, a member of the Bengalee Christian community of Calcutta, went as Editor of this paper to Sylhet, and he was mainly instrumental in getting up this Sanskrit address and publishing the text of it in his paper. It seemed to us, young Sylhet students in Calcutta, a very poor production, unworthy of the reputation which Sylhet had from olden times of Sanskrit culture. We raised our voice against it and publicly condemned it through the columns of the *Sreehatta Prakash*. The Editor published a rejoinder. And thus started a controversy over the merits of this Sanskrit address. We were all young students, and could not possibly pose as authority in Sanskrit versification or rhetoric. We, therefore, approached Pandit Shivanath Shastri for his opinion. Shivanath Shastri was at that time employed as Head Pandit of the Hare School. He was believed to have already been marked out for the chair of Sanskrit in the Presidency College and ultimately for the post of Principal of the Sanskrit

College itself. He characterized the Sylhet Pandits' address frankly as a doggerel. This introduction to Shivanath Shastri very largely determined the future course of my religious and social evolution.

Shivanath had won high distinction in the University. He had taken his M.A. degree from the Sanskrit College, and had received the title of Shastri from his Alma Mater. His father had been a Sanskrit Pandit of the old type. His maternal uncle Dwarkanath Vidyabhusan had been a teacher in the Sanskrit College. Vidyabhusan was also the Editor of the premier weekly Bengalee newspaper of those days, the *Somprakas*. Government servants were not as yet strictly forbidden to have any manner of connection with the newspaper press. Babu Bhudeb Mukherjee had started a weekly newspaper of his own, namely, the "Education Gazette." He also owned the press from which this "Education Gazette" was issued. Though it was specially devoted to the discussion of educational topics and circulation of the news of the Government Education Department, the "Education Gazette" did not absolutely exclude the discussion of general topics of public interest, including politics. *Somprakas* was, however, a professedly political newspaper, and it had always been absolutely outspoken in its criticism of public policies and measures. And Shivanath had been trained by his uncle as a Bengalee writer. Dwarkanath Vidyabhusan never joined the Brahmo Samaj and always criticised what was regarded by him as the revolutionary doctrines of Keshub Chunder Sen and the progressive Brahmos. But the *Somprakas* had at one time, before the revolt of Keshub against Devendra Nath, been a supporter of the old Brahmo Samaj. I think, like Pandit Iswar Chandra Vidyasagar, Dwarkanath Vidyabhusan was also a member of the *Tattvabodhini Sabha.* Vidyabhusan exerted very considerable influence in the making of Shivanath's mind and character.

After passing out of the University with high distinction Shivanath started life as a school master at Bhowanipore, where he was the Headmaster of the South Suburban School. From there he entered the Government Education Service and was posted as the senior Sanskrit teacher in the Hare School. It was about this time that I made his acquaintance. He was living then at the back of the Presidency College in Bhawani Charan Dutt's Lane. Our first visit to him was repeated even after the question of the address presented to His Royal Highness by the Sylhet Pandits had ceased to engage our attention. In that address Oxford had been rendered into Sanskrit as *oxavataran.* Shivanath, asked concerning the correctness of this translation, said that almost any combination of sounds in any language could be given a meaning in Sanskrit. Years after, speaking on this subject he cited an anecdote. A lady missionary one day placed a Bengalee Christian tract in his hand. In this tract Jesus Christ was described as *Narayana.* Shivanath smiled at this attempt to Hinduise Christianity. The lady missionary pointedly asked him what was it that drew that smile from him. He referred to the use of the word *Narayana* to describe Jesus. What is wrong, asked his hostess. *Nara*, she went on, means humanity, and *ayana* means refuge; *Narayana* means the refuge of mankind, and that is exactly the position of Christ in Christian thought and culture; He is the refuge of mankind. Shivanath said, there is no word in the English or in any other language which could not be interpreted by Sanskrit grammar and lexicon. As examples, he cited the English word rascal. Following the method by which *Narayana* has been made to mean Jesus Christ, the word rascal might very well apply to Sree Krishna of the Hindu pantheon. *Rasa* means the particular kind of dance referred to in the *Bhagabata*. Shree Krishna used to sport with the *gopinees* in this *rasa* dance. He who sports in the *rasa* dance is in Sanskrit *rasakela* or rascal. The lady asked if he could give a Sanskrit meaning to her name. Yes, why not, replied the Pandit; tell me your name, and I shall explain it in Sanskrit. Her name was Emmi Barbara. Shivanath replied Emmi means come, Barbara means one whose greatest element is water, in other words, a fish. Emmi Barbara means that which has come from the fish. Continuing he said that the very common word 'stupid' in English bears practically the same meaning in Sanskrit also. He who pulverises or tramples under foot his own good is according to Sanskrit grammar and lexicon a stupid.

Shivanath, though one of the proudest products of his college in our University, was in his conduct and conversations almost as simple as a child. He never gave himself any airs, and we young men who went to him for his opinion on the Sanskrit address of the Sylhet Pandits were strangely drawn to him by his geniality. That first visit was repeated until some of us became almost like members of his family. Shivanath's Brahmoism was more attractive to me than that of Keshub and his missionaries. It had in those days a stronger note of rationalism than the prevailing Brahmo doctrines. Above all, Shivanath's Brahmo ideal was more instinct with the spirit of freedom and individualism of middle 19th century European culture than the ideal of Keshub Chunder Sen and his intimate missionary group. Shivanath's piety was of the type preached and cultivated by Theodore Parker, particularly in his volume of Sermons. Social freedom and national emancipation were both organic elements of Shivanath's religion and piety. In all this there was very close affinity between our youthful ideals and those of the Brahmo Samaj, as represented by Shivanath. Endowed with a very high order of poetic genius, Shivanath had already secured a place for himself in the renaissance literature of Bengal. To him belonged the great distinction of bringing to our new patriotism and politics the inspiration of a lofty ethical ideal. Some of the utterances from his first lyrical publication *Pushpamala* had become current coin in the thoughts and ideals of young Bengal. Educated Bengalees of those times were, as a class, living a very free life of undisciplined appetites and unrestrained passions. The drink habit had, as I have already noted elsewhere, in reference to the temperance propaganda of Peary Charan Sircar, got its strangle-hold on the finest flowers of our University. Dinabandhu Mitra's *Sadhabar Ekadashee* immortalised the type of educated young Bengal as familiar with Shakespeare and Milton as with the strong wines of European vineyards. Shivanath used his pen with relentless sarcasm against the Indian patriot who sang the glories of his motherland and dedicated his life to her service during the day and at night gave himself up to all sorts of self-indulgences. Slaves of their appetites and passions, cried Shivanath, how can they be serious about their country and their nation? Political emancipation is impossible without social emancipation and personal purity. Freedom is one and indivisible. The political freedom of the social or the sacerdotal slave is a myth and a fancy. However pleasant it may be to the sentimentalist, it can never be either attained, or if attained through some chance it can never be sustained, by a people who are not emancipated in their mind and who do not follow the same principles of freedom in their personal, their domestic and their social life. This was the main teaching of Shivanath's new poetry. In this, as a matter of course, he gave voice to the high ideals of the Brahmo Samaj. Here he was at one with Keshub and his missionary group. With Shivanath, however, not only was political emancipation impossible without personal purity and social reconstruction built upon the principles of liberty, equality and fraternity, but even the realisation of man's spiritual destiny or his salvation, as it was called by all the ancient religions, was equally impossible unless these ideals of equality, liberty and fraternity were fully organised in his personal life, his social relations and in the constitution of his national State. It was here that Shivanath's ideal of piety differed, though perhaps not in theory but certainly in emphasis and practice, from the prevailing ideals of even the Brahmo

Samaj under the leadership of Keshub Chunder Sen and his missionary group. It was this larger and completer ideal of freedom of Shivanath Shastri that drew me to the Brahmo Samaj far more powerfully than the preachings of Keshub had been able to do.

About the middle of 1876 we organised under Shivanath's leadership a society of our own that differed from the political societies organised under Surendranath's inspiration in this that it combined the religious and social idealism of the Brahmo Samaj with the political idealism of Surendranath.

In fact, the political aspect of it was distinctly subordinated to its ethical and spiritual aspects. The political ideal was governed by the ideals of personal freedom and social equality. The original copy of the pledge which we signed was lost many years ago, how we never found out. It was a remarkable document drawn up by Pandit Shivanath. The first article of it pledged the members to put up a strenuous and uncompromising fight against current image-worship and caste-domination in the Hindu society. This was called for by the supremacy of individual reason for the determinaion of religious faith and duty. It was equally an assertion of the absolute supremacy of the individual conscience in the determination of all ethical questions and the regulation of all social relations. This fight was called for in the pursuit of the modern ideal of Equality, Liberty and Fraternity. The next article of this pledge was distinctly political. It started with the declaration that "self-government is the only form of political government *ordained by God*." The first implication of it, though not explained in so many words in the pledge, was that the existing Government in the country not being self-government in the sense of government of the people, by the people and for the people, was not really ordained by God, and this Government had therefore no moral title to the allegiance of the people. This was practically a declaration of revolt. But Pandit Shivanath and those who were with him did not ignore existing actualities. These actualities, they believed, were really responsible for their foreign subjection. Self-government was the ideal. It was the only form of State organisation supported by the higher moral law. But the country was not yet fit for self-government. The main cause of its unfitness was the mechanical pursuit of religion and the consequent subservience to un-understood scriptural authority and degrading priestly domination. The removal of these religious and social evils must be the condition-precedent of the reconstitution of the national State upon a truly democratic basis. Pandit Shastri and those who joined him in this small organisation, therefore, while boldly asserting India's right to self-government, recognised at the same time the duty of Indian politicians striving for full self-government for their people, to render lawful obedience to the laws and institutions of the present Government, though it could not really claim their moral allegiance. But they added a significant rider to this political declaration to the effect that while obeying the laws and institutions of the present foreign Government in the country, they would not, even if faced with extreme poverty and economic destitution and all the miseries consequent upon it, "take service under this Government." The exact Bengalee words were "never to agree to accept the *slavery* of this foreign Government." The whole idea was that while they refused moral allegiance to this Government, from practical considerations they were willing to accept its authority out of regard for existing actualities and the future well-being of the people. But this was the utmost limit of their association with this Government. But their sensitive conscience as well as their newly-awakened national self-respect prevented them from making any manner of personal profit through association with an Administration, the very foundations of which were fundamentally unmoral, being based upon what is called the Right of Conquest, which meant the assertion of the supremacy of sheer brute force over the universal moral law. The next article in this pledge discussed ways and means for advancing the country to this goal of self-government. Education came here first, the education of the masses, including the education of women; the removal of the disabilities under which the Hindu widows labour in regard to remarriage, and the breaking down of the *purdah* system. The signatories of this pledge offered to consecrate their lives to these religious and social reforms. But they did not forget or ignore the physical side of national self-government. A people, who do not with their own arms defend their hearth and home against outside invasion, or protect themselves against internal lawlessness and disorder, have no right or claim to govern themselves. The national physique must therefore be simultaneously cultivated and improved along with the national intellect. And every adult member of the nation must be trained in the efficient handling of all instruments and engines for physical struggle. The signatories, therefore, pledged themselves lastly to learn to ride and shoot and preach the duties of acquiring these military trainings and aptitudes to their fellow-countrymen. There was as yet no Arms Act; that Act was passed two years later; and every Indian like the citizens of every free State could keep and learn the use of fire-arms.

It will thus be seen that the ideal which inspired Shivanath Shastri and his youthful friends was on the religious and the spiritual side much fuller than the prevailing ideal even of the Brahmo Samaj itself. It accepted the theology of the Brahmo Samaj of Keshub Chunder Sen, but refused to be restricted in the pursuit of the fullest personal and social freedom. Keshub had accepted fourteen as the minimum marriageable age for girls and eighteen for boys as laid down in the Civil Marriage Act of 1872. But Shivanath and his youthful following pledged themselves not to marry (if they are unmarried) before the age of twenty-one, nor marry a girl before the age of sixteen nor in any way to help or be associated with marriages wherein the bride was below the age of sixteen and the bridegroom below twenty-one. Keshub and his missionaries did not quite approve of the removal of *zenana* seclusion from the Brahmo Samaj, while this new band of idealists declared openly against every social custom or convention that interfered with the legitimate freedom of social intercourse between the sexes. This new group of young men led by Shivanath Shastri all belonged to the Brahmo Samaj. But the ideal that moved them was much fuller than even the Brahmo ideal of those days. The Brahmo Samaj under Keshub Chunder Sen had hardly any clear political ideal. Its ideal of freedom was practically confined to the religious and the ethical life in the narrow sense of these terms. The Brahmo Samaj under Keshub feared to pursue the fundamental logic of their theology and ethics in the social life to the fullest extent and practically left the political life outside the limits of the religious and the ethical ideals which they pursued. If anything, Keshub's politics accepted the British subjection of India as due to the intervention of God's Special Providence for the salvation of India. He never seemed to have recognised the initial wrong which the political domination of one people over another universally and inevitably inflicts. The very thought of despotic political government in any part of the world deeply wounded the inner susceptibilities of Raja Ram Mohan Roy. Shivanath felt similarly at the sight of political despotism, whether it be in Russia or any other part of the world that had absolutely no reference whatever to his national life; and with him the ideal of self-government in India was as much an organic element of his personal religion and piety as was his repudiation of popular Hindu ceremonialism and the prevailing system of Hindu castes.

Shivanath dreamt of consecrated lives, vowed like the Catholic priesthood not to celibacy but to poverty. Those who joined this group were expectd to earn nothing for themselves or their family but to put whatever wages their consecrated work might bring into a common purse from which the wants of themselves and their families would be met. The idea was to form a communist group more or less like the early Christian communists. This idea, however, failed to materialise itself. In fact, no serious attempt was ever made by those who joined this group to practically follow this communist ideal. But the other pledges they have followed except just in one instance, where one of the signatories was soon overtaken by an overpowering religious and social reaction, that forced him back to the old orthodox fold. But even in his case his change of opinion was absolutely honest and he has been as earnest and uncompromising and as much regardless of whatever consequences the pursuit of his new ideals might lead to in regard to his personal life or the pecuniary prospects of his family as he had been in his ardent youthful days in the Brahmo Samaj. It was a new movement which combined the religious and ethical idealism of the Brahmo Samaj under the ministrations of Keshub Chunder Sen with the new political ideal of which in a special degree Surendra Nath was undoubtedly the greatest apostle. There were Brahmo idealists who were left absolutely cold by the new political inspiration of our educated intellectuals. There were ardent politicians—and their number was very large—who were eagerly desiring the removal of British subjection from their national State and Administration, but who were untouched by the spiritual and ethical idealism of the Brahmo Samaj. To Shivanath belongs, in a special measure, the credit of realising the impossibilty of attaining the moral and spiritual objective of the Brahmo Samaj without a radical reconstruction of our social life and political government as well as the impossibility of reaching the political goal of democratic self-government unless our national politics was wedded to the ideals of spiritual and social freedom for which the Brahmo Samaj openly stood.

I forget the date, but it was sometime in the autumn of 1877, that we took our oath of initiation as members of this group. Shivanath was then employed as the senior Sanskrit teacher in the Hare School. He used to sleep in one of the rooms of the first floor of the school building. One night, or more accurately, in the small hours of one morning, we assembled in one of the rooms of the first floor of the Hare School for our initiation. The poet in Shivanath could not rise above the spectacular value of all sacraments. He could not ignore the place and importance of symbolism in all cults and cultures, however rational these be. Through these symbolisms religion universally appeals to our emotions and helps in the cultivation of the consciousness of the Unseen. So he did not hesitate, his uncompromising rationalism notwithstanding, to have recourse to an imitation of ancient Hindu ritualism in our initiation ceremony. We made a fairly big fire, collected some green banyan leaves, wrote on these leaves words indicating our different passions and appetites, such as lust, anger, envy etc., as well as those which stood for the more glaring social evils about us like, for instance, caste, *zenana* seclusion and the meaningless ceremonialism of popular Hinduism. Dipping these in pure clarified butter we went round this fire, and chanting a hymn specially composed by Shivanath for this occasion, we threw these leaves into this fire, and then, after offering a fervent prayer to the Lord to lead us to our ideal, we signed this pledge. Shivanath, however, could not accept this initiation or sacrament on this day, because he was still in Government service. He did so six months later. The original members of this group were (1) Babu Sarat Chandra Roy, (2) Babu Ananda Chandra Mitra, (3) Babu Kali Sankar Sukul, (4) Babu Tara Kishore Choudhury, (5) Babu Sundari Mohan Das, and (6) myself. In January 1878 three members were initiated, (1) Pandit Shivanath Shastri himself, who had in the meantime resigned from the service of the Government, (2) Babu Umapada Roy, and (3) Babu Gagan Chandra Home. Babu Sarat Chandra Roy was a remarkable character. He had joined the Brahmo Samaj at Mymensingh where he was running a book and stationery shop. This shop was the centre of a powerful Brahmo propaganda among the youthful students of the town, and it was the personal character of Babu Sarat Chandra that attracted these youthful reformers to the movement. The strangest thing about Babu Sarat Chandra was that he had never been to an English school, and even in Bengalee he was by no means a scholar. Not his intellect but his transparent honesty and deathless devotion to what appealed to him as true and good were the source of the strength and fascination of his personality. He was, with the possible exception of Pandit Shivanath

Shastri, the oldest member of this new group. He has gone to his rest. But those who knew him can never forget the quiet strength and the persistent sweetness of his character. Babu Ananda Chandra Mitra was also much older than the majority of us. He had made his mark even when working, I think, as a school master at Mymensingh, as a Bengalee poet of great promise. He had joined the Brahmo Samaj at Mymensingh and at the time of his initiation he was living in Calcutta. If I mistake not, he had been almost a regular writer in Shivanath's monthly magazine, the *Samadarshee*. He too has passed on to the other side. Babu Kali Sankar Sukul was not a Bengalee by birth, though his father was a resident of Mymensingh where he carried on some flourishing business. He was by birth an up-country Brahmin. His native place, or more correctly, his family residence was in Unao in the district of Cawnpore. He was one of the most brilliant students of the Mymensingh Government School of his time, and passing the Entrance Examination from there with some distinction he came and joined the Presidency College in Calcutta in 1874. He had been slowly drawn to the Brahmo Samaj at Mymensingh mainly, I think, through the influence of Babu Sarat Chandra Roy. Coming to Calcutta, he openly joined the Brahmo movement throwing off his Brahminical thread. He came to our small group through the influence of his two old Mymensingh friends, Babus Sarat Chandra Roy and Ananda Chandra Mitra. He made his mark in the University also, and when Surendra Nath came and joined the Students' Association, Kali Sankar became a prominent member of it. When he joined this new organisation, he was studying for his degree. Passing his M.A. examination in '78 or '79, Kali Sankar joined the City College as a Professor. Subsequently, he left the City College to take full charge and complete financial responsibility of one of the branches of the City School in the northern part of the town. It was when running this School that death overtook him. He died young. Tara Kishore Choudhury's is a most remarkable personality. He belongs to my own native district of Sylhet. He came off a most respectable Brahmin family, whose traditional pride was that they never accepted any gift from a Sudra. He passed the Entrance Examination of the Calcutta University in the same year with me, and secured a scholarship of Rs. 15 from the new Assam Government. Coming to Calcutta, he joined the Metropolitan Institution. Here he soon came under the influence of Surendra Nath. Gradually he was drawn to the Brahmo Samaj also. Tara Kishore is so made that he can never do anything by half. When he felt drawn to the Brahmo Samaj, without a moment's hesitation he threw off his Brahminical thread and started to practise, regardless of all costs or consequences, everything that was considered right or good in the ideals and estimates of the Samaj. The same fidelity to what appealed to him as true that had drawn him to the Brahmo Samaj, drove him a few years later back to the old Hindu orthodoxy. From an aggressive and radical Brahmo Tara Kishore became in later life a sincere Hindu, strictly following all the disciplines, physical, psycho-physical as well as social and ethical, enjoined upon every devout Brahmin by ancient Hindu law and scripture. Starting life as a school master he soon entered the profession of law, and after practising it for a few years in his native district of Sylhet he came to the Calcutta High Court and soon made a fairly good practice on the Appellate side of this court. Though his practice was not as large as that of some of his contemporaries in the Calcutta High Court, he was recognised as one of the very best lawyers in the profession, taking his place in the estimates of many of those who worked with him, only next to that of Sir Rash Behary Ghosh. But financially he did not succeed as well as some other Vakeels in the front rank of the profession. And the reason was that Tara Kishore never allowed his legal work to interfere in any way with the regular pursuit of his religious duties. Later in life he came in contact with one of the most pious and renowned Vaishnava saints of our time, Kathia Baba, and became a disciple of his. From this time forward he consecrated all that he owned, his bodily energies, his thoughts and emotions, absolutely to the leading and service of his Guru. Upon attaining the age of fifty, according to ancient Hindu ideals of life, Tara Kishore retired from all secular activities, giving up his practice at the Bar, and devoted himself entirely to the pursuit of the religious life. After the passing away of his Guru, Tara Kishore went to Brindaban and took charge of the service in his Guru's Ashram. All his earthly savings were dedicated to this service. He built a magnificient temple here and himself became its custodian. His piety and devotion has been recognised by the Vaishnavic brotherhood of the whole of India, and they have conferred on him the rare distinction of the title "Braja-videhi." He is now known as Braja-videhi Baba Santdas.

In the very nature of things a large number of recruits could not be expected in a movement like this. The ideals of this small group were far in advance even of the progressive section of the Brahmo Samaj. Indeed, a prominent member of the Samaj had come to one of our initiatory services fully prepared to join us. But at the last moment he withdrew because he found it impossible for him to take the vow of not only not to marry himself before the age of twenty-one, but also not accepting as his spouse any girl below the age of sixteen, and particularly the obligation to discourage early marriage by refusing any manner of association with even Brahmo marriages, the ages of the parties wherein were below twenty-one for the bridegroom and sixteen for the bride. But other circumstances also soon intervened and prevented the growth of this movement. Chief among these was the marriage of Keshub Chunder Sen's daughter with the minor Maharaja of Cooch Behar and the schism in the Brahmo Samaj, to which it led. The establishment of the Sadharana Brahmo Samaj in the summer of 1878, within less than six months of Pandit Shivanath's acceptance of this initiation, opened up before him a large field of public usefulness as a minister and missionary of it. This completely absorbed all his time and energies and left him but little leisure to nurse the infant society which he had inspired and practically created. Of this small band Tara

Kishore Choudhury had long separated himself from it, and two of us only, namely, Sundari Mohan Das and myself, are at present the only survivors. This small organisation had, however, a very large hand in shaping the whole course of my life. Though I have been slowly drifting towards the Brahmo Samaj, it was this organisation and the vow which I took in joining it that almost immediately forced me to openly cut myself off from the old Hindu orthodoxy, creating a permanent breach between my father and myself, and making me a member of that section of the Brahmo Samaj, which tried to regulate the personal, the domestic and the social life of its members in accordance with the Brahmo ideals of rationalism and freedom, popularly known as *anusthanic* Brahmos.

CHAPTER XVI.

FATHER AND SON

Between 1875 and 1877, when I received my initiation through this small organisation into the Brahmo Samaj, I had been home to Sylhet twice, once during the summer of 1875, when I lost my mother, and again in the winter of 1876. My mother's death practically removed the bands that had tied my heart and my life to my family and home. And this very considerably made it easy for me to cut myself off from the old orthodox society which I was compelled to do by openly joining the Brahmo Samaj.

In the winter of 1876, that is, before my initiation into the little group organised under the leadership of Pandit Shivanath Shastri, I went once more to spend a few days with my father in Sylhet. I was, however, still within the Hindu communion, though I had no respect for the restrictions of Hindu orthodoxy in regard to eating and drinking. Even my father knew it, though he never asked me about it, and I made no confession to him of my lapses. My father knew that neither he nor anybody else could possibly prevent the inevitable dissolution of Hindu orthodoxy under the disintegrating influences of English education and the modern spirit which our people imbibed through it. I remember one evening during this, which was practically my last visit to our home in Sylhet, while I was sitting by him, a Brahmin guest of his came and complained to him how young boys of the neighborhood showed no respect for his age or caste and freely washed their hand and mouth after their meals at the platform of the tank in our compound while this Brahmin was performing his daily devotions, and my father replying that these things could not be prevented. They were due to the omnipotent Time-Spirit, and pointing his finger towards me he said, "How can I interfere with other people's sons when I cannot control my own son in regard to these matters. He is sitting there. Now, do you think that he starved all the way from Calcutta to Sylhet or lived on parched rice during his journey on board the steamer between Goalando and Sylhet? Knowing all this how can I chastise other people's sons for the slight offence which they have given you?" This frank confession silenced our Brahmin guest, and incidentally it revealed to me a new mentality and an unexpected spirit of toleration in my father.

But while he was evidently ready to tolerate the inevitable breach of Hindu orthodoxy in my personal habits of life, he was not willing to put up with any open revolt against the Hindu society, and when I challenged social authority and publicly commenced to disobey the restrictions of caste, my father was the first person to excommunicate me and gradually to disown and disinherit me for my apostacy. This happened in 1878, that is, after I had been initiated into the larger Brahmoism of Pandit Shivanath Shastri.

All through 1877, my father repeatedly urged me to go home during the summer, the Puja and the winter recesses. I did not like to cause an open breach with him. As long as I was in Calcutta, it mattered absolutely nothing to my father and my family whether I observed the rules of Hindu orthodoxy or not. But my new faith would be put to a practical test the moment I went home. So I avoided it. But my father was not left in ignorance of the new developments in my thought and life. He had come to know, though not directly from me, because he never asked me any unpleasant questions regarding my faith and life, but from fellow-students belonging to my district who were studying in Calcutta at the time, that I had joined the Brahmo Samaj, and was not likely to continue inisde the Hindu fold. I was his only son. He had built up his earthly hopes on me. Though he rarely or never gave outer expression to his deep affection for me, he had, like Hindu parents of his generation, devoutly prayed for a son who would continue the line of his ancestors and by his learning, wealth, social distinction and character, add fresh glories to the family history. His affection for me was something intensely religious, if not spiritual. To bring up sons was to the ideals of the generation to which my father belonged a sacred religious obligation. It was discharging a debt which he owed to the unremembered line of his forbears, called in Sanskrit *pitri-reena* or the debt to the *pitris* or the manes. It was, to use modern phraseology, the obligation of the individual to help race preservation. But it was more. To produce progeny and then to bring them up in the ways and wisdom of the race was an equally sacred obligation imposed upon every householder. This was called *deva-reena* or the debt to the

Gods, which was discharged by the preservation of the ancient rituals of the race, and *rishi-reena* or debt to the *rishis*, who were the repositories of intellectual illumination and the ethical and spiritual ideals of the race. This last debt was discharged by acquiring the inherited wisdom of the ancients and contributing to it by personal culture of the supreme wisdom. These were the debts under the burden of which every Hindu was born, and for the due discharge of which he entered the marital life and became a householder. My father was brought up in the ideals and traditions of this old Hindu social economy. Marriage and the rearing of issue, particularly of male issues, were thus part of the religion of the Hindu householder of the higher and educated classes, of the generation to which my father belonged. This idealism formed really the foundation of a highly developed science of eugenics in our society. My father prayed for my coming. When I came, he accepted me as a sacred gift from Heaven. He tended me in my infancy almost as if I were his God. When I grew up he no doubt chastised me sometimes very severely but he never lost sight of this ideal even in my upbringing in boyhood. He was consciously working to bring out the highest possibilities of my mind and body. He had also, quite naturally, his social ambitions. Years after, a few days previous to his passing away, he explained to me why he christened me as "Bipin Chandra". Bipin in Bengalee and Sanskrit means a jungle or a wilderness; Chandra means the moon. Bipin Chandra means the moon of a jungle or a wilderness; and my father told me that his village was more or less of a wilderness in those days. It was an obscure place, unknown to the outer world, and he deeply desired that his son should illumine some day this wilderness and bring name and fame to it. This is why he gave me this particular name. By joining the Brahmo Samaj, making myself thereby an outcaste from home and society, I had taken up by the roots those tender hopes and ambitions of my father. And it was in the desolation of his heart caused by my apostacy that he referred to the secret of his father-love in course of a chance conversation on this occasion. And I felt then the height and depth of the parental love which I had outraged by breaking away from my father and the old Hindu communion. This brought home to me that I was not the fruit of my father's sex-passion but was in his eyes a gift of the Gods, given in response to his profound religious and spiritual longing, what is called in Sanskrit *tapasya* There is no word in the English language able to convey the significance of this Sanskrit word *tapasya*. People perform *tapasya* to win heaven; they perform *tapasya* to attain *moksha* or salvation, which is higher than heaven; others perform *tapasya* for the acquisition of wealth or earthly power. My father performed *tapasya* to have a son, and I was the fruit of that *tapasya*. I did not understand all this in my early youthful days. Looking back, however, upon those early experiences I am able to somewhat understand the lofty idealism that stood behind my father's restrained and chastened love of his ungrateful and unworthy son.

I was not directly initiated into the Brahmo Samaj. But by joining the small group organised by. Pandit Shivanath Shastri I was forced to cut myself off from the orthodox Hindu communion. I would never have done this at the call of any sectarian religion or theology. It was the fuller ideal of freedom of our small group that led me to repudiate ancient caste and customs. After my initiation into this small group, it became absolutely impossible for me to go home. That would inevitably hasten the crisis between my father and myself. He had built up great hopes on me. He had thought that I would maintain, even if I could not improve, the old family status. He had felt the handicap under which he worked in his profession owing to his ignorance of English, which was rapidly replacing Persian as court language in Bengal, and that was one of the strongest reasons which weighed with him in giving me an English education. In sending me to the University after I had passed the Entrance Examination, my father eagerly looked forward to the day when I would take my law degree and go to Sylhet and succeed him in the high position which, notwithstanding his ignorance of English, he had secured at the bar. But all these hopes were shattered by me. When rumours of my apostacy reached him, the first action that he took was to stop supply. He did it in the hope that I might be forced thereby to go home. But I did not. I continued to struggle in Calcutta. The next step that he took was to marry again at the age of sixty-four. He had placed on me his hopes of carrying on the family tradition. I was his only son. Like myself he also had been his father's only son. He had no brothers, and no nephews who could fill up my place in the family scheme. And it was this which drove him to marriage at this advanced age. For about six months he sent me no remittance. But immediately after his marriage, he sent me in a lump all the arrears of this half a year. In doing so, he wrote to me a long letter the contents of which I have not forgotten in course of the last fifty years and which I shall never forget as long as memory lives. I did not preserve it. But I am able to reproduce it even after this long lapse of time almost word for word.

The very form of the address was remarkable. He addressed me not as *kalyanabareshu*, meaning the object or recipient of the highest blessings or good, but as *pranatulyeshu* which meant 'the very life of my life.' This was really not the usual form of address from father to son even in those days, and it showed the peculiar tenderness with which my father cherished me. In our ancient books it is said that the father is re-born in the son. It is the self or life of the father which is born as the son. The address, which my father adopted in this letter though not common, was, therefore, in absolute consonance with the ancient ideal of the relation between father and son. If I remember aright, I think my father had never before addressed me in these terms, and that he should have done so on this occasion, proved the deep wound which I had inflicted in the tenderest part of his self by this open repudiation of almost everything that he held not only of supreme social but also of very great spiritual value. In this letter, he gave a brief resume of his life in relation to me. He first referred to the high hopes that he had placed on me and my future, and now that those hopes had been dashed to the ground, he recounted one by one what he described as the greatest mistakes of his life. He wrote: "My first mistake was to send you to an English school. My second mistake was to resign from the judicial service with a view to find facilities for your English education. Had I continued in that service, I would have, like my contemporaries in the service, retired from the position of a Subordinate Judge today with a pension of Rs. 500 per month. My third mistake was to send you to Calcutta after you passed the Entrance Examination; and I have committed a fourth blunder by marrying at this age. But I hope that by this marriage I have created unexpected opportunities for the pursuit of your religion, so that you may, like Durga Mohan Das, have the satisfaction of giving your own widowed step-mother in marriage." I wish I could reproduce in the original that letter, so full of pathos, so subtle in its irony and its pathetic humour, for even in this unspeakable anguish of his soul my father could not overcome his inborn sense of humour. The whole letter laid bare his wounded soul. He had stopped my remittances in the hope of forcing me to go home to him, but when I quietly ignored this, evidently in a fit of anger he married at that age. When that fit passed away, he realised the wrong that he had done to me, and as some little reparation for it he sent me the accumulated arrears of my monthly remittance. This was the last letter that I had from my father. With this letter he shut his door against me. But it was not yet barred and bolted. That came later on.

CHAPTER XVII.

THE SADHARANA BRAHMO SAMAJ

With the establishment of the Sadharana Brahmo Samaj in 1878 my association with the movement of religious and social revolt became increasingly intimate. In fact, though I had been attending the Sunday Services of the Brahmo Samaj of India, led by Keshub Chunder Sen, I was all along practically a mere "worshipper at the gate" in that temple. I never came in personal contact with the Minister. I was not personally acquainted with any of his missionaries either, with the solitary exception of Bhai Amrita Lal Bose, who was the Superintendent or the missionary-in-charge of the Brahmo Niketan, the Brahmo students' mess located in 13 Mirzapore Street, or was it 12 ?. Babu Sitanath Datta, who came from my native district of Sylhet, and his cousin Babu Srinath Datta were inmates of this Niketan; and through them I gradually came to know Babu Amrita Lal Bose. When we started a prayer meeting in our mess in 1876, Amrita Babu used sometimes to come and lead us in our devotions. This was practically my only association with the leaders of the Brahmo Samaj of India.

When in March 1878 a storm broke upon the Brahmo Samaj of India over the marriage of the eldest daughter of Keshub Chunder Sen with the minor Maharaja of Cooch Behar, I was drawn into this protest movement. Both the bride and the bridegroom were below the minimum marriageable age fixed by Act III of 1872, which had been passed at the special desire of Keshub Chunder Sen and his following of progressive Brahmos. Keshub had indeed asked for a special Act to legalise the marriage of the members of the new reformed church or community. They had broken away from the old and orthodox Hindu community by discarding both caste and image-worship. They had removed from their own community the ban on the re-marriage of widows. They had commenced to contract inter-caste marriages and encourage widow marriages. These marriages were performed without the presence of the Hindu symbol, *Salagram*, as witness, and without the Brahmin as the presiding priest. The first widow and inter-caste marriage in Calcutta under the auspices of the Brahmo Samaj created such a tremendous sensation in the local Hindu community that the bridegroom's party had to proceed to the bride's house under police protection. These marriages could not claim to be Hindu marriages. They were of doubtful validity under the Hindu law, which had no sanction for inter-caste marriages, particularly between a bride of a higher caste and a bridegroom of a lower caste. Faced with these difficulties the small band of advanced social and religious reformers belonging to the new Brahmo Samaj of India wanted through their leader a special law for legalising these marriages. Lord Northbrook was then the Viceroy. Sir Henry Sumner Maine was the Law Member in the Government of India, and both the Viceroy and his legal adviser recognising the justice and necessity of a special law for the Brahmos proposed to pass a Brahmo marriage law. This was stoutly opposed not only by the orthodox Hindu community, as offering official encouragement to the disrupting forces in the Hindu society, but also by the older section of conservative Brahmos themselves belonging to the congregation of Maharshi Devendra Nath. The Maharshi had eschewed all form of idolatry in the marriage of the members of his own family. No *Salagram* was brought as witness in these marriages. The ritual was unobjectionable from even the Brahmo point of view; and the objection of his wing of the Brahmo Samaj to the proposed marriage law was that if such a law was passed, it would by implication invalidate all the marriages contracted and celebrated by the members of the Adi Samaj, and more particularly in the family of Maharshi Devendra Nath himself. In the face of this dual opposition to a special Brahmo Marriage Act from Brahmos and Hindus alike the Government was forced to drop the original Bill. All that they could do to meet the situation was to enact a special Civil Marriage Act for India that might be availed of by all people who did not follow the Hindu, the Christian, the Buddhist, the Moslem and other established religions. This was Act III of 1872, and though not called a Brahmo Marriage Act, the advanced section of the Brahmo Samaj under the leadership of Keshub Chunder Sen practically accepted it as their own marriage law. This Act placed certain restrictions upon the civil marriages that might be contracted in accordance with its provisions. The first was that no marriage should be performed until the bridegroom had completed his eighteenth year and the bride her fourteenth year of age. This was the minimum marriageable age fixed by this Act. But in marriages between parties, particularly of a girl of this minimum age, the consent of her parent or guardian was absolutely necessary for its legalisation. When a bride attained the age of twenty-one the sanction of her parent or guardian might be dispensed with. In the case of a widow, however, who was believed to be without any legal guardian, she was free to marry whomsoever she liked even without the consent of her parents or other relations, provided she was above the age of fourteen. Another provision of this Act was that at the time of their marriage parties uniting in lawful wedlock under this law must be either maidens, spinisters or bachelors or widows and widowers. The marriage of the eldest daughter of Keshub Chunder Sen with the minor Maharaja of Cooch Behar violated the provisions of this Act in regard to the age of the parties. Keshub Chunder Sen's daughter was below fourteen and the Maharaja of Cooch Behar had not as yet attained his majority. This was the first and initial objection to this marriage. Keshub, however, waived it, possibly in consideration of the help that the acceptance of the Brahmo Samaj as the State religion in a Hindu principality would bring to his movement. And it would not be unfair to imagine that in giving his sanction to this marriage Keshub interpreted it only as a formal betrothal. The Maharaja of Cooch Behar was going to England to finish his studies. His guardians naturally wanted that to prevent future complications he should be married before he left for England. The same motive might have possibly influenced Keshub in looking upon this marriage only as a betrothal and nothing more, the actual nuptial being left to be celebrated when the parties came of age. It must have been in this view that Keshub accepted this proposal of the Maharaja's party. They assured him that so far as the ritual was concerned, it would be in complete consonance with the principles of the Brahmo Samaj. When, however, Keshub arrived at the head of the bride's party at Cooch Behar, the authorities discovered that for the legality of the minor Maharaja's marriage the ancestral custom of the Raj must be followed. It meant the observance of all the details of the orthodox Hindu marriage ceremony, including the installation of the symbol *Salagram* as witness of it, and also the due observance of the rules of caste. By his visit to England Keshub had openly and definitely put himself out of caste; he could not, therefore, give his daughter away himself; his younger brother Krishna Behari Sen could however be regarded as being in caste and he would have to act for his elder brother in the marriage ritual. These surprises were sprung upon Keshub in open violation of the assurances given him by the Maharaja's representatives in Calcutta. And Keshub found himself helpless, as he believed, to oppose the wishes and the machinations of the Maharaja's guardians. The marriage was thus not only a violation of Act III of 1872, but it was equally an outrage against the very foundation-principles of the progressive section Brahmo Samaj of which Keshub was the universally acclaimed leader.

Naturally enough, it provoked almost universal protest from his following all over the country. At first, even his intimate missionaries felt sorely grieved by these happenings. As soon as the settlement of the marriage was announced, prominent members of the Brahmo community submitted a written protest against it to the Minister. But it was not even courteously acknowledged, and Keshub with the bridal party left for Cooch Behar with such pomp and circumstance as the marriage of a Prince naturally called for. The indignation in the Brahmo Samaj deepened and expanded at this open disregard of the sanctities and sentiments of the Brahmo Samaj by its accredited leader. When the report of the manner in which the marriage was performed became public, this indignation developed into a wild storm of protests against the action of the Minister. Public meetings were held in Calcutta and the Mafassil to give organised expression to the sentiments of the Brahmo community in regard to this matter.

A meeting of youthful students of Calcutta was held in the premises now known as 13 Cornwallis Street, which stands opposite the Sadhharana Brahmo Samaj, which at that time was the location of a High English School, called the Training Academy. I was charged with the duty of seconding the resolution of protest against the Cooch Behar marriage, which, if I remember aright, was moved by Babu Sitanath Datta, better known now as Pandit Sitanath Tattvabhusan. We adopted the following letter of protest at this meeting:

"To the Very Reverend Babu Keshub Chunder Sen.

"Most Reverend Sir,—We, the undersigned Brahmo students of Calcutta, have heard, with deep despair, the news of the intended marriage of your daughter with His Highness the Maharaja of Cooch Behar, a Prince not yet in his sixteenth year, while your daughter has passed thirteenth year only. We need hardly say that the consequences of such a step, if taken by you, would be disastrous on the minds of the rising generation of Brahmos. It was principally through your exertions that Act III of 1872 was passed, and a higher platform gained with respect to marriageable age ; but such conduct in you would inevitably neutralize the effects of that law, and lead many weak minds amongst us to fall early victims to the increased importunities of guardians and friends.

"Secondly,—Such a step will seriously compromise the character as a leader of social reform attained by our Church through so many years of struggle and self-sacrifice.

"Thirdly,—The fact of giving your daughter in marriage to a person who was never known before to be a Brahmo would lead young men to attach secondary importance to considerations of religious faith in matters of matrimony.

"Under these circumstances, we beg to entreat you, Most Reverend Sir, to take into consideration the grave nature of the step you are about to take."

This protest was signed, among others, by Babu Krishna Kumar Mitra and Sitanath Datta. This was my first public association with the Brahmo Samaj. Ours was only one of a very large number of protests submitted to Keshub, personally, or by letter or by wire, beseeching him to withdraw from an arrangement that was directly opposed to the accepted principle in regard to the minimum marriageable age of boys and girls belonging to the Brahmo Samaj. Though the protesters represented practically the entire body of the elders of the Brahmo Samaj, their protests were treated with scant courtesy, if not indeed with open and insulting defiance. The marriage was gone through in the way already noted, and Keshub's practical submission to the idolatrous ceremonies forced upon him by the authorities at Cooch Behar roused profound pity and universal indignation in the Samaj and lowered it very seriously in the estimation of the educated community of India, who, whether they entirely accepted the doctrines of the Brahmo Samaj or not, looked upon it as a great moral power and an effective instrument for the social emancipation and uplift of the Indian and particularly the Hindu community. At the requisition of the protesters in Calcutta a special meeting of the Congregation of the Brahmo Samaj of India was held to consider the conduct of its Minister in regard to the marriage of his eldest daughter. I was present at this meeting in the belief that as a regular attendant at the Sunday Services in the Mandir I was also a member of the Congregation, though I never paid any subscription and did not even know that payment of such subscription was at all a condition of membership of the Congregation. Indeed, as it came out in course of this controversy, the Calcutta Congregation, of which Keshub was the Chief Minister, had hardly any well-defined constitution of its own. There was, it seems, some kind of a register of membership, but this register was filled up and kept by one of the missionaries, and the congregation was never consulted in enrolling members. Keshub was the President of the Congregation and the Rev. Pratap Chandra Majoomdar was its Secretary. The meeting was divided into two camps, in one of which stood the personal friends of the Minister, most of whom belonged to the missionary body of the Samaj; on the other, were ranged practically the entire body of the laity. As Keshub's conduct in regard to his daughter's marriage was the subject of consideration before this special meeting, Babu Durga Mohan Das, one of the leading protesters, was proposed to the chair. But it was opposed by the missionary group, and Keshub himself in virtue of his office as permanent President took the chair. This led to great confusion. A division was called for to decide as to the opinion of the meeting on the question of its president. The motion that Babu Durga Mohan Das should take the chair was carried in this division by an overwhelming majority of those present. At this Keshub with his missionary-following and the few friends who stood by him among the laity left the meeting, which carried unanimously a resolution condemning the action of the Minister and calling for his resignation. This was only the beginning of the fight. Keshub and his friends denied the validity of this meeting and refused to accept its decision as constitutionally binding on them. Then followed a most unseemly struggle for the occupation of the Prayer Hall from which, however, the protesters were kept out by force and intrigue. The organisation of a separate Congregation thus became inevitable. Driven from the old Mandir the protesters started their weekly prayer meetings in a private house, a couple of doors removed from their old place of worship. A provisional committee, called the Brahmo Samaj Committee, was formed with Mr. Ananda Mohan Bose as President, to take such steps in consultation with the Mafassil Congregations as might be deemed necessary and desirable for the protection of the purity of the Samaj and to secure a Prayer Hall of its own. This Committee convened a general meeting of Brahmos in the Town Hall of Calcutta and at this meeting was formally established the Sadharana Brahmo Samaj in May 1878. I became a member of it and threw myself into such activities of the Samaj, mainly literary, as were open to me. In August 1878 the Sadharana Brahmo Samaj celebrated its first *utsava* or spiritual festival in commemoration of the establishment of the original Samaj by Raja Ram Mohan Roy and at this *utsava* some of us among the younger members of the Samaj were asked to read suitable essays. Sundari Mohan read one, and I also read a paper on fidelity to truth in the face of severe trials and persecutions, drawing my inspiration mainly from Fox's Book of Christian Martyrs. The new Brahmo Samaj had started upon a militant propaganda as much against Hindu orthodoxy as against the organised autocracy of the Brahmo Minister.

This autocracy had grown in the Brahmo Samaj of India mainly if not entirely owing to the lack of a regular democratic constitution of that body. Those who broke away from Maharshi Devendra Nath Tagore because they could not stand his autocracy failed however themselves to provide against this evil in their new Samaj by giving it a regular constitution and seeing to it that this constitution was maintained in full vigour. The young men who broke away from Devendra Nath were fired with an enthusiasm for truth. They stood up for their conscience and devoted themselves almost exclusively to the building up of their personal character and piety in consonance with the dictates of their reason and their conscience. And in this work of character-building Keshub had naturally been their guide, philosopher and friend. Keshub was endowed with very considerable personal magnetism, and this drew to him the entire body of youthful reformers and kept them with him by weaving around them silken bands of personal affection and regard. The very idea that Keshub might, at any time, fall away from the lofty idealism of the movement which owed so much of its initiation, strength and inspiration to his personal character and culture, was dismissed immediately it rose in the minds of his following, if it did rise at all, and in the preoccupation of their ethical and religious exercises the question of giving a regular constitution to the new Samaj never received the serious attention of its members. This was neglected to such an extent that though the Prayer Hall in Mechua Bazar Street was built by public subscription, no body cared to have a trust-deed of this property drafted and registered. The title-deed of the land on which the Prayer Hall was built remained in the name of Keshub. All this came out in course of this struggle for occupation of the Mandir by the protesters. The first concern of the new Samaj was, therefore, to prepare a regular constitution of its own. Ananda Mohan was entrusted with this duty along with a few members of the new Samaj of whom Shivanath Shastri was one. In drawing up the constitution of the Sadharana Brahmo Samaj Ananda

Mohan was moved by a much larger ideal than that of building up a religious congregation only. We, young men belonging to the small group led by Shivanath Shastri, had already caught the larger inspiration of freedom, personal, social, as well as political. We had commenced to dream dreams of the future of our country which would realise, as much in the personal purity and character of its children as in their social life and institutions and in the organisation of their State and the constitution of their Government, the largest and highest ideal of freedom that moved us. In this we stood more or less apart from the older members even of the new Brahmo Samaj. Ananda Mohan, though not openly identified with us, had yet seen this larger vision of national freedom and sovereignty, and in drafting a constitution for the Sadharana Brahmo Samaj he was moved by this larger vision and wanted to give to this new Brahmo Samaj a constitution that would some day furnish a model for the constitution of the future National State of India. Once bit twice shy—practically guided the framers of this constitution. The makers of this constitution for the Sadharana Brahmo Samaj carefully devised checks and counter-checks to prevent the growth of any manner of autocracy in this Samaj. The central idea of the makers of this constitution was to prevent the development of any manner of leadership of any individual, howsoever endowed he might be, in the control and direction of its affairs. This was, no doubt, necessary at that time; but every good has its counterpoise of evil, and while this new constitution maintained to the fullest extent the democratic character of the Samaj, it certainly stood in the way of the development of that large spiritual personality in the guidance and education of the Congregation, which is so essential for the preservation and development of a religious body.

The new Brahmo Samaj immediately after its establishment applied itself to the organisation of its mission work. Of the older missionaries of the Brahmo Samaj of India, only one, Pandit Bijoy Krishna Goswami, left Keshub and joined the protestant organisation, and he was among the very first to be accepted as a missionary of the new Samaj. Pandit Shivanath Shastri, who had already resigned from public service (at the beginning of the year 1878) was also ordained as a missionary of the Sadharana Brahmo Samaj. Pandit Ram Kumar Vidyaratna, who had been associated with Maharshi Devendra Nath Tagore in the Adi Brahmo Samaj, joined the Sadharana Brahmo Samaj almost as soon as it was organised, and was ordained as one of its missionaries. Babu Ganesh Chandra Ghosh had been working as an official in the postal service in Bengal, and he felt the call of the new Samaj, and retired from his service with a view to devote himself exclusively to its mission work. Babu Nagendra Nath Chatterjee, who had been wanting to consecrate his life to the mission work of the Brahmo Samaj before the Cooch Behar marriage, but whose spirit of freedom and liberal social ideas did not find favour with Keshub's missionary brotherhood, became, on the establishmnt of the Sadharana Brahmo Samaj, one of its most popular and powerful propagandists and was soon ordained as a missionary.

From the beginning of this struggle, the leaders of the protest movement keenly felt the want of an organ of their own in the public press. Keshub Chunder had his English organ, the *Indian Mirror*, and the Bengalee organ of the Brahmo Samaj of India entirely controlled by his missionaries, was a fortnightly, the *Dharmatattwa;* while he had also a Bengalee weekly, (the first Bengalee pice paper) the *Sulabh Samachar*. And all these organs of his commenced to try to prejudice public opinion against his opponents. The new Samaj had therefore to start first an English organ of its own, called the *Brahmo Public Opinion*. Indeed, it was already started with the beginning of the protest and before the establishment of the Sadharana Brahmo Samaj. It was financed by Babu Durga Mohan Das and Mr. Ananda Mohan Bose. Babu Bhuban Mohan Das, an attorney of the Calcutta High Court, Durga Mohan's younger brother, was placed in editorial charge of it. Immediately after the establishment of the Sadharana Brahmo Samaj, a Bengalee fortnightly organ of it was started under the name of the *Tattwa-Kaumudee*. This name was selected by combining the title of the first organ of the new movement under Raja Ram Mohan Roy, which he called *Kaumudee*, and the name of the organ of the revived Brahmo Samaj under Devendra Nath Tagore, which he called, *Tattwa-Bodhinee*. The *Brahmo Public Opinion* was subsequently set free from direct association with the Samaj in 1883, when the *Indian Messenger* was started by the Samaj itself as its own organ, and the *Brahmo Public Opinion* became a general weekly newspaper and review under the name of the *Bengal Public Opinion*. Babu Durga Mohan Das and his younger brother Bhuban Mohan took up the entire financial responsibility of the new undertaking. The *Bengal Public Opinion* lived an independent existence for two years, and in the third year it was merged in or incorporated with the *Bengalee* (weekly), which had passed a few years previously into the hands of Surendra Nath Banerjee. It was in this paper, the *Bengal Public Opinion* that I served my regular apprenticeship in English journalism.

There was one other Bengalee weekly, the *Bharat Samskaraka* which though not directly owned by the Sadharana Brahmo Samaj, identified itself with the protestant Brahmos. It had originally been started as the organ of the Indian Social Reform Association, which was established by Keshub upon his return from England in 1872. Babu Umesh Chandra Datta was placed in charge of it. About 1878 when the schism in the Brahmo Samaj took place the *Bharat Samskaraka* was jointly owned and edited by Babus Kalinath Datta and Umesh Chandra Datta. After the establishment of the Sadharana Brahmo Samaj, I had the honour and the privilege of being invited to join the staff of this paper as an honorary contributor by the editors, and this was my first regular apprenticeship in Bengalee journalism.

The new Samaj was in need of workers. The regular missionaries were few, and these few could hardly cope with the requirements of the very large field extending over the whole of Bengal, including Behar and Orissa and Assam, that cried for the new light. Young men who had just passed out of college or were preparing to pass out of it had to be trained for this work. They had also to be provided for not only during their period of probation and training but also after they joined as whole-time workers. The mission fund of the Samaj was too poor to find all this money. Other sources of income had, therefore, to be created. High education had already become the crying need of the province. The new education policy of the Government of Bengal initiated by Sir George Campbell wanted, on the other hand, to check the spread of this costly high education, and divert the public funds thus set free, to the education of the masses. This new policy of the Government drove increasing numbers of our educated people to start private educational institutions to counter this mischievous move on the part of the Government. The experiment of this private educational movement promised, almost from the very beginning, a large measure of financial self-sufficiency, if not success. The authorities of the Sadharana Brahmo Samaj recognised here an excellent way out of the difficult problem which faced them for training their workers and maintaining them. With this object the City School was opened at the beginning of 1879 or towards the end of 1878. Babu Umesh Chandra Datta, who had already secured very considerable distinction as Headmaster first at Harinabhi, a village to the south of Calcutta, and next at Konnagar, a small town next to Serampore on the East Indian Railway, was invited to take charge as Headmaster of this school. Pandit Shivanath Shastri had also won high distinction as a successful Headmaster in the southern suburb of Calcutta, from which position he had been drafted into the Education Service of the Government and appointed as head Sanskrit teacher in the Hare School. After his ordination as missionary of the Sadharana Brahmo Samaj, Shivanath would not tie himself up with any regular office in the new school, but he became its first Secretary, and Ananda Mohan became its President. The school was started in 13, Mirzapore Street with a small sum advanced by Ananda Mohan Bose to meet initial expenses. But from the very first month, it proved a financial success, and the money advanced by Mr. Bose for its furniture was returned to him at the close of the first month. Babu Kali Sankar Sukul joined the City School as assistant teacher. From the very first this school was staffed by a number of highly qualified and experienced teachers.

I knew, as already mentioned, that I could not expect any help from my father now that I had openly and definitely cut myself away from the parent society and thereby outraged his tenderest affections and loyalties. So I was looking out for some employment by which I might find my own bread and devote myself to the work to which I had pledged my life by joining the small group formed by Pandit Shivanath, and I was eagerly looking forward to find an humble place in the City School staff. But, for one thing, I had little or no University qualification, having failed to pass the F.A. Examination for the second time in 1878, and for another, I had received my school education in far away Sylhet, and the authorities of the

City School found it impossible to trust me to keep order and discipline over metropolitan school-boys. In those days young men coming to Calcutta from Eastern Bengal were the butt of ridicule of the Calcutta boys and young men. And for fear lest I should betray by provincial intonations my Eastern Bengal nativity, and thus fail to command the respect and confidence of the young boys in this new institution, my application for a place in it had to be turned down. It proved, however, though I was sorely disappointed at first, a real blessing to me in disguise. If I had been taken into this School, I would have to be placed at the lowest rung of the ladder; and looking back upon that disappointment I recognised in the course of a year or two how my whole life would have been cramped by being placed in the lower grade of the teaching staff of the City School from which owing to absence of any high University qualification, it would take me a long life time to get into any responsible position in the teaching staff. As it was, when my application for a very junior teachership in the City School did not meet with success, Providence, to my surprise, opened before me the very responsible post of Headmaster in an Entrance School at Cuttack. It came in this way. A Brahmo friend, Babu Jadumani Ghosh, who had joined Keshub in the hope of being ordained as a missionary and had trustfully placed all his capital unreservedly in the hands of the mission committee—it counted in five figures or about Rs. 20,000, a very large sum in those days—joined the Cooch Behar protest and came out of the mission home of the Brahmo Samaj of India; he was asked by the authorities of this High School in Cuttack to find some Brahmo young man to take charge of it on a more or less subsistence allowance. Jadumani Babu had great confidence in me. Though I had failed to pass the Intermediate or F.A. Examination, Jadumani Babu believed that my knowledge of English was quite sufficient to enable me to take charge as Headmaster of this school. So he offered me this place. He also wanted a second and a third master for this school. As the Headmaster would be in charge of English language and literature, so the second master would have to teach mathematics and the third master history and geography. These two places were offered by him to two of my friends, who also had like me got plucked in the F.A. Examination. One was Babu Brajendra Nath Sen, who came from the district of Dacca; the other was Babu Raj Chandra Choudhury, who came from my own district of Sylhet. Brajendra became second master in charge of mathematics, and Raj Chandra the third master of this High English School at Cuttack. And we three, who had been thrown adrift by their families for joining the Brahmo Samaj, left together for our new field of work at the beginning of 1879. I was to get Rs. 30 a month and free quarters, and I think my two companions were promised either the same pay or just a little less than what I was to get.

CHAPTER XVIII.

ORISSA FIFTY YEARS AGO

At the beginning of 1879 I thus found myself at Cuttack. Orissa had not as yet been connected with Bengal by rail. People had, during my boyhood and early youth, to walk all the way from Bengal to Puri along the old pilgrim-way mentioned in sixteenth century Bengalee literature. In the seventies of the last century steamer communication had however been opened between Calcutta and the port of Chandbali in Orissa. My first trip to Cuttack was made on board the ill-fated s.s. "Sir John Lawrence," which was lost a few years later in the Bay of Bengal while making its weekly trip from Calcutta to Chandbali. It was a rickety old thing, hardly seaworthy, and no one who had any experience of it had any cause for surprise when it went down with a full complement of passengers during the pilgrim-season and not a sign could be traced of either its men or its materials. That was my first experience of the sea, and though it was winter time and the sea stood calm and placid almost like a lake, I did not entirely escape the discomforts of crossing the black water. We left Calcutta early in the morning and reached Sagar, the mouth of the Ganges, at about sun-set. It took us about six hours to cross from here to Chandbali, which stands at the mouth of the delta of the Mahanadi. From Chandbali passengers, who cared to travel by boat, could do so by getting on board a canal steamer.

This steamer had no first or second class accomodation, which was supplied in green boats towed by it. I took a second class ticket from Chandbali to Cuttack and found myself in one of the green boats, the sole occupier of a two-berth cabin. The kitchen, presided over by a Madrasi cook, was next to my cabin, and for want of better occupation I opened the window between my cabin and the kitchen and commenced to take my lessons silently in Madras cookery. Cooking was a hobby of my father's, who used, whenever he found leisure to do so, to cook many delicacies himself for our family breakfast or dinner. I must have inherited my father's passion for cooking, and the opportunities of learning the art offered by the boat that took me to Cuttack brought out my latent love of cooking and laid the foundations of my not altogether negligible proficiency in this art. Throughout my long life I have always tried to prepare something myself for friends whom we invited to breakfast or dinner to our house.

It took, so far as I remember, about twenty-four hours to reach Cuttack from Chandbali by these canal boats. This canal was the legacy left by the terrible Orissa famine. At one end of this canal, there is the Bahmani, one of the branches of the Mahanadi, and the Baitaranee, while at the other end, below Cuttak, there is the Mahanadi itself. This canal not only found convenient river transport in these parts of Orissa but was also of very great help to the irrigation of these parts. There was an anicut on the Mahanadi near Cuttack which helped to store up the waters of this great river when it overflowed during the monsoon. The canal drew its supply from this storage.

Cuttack stands at the junction of the Mahanadi and its tributary, the Katjuari. The Mahanadi flows by the north of the town, while the Katjuari branching off from it at a distance, I fancy, of four or five miles from the western boundary of the town, flows along its southern limit. The Katjuari, though more or less a dry sand-bed during the greater part of the year, is, however, subject to wild fits of turbulence during the rains, and is, therefore, almost a perpetual danger to the town during these floods. From before the occupation by the British, Cuttack had tried to protect itself against the outbreak of the Katjuari by an embankment, the engineering skill and masonry of which challenged, when I first went to Cuttack, all the skill and resources of the British P. W. D. This embankment appealed to our young pride of race as a remarkable achievement of indigenous engineering. Was it Moslem or was it Hindu, we never asked, though Cuttack had been a chief town of Orissa under Hindu rule also. It was sufficient to our youthful patriotism that this achievement was Indian, and not British.

When I first went to Cuttack fifty years ago, neither the classes nor the masses there had developed any separatist provincial consciousness. Orissa formed then a part of the Bengal Administration. The Administration of Bengal was composed of the three provinces of Bengal, Bihar and Orissa. Bihar, though inside the administrative province of Bengal, had a distinct linguistic and cultural individuality of its own. But for more than five hundred years past a process of inter-provincial fusion had been at work between Orissa and Bengal. During the life-time of Shree Chaitanya, the *Avatar* of Nadeeya and the founder of the Bengal School of Vaishnavism, Puri and Nadeeya were regarded, as Chaitanya's mother put it in her homely way, as "this house and that house" inside the same homestead. There was in those days an almost constant flow of pilgrims from Bengal to Orissa. This helped to spread the culture and with it also the literature of Bengal among the Oriyas, and bring back to Bengal in return valuable elements of Oriya culture and literature. The movement of Shree Chaitanya exerted perhaps deeper and wider influence among the people of Orissa than even among the Bengalees themselves. The element of protest against Brahminical caste and ritualism of Shree Chaitanya's movement was soon overwhelmed by the influence of the Bengal Brahmins, who captured even during the life-time of Shree Chaitanya, the leadership of the movement. There are ample evidences of it all through in the sacred literature of Bengal Vaishnavism created or collated within a very few years of the ascension of its originator. Brahminical influence is unmistakable in "Shree Chaitanya-Charitamrita," the universally accepted Bible of the Bengal Vaishnavas. The most powerful cultural influences in the new cult were the two brothers, Rupa and Sanatana, and their nephew Jeeva, who developed the new philosophy and art of Bengal Vaishnavism, inspired by the life and experiences of its great founder, Shree Chaitanya Mahaprabhu; and both Rupa and Sanatana repeatedly confessed to their low origin and untouchable caste. This is interpreted by later Brahminical apologists not as something which was literally true but as the expression of the Vaishnavic spirit of humility, and as a confession of the degradation to which these Fathers of the new Vaishnavic Church subjected themselves by taking service under and accepting the wages of the Moslem rulers of Gauda. They fell off from their Brahminical sanctity through association with the *mlechhas*. Whether these two brothers and their nephew Jeeva were really Brahmins or not, seems to be doubtful, though all the Vaishnava writers have made strenuous efforts to prove that they were really Brahmins. In any case, if Brahmins at all, they must have been Brahmins who had fallen off from Brahminical purity and relegated to the level of the untouchables in Hindu society like the *peerali* Brahmins of our own day. While we find this attempt to Brahminise the non-Brahmins in Bengal Vaishnavism, in Orissa we find the contrary process of non-Brahminisation, so far as this could be, of the Brahmins themselves. In Orissa there are the holiest of holy Brahmins, the priests of the temple of Jagannath, whose family title is *Dasa*. *Dasa* is the title of the non-Brahmins; literally it means a servant or a slave. And that the Vaishnava Brahmins of Orissa should have adopted this surname or title seems to my mind to be an incontrovertible evidence of the greater hold of the followers of Shree Chaitanya in Orissa on the divine democracy which he promulgated than in Bengal.

What the Lutheran movement did in the history of the Christian Church that was done by the movement of Shree Chaitanya in the evolution of Hinduism in Bengal. All the religious books of the Hindus were written in Sanskrit, starting with the Vedas and ending with the Puranas. All the sacred *mantrams* or texts used in worship and the cultivation of the spiritual life were in Sanskrit, and even these Sanskrit texts were not easy of comprehension. The ancient formula of Brahminical worship, the *Gayatree* taken from the Vedas, universally used by the Brahmins all over India, was hardly understood by the multitudes who mechanically repeated it three times a day. Shree Chaitanya however offered a simple substitute for this difficult and un-understood formula. The repetition of the name of the Lord, he declared, was more than enough to acquire the knowledge and the love of the Deity. All or almost all the literature of the Chaitanya religion were composed in the current vernacular of the province, and this found a new incentive to the large and growing congregation of Vaishnavas to acquire sufficient knowledge of their own vernacular to be able to read their holy books, as this was enjoined as part of their daily devotional exercises. The immediate result of it was a remarkable spread of literacy among the Vaishnavas of Bengal. Vaishnavism in Bengal had from the time of Shree Chaitanya himself been divided into two camps; in one camp stood the followers of the Mahaprabhu belonging to the so-called higher castes who, while accepting his religious and spiritual message, quietly ignored the great message of social democracy which he delivered to them and who, therefore, while they even worshipped him as the very God of Gods, continued still to follow in their domestic and social life and disciplines, the law of Manu and other Brahminical law-givers. They were known as Vaishnavas who still stuck to the *Smritis*. Side by side with these there was another class of Vaishnavas, who not only accepted the religious and spiritual teachings of the Master, but also loyally followed the social law of freedom and equality inculcated by him. These were known as "caste Vaishnavas," who stood practically outside the heirarchy of Hindu castes and were therefore relegated by the Brahmins to a lower and almost untouchable social grade. I do not know if the Vaishnavas of Orissa practically adopted the social code of Shree Chaitanya and whether there exists among the Oriyas a section of Vaishnavas corresponding to the "caste Vaishnavas" of Bengal. But whether the ideal of social democracy of the movement of Shree Chaitanya was practically adopted by his followers in Orissa or not, the moral influence of it is still seen in the repudiation of all Brahminical titles and family names by them, such as we do not find in Bengal. The only attempt made in this direction by the Bengalee followers of Shree Chaitanya was not towards social democratisation but on the contrary rather towards social aristocratisation. Every Vaishnavic teacher to whatever caste, Brahminical or non-Brahminical, he might belong, became a *Goswami* or "lord of the earth." Even the so-called untouchables, not to mention of mere non-Brahmins, thus became Gosains or Goswamis in Bengal; while in Orissa the highest Brahmins abandoned their Brahminical patronymic or surname and styled themselves as *Dasa*, which was the general title of the Sudras. This to my mind conclusively proved the stronger and deeper hold that the Chaitanya movement had upon the people of Orissa than even upon the people of his own native province.

It helped also to a closer racial and cultural fusion between Bengal and Orissa than was found between any other neighbouring provincialities. This old process of inter-provincial union or fusion was further advanced under British rule by the establishment of a common Administration over these two provinces. Bengalee promised to become the cultural language of Orissa when I first went there. Bengalee was in many places the second language in the Orissa schools, as in Bengal proper. There was as yet no jealousy of the Bengalee among the people of Orissa. In fact, the makers of modern Orissa were, almost without a single exception, domiciled Bengalees. The cry of Orissa for the Oriyas had not as yet been raised, and economic competition had not commenced as yet to create a serious bar to inter-provincial fusion and unity. Educated Bengalees had themselves no conceit of provinciality, and looked upon Orissa as much as their own mother-country as they did upon Bengal proper. The old Oriya language and literature were indeed closely akin to the ancient Bengalee language and literature. When I first went to Orissa in 1879, my contact with Oriya language and literature created the impression upon me that these represented only an ancient and archaic type of Bengalee language and literature itself. The rising generation of Orissa were as eager to study the Bengalee language and literature as they were to cultivate their own mother tongue.

Cuttack had been from of old the seat of the Hindu Government in Orissa. Under the British also Cuttack continued to be the principal city in Orissa. It was the seat of the Commissioner of the Orissa Division. Cuttack was also the centre of the intellectual and cultural life of the province. As early as 1841 an English school had been established in Cuttack. This was raised to a High School affiliated to the Calcutta University in 1868. Eight years later, in 1876, Cuttack was endowed with a full-fledged college teaching up to the M. A. degree examination of the University of Calcutta, supported by Government and controlled by the Department of Public Instruction, Bengal. The college was named after Mr. Ravenshaw, who was Commissioner of Orissa at one time.

The most prominent public man in Cuttack, when I went there was Babu Gouri Sankar Roy, who edited a Oriya weekly, the "*Utkal Darpan*," and was Secretary of the Cuttack Printing Company. This company not only owned a printing press and the weekly newspaper, but also had built a public hall, the Cuttack Printing Hall, in which was located a public library. This Printing Hall was a great influence in those days in the cultural life of young Oriyas; and it was here that I came in close contact with the representatives and leaders of the new intellectual and national movement in Orissa.

The school to which I was appointed as Headmaster was a private school. In those days private schools were springing up almost all over Bengal to meet the increasing demand for English education of our people. Even where we had Government schools these were not adequate to meet the educational requirements of the localities where they had been established. There was not sufficient accomodation for the large and increasing number of students eager to have English education. They were also comparatively more expensive than the private institutions. Public spirited young men, who had themselves received a fairly high education and who were moved by the new spirit of patriotism and public service, oftentimes set up these schools, and found their life-work here. Babu Peary Mohan Acharya, the founder and proprietor of the Cuttack Academy, belonged to this type of our old educated countrymen. Passing out of college before taking his degree he started this school, and became himself its Rector. He had a fairly good income from his landed properties, and had therefore no imperative need to seek Government service. He had been drawn to the Brahmo Samaj and was a leading member of the local Brahmo congregation. In inviting me to take charge of his school, Babu Peary Mohan was moved also by a desire to get a Brahmo worker in his town.

The Ravenshaw College, Cuttack, was then manned practically by Bengalees. Babu Sashi Bhusan Datta, who subsequently rose to a senior place in the Bengal Educational Service, and was a senior professor in the Presidency College, Calcutta, at the time of his retirement some years ago, was Professor of Philosophy in Cuttack in the early seventies. Babu Kshirode Chandra Roy, a well-known Bengalee man of letters and the first Bengalee anthropologist, had been for many years Headmaster of the Collegiate School in Cuttack. He was Headmaster of the Puri High School when I went to Cuttack. Both Babu Sashi Bhusan Datta and Babu Kshirode Chandra Roy were members of the Brahmo Samaj. They had both been initiated in 1870 or '71 by Keshub Chunder Sen. Babu Bhairab Chandra Banerjee was the leader of the District Bar in Cuttack in those days, and he too was, though not a member of the Brahmo community, an honest sympathiser of the movement, and if I remember aright, he occasionally officiated as Minister of the Brahmo Samaj in Cuttack. His relations, however, were more intimate with Maharshi Devendra Nath and the Adi Brahmo Samaj than with the Brahmo Samaj of India. It was here at Cuttack that I made the acquaintance of Principal Girish Chandra Bose and the late Mr. Byomkesh Chakravarty. Mr. Bose had, I think, his first appointment in the Bengal Education Service as Professor of Science and was posted to the Ravenshaw College. Mr. Chakravarti also went at the same time to Cuttack as Professor of Mathematics. It was here at Cuttack that I entered public life as Minister of the local Brahmo Samaj and general lecturer on both social and political subjects. Among those whose friendship I was privileged to have at Cuttack were the late Babu Radhanath Roy and the late Babu Madhusudan Rao. Radhanath Babu was at that time Deputy Inspector of Schools in Cuttack and Babu Madhusudan Rao was an assistant teacher in the Collegiate School. Babu Radhanath was already a recognised Oriya poet. Though not a member of the new Brahmo community, he had, like the majority of English-educated Bengalees of that generation, sincere sympathies with the Brahmo

Samaj movement. Babu Madhusudan Rao, as his name shows, was a domiciled Mahratta. He was practically a pioneer of the Brahmo Samaj in Orissa, being among the very first domiciled Brahmos in Cuttack who discarded the Brahminical thread, educated his daughters and when they were of age gave them in marriage in accordance with the Brahmo ritual. He was also a recognised Oriya writer and like Babu Radhanath left his impress upon the development of modern Oriya literature. Madhusudan Rao rose to a high position in the Education Service in Orissa, and retired from the post of the Head-master of the Cuttack Normal School. Though Government servants, both Babu Radhanath Roy and Babu Madhusudan Rao were among the leaders of the public life of Cuttack, if not of Orissa, in the eighties of the last century.

I was at Cuttack only for a year, or more correctly for ten or eleven months. As Head-master it was my duty, as it was also my right, to make selections of the candidates who would be allowed to appear at the Entrance Examination of the University from the Cuttack Academy. The test examination was held before the Puja vacation, and I selected, so far as I remember, four candidates for appearing at the University Examination the following November, and having filled up and signed their application forms I left these with the fees collected from them with the proprietor Babu Peary Mohan Acharya and came for the Puja vacation to Calcutta. On my return after the Pujas I found that one of the boys whom I had refused to send up for the Examination had got his application form certified and signed behind my back by the proprietor, who had also thrown away the other application forms signed and certified by me replacing these by fresh forms which were signed and certified by him. It was a denial of my right and my authority as Headmaster which I could not possibly submit to. Immediately upon my return to Cuttack I tendered my resignation and came back to Calcutta. One of the four students whom I had selected for the Entrance Examination from the Cuttack Academy stood first in the whole of the Orissa Circle at the Examination of 1879. Thus ended my first career as a school master. Short as it was, it was my first stepping-stone to public life, and I shall always be grateful to Providence and those who were His instruments in securing my first post as Headmaster of a High English school.

CHAPTER XIX.

"NATIONAL" EDUCATION AND PUBLIC ACTIVITIES IN SYLHET

Leaving Cuttack I came back to Calcutta not knowing exactly to what I should turn my idle hands now. As far back as 1874 young students from Sylhet reading in the Calcutta University had organised an association under the name of the Sylhet Union. Its main object was to promote closer relations between the different individuals belonging to Sylhet living in Calcutta for study or business. But it was recognised that such unity could not possibly be secured without active co-operation with one another in the pursuit of some common object. This object was found in the promotion of education, particularly female education, in the district from which they came. They were receiving a fairly high standard of modern education. They realised the value of this education to themselves and to the family from which they came. Naturally enough, they wanted their neighbours and less fortunate countrymen to participate in these benefits. Under inspiration of this patriotic motive these young students banded themselves into this Union for self-culture and patriotic service. Babu Jay Gobinda Shome became the President of this Union. With his association and under his guidance the Sylhet Union within a very short time received the recognition of the educated community of Sylhet. When I resigned from the Cuttack Academy Babu

Brojendra Nath Sen and Babu Raj Chandra Chaudhury also tendered their resignation; and the three of us came back to Calcutta. The Sylhet Union saw in our unemployment a splendid opportunity for opening a High English School in Sylhet. We offered our services almost as honorary workers in the proposed school. We went even further, and agreed to shoulder the financial responsibilities of it if only the Union would find funds for the initial outlay in house and furniture. We were sanguine of the success of the new institution. When the Sylhet Union was seriously considering this scheme, news came from Sylhet that a private Entrance School run by a Mahomedan gentleman and called the Mufti School had decided to close its door with the beginning of the next year (1880). Friends in Sylhet coming to know that I had left Cuttack wired to me forthwith to go to Sylhet and start a school there in place of the Mufti School. I handed over this telegram to the committee of the Sylhet Union, who replied that the Union was prepared to send me and my colleagues immediately to Sylhet and bear all our expenses provided the local gentry undertook to find or construct a school house and provide it with the requisite school furniture. This was undertaken by the educated leaders of the town. Thus when after leaving Cuttack I found myself practically at sea Providence opened a new field of service and self-fulfilment before me. About the middle of December, if I remember aright, I found myself once more in my native district. Both of my old colleagues from Cuttack went also with me.

In the summer of 1879 I had been to

Sylhet to meet my father. After I left the University and took service my father saw that he could not bring me back to the orthodox Hindu fold by cutting off supplies. When leaving Calcutta for Cuttack I wrote to him about it. He asked me to go home once to see him. This I did during the summer recess of my school. I had heard at Calcutta on my way back from Cuttack in May 1879 that my father was at our village home in Poil. So instead of going directly to Sylhet I went to Poil, leaving the steamer at a station near Habiganj, the Sub-Divisional headquarters of south-western Sylhet. But my father had already gone back to Sylhet. I had thus to travel by boat from our home at Poil to Sylhet. During summer the waterways in Sylhet get dried up and one travelling by boat has to follow the meandering course of the rivers which takes a much longer time than travelling by road or by boat during the rainy season. My father had been expecting me in Sylhet long before I actually reached it. And I heard it from friends that for almost a week previously he used to go to the river-ghat every evening in the hope of meeting my boat. I arrived one evening at about nine or ten. It was a tragic meeting between father and son. This was our first meeting after my mother's death about five years previously. During these five years I had not gone to Sylhet. During these five years my father had married again for the third time, because I had joined the Brahmo Samaj. He wanted to make a last effort to win me away from the Brahmo Samaj. A few minutes after I reached our home in Sylhet he called me to him, and said, "I know you must be very hungry after this long journey. But I have not as yet been able to decide what I should do with you, and I have therefore arranged only for some light refreshments for you. So you will take these things here in this room and pass the night. Tomorrow I shall decide whether I shall admit you into your rightful place in this family." Now that I have myself become a father I can very well realise how my father must have felt when for conscience' sake he could not receive me and dine with me that evening. The next morning he sent word to Mrs. Navakishore Sen, who occupied the same building with my father, and also to his close neighbours that if they received me in their own house and admitted me into their kitchen or dining room he would be forced to deny himself the pleasure of dining with them in the future. Mrs. Sen was four or five years older than myself. She used to call my mother as 'mother', and she always treated me as a younger brother. As soon as she heard that my father had practically put me out of caste, she sent for me and forcibly drew me inside her kitchen saying whatever my father might do, had my mother been living she would not let me go without my food the previous night or serve my meals as to an outcaste. "I am not willing to obey him in this matter, though he is almost a father to me,"—she declared. My father called me and told me that he would not take any notice of my conduct when I was away from home, but he desired this that as long as I was with him in Sylhet I should observe the rules of caste. I told him how could I observe what I believed to be false. Of course, I would not go out of my way to outrage his feelings, I assured him. But if a low caste person or a Mahomedan should enter my room when I was drinking a glass of water, I would neither throw that water away nor ask him to go out. My father held no further argument with me. He did not even utter a single angry word at the outrage I was committing on his social loyalties. He held out no threat to me. But telling a cousin of mine who was present at the interview and who lived in the same compound with my father with his family that he should provide my meals but must under no circumstance let me into his kitchen or dining room, as long as I was in Sylhet, my father walked away and the same evening left for his village home. Thus the breach between father and son became complete.

I believed, when called to take up this new work in Sylhet, that my father was away in our village home at Poil, having retired from his practice, and there was little chance of his coming to town at least immediately. So there would be no difficulty in taking up my residence, in any case for the first few days, in our own house in Sylhet. But as soon as my father heard that I was going to Sylhet to take up this new educational work, he wrote to Babu Navakishore Sen, who occupied part of that house, that under no circumstance I should be allowed to stay there. Thus I found myself in Sylhet in January 1880 openly excommunicated from society and formally and publicly cut off by my father.

We three, myself, Brojendra Nath Sen and Raj Chandra Choudhury, all Brahmos, excommunicated from the parent Hindu society, had thus to take a separate house. Our first difficulty was about domestic service. No Hindu would serve us. An old retainer of my father's agreed to do the necessary shopping for us and even cook our food provided we did not enter the kitchen, but he could not for fear of losing his own caste touch the leavings of our food, or wash and clean our plates and glasses. But after a few days even this help was refused us. His affection for me was deep and genuine, but the fear of losing caste on account of his close association with me was stronger; and almost with tearful eyes he came and asked my permission to take up his lodgings elsewhere, while he was ready to loyally serve as an orderly in the school. We then secured a so-called untouchable to do our shopping and cooking; but even he would not touch our leavings or clean and wash our platters and glasses. We had to engage a Mahomedan to do these works for us. He was employed as groom in Babu Navakishore Sen's stable. He used to come and clean and wash our plates twice every day. But this gave offence to many of our Hindu friends, who felt deeply hurt by our engaging a Mahomedan even for this work. Yet there were very few among English-educated Hindus of the town, who did not come and take their meals not exactly in strictest secrecy but almost in open secrecy with us, particularly every Saturday evening when we used to have a regular feast in our house on all sorts of forbidden delicacies ordered from the Mahomedan butler of the local Dak Bungalow. And it was the common talk of the town that the Mahomedan *syce* who came to clean and wash our plates and glasses found as many as twelve or fifteen plates and glasses put out for him every Sunday morning while his masters were only three. How three gentlemen could eat and drink out of as many as ten to fifteen plates and glasses was absolutely beyond his comprehension. The fact of the matter really was that almost every body in the local Hindu community knew who were our regular guests at these heterodox dinners, but no one dared or cared to kick up a row over it. This was in 1880, while ten years previously in 1870, people had been put out of caste for taking biscuits!

Our new school, which was christened as the Sylhet National School, was opened about the first or second of January 1888. By the end of March we had on our rolls about four hundred boys, or only just less than fifty of the number on the rolls of the old and well-established Government School. This was an achievement far beyond our wildest dreams. I was the Rector of this school, Babu Brajendra Nath Sen was mathematical teacher and Babu Raj Chandra Chaudhuri was teacher of history and geography. Another friend, Babu Radha Nath Chaudhuri, soon joined with the same status as ours, that is, as missionary workers, not engaged on any fixed salary but who agreed to take what remained from the collections after the other teachers had been paid and other incidental expenses had been met, in equal proportion as Brajendra, Raj Chandra and myself.

The advent of three full-fledged Brahmos, excommunicated for their loyalty to their convictions from the parent society, naturally lent new strength and inspiration to the

Sylhet Brahmo Samaj. I was soon elected a Minister of this congregation. Our activities were, however, not confined to the school and the Brahmo Samaj only. The ideal that possessed us was much larger. It was also social and political. The vow which I had taken to devote myself to the spiritual and religious regeneration of myself and my country as well as to secure the uplift of our people intellectually, morally, socially, and politically, aiming at the development of the highest ideal of Freedom personal, social and political, drove me at once to every field of our new public life in Sylhet. Even before I went to Cuttack, I had discovered my gifts of public speaking. At Cuttack I had found my first field for the cultivation of this gift. In Sylhet I found myself soon the public lecturer, who was requisitioned for every occasion, from the public meetings organised by local officials in furtherance of their own objects to demonstrations against official high-handedness or official measures distasteful to the people. I remember how I was invited by the District Magistrate to address a meeting convened by him with the Chief Commissioner of Assam in the chair to collect subscriptions in aid of the so-called Patriotic Fund which had been started by Lord Lytton's Government to help the families of the dead and disabled sepoys in the Afghan war.

But my first love was, of course, the Brahmo Samaj, and a systematic platform propaganda was started immediately I was established in Sylhet both among the youthful students and the general public which I had very largely to carry on myself. Nor was this all. A new political association of the name of the Sylhet Association was also started about this time with my old friend—alas now no more on this side—Nabin Chandra Sharma, a leading member of the District Bar, as Honorary Secretary, while I was appointed as its Honorary Assistant Secretary.

Sylhet had, as already recorded, a weekly Bengalee newspaper, the "Shrihatta-Prakas," founded by Babu Peary Charan Das. But it had, however, seen its best days. When I went back to Sylhet in 1880, this paper was in a moribund condition. Besides, the new thought and life in the town could hardly be put into this old bottle. So a small limited liability company was started with a realised capital of Rs. 2,500/-, with which a hand-press and necessary types and accessories were bought and taken from Calcutta. There were very few compositors and pressmen available in Sylhet in those days. Those who had learnt press work, three or four persons, were all employed in the Shrihatta Prakas Press, which even though the weekly news-sheet had ceased publication, still was working for printing notices and zemindary forms and returns etc. When this new press was bought, printers and compositors had to be taken along with it from Calcutta, while a pressman was imported from the neighbouring town of Mymensingh where already they had established a flourishing printing business round the weekly newspaper, "Bharat-Mihir," edited by the late Anath Bandhu Guha. Though a Maffassil publication, the "Bharat-Mihir" had from the very start secured for itself a high place in the Bengalee journalism of those days. Later on, about 1883 or '84, the "Bharat-Mihir" was brought down to Calcutta from Mymensingh. But it never got back its old place in Bengalee journalism. The "Bharat-Mihir" press however flourished in Calcutta and its proprietor, Babu Kali Narayan Sannyal, left behind him not only a rich printing establishment but also a premier type foundry in Bengal.

With the new men and printing materials a new Bengalee weekly was started in Sylhet about the middle of 1880, and I was invited to be its editor. When my father practically sent me away from his house in Sylhet, I with my Brahmo colleagues, Brajendra Nath Sen and Raj Chandra Chaudhuri, took up our quarters in a two-storied small building on the eastern bank of our local Lal-Dighi, at the back of our chief bazar, called "Bandar Bazar." This press was also housed in this building; while we occupied the first floor of it, the ground floor was given to the press. The name of our new Bengalee weekly was "Paridarshak" and the press was also registered under that name. Like the "Bharat-Mihir" of Mymensingh, the "Paridarshak" of Sylhet also almost from its birth commanded public attention and soon became one of the most powerful exponents of educated public opinion not only of the district of Sylhet but more or less of the whole province of Bengal. Brajendra, Raj Chandra and, later on, Radhanath Chaudhuri, all of us, worked both at the new National School and at this newspaper and press also. It was my first independent charge in journalism, and my subsequent career in this line has been very largely indebted to this first opportunity that my Sylhet friends found me. The Paridarshak Press initiated me also in the art of printing. Because, from the very first day that I was placed in charge of the "Paridarshak," I found that if we were to carry on this work regularly and efficiently, we would have to work out our freedom from the domination of the men who had been imported from Calcutta; and the only way to secure this was for us to learn and, if possible, master the printer's work, setting up matter, correcting proofs and even working the printing machine. And we all of us, more or less, soon mastered this art, and this had a very great moral influence upon our composing and printing establishment, who soon came to realise it that should they strike work or misbehave and force us to dismiss them for wilful misconduct, we could immediately wire for a fresh set of compositors from Calcutta and during the week or two that might take the new men to reach Sylhet, we would be able to maintain the regularity of our weekly issue.

During my stay in Sylhet in connection with the National School and the "Paridarshak," the wave of the new Hindu revival and reaction touched our little town also. While we were carrying on a somewhat vigorous religious and social propaganda along the lines of the Brahmo Samaj, a section of our educated fellow-townsmen started a counter propaganda in support of current Hindu ceremonials and institutions. For some time before the Cooch Behar marriage the Brahmo Samaj had been rapidly losing its hold on the educated Bengalee, and a movement of social and religious reaction had slowly been making head as a counter-blast to the Brahmo propaganda. The leader of this movement was my old friend the late Babu Bipin Behari Das. He had at one time joined the Brahmo Samaj and was one of the many young men of our University who enthusiastically welcomed Keshub Chunder Sen back home to Calcutta after his English visit. I had read a poem composed on that occasion by Babu Bipin Behari before I came to Calcutta. He was one of the most successful students in the University from our District. He had passed the M.A. degree examination early in the seventies and after taking his law degree he had joined the District Bar before I went back to Sylhet to take up this educational work in the new National School. In Calcutta Bipin Babu was more or less with Sundari Mohan and myself in our social reform activities. He belonged to the Shaha caste, who had in those days been regarded as untouchables by the higher caste Hindus. We refused to observe this iniquitous custom and freely dined with Shaha students who came from our District. Bipin Babu and his fellow-castemen openly commended us for our courage and liberalism as long as they were in Calcutta. But they took up a different attitude towards us in Sylhet. They too treated us as outcastes just as our Hindu relations did. Gradually Bipin Babu started with some others of his own caste a definite Hindu propaganda with the obvious object of fighting the movement of religious and social reform which the Brahmo Samaj represented and which in Sylhet we openly and somewhat vigorously tried to advance among the rising generation of our people. The strangest thing, however, which I soon discovered in this quarrel between us of the Brahmo Samaj and Babu Bipin Behari Das, advocating the cause of popular and orthodox Hinduism, was that the sympathy of practically the whole of higher caste Hindus was with us instead of being with Bipin Babu and his movement. And the reason of it was, as an old relation of mine one day frankly gave out, that even though I and my friends had abjured our ancestral faith and had openly broken away from the regulations of caste and ancient customs, our kinsmen could not get rid of their partialities for us. This relation of mine plainly told me, when I asked him how was it that he sided with me as against the defender of his own faith in this controversy, that notwithstanding anything that I might believe or do, I was one of them, while Bipin Babu was an untouchable and could set up no manner of pretensions to preach to the higher castes. It showed how in those days caste had completely usurped the place of religion in our old society.

During this controversy between us of the Brahmo Samaj and Babu Bipin Behari Das an interesting incident happened that unexpectedly brought new strength to our elbow. Rama Bai Sarasvatee, the well-known Brahmin lady, who in the company of her brother had come to Bengal from the Maharashtra and had been holding disquisitions with our Brahmin-Pandits and had won universal commendation as exceptionally learned, came on her second visit to Sylhet about this time. This encouraged our opponents who commenced to organise public addresses by Rama Bai and her learned brother on Hindu religion and traditions. When this new propaganda was going on, news came of the arrival in our distant town of a very learned Pandit from the Maharashtra, and he was immediately captured by the party of Babu Bipin Behari Das, and a public meeting was advertised to hear him. He was believed to be an orthodox Pandit who knew no language except his vernacular and, of course, Sanskrit. He was, therefore, advertised to deliver a lecture in Sanskrit on Hinduism. The hall was literally overcrowded not only by the English-educated residents of the town, but even orthodox Brahmins, who knew not a word of English and who were more or less untouched by modern influences flowing so strongly about them, came in large numbers from far and near to see and hear this great Pandit who could handle the divine language with the same ease and freedom with which people handle their vernacular. I and my friends of the Brahmo Samaj also went to hear this unknown Pandit. But naturally we took back seats at this pro-orthodox demonstration. From the very commencement of his address we were profoundly impressed by the wonderful facility with which he spoke in simple Sanskrit, as if instead of being what is called a dead language it was to him almost as much living as our own mother-tongue. This impression deepened more and more as he proceeded until the subject matter of his discourse revealed to our wondering mind that he was no mere Pandit as Pandits go, but possessed a very wide knowledge of modern researches and investigations. In fact, though he had been advertised to lecture on Hinduism, he commenced to tell us how through the discovery of Sanskrit, the thought of the whole world was rapidly being revolutionised. He commenced to severely criticise our ancient methods of education and put forward a powerful plea for a more intelligent study of our own ancient language and literature. In fact, his lecture seemed to deal not with Hindu religion at all but with modern comparative philology. This seriously upset Babu Bipin Behari Das and the other conveners of this meeting. Pandit Shrinivasa Shastree, Pandita Rama Rai's brother, had been put on the presidential chair. As the lecturer commenced to develop his theme, the organisers became more and more impatient and repeatedly slip after slip commenced to pass from Bipin Babu to the president urging him to pull the lecturer back to his theme of Hindu religion. When this was being insisted upon, the lecturer suddenly broke out in English, and so pure was his language and so perfect his intonation that he literally took the breath of his audience away by this revelation of his education and modern culture. Without wasting a moment's time, he said: "Gentlemen, I must no longer conceal my identity. My name is Shreepada Babaji Thakur. I belong to the Bombay Civil Service. I had been to England to pass the usual competitive examination to enter the Civil Service." And having thus introduced himself to the audience, he spoke in English on comparative philology and the necessity of a more intelligent and critical study of our ancient language and literature not only to learn the niceties of grammar and lexicon but what was far more important, to realise how these old books gave ample and incontrovertible evidences of the outer historical and commercial no less than cultural relations of our mother-country with all the advanced countries of the ancient world. This lecture completely turned the table against those who had got it up with the hope of strengthening their reactionary movement and putting down the Brahmo propaganda. Shreepada Babaji Thakur became from the next day our guest, was housed in the furnished and commodious garden house of one of the leading Mahomedan zemindars of the town.

The secret of his romantic adventure soon came out. He had come to Sylhet *incognito*, not to preach Hinduism or out of idle curiosity to see this out-of-the-way town among the hills of Cachar and Jaintiya, but to woo and if possible win the fair widow, Rama Bai Sarasvatee, for his wife. His object in agreeing to lecture to us in Sanskrit was to meet Rama Bai on the same platform and conquer her, if possible, by establishing a strong intellectual kinship with her. But this was not to be, because, somehow or other, Rama Bai refused to attend his lecture. Thus disappointed he found that he had no reason to continue to conceal his identity. He stayed as our guest for a couple of days, and then went back to Bombay, a disappointed suitor for the hand of the famous Pandita.

The real cause of his disappointment came out in course of the next month or two. When Shreepada Babaji Thakur went to Sylhet Rama Bai's heart had already been either captured or was in the process of being captured by Babu Bipin Behari Das. Bipin

Babu had a commanding presence. Tall of stature, strong of limbs, well-knit and well-proportioned physique, he was so made that his very sight had a fascinating appeal even to men, how much more was it likely to appeal to a woman. To this physical presence was added intellectual acquisitions of no mean order, and these must have combined to capture the senses and the intelligence of the learned Pandita. Bipin Babu followed her from Sylhet to Dacca, and his pertinacity was ultimately rewarded. In the autumn of 1880 the Pandita was joined in wedlock to this Bengalee from Sylhet. The marriage took place at Bankipore, and was registered under the Civil Marriage Act, Act III of 1872. Mr. Beveridge and his wife, who had themselves been married under this Act, helped the marriage of the Pandita by their presence and patronage. Mrs. Beveridge had come out to India to take charge of the Banga Mahila Vidyalaya started by Babus Durga Mohan Das and Ananda Mohan Bose to provide high liberal education in English to the ladies of the progressive section of the Brahmo Samaj. Her maiden name was Miss Ackroyd. Mr. Beveridge had always great sympathy with the movement of social and religious freedom represented by the Brahmo Samaj, and this common sympathy brought him and Miss Ackroyd together, ultimately leading to their marriage. Babu Bipin Bihari Das's marriage with Pandita Rama Bai Sarasvatee and his consequent excommunication from his caste and community was an instance of poetic justice.

During my stay in Sylhet in connection with the new National School my father made one more attempt to win me back. About the middle of the year he came to the town for this purpose. The ostensible object of his visit was to make his last will and testament disinheriting me. All his friends in Sylhet, members of the Subordinate Judicial and Executive Services, as well as his colleagues at the Bar, tried hard to dissuade him from taking this step. But he was as firm as adamant. The utmost that he was induced to do was to agree to allow me to continue my work in the School, the Brahmo Samaj and on the "Paridarshak", and make an allowance of Rs. 100 a month as my pocket money if I went and took up my residence in his town house by myself. His object was to separate me from Babu Raj Chandra Choudhury, who had discarded the Brahminical thread and had thereby openly broken away from the Hindu communion. Association with him made me liable to the same punishment. As a non-Brahmin I had no sacred thread to throw away. So far my repudiation of my allegiance to Hindu orthodoxy had been more or less verbal. I was no doubt publicly taking forbidden foods and drinks, but Hindu society had already commenced to tolerate these petty lapses in her rebellious children. Some of my relations and friends freely dined with us and enjoyed these forbidden victuals. All this was well-known, but nobody caused any trouble over these violations of orthodox rules. My father saw that society would equally similarly tolerate my lapses also if only I separated myself from my friend, Babu Raj Chandra Choudhury, who had burnt the bridge behind him. My father's friends tried to persuade me to accept this generous offer of his. I was then suffering almost perpetual privations, the income from the School left very little to us, that is, Brajendra Nath, Raj Chandra and myself, after the other teachers had been paid. The "Paridarshak" was also not as yet a paying concern, and I received nothing for my work as its editor. It so happened therefore that many a day we had to live on one meal only. In the face of these difficulties and privations an allowance of a hundred rupees a month would certainly be a great help to me and to my work. This is how my father's friends put the case before me. But I was mortally afraid of accepting this help from him, particularly as his offer was conditional upon my separating myself from Raj Chandra Choudhury. My privations and sufferings were themselves a source of very great moral strength to me. If I accepted my father's offer and entered a life of comparative ease and physical comforts, my inner strength, I felt, would commence to decrease; and on the other hand my father also would be encouraged to turn the screw more and more until my defeat was completed and I deserted the Brahmo Samaj and the cause for which it stood openly for the lure of physical comforts and worldy conveniences. These considerations saved me by the grace of God from walking into this trap. My reply to my father's offer was that if he allowed me to go to his town house and take up my residence there with my Brahmo colleagues I would gladly and gratefully do so. But to accept his offer with the condition attached to it would mean open disloyalty to my conscience and to my religious principles. I could not, therefore, honestly accept that offer. This was my father's last attempt to win me back. When I refused to accept this offer he made his will. By this will he directed that after his death his main properties would be devoted to the maintenance of a school and a hospital in his native village. As for my step-mother and widowed sister and her little daughter, they would be entitled to an allowance adequate for keeping them in the station of life to which they belonged. Further, it was also provided that the continuance of the family worship and *pujas* would be secured by the income of his property. My father's friends, who were anxious to protect my interests, failing to dissuade him from disinheriting me completely, made a last appeal to him to dispose of his property just as he liked, but only as a mark of his affection for and confidence in me, to nominate me as the executor of his will. At this my father made a characterstic reply, saying, that it would be quite in the fitness of things that in arranging for the annual Durga Puja his family would have to come to a *Cazi* or a Moslem judge, to secure his sanction. This silenced those who were fighting for me, and the separation between father and son not only during his life but even after his death was thus completed. From this time my father would not hold any communication with me. He refused to accept my letters. He would not permit me to go near him, not even when, as happened during his short stay at Sylhet about the middle of 1880, he was ill and I wanted to see him.

The rather heavy strain on my strength, caused by hard work and insufficient nourishment, soon commenced to tell on my health.

In June or July 1880, Keshub Chunder Sen completely cut himself off from the old ideals and doctrines of the Brahmo Samaj, as we then thought, and proclaimed the advent of his Nava-Vidhan or New Dispensation. This provoked a new and vital conflict between him and his following on the one side and the general body of Brahmos on the other. The wave of this new moral and theological war did not take long to reach us even in far distant Sylhet. We had in the local Brahmo Samaj a few loyal followers of Keshub. And a debate was proposed to be held between them and us, who were members of the Sadharana Brahmo Samaj. This meeting was held one evening, and practically the entire educated community of the town, numbering over five hundred, gathered to hear this debate. At this debate I was on my legs from seven in the evening to nearly eleven at night. The whole audience sat out this long meeting and listened to our discussion with absorbing interest. The next morning I started spitting blood, not in large quantities but in deep red streaks. This frightened the local doctors, who ordered me to take leave of my school immediately, and as the damp climate of Sylhet was considered extremely dangerous for one who was suspected of pulmonary affections, I was forced to come to Calcutta for treatment. Thus was prematurely cut off my educational and journalistic and missionary career in my own native District. I had not the wherewithal to meet the expenses of this change and rest. These were found by friends, and I found myself back in Calcutta by the end of July 1880. Sundari Mohan without consulting me wrote to my father immediately he came to know of my condition asking for his help. My father replied that he did not recognise me as his son and accepted no manner of obligation for my health or my life. God's will must prevail in this matter. However, if I agreed to perform expiation and re-enter Hindu society, he would immediately come down to Calcutta with his family and take charge of my treatment and nursing. This was his last offer. If I refused to accept it, he would on his part completely wash his hands of one who had wilfully deserted his proper place and who was no longer his son. Expert medical opinion in Calcutta, however, did not find any reason to suspect any pthisical tendency in me. But the doctors here did not advise me to go back to Sylhet. So I had to definitely abandon my post in the Sylhet National School, my place being gradually taken up by Babu Radha Nath Chaudhuri, who conducted it until his death at an early age, about the middle of the eighties of the last century. After his death the Sylhet National School was taken over by Raja Girish Chandra Ray, and became the foundation of the present Murari Chand College. And as for myself, I soon found a new place at Bangalore in Mysore, where I went about the end of August 1881, as Headmaster of Rai Bahadur Arcot Narayanswamy Mudaliar's High English School.

CHAPTER XX.

MADRAS FIFTY YEARS AGO

Madras and Bengal have come very close to each other today. When I first went there in 1881, it was more or less an unknown land to us. I think, Keshub Chunder Sen was the first educated Bengalee to visit Madras in the late sixties of the last century. That visit of the young Brahmo leader was followed by that of Bhai Amritalal Bose, who made a fairly extensive tour and long stay in that Presidency in connection with the missionary propaganda of the new Brahmo Samaj of India. He met with cordial reception from some sections of the people, particularly the Kanarese. When Amrita Babu went to Bangalore, he found a strong colony of Kanarese residing in the cantonment there. They were drawn to the Brahmo Samaj by the preachings of Bhai Amritalal and established a Brahmo congregation in Bangalore. With the transfer of their regiment from Bangalore to Mangalore, this congregation was also removed to that town where there is now a strong Brahmo Samaj, the members of which follow the Brahmo laws of domestic and social life. The next Bengalee who visited Madras was Pandit Shivanath Shastri. After his ordination as Minister and missionary of the Sadharana Brahmo Samaj, Pandit Shastri went on a missionary tour to the Southern Presidency. In course of this tour he visited both the city of Madras, and Bangalore among other Mafassil places. This first visit of his was followed, I believe, by other missionary tours in that Presidency. And it was through him that I secured the post of Headmaster in Rai Bahadur Arcot Narayanswamy's High School at Bangalore. Mr. Gopalswamy Iyer was at that time the Headmaster of the Regimental School at Bangalore. This school was maintained by the Military Department for the benefit of the members of the Indian regiment stationed at Bangalore and their boys. Mr. Gopalswamy was associated with the local Brahmo Samaj, originally established by the leaders of the Canarese sepoy colony when that regiment had been stationed at Bangalore. Gopalswamy was a fairly educated man and had the qualities of popular leadership to some extent. Though a poor school master, Gopalswamy was a recognised public man in the civil and military station of Bangalore, commanding by his character considerable influence over the educated community of the place. It was mainly through his influence, I believe, that Rai Bahadur Arcot Narayanswamy Mudaliar, one of the multi-millionaries of the place, had been drawn to the Brahmo Samaj. Narayanswamy started life in humble circumstances. The famine of the early seventies, that decimated the whole Presidency of Madras, found him his opportunity. Starting with some petty contracts for the supply of rice to the famine-stricken people in connection with Government relief measures, Arcot Narayanswamy soon rose to a high position as Government contractor, and it was by this work that he gradually built up his large fortune. At the close of the famine operations, Arcot Narayanswamy found himself the owner of many lacs and the proprietor of the largest and richest miscellaneous stores in Bangalore. His services in connection with famine relief in his district were rewarded by the Government by a Rai Bahadurship, which has become very cheap today but which was a rare and, therefore, much coveted distinction fifty years ago. Narayanswamy encouraged by this recognition, and moved, I have no doubt, equally by the desire to devote some portion of his unexpected fortune to the service of his God through service of His children, established and endowed this High School. Though not socially a Brahmo, Rai Bahadur Arcot Narayanswamy had imbibed deep respect for the ideals of the Samaj and held the character of the Brahmos in very high regard. Pandit Shivanath had been to Bangalore in 1879 and '80, when he made the Rai Bahadur's acquaintance. The Rai Bahadur was anxious that the rising generation of his countrymen should come under the moral influence of the Brahmo Samaj and therefore asked Pandit Shivanath to find a Brahmo young man from Bengal to take charge of his school as headmaster. When I came back from Sylhet to Calcutta and was without any employment, Pandit Shivanath asked me to take up this work and go to Bangalore as Headmaster of this school where, he said, I would find a large and virgin field for Brahmo mission work also.

When sending me off to Bangalore Pandit Shivanath Shastri told me that I would find there a group of educated young men who cut their hair like ourselves and used boots and shoes. I asked him what was the meaning of it. He smiled and said, "They are the advanced reformers in Madras." Cutting the hair instead of shaving the head as orthodox

Brahmins did and using boots and shoes instead of slippers and sandals indicated social revolt in the Madras Presidency. That was the state of things in Madras when I first went there in the autumn of 1881. I took train at Howrah. If I remember aright I travelled by the Punjab mail. Locomotion was much slower then than it is to-day. It takes now about fifteen hours to reach Allahabad from Calcutta. When I first went, it took about twenty-four hours to get to Allahabad. From Allahabad, after a halt of nearly an hour, the train for Bombay recrossed the Ganges and coming back to Naini branched off towards Jubbulpore. Jubbulpore was reached, if I remember, the next evening. At Jubbulpore I had to transfer myself to the G. I. P. train, and after thirty-six hours arrived at Bombay in the morning of the third day from Jubbulpore. The journey though long was, however, not at all tedious to me because of the new experience that I was getting. The greater part of the way from Jubbulpore to Bombay was in those days through extensive and more or less dense forests. All that wilderness has been practically cleared to-day. Mr. Rajani Nath Ray, who at the time of his death in 1906, was officiating as Accountant General, Bengal, was Assistant Accountant-General in Bombay in 1881. Babu Rajani Nath was a member of the Brahmo community. After an exceptionally brilliant career in the Calcutta University from which he passed with honours in mathematics, taking the first place in the examination of his year, Rajani Nath was appointed to the Finance Department of the Government of India. Before he passed out of the University he had publicly joined the Brahmo Samaj, having been initiated by Keshub Chunder Sen either in 1870 or '71. After passing his final examination in the University, Rajani Nath married Sreematee Bidhumukhi in accordance with the new Civil Marriage Act, his marriage being one of the earliest to have been performed under that Act. The life-story of Bidhumukhi was highly romantic. It was the subject of a small book "Bidhumukhi-charit," which was very popular at one time, particularly among members of the Brahmo Samaj. It was the story of a *kulin* girl of Bikrampur, Dacca, who was rescued from marriage with an old man with many wives, and who found rest and shelter after an anxious chase by the emissaries of her guardians in the Brahmo home for missionaries and workers, called the Bharata-Ashrama, in Calcutta. She was secretly helped out of the family residence of her people by two young relatives who had already joined the Brahmo Samaj. They were two brothers, Sarada Nath and Baroda Nath Halder. Saroda Nath died young; Baroda Nath married in the Brahmo Samaj. Basanti Devi, Mrs. C. R. Das, is Barada Babu's eldest daughter. Mr. S. N. Halder, Barrister-at-law, is Baroda Babu's second child and only son. They rescued Bidhumukhi at the risk of their very life, because Bidhumukhi's guardian was a man of great power and influence in his locality in those days. Law and order had not as yet been fully established in the Mafassil parts of Bengal even in the early seventies of the last century, and the local zemindars oftentimes held not only the person and property but even the very life of their neighbours in the hollow of their hands. As soon as it was discovered that Bidhumukhi had been secreted away from her home by the young Halders, messengers were despatched on all sides in pursuit of them. If they had been caught before they got into the railway train at Kusthia, it was practically certain that all three would have been murdered and their dead bodies thrown into the Padma, and if discovered subsequently, nobody would know as to how or by whom they came to their end. After the break-up of the Bharata Ashrama, Bidhumukhi found a home with Mr. Durga Mohan Das. She was brought up by Mr. Das along with his daughters in the Banga Mahila Vidyalaya. Rajani Nath also came from Dacca and the element of romance in the earlier life of Bidhumukhi was not absent even when she accepted Rajani Nath's offer of marriage. But their marriage could not be immediately performed owing to the fact that Bidhumukhi had not as yet attained the twenty-first year of her age, and her natural guardian, not being a member of the Brahmo Samaj, could not possibly be induced to give his permission for this marriage, as was required by the terms of the new law.

When, on my way to Madras, I landed at Bombay,—that was the only route then from Calcutta to Madras by land and rail, neither the East Coast Railway from Madras to Waltair, nor the Bengal Nagpur Railway had then been opened, it is doubtful if these had even been under contemplation,—I found Mr. Rajani Nath's carriage waiting at the station for me. Mr. and Mrs. Ray were then living at Bandora, one of the suburbs of Bombay. I was their guest for about a week. That was a new and really inspiring experience to me. Bombay was socially far ahead of Bengal. Bengal, or the new Bengal which was building before our eyes, was the creation, really of the British. All our progressive movements had been born of the inspiration of freedom and democracy caught by us from our contact with modern European, particularly modern British, culture through our schools and colleges. But Bombay was different. Bombay had very recently a national State and Administration. In Maharashtra the Peshwas governed the people to almost the middle of the nineteenth century, that is, about fifty years or thereabout before I first saw it. And this national State had developed certain traits in the Mahratta people and called into being certain social institutions and customs under pressure of what can be best described as the biological requirements of the Marhatta society, which we had no knowledge of in Bengal. Female education and the freedom of social intercourse and movement of respectable Mahratta ladies was a new and inspiring experience which I had in Bombay. Both the Parsis and the Mahrattas did not observe the *zenana* seclusion or the *purdah*, which is universal among higher class Hindus and Moslems in Bengal and Upper India. While we in Bengal were fighting even in the Brahmo Samaj for higher education of ladies and the removal of the *purdah*, these social evils were practically absent from the Indian community of Bombay. And all this made a very profound impression upon me during my first visit to this city.

I took train at Bombay for Madras. The

railway route between Bombay and Madras passes across the Ghats. The scenery between Kalyan and Poona is perhaps the most beautiful to be found in any railway in India. The engineering skill displayed in building up this section of the Great Indian Peninsula Railway is also of the very highest order. I did not halt anywhere on my way from Bombay to Madras. I saw Poona some years later, on my way from Madras to Lahore after the Madras Congress of 1887. This time I went straight to Madras, changing at Raichur into the Madras Railway. If I remember aright, it took me about forty hours to reach Madras from Bombay. There was already a small Brahmo Samaj at Madras. A Telegu Brahmin of exceptionally simple habits and devout soul was the principal member of this Samaj. He was its Secretary and Minister. Pandit Shivanath Shastri knew this gentleman very intimately. His name was Butchia Pantalu. He came to receive me at the station, and I was his guest for two or three days until I took train for my destination. The Bangalore Mail, by which I travelled used to leave Madras in the evening and reached Bangalore early in the next morning. Thus one fine and sunny morning in the month of September I found myself at Bangalore. Mr. Gopalswamy Iyer came to the station and offered me a cordial welcome and practically took charge of me. As Headmaster of the Regimental School, Mr. Gopalswamy lived in Regimental quarters, and he found a room for me in the quarters of the Head Clerk of his school, Mr. Narayanswamy Mudaliar. There were two houses in these quarters. One was attached to the school itself, and the other stood facing it on the opposite side of the court-yard. Mr. Narayanswamy occupied this latter house with his family, while I was put up in the other house or room which had an ante-room or covered veranda that served as my kitchen.

Mr. Gopalswamy had asked one of his students, or more correctly one of his pupil-teachers, who lived in the school premises, to look after me. This was really very kind and considerate of him. Because I did not know a word of Tamil or Telegu or Kanarese, the three predominant vernaculars of the Mysore State. And it was absolutely necessary for me to have some one about me in my house who knew sufficient English to act as interpreter between me and the local domestic who kept house for me, acting both as cook and maid. My first experience in Bangalore was of such an amusing character that I have never been able to forget it. The second day of my sojourn in Bangalore early in the morning I suddenly woke at the sound of my name which was being cried from the street running by my house. It was—"Pal, Pal, O". I thought somebody was calling me. But for the life of me I could not understand who this somebody could possibly be. I knew no one as yet in this strange place. Those whose acquaintance I had made in course of the previous day, were not sufficiently familiar with me to address me as mere "Pal". When the next morning I asked my friend Mr. Narayanswamy, who could it be that called me early at the very break of day by my name, crying 'Pal, Pal, O', he laughed out and said, it must have been the milk-maid.

but she was not serenading under your window, fascinating young man, but only hawking her milk. *Pal* or more correctly *palo* is Tamil and Telegu for milk.

Before leaving for Bangalore I had been introduced to Sreematee Nritya Kali, a ward of Pandit Shivanath Shastri. Her's also was a romantic story. Married at the age of eight, she became a widow at nine. She came of a very respectable and high-caste Brahmin family. Her eldest brother was employed in the Government Telegraph Department. Early in the seventies of the last century, he was stationed at Allahabad. Like many a soft-hearted Hindu of that generation, he inwardly rebelled against the disabilities imposed upon young Hindu widows, and especially on those who were condemned to lifelong widowhood even before they knew their husbands or were of the age when they might be expected to realise the superb romance of married love or the sanctity of the marital relation. Like the general body of English-educated Bengalees he too had come under the influence of the Brahmo Samaj. Naturally he inwardly felt a desire to get his young sister remarried if that could be arranged. It so happened that at Allahabad he found for his immediate neighbour a Brahmo family, the mistress of which had been a Brahmin widow, coming from the same class to which he himself belonged, and who had been remarried in the Brahmo Samaj. This lady was the younger sister of the late Babu Chandi Charan Banerjee, the biographer of Pandit Ishwar Chandra Vidyasagar, and a well-known Bengalee writer. Negotiations were opened by Nritya Kali's brother to try if she could be similarly brought to the Brahmo Samaj with a view to her re-marriage. Of course, this could not be done publicly, as it would involve excommunication to her brother, who was not prepared to face it even for his sister's future happiness. In the meantime, Chandi Babu's sister commenced to work upon the tender mind of Nritya Kali and gradually induced her to leave her brother's home and come to the Brahmo Samaj. Her brother all along knew all this, though he dared not openly do anything in the matter. At last the situation seemed to have been seriously and suddenly complicated by some breach between Nritya Kali and her sister-in-law. This set fire to the train that had been slowly laid, and one day she left her brother's home and came to the house of Chandi Babu's sister determined to stay with her and thus cut herself free from the bondage of caste and custom, because Chandi Babu's brother-in-law was not a Brahmin but came from the carpenter caste. But this Brahmo family dared not accept her for fear of her brother and his friends. So she was at once removed to the family of a sympathiser of the Brahmo Samaj, who indeed was expected at that time to completely cast his lot with this new community of religious and social reformers. He was the late Babu Bipin Behari Bose, at that time working as Headmaster of the Government Collegiate School at Allahabad. This caused quite a storm not only in the Bengalee Hindu community of Allahabad but more or less all over Hindu Bengal. From Allahabad she was brought to Calcutta and placed in the family of Pandit Shivanath Shastri, where she soon won the place of almost a daughter of the family. I was soon accepted as a suitor of his adopted daughter by Pandit Shivanath and his wife, and before I left for Bangalore, we were formally engaged to be married. The idea was that after I had settled in my new place of work, I would return for a few days to Calcutta and after getting married go back to Bangalore. But Mr. and Mrs. Rajani Nath Ray wanted to have a Brahmo marriage in Bombay. So they arranged with Pandit Shivanath Shastri, who was going South on a mission tour, to bring his ward with him to Bombay and wanted me to come there during the Christmas vacation. Thus it was that mine was the first Brahmo marriage in Bombay though both the bride and bridegroom were not of Bombay but Bengalees. The marriage took place in the Prarthana Samaj Mandir at Girgaum. And after the ceremony my wife and myself were the guests of Mr. and Mrs. Madhodas Raghunathdas, who were the pioneers of the widow marriage movement in Bombay. It was here during my marriage that I first made the acquaintance of Mr. Chandravarkar, who soon became one of the leaders of Bombay public life and having succeeded Mr. Ranade in the High Court as a puisne judge, was knighted. Mr. Chandravarkar was at that time a junior Vakil in the Bombay High Court, though as editor of the bi-lingual weekly, "Indu-Prakas," that held more or less the same position in Mahratta journalism which our "Hindoo Patriot" held in Bengal, he was already a well-known public man in his province.

The life-story of Mr. Madhodas Raghunathdas had a fascinating romance about it. Madhodas Raghunathdas belonged to the Guzrati Bania community. He had acquired a fairly large fortune in his business as silk merchant. One day during the hot summer months while walking along the streets of Bombay he stopped at a road-side house, and asked for a drink of water. It was brought to him by a youthful widow, who at once moved him to pity at the contemplation of her miserable life as a Hindu widow. She was of his own caste. She was of attractive appearance. And then and there Madhodas, who had lost his wife and was himself a widower, made up his mind to woo and win this comely young widow for his wife. It was really what poets call love at first sight on both sides. Thus Dhankar Bai became Madhodas's wife. Their home gradually became the centre of the widow marriage movement in Bombay. Mr. and Mrs. Madhodas were very intimate friends of the Rays, Dhankar Bai was a particular friend of Mrs. Ray. And it was through her that my wife before her marriage became intimate with Dhankar Bai. This was how after our marriage we came to be the guests of Mr. and Mrs. Madhodas Raghunathdas. Their house stood next door to the Prarthana Samaj Mandir, and as Mr. and Mrs. Ray lived in the suburbs, the guests were entertained to dinner by Mr. and Mrs. Madhodas in their house after the ceremony in the Mandir. Mr. Madhodas subsequently built a new Hall in his compound and named it the Widow-Marriage Hall. Mrs. Madhodas after her husband's death, as in his life-time, offered shelter in her home here to many a young widow and helped to give them suitably in marriage. The last time I met her was in 1901, when I was present at a widow marriage celebrated in the Widow Marriage Hall. The bridegroom was a Guzratee Brahmin, Mr. Govindjee, whose "Atanka Nigraha" patent pills had already won very wide publicity in the country through advertisements that appeared in almost every newspaper and periodical all over India. I was then in charge of "New India" which also had been publishing his advertisement. Mr. Justice Chandravarkar, Mr. Bhajekar, and almost all the supporters and workers of the social reform movement in Bombay were present at this marriage which was celebrated with great *eclat*, Mrs. Madhodas standing as hostess at the reception and dinner that followed. That was the last time when I met her. She passed away a few years later, and with her passed a fascinating and powerful personality in the Social Reform Movement of Bombay. After my marriage my wife told me that Dhankar Bai preserved, as a holy memento the vessel or *lota* with which she first gave that drink to her future husband. I think she proudly showed it to me also.

After Christmas (1881) I went back to Bangalore. On my way from Bombay a rather strange incident happened which I have not been able to, and shall never, forget. Pandit Shivanath Shastri came to the Boree Bunder station to see my wife and me off. As the train moved he suddenly asked me if I had enough money with me to comfortably reach Bangalore. I said that I had, or that I would manage to reach Madras with what I had. As a matter of fact this was not the strict truth, though I had made up my mind to manage with what I had. The luggage charge had been overlooked and it was rather heavy. After paying for this, I actually found myself in possession of just fourteen annas to pay our way from Bombay to Madras. In those days they did not allow ladies to travel with their male escorts in third class between Bombay and Poona; because the train passed through a number of tunnels on this part of the journey, and third class carriages were not provided with lights during day time. So we were separated during this part of our journey to Madras. In the loneliness of my compartment I commenced to cast about as to how I should find necessary refreshments for my wife and myself with just fourteen annas from which I would have to pay also for coolies at the changing station, Raichur. So I decided to keep the condition of my purse from my wife and pretending that I had no desire for food, I would spend, in any case that evening, what was needed for her only. But we were rather punctilious in those days about our veracity. I could not, therefore, tell a lie to my wife that I was not hungry if really I was not full. So the first thing that I did on gettng down from the train at Poona was to drink a lot of water, after which I went and brought my wife to my compartment, or more accurately to an empty compartment into which the guard taking pity on this solitary young couple, put us. I then asked her what she would like to take. She asked me what I should desire. I told her that my stomach was full and I would not take anything that night. At this, she also said that she would have nothing unless I shared it with her. Her determination to do this forced me to make a clean breast of the ugly predicament which my want of calculation and foresight had placed me in. She put courage in me, saying, never mind, we could even manage with what we had. We would take that night cheap fruits and fried gram and the like, and spend something the next day, braving it out at night when we could fast in the hope that morning would take us to Madras where friends had already invited us to break our journey as their guests. Next morning we had some tea and biscuits and I had just a couple of annas in my pocket after paying the cooly who took our things from the G. I. P. train to the Madras train at the Raichar Junction. Having put our things in an empty compartment into which the guard very kindly put us, we were walking up and down the station platform, when a telegraph messenger approached me and asked if my name was Babu Bipin Chandra Pal. I said it was so, and at this he took out a telegram addressed to me and placed with it a ten-rupee note in my hand. I found that this telegram had been sent by Pandit Shastri with this money. Postal Money Orders had not as yet been introduced in India. Registered and insured covers used then to convey money from one part of the country to another. In case of emergency money could be sent by wire but not as money, but only as reply prepaid for the return message. The telegraph office sends now reply forms in these cases, but in those days, it used to deliver the amount deposited with the office of despatch in cash to the addressee of the telegram. The receipt of this money by wire struck me as a direct intervention of Providence. When I met Pandit Shivanath Shastri some months later, I asked how was it that he sent me to a roadside railway station this money. He told me that though I had told him that I would manage with what I had to reach Madras, he could not get a wink of sleep that night for us, thinking that we had no money to pay for our food on our way. So the first thing that he did the next morning was to send this money by wire to me at the first important changing station through which I would have to pass.

Looking back upon this incident I felt often that Pandit Shivanath was a fairly developed psychic subject, as our friends of the Theosophical Society would say. Indeed I had heard from Pandit Shastri himself of another experience of his which seemed to corroborate this view. At one time, before the birth of the Sadharana Brahmo Samaj, when spiritualism was much in vogue among some of our educated countrymen in Calcutta, Pandit Shastri was invited to attend a spiritualistic seance at the house of a friend interested in these experiments. Pandit Shastri commenced to write automatically, and the detailed story of a grave family scandal of a neighbour came out through his hand. He had no intimacy with this family and knew absolutely nothing of this scandal. But those who knew said that it was all true. This also proved his psychic endowments. But this strange revelation of a grave secret affecting the honour of a respectable family so staggered him that from that day he resolved never to dabble in spiritualism.

The Brahmo friends at Madras, headed

by Mr. Butchia Pantalu, had arranged almost a royal reception for us. They had specially hired a house for us, and here we stopped for five or six days, being entertained by them. They had indeed a fairly big "love-feast" in our honour to which almost all the members and sympathisers of the Samaj were invited. Besides, we were invited by individual friends to their homes and received presents of *saries* for my wife and *dhoties* for myself from them. I never dreamt when I went to Madras that I would find so many friends in that city and would be so warmly welcomed into their homes. This was specially unexpected, because many of those who did this for us had not cut themselves off from the old and orthodox society as we in Bengal had done. Our visit, however, loosened the old bonds of caste very largely among our Madras friends, and for this we felt sincerely grateful.

My stay in Bangalore was, however, not very long. I went there in August 1881, was married in December of the same year, but had to leave my post there in December 1882. Certain incidents happened about October or November 1882, which wounded my self-respect. It might not have been intentional but it destroyed the old relations that had grown up between the proprietor of the school where I was employed and myself. And I felt I could not continue in his service. So I sent in my resignation, not knowing anything of my future. Just about this time Babu Durga Mohan Das went to Madras to put his second daughter, the present Lady Bose, wife of Sir Jagadish Bose, who had passed the Entrance Examination of the Calcutta University that year, into the Madras Medical

College, which admitted Matriculates of any Indian University for medical studies and the medical degree. After settling her there in the family of a pious Danish missionary, Durga Mohun Babu went to Bangalore to see the place. He knew that I was living there and so came to see me. He sent his card to me and this took me by surprise. He had put up at a local European hotel. I insisted upon his coming to my humble quarters which he did the next day. My wife was then in a very poor state of health. Asked about the reason of it, I said that the climate of Bangalore did sot seem to quite agree with her. Durga Mohan Babu said that I must take her away from that place. I replied, how could I? I would have, for one thing, to find some other work for me, and for another, I had not even the wherewithal to pay for our passage to Calcutta. At this he assured me that all this would come. He then invited me to take charge of the education of his two younger sons, Satish Ranjan and Jyotish Ranjan whom he wanted to send to England to compete for the Indian Civil Service and would like to prepare them for it by withdrawing them from their school and placing them under a whole-time tutor. And he offered me this job and agreed to pay for our passage back to Calcutta. Thus quite unexpectedly succour came to me, and by the end of December 1882 I found myself once more among old friends in Calcutta.

I parted with sincere sorrow from the fairly large circle of friends whom we had acquired at that distant land. The credit was really not mine but my wife's. She had a personal magnetism that drew both men and women to her. Though she did not know English, yet her familiarity with Hindustanee which she had acquired during her sojourn with her brother in the United Provinces gave her a good medium of communication. But it was not her conversational powers, but the silent force of her character that really attracted those who came near her. And our departure from Bangalore so worked upon the feelings of the fairly large circle of our friends, both Hindu and Mahomedan, that for a full fortnight previous to our departure we were not permitted to keep our own house but were practically forced to take up our residence in a new and well-furnished house of a friend, Mr. Singaravelu Mudaliar, at that time employed in the office of the Mysore Dewan. This fortnight every evening there was one function or another, generally a dinner at the house of some friend, to which the entire group that had formed around us were invited. At these dinners Brahmins and non-Brahmins sat down together and there was also one or two Mahomedan friends who were never excluded from these. When we took train for Madras some of our friends accompanied us part of the way and I cannot recall at what distance from their home they took leave of us literally with tearful eyes and choking voices. Thus ended my life in Bangalore. It was a most tender and inspiring experience, and even today I cannot send my mind back to those happy and hopeful days without deep emotion.

CHAPTER XXI.

LORD RIPON AND THE NEW POLITICAL AWAKENING

In 1880 there was a change of Ministry in England. Lord Beaconsfield was defeated at the General Election of 1880. The most remarkable feature of this election was Gladstone's Midlothian campaign. The wave of enthusiasm created by that historic campaign in Great Britain touched even us in India. Indian politicians were particularly interested in this election because they had found reasons to believe that if Gladstone came back to power, he would try to undo all the evils that had been done by the Beaconsfield-Lytton Government in India. The Afghan war had already been condemned by the Liberal Opposition in Parliament. Lord Lytton's Indian Vernacular Press Act and the Arms Act had both found material for repeated attacks on the Government in the House of Commons. These were prominently dealt with by Mr. Gladstone in his indictment against the Beaconsfield Administration in course of his electioneering campaign. For the first time the Administration in India got incorporated into the policy of the Liberals in the House of Commons. I think for the first time, India became, during Gladstone's electioneering campaign, openly a party question. The victory of the Liberals roused considerable hope and enthusiasm in India. These were strengthened by the appointment of Lord Ripon to the Indian Viceroyalty to succeed

Lord Lytton. Lord Ripon was perhaps even better known as a religious man than as a politician. His entrance into the Catholic church created almost as much of a sensation in England as the conversion of Newman. It showed his courage of conviction. That fact created a favourable impression upon the educated mind in India. The genuineness of his piety was further proved by the selection of his Private Secretary, Col. Gordon. Unfortunately, however, Gordon resigned from his post before landing in India. It was believed that the character and traditions of the Indian Civil Service convinced him (with which evidently he became acquainted more intimately from his preparatory studies for equipping himself for his new responsibility during the voyage) of the stupendous difficulties, if not the utter impossibility, of establishing a righteous and Christian administration in India with such materials and under such influences. This was believed to be his reason for turning back from the very gate of India where he was coming to help the new Viceroy. These gossips were widely circulated at the time, and they helped to create favourable prepossessions in regard to the new Viceroyalty. Besides, Gladstone's Midlothian campaign had also created very large hopes in the political mind in India that the reactionary and repressive measures of the Government of Lord Lytton would be reversed by Lord Ripon, who was believed to have been specially commissioned by the Liberal Prime Minister to regain the lost loyalty of the Indian people to the British Power.

Lord Ripon did not take very long to give practical evidence of the new policy which he was charged to initiate. One of the very first measures of the new Viceroy was an Act repealing Lord Lytton's Vernacular Press Act. It evoked almost universal enthusiasm among our politically-minded. It was hoped that Lord Lytton's Arms Act would also be gradually repealed, as both these Acts had found materials to the new Premier for his indictment of the previous Administration. But while the Vernacular Press Act was repealed, Lord Lytton's Arms Act was allowed to stand on the Statute Book. But this disappointment was soon thrown into the background by other measures of a very far-reaching character initiated by the new Viceroy, directed towards the gradual evolution of a frankly democratic constitution in British India. Lord Ripon was, I think, the only British Viceroy in India who made an honest attempt to translate the principles and ideals of the Queen's Proclamation of 1858 into practical measures of the Indian adiministration. This was proved by his ill-fated Ilbert Bill. Those Englishmen who may be surprised at the later developments of political agitations in India might profitably turn to the history of the Ilbert Bill agitation to trace the psychological and moral origin of these. Our people really learnt the A. B. C. of seditious campaign against the Government from the agitations organised by their British fellow-subjects in India against the Government of Lord Ripon and particularly against the Viceroy personally. The Ilbert Bill was intrinsically a very insignificant measure. It was initiated by a minute by Mr. B. L. Gupta, an Indian member of the Covenanted Civil Service, one of the first three Bengalees (the other two were Mr. Romesh Chandra Dutt and Mr. Surendra Nath Banerjee) who had successfully competed for it. At that time he was the Police Magistrate of Calcutta. But owing to his race he was disqualified for trying European British subjects. This disqualification was unjust, and sought to cast a needless discredit and dishonour upon India-born members of the Covenanted Civil Service. They had not only passed a very rigid test on the same terms as the British members of the Service, but had spent the very best years of the formative period of their youth in England. Upon their return to their homeland, they practically lived in the same style as their brother Civilians, and almost religiously followed the social conventions and the ethical standards of the latter. In those days the India-born Civilian practically cut himself off from his parent society, and lived and moved and had his being in the atmosphere so beloved of his British colleagues. In mind and manners he was as much an Englishman as any Englishman. It was no small sacrifice for him, because in this way he completely estranged himself from the society of his own people and became socially and morally a pariah among them. He was as much a stranger in his own native land as the European residents in the country. Quite naturally, therefore, the India-born Covenanted Civilian felt keenly the indignity of the invidious distinction which the Criminal Procedure Code made between him and the British members of his Service in the matter of presiding over the trial of European British subjects in India when accused of any crime. Mr. B. L. Gupta's minute touched the sensitive conscience of the new Viceroy. Sir C. P. Ilbert was then his Law Member. And a small Bill was introduced by him into the Viceregal Legislative Council to remove this invidious distinction between Indian and British members of the Covenanted Civil Service. The introduction of this apparently just and inoffensive measure was the signal for a tearing agitation among the European residents in the country, who were literally maddened by this attack on what they believed to be one of their fundamental rights as European British subjects. They offered an open challenge to the authority of the Government "by law established in British India," a phrase which has since become familiar to the political history of this country in connection with prosecutions for seditious libels. The Government of Lord Ripon suffered all the abuse heaped upon them by the spokesmen of the European community in the country. They even threatened personal violence to the Viceroy, declaring that should this measure be persisted in they would even go to the length of capturing by force the person of Her Majesty's representative in India and packing him back to England. With rare Christian forbearance Lord Ripon calmly tolerated all this persecution by his own countrymen in India.

This Ilbert Bill agitation was marked by two incidents that had a far-reaching influence not only upon our political but also upon our social history. One was the speech of Mr. Branson, a member of the Calcutta High Court Bar, at Dacca, against this measure. In course of this speech Mr. Branson made a most savage attack upon Indian culture and character citing our mediaeval social institutions of caste, child-marriage, *zenana* seclusion and the prohibition of widow re-marriage as conclusive evidences of our moral degenaration, that branded us with absolute disqualification to sit in judgment upon European criminals. In those days we had no law in British India against the setting of class against class or Mr. Branson would have been hauled up for that highly inflamable and offensive speech of his. That speech immediately reacted upon our social reform propaganda, and helped very powerfully to strengthen the hands of our own social reactionaries. Politically, that speech almost immediately provoked a powerful reply delivered in Dacca itself by Mr. Lal Mohan Ghosh. Lal Mohan's refined oratory was more than equal, even in the strength of its vituperations, to the vulgar exhibitions of Mr. Branson. The Ilbert Bill agitation, however, left its mark upon the course of Indian political agitation. It burnt into the mind of the Indian politician the fateful lesson that if India is to protect her liberties and secure an expansion of her legitimate rights, she must inititate as violent an agitation as enabled the European residents in the country to compel the Government of Lord Ripon to practically throw out that proposed measure.

Though the Ilbert Bill caused almost wild sensation and roused angry passions in both the communities, the really progressive measures during the Viceroyalty of Lord Ripon were his amendment of the Bengal Rent Regulations and his Local Self-Government Act. Lord Cornwallis' Permanent Settlement in Bengal was clearly moved by one single object, namely, to ensure a fixed land revenue and relieve the Government of the East India Company of the troubles of collecting it from a large number of individuals enjoying land-tenures. It certainly contributed to develop the agricultural wealth of Bengal to an extent not found in any other Indian province. It saved Bengal from the increasing exactions of periodical settlements that have been one of the causes of the poverty of the other provinces as compared to Bengal. Owing to this Permanent Settlement in Bengal we never had the painful necessity of special measures like, for instance, the Bombay Agricultural Relief Act. The growth of a class of landed aristocracy in Bengal, the majority of whom were Hindus, subject to the Hindu social order of caste, that gave precedence to birth over wealth and enabled oftentimes the poorest members of the community to claim social superiority over the richest of their class, very materially helped to develop a kind of democratic freedom devoid of the degrading class-envy and class-conflict associated with the evolution of democracy in Europe and America. Realised wealth was accumulated in a comparatively few hands, but the ramifications of their social relations covering practically the whole body of the higher castes prevented the use of this wealth to advance this wealthier class to any manner of social and much less economic domination over their fellows. Menial service was rendered by certain castes only. The higher castes would not stoop to these personal services. They have therefore necessarily to seek their means of living in the service of the Government for which they had to qualify themselves with the new education which their British masters had introduced into the country. One of the indirect results of the Permanent Settlement in Bengal has certainly been the premier position which this province attained in the matter of the new English education and modern culture. On the other hand, this Permanent Settlement leading to the accumulation of wealth in large owners of land, very seriously interfered with the growth of industrial and commercial enterprises in the people. Trade inevitably fell into the hands of hereditary castes, who had been condemned from of old to a lower social status. And this caste domination stifled the ambition of these trading classes, restricting very seriously their economic enterprise. This Permanent Settlement could not certainly prevent the division of land among an increasingly large class of small landlords and sub-tenure holders, mostly belonging to the higher castes. But the great mass of the agriculturists were placed almost absolutely at the mercy of their landlords, both big and small. This created an anxious agrarian problem. With the gradual development of a sense of personal dignity and liberty, due to the new system of administration of justice established by the British and the reign of law that replaced the old rule of caste and class domination, a clash between the tenants and their landlords became inevitable. This problem had to be solved, and from time to time attempts had been made to indirectly amend Lord Cornwallis' Settlement by the imposition of new rural cesses, like for instance, the Road Cess, on the one side, and the passing of new land legislations, on the other, defining more and more strictly the rights both of the zemindars and their tenants. These, however, were found inadequate to meet the requirements of the situation. They failed to put a stop to the exactions of the zemindars or prevent conflicts between the zemindars and their tenants. A more radical measure for the regulation of the relations between the landlords and the tenants was called for. The Bengal Tenancy Act amendment of Lord Ripon's Government was framed to achieve these ends. It was naturally opposed by the representatives of the zemindary interests in Bengal and Bihar. And though considerably mauled by them in its passage through the Legislature, Lord Ripon's Government was able yet to place on the Statute Book a measure of very definite advance towards securing the legitimate rights of the tiller of the soil to the land that he brings under cultivation and nurses to yield considerable produce for the benefit of himself and the community. Since then land tenure in Bengal has received a measure of security which it had not before.

But the most important of the progressive legislations of Lord Ripon's Viceroyalty was his Local Self-Government Act. While the Ilbert Bill wanted to remove an obvious injustice based upon racial discrimination and the new Bengal Tenancy Act sought to advance the legitimate rights of the agriculturalist population of Bengal to the land upon which they spent all their labour and substance, Lord Ripon's Local Self-Government scheme was directed towards a more permanent and national objective. Unending subjection of the people of this country to their British political masters had never been the acknowledged aim of British Administration in India. From the days of Lord Macaulay British statesmen in charge of Indian affairs had worked, so far as might be consistently, of course, with the protection of their own national interests, to train the people of India in the art of Parliamentary or Representative Government which had found its original home in the modern world in Great Britain. This self-government was really built upon institutions of local government worked by the elected representatives of the people. If India was ever to have a system of government similar to that obtaining in the British Isles and also in the British Colonies, then the foundations of it would have to be laid deep and strong in institutions of local self-government. Lord Ripon clearly realised this. The Indian intelligentsia, particularly the leaders of the new political thought in Bengal, had already raised the cry of self-government or Parliamentary or Representative government as the goal of their political endeavours. Though this political awakening was confined at the time to the rising generation of educated intellectuals, the masses were slowly but surely coming into line with them; and if the British connection with India were to endure, the political aspirations of the people must be satisfied by timely reconstruction of the system of government in this great Dependency. Lord Ripon clearly recognised all this with the instinct of the far-seeing statesman, and he promulgated a Resolution proposing to build up by degrees a modern system of local self-government upon which gradually the stately structure of modern democratic national self-government might be reared. Lord Ripon thought not in the terms of the actual state of political consciousness and education of the people but in the terms of the still distant future when the ripples of the new consciousness would grow and gather strength and volume and render a radical change in the system of Indian Government imperative and inevitable. But unfortunately lack of vision and far-seeing statesmanship in those upon whom, as a matter of course, the practical working of Lord Ripon's scheme fell, prevented us from reaping the results of it. Nearly forty years after, the Montagu-Chelmsford report had, therefore, to frankly confess that the ideal towards which Lord Ripon wanted his scheme to move was sacrificed in its working to the demands of practical efficiency. The educational object was lost sight of in the pursuit of immediate administrative efficiency, and the institutions of local self-government established under Lord Ripon came to be dominated by the all-absorbing British Bureaucracy in the country depriving the people of those educative opportunities which Lord Ripon had wanted to offer them through his Local Self-Government Act. The tedious process of educating the people of this country in the unfamiliar methods of rural and municipal self-government was not liked by the impatient members of the Indian Civil Service, who deliberately usurped the powers that were meant to be transferred gradually to the representatives of the people; and Lord Ripon's Self-Government measure inevitably came to be treated with contempt as "local slough." But though it failed in its practical working owing to obvious reasons, the farsight and liberal spirit of its author must be frankly acknowledged and recorded by the historian of Lord Ripon's Viceroyalty in India.

That Viceroyalty, though not directly responsible for it, was incidentally associated with another movement that had a profound influence upon the evolution of Indian history and politics during the half-a-century that has elasped since his lordship left the Indian shores. It was about 1880 or 1881 that Djemal ed Din, the founder of the Pan-Islamic movement, came from Afghanistan to India, and had confidential conversations with the leaders of the Mahomedan community in this country. He came to Calcutta and met the late Nawab Abdul Latiff and the small group of educated Mahomedans associated with him, including the late Justice Ameer Ali, and inoculated them with the virus of his Pan-Islamism. Before Djemal ed Din's advent the educated Indian Mahomedans, particularly in Bengal, had been loyally co-operating with their Hindu fellow-subjects for the common advancement of national political interests. But after his visit they commenced to draw themselves away from the political activities of their Hindu fellow-subjects until gradually a wide gulf was created between the Hindu and the Moslem intellectuals in the country in regard to our national endeavours.

Lord Ripon was the most popular Viceroy that India had. His popularity, however, was more due to his personal character and piety than perhaps to even the liberal policy which he tried to initiate or his far-seeing statesmanship. This last, no doubt, contributed very materially to allay the popular discontent created by the acts and policies of the Lytton Administration. But these alone would hardly have been sufficient to earn for him that enthusiastic and almost affectionate regard which became manifest in the unprecedented demonstration that marked his departure from India. Both in Calcutta and Bombay impressive farewell functions were held in which all classes of the community joined. He was the only Viceroy who received the unique distinction of being voted a statute practically by the educated Indian community only. The farewell demonstrations held in his honour compelled the "Pioneer", the spokesman of the European community in India, to ask in a remarkable article: "If It Be Real, What Does It Mean?" The article was anonymous, but was believed at that time to have been written by Mr. A. O. Hume, who was then Chief Secretary to the Government of India, and who upon his retirement from office helped to initiate the historic movement of the Indian National Congress.

Lord Ripon belonged to that old generation of British administrators in India who honestly believed in England's mission in this continent. That mission was to help an ancient and decadent people to a rejuvenascent national life under modern conditions. No British statesman could desire the break-up of India's British connection, neither did Lord Ripon. But he saw that if England's connection with India was to endure it could only be through the complete reconciliation of India's natural desire for national autonomy with the British connection. The British Colonies enjoyed practical self-government. This Colonial Self-Government was, therefore, the objective for which British statesmen of the class of Lord Ripon deliberately and sincerely strove. The Dominion ideal had not as yet dawned upon the consciousness of Imperial statesmanship. That was revealed towards the close of the last century in the light of the experiences of the Boer War. But those who knew Lord Ripon cannot possibly doubt it that had he lived to this day his far-sighted statesmanship would have recognised the safety of the British Empire in India in the admission of this great Dependency into the Commonwealth of Nations composing the White members of that Empire upon terms of absolute equality with the other members of it. And frankly accepting this objective Lord Ripon would have steadily worked for the education of the Indian peoples to qualify themselves for their legitimate place in the Federation of Free States wherein the present British Empire must seek and find its permanent safety and ultimate destiny. Lord Ripon's Indian policy has been interpreted in some quarters as prompted more by cunning diplomacy than by honest regard for India's legitimate political freedom in the modern world. It did, no doubt, help to strengthen and prolong the hypnotic spell which the British had cast over our people. But those who knew Lord Ripon personally could find no support for this suspicion in his mind and character. And history must give to the most popular Viceroy that India had a high place among the makers, politically, of modern India. The immediate result of India's awakening under Lord Ripon was the birth of the Indian National Congress about a year after he retired from the Indian Viceroyalty.

CHAPTER XXII.

HINDU RELIGIOUS REVIVAL AND SOCIAL REACTION

At the close of 1882, I found myself again in Calcutta. I came from Bangalore, as I have said, to take charge of the education of the two younger sons and the third daughter of Babu Durga Mohan Das. Upon my arrival, however, I found, though in an honorary capacity, more congenial occupation along with that of private tutor, as assistant to the Editor of the "Bengal Public Opinion." The "Bengal Public Opinion" was under a new name really the old "Brahmo Public Opinion" started as the official organ of the Sadharana Brahmo Samaj. The "Brahmo Public Opinion" was a general newspaper and review with a few columns specially devoted to the news of the Brahmo Samaj and the discussion of topics of special interest to the Brahmo community. It was very largely patronised by the advanced sections of educated Bengalees, and men like the late Mr. Nagendra Nath Ghose, better known as Mr. N. N. Ghose, Barrister-at-Law and Principal of the Metropolitan Institution, were regular contributors to the columns of this paper. From the very first it became the organ in politics of the most advanced democratic ideals in this country. During the amendment of the Bengal land or rent law, the "Brahmo Public Opinion" took up the cause of the ryots as against the vested interests of the zemindars and lent its influential support to Lord Ripon's policy as embodied in the new Rent Bill. When first started, the "Brahmo Public Opinion" was financed by Babu Durga Mohan Das and Mr. Ananda Mohan Bose. But it did not satisfy the so-called religious needs of the Brahmo community. The ideal of this paper, under Babu Bhuban Mohan Das, was more liberal and rational than what was liked by the general body of Brahmos, still obsessed by mediæval notions about religious life and duty. To Babu Bhuban Mohan Das, as it was also to his elder brother Durga Mohan, religion was not merely a matter of the culture of the emotions or of mere prayers and adorations to the Deity. Religion, and particularly the religion which the modern man especially needed, was something that covered every department of man's personal life and social duties, including his duties towards the State or his political duties and obligations. Among the earlier teachers of the Brahmo Samaj none counted higher than the American Unitarian Minister, Theodore Parker. Parker's "Sermons" were in a somewhat special sense the scripture of our new religion. And the ideal of the more advanced and rational section of the Brahmo Samaj, the section which was most largely represented in the Sadharana Brahmo Samaj, was that set up in the first of these sermons, headed "Solid Piety." "The harmonious development of all the faculties of our manhood" was the soul and essence of his ideal of "Solid Piety." But there were men among us in the Brahmo Samaj, who favoured the ideal of the old and orthodox devotional, or contemplative and emotional life more than the life of active service of God through service of man and the simultaneous cultivation of all our faculties, our Reason, our Conscience or the Social Sense, our Emotions and our Will with a view to reach out to the most perfect type of manhood. Keshub Chunder Sen had already developed the tendency to advance the emotional side of religion to the more or less open neglect of its rational and practical side. And even among those who had rebelled against Keshub's authority in the Samaj and had joined the Sadharana Brahmo Samaj, there were not a few, especially among the elders, whose partiality for mediaeval religious ideals was open and emphatic. They did not quite favour the "Brahmo Public Opinion" as the official organ of the Samaj. They wanted a more pronounced Brahmo propagandist than what the "Brahmo Public Opinion" seemed to be in their eyes. Even Pandit Shivanath Shastri had commenced slowly and imperceptibly to shed his earlier rationalism; and what he was before the schism as Editor of the "Samadarshee", he no longer was as Minister and Missionary of the Sadharana Brahmo Samaj. He too felt that the "Brahmo Public Opinion" was not sufficiently "religious and spiritual" to continue to be the official organ of the Samaj. Mr. Ananda Mohan Bose also lent his support to this view. And the result was that the "Brahmo Public Opinion" ceased from the beginning of 1883 to be the organ of the Brahmo Samaj. The "Indian Messenger" succeeded it in this office, with Pandit Shivanath Shastri as its formal Editor. The "Brahmo Public Opinion" changed its name into "Bengal Public Opinion" with Babu

Bhuban Mohan Das as Editor, and the two brothers, Durga Mohan and Bhuban Mohan, undertook the financial responsibility of it. It was on this paper, upon my return to Calcutta from Bangalore at the beginning of 1883, that I found my first regular training in English journalism. Though Babu Bhuban Mohan was its Editor, within a few weeks of my joining it I became practically the chief writer on its staff and gradually the editorial function also came into my charge without editorial responsibility.

When in 1879 I left the University and went to Cuttack, the Brahmo Samaj was still a great intellectual and moral force in the country. Middle-Nineteenth Century Rationalism and Individualism of European culture were still the dominating ideas in the life and evolution of modern Bengal. But the conflict of political interests between the new generation of English-educated Indians and the British officialdom in the country, and the more fundamental cultural conflict between European modernism and Indian mediaevalism soon provoked a new revolt against this foreign domination in the wake of which rapidly followed a new national self-consciousness which, in the first flush of its new-found pride of race and culture, commenced to repudiate whatever was foreign, irrespective of the intrinsic reason and value of it, and set up a new defence even of those social institutions and religious and spiritual tendencies that had previously been openly repudiated as false and harmful. Many things contributed to this reaction. The revival of mediaevalism in the Brahmo Samaj itself was certainly by no means the least powerful of these. In

1876 or thereabout Col. Olcott and Madame Blavatsky landed at Bombay with a new message and a new mission. And the Theosophical Society which they founded was perhaps the most powerful of the forces that brought in this movement of Hindu religious revival and social reaction. This Society told our people that instead of having any reason to be ashamed of their past or of the legacies left to them by it, they have every reason to feel justly proud of it all, because their ancient seers and saints had been the spokesmen of the highest truths and their old books, so woefully misunderstood today, had been the repositories of the highest human illumination and wisdom. Our people had hitherto felt perpetually humiliated at the sense of their degradation. This new message, coming from the representatives of the most advanced peoples of the modern world, the inheritors of the most advanced culture and civilisation the world has as yet known, at once raised us in our own estimation and created a self-confidence in us that commenced to find easy expression in a new propaganda which, instead of apologising for our current and mediæval ideas and institutions and seeking to reform and reconstruct these after modern European ideals, boldly stood up in defence of them.

In Bengal this movement of Hindu religious revival and Hindu social apologetics and reaction, found expression through the school of Bankim Chandra on the one side, whose new organ was the small propagandist monthly, the "Prachar," and through the school of Pandit Shashadhar Tarkachudamani, who soon found a ready-made organ in the popular Bengalee weekly, the "Bangabasee." Other schools also, more or less identified with either the line of Bankim Chandra or of Pandit Shashadhar, were fast springing up under the inspiration of this new revivalist and reactionary thought. Foremost among these was the "Navajeevana" started and edited by Babu Akshay Chandra Sarkar. All these new organs, more or less, followed the line of propaganda of the Brahmo Samaj. Bankim Chandra openly attempted a "re-explanation, a re-interpretation and a re-adjustment" of our old theology and ethics in the light of the most advanced modern thought and in accordance with the new rules of literary criticism and scriptural interpretation that had been so powerfully influencing current religious life and thought in Christendom itself. In this work of re-explanation re-interpretation and readjustment, Bankim Chandra very closely followed the canons of Renan in his studies of the life of Jesus and the early history of Christianity. Bankim Chandra followed, or more correctly, closely imitated Renan in his presentation of Shree Krishna. Like Renan, who had formed in his mind a picture of Jesus Christ in accordance with the moral and spiritual ideals presented through the Gospel narratives and then applied this picture of Christ to critically examine the Gospel narratives themselves, accepting as true only such portions of these narratives as seemed to be in consonance with his own fancy-picture, and rejecting as false and spurious additions all those things in these narratives that were inconsistent with this picture of the character of the Master, Bankim Chandra also first formed in his own mind a picture of

Shree Krishna as the Ideal Man; he applied this picture to his examination of the Krishna legend current among our people, and rejected everything that did not harmonise with it. Bankim Chandra's *Anusheelana Dharma* was really the Brahmo Samaj ideal of what Theodore Parker called "Solid Piety", the ideal, namely, of the harmonious development of all the faculties of man, physical and mental, through his personal and social life, and he preached it only without the unpopular Brahmo name. Akshay Chandra Sarkar through his "Navajeevana" presented a somewhat different line of Hindu apologetics and exegeses. While Bankim Chandra was more critical and rational or logical, Akshay Chandra was more emotional. Bankim Chandra followed more or less in the footsteps of our old Mimansakas, like Jaimini for instance, or more correctly like Badarayana in his Brahma-Sutras. Akshay Chandra followed the Bhaktivada schools and laid greater emphasis on the direct realisations of saints and seers, both ancient and modern. But both were high-priests of the movement of Neo-Hinduism and Hindu social reaction that followed as a protest against the pretensions of aggressive Christian propaganda and more particularly against the cultural domination of the "stranger within our gate," who had captured the machinery of our State and Administration.

All these revivals and reactions were more directly the fruit of the previous movement of religious and social revolt led by the Brahmo Samaj itself. In this sense, they were not merely destructive of the Brahmo propaganda, but also at the same time, partially corrective of and supplementary to it. Most, if not all the protagonists of this new Hindu religious revival and social reaction had been in their early life connected with the Brahmo Samaj. And the new revival movement that openly declared war upon all the fundamental progressive ideals of the Brahmo Samaj, whether consciously or unconsciously, practically took up the cause of modern religious and social reconstruction in Bengal at the point were the Brahmo Samaj had already brought it. Religious ritualism, though sought to be defended by psuedo science, such as was found in the exegeses and apologetics of Pandit Shashadhar Tarkachudamani and the Theosophists, practically initiated a new movement of inner spiritual and religious culture which was distinct from all outer rituals and formularies. Hinduism in my boyhood was almost exclusively a personal religion with a social aspect that was organised in the festivities of the external *pujas*. The only form of what might deserve to be called congregational worship was found in the Vaishnava *keertanas* and in the Vaishnava *Mahotshavas*. The higher and the more educated classes had no participation in these. It was the Brahmo Samaj which first introduced congregational worship in modern India. With this Hindu revival and reaction, *Hari Sabhas* commenced to grow up everywhere which inaugurated a kind of congregational worship. At meetings of these *Sabhas*, scripture texts were read and expounded by some Pandit and hymns or *bhajans* were sung. All this was clearly a reproduction of the Brahmo mode of worship. Indeed, this was originally what Raja Ram Mohan wanted to be the form of Divine Worship in his Brahmo Samaj. He advised the reading and exposition of sacred texts for the mental worship of the Supreme Being. But while this revival and reaction movement adopted or adapted the spirit and even the form of Brahmo Samaj religion and worship, it stood up violently against the social idealism of the Brahmo movement. It was really here in its social gospel and in its war upon caste and custom that denied to man on account of his birth or heritage his rights as man and a social being, that the Brahmo Samaj struck at the very life of the old Hindu social hierarchy. This social reaction, therefore, put up a most determined opposition to the Brahmo movement.

This revival and reactionary propaganda in the periodical press was very powerfully supplemented by the new Bengalee stage. While Bankim Chandra's "Prachar" and Akshay Babu's "Navajeevana" tried to combat Brahmo rationalism by argument, the Bengalee stage sought to kill the social idealism of it by satire and ridicule. The readers of "Prachar" and "Navajeevana" could be counted only in three figures, but those who crowded the Calcutta theatres week after week numbered thousands. They were hardly an educated or discriminating audience. They enjoyed the vulgar ribaldries of the actors and actresses who represented Brahmo men and women on the stage. All this created a very violent antagonism to the Brahmo Samaj about the time when I found myself once more in Calcutta. And I was soon drawn into this new fight for faith and freedom against reactionary forces let loose about us.

When Bankim Chandra started his "Prachar" and Akshay Chandra his "Navajeevana", a few young men of the Sadharana Brahmo Samaj started a small monthly, the "Alochana." Though not formally its editor, I was practically called upon to share the bulk of the work and responsibility of the editorial chair. A few rupees were collected from a few friends to meet the initial outlay. Lady Jagadish Chandra Bose, before her marriage Miss Abala Das, as she was then known, who was then reading for a medical degree at Madras, helped us with a little money. Babu Paresh Nath Sen, who subsequently entered the Educational Service of Government in Bengal and has retired on a pension from the chair of English literature in the Bethune College, was another of the helpers or proprietors, if this term may be applied to people who had no pecuniary or indeed any other interests in this paper and whose only motive was just to see an organ of advanced social and religious ideas and ideals in current Bengalee periodical literature that would try to offer some corrective, however feeble, to the growing forces of religious and social reaction in the country. The "Alochana" was able to secure contributions from such eminent Bengalee writers as Raj Narayan Bose, Shivanath Shastri, and I think both Dvijendra Nath and Rabindra Nath, though they had their own family monthly the "Sadhana", occasionally contributed to the pages of this new paper as a public acknowledgment of their sympathy with the cause which it had so courageously espoused against such tremendous odds, both financial and intellectual. Babu Gagan

Chandra Home was the managing editor. He looked both after its business side as well as its literary side also. "Alochana" did not live long, it ceased publication after about a couple of years, probably within that period. But it did help, as long as it lived, to keep the flag of progressive thought and rational life flying.

Upon my return to Calcutta in 1882, I found a new development in Bengalee journalism. During my sojourn in far away Bangalore, a new Bengalee weekly had come into being, which exerted very considerable influence over current life and thought in our province for nearly quarter of a century. It was the "Bangabasee." When it was first started, the Brahmo Samaj was still a force in Bengalee thought and life. Shivanath Shastri, Dwarka Nath Gangulee, Umesh Chandra Datta, Editor of "Bharat-Sanskaraka" and "Bamabodhinee," these prominent Brahmos belonging to the Sadharana Samaj, were all Bengalee writers of established reputation. The proprietor of the "Bangabasee," wanting to publish a first class Bengalee weekly, could not think of it without them as regular contributors. So he approached them all and they all readily offered their help and co-operation in this new journalistic venture. Babu Jnanendra Lal Roy was the first editor of this paper. Jnanendra Lal, though not a professed Brahmo, had genuine regard for the cause which the Brahmo Samaj represented. Owing to him and these Brahmo contributors the "Bangabasee" became a powerful organ of liberal thought in Bengal. But this was not continued for very long. Babu Jogendra Chandra Bose, the proprietor of the "Bangabasee", himself had no especial predeliction for Brahmo liberalism. His aim was to unite all the best intellects of Bengal in his weekly with a view to make it the most popular journal in the province. As he approached therefore men of advanced social views like Shivanath Shastri and Dwarka Nath Ganguly to write in his paper, so he invited contributions also from eminent social reactionaries like Chandra Nath Bose and Indra Nath Banerjee. Chandra Nath had secured by his "Sakuntala-tattwa," an attempt at a psychological study of the world-renowned production of Kalidasa, a very high place among Bengalee writers as an essayist and literary critic. Indra Nath leapt to fame as a remarkable satirist by his "Bharatoddhar." He turned his shafts on the ideals of female emancipation of the Brahmo Samaj. An exceedingly offensive attack on educated Brahmo ladies appeared one day in the "Bangabasee." Babu Dwarka Nath Ganguly immediately demanded a public recantation and apology for it from the "Bangabasee." This was refused with the result that the Brahmo contributors of the "Bengabasee" boycotted it at once, and in a few days started a Bengalee weekly of their own, the "Sanjibanee," with a view to counter the pernicious influence, from their point of view, of the "Bangabasee." This open breach with the Brahmo Samaj instead of weakening the growing popularity of the "Bangabasee" helped materially to increase it and soon converted it into the organ of the most hide-bound conservatism, both theological and social, of the Bengalee Hindu society. The "Sanjibanee's" influence was more or less confined to the members of the Brahmo Samaj and their sympathisers. It was this division which gradually drove the "Bangabasee" to an extreme position on the side of Hindu orthodoxy on the one hand, while it drove the "Sanjibanee" also to the other extreme of Brahmo orthodoxy. Contemporary Bengalee thought and life, divided practically into these two camps, was thus deprived of reasonable reconciliation and synthesis in which alone these conflicts of ideals could possibly find their final settlement and solution. The movement of social and religious progress represented by the Brahmo Samaj suffered most seriously, at least for the time being, on account of this separation and conflict. Practically, the whole decade, 1880 to 1890, was marked by a strong current of religious revival and social reaction, which positively set back the movement of progress not only in Bengal but all over India.

These years (1880 to 1890) were also marked by the birth of a new political conflict, which was initiated first by the ill-fated Ilbert Bill. In 1883 Surendra Nath was sentenced to simple imprisonment, on the civil side of the jail, for two months on a charge of contempt of court. It arose out of certain criticisms of the conduct of one of the High Court judges, Mr. Justice Norris, who had ordered to be produced before him for examination the Hindu religious symbol or ikon, the *Salagram*. This matter was first brought to public notice by the "Bengal Public Opinion." Surendra Nath had already acquired the "Bengalee," and was its responsible editor. Commenting upon the information published in the "Bengal

Public Opinion," the "Bengalee" wrote that "we have now however amongst us a judge who, if he does not actually recall to mind the days of Jeffrys and Scroggs, has certainly done enough within the short time that he has filled the High Court Bench, to show how unworthy he is of the high office and how by nature he is unfitted to maintain those traditions of dignity which are inseparable from the office of judge of the highest court in the land." These remarks were prompted by the following paragraph of the "Bengal Public Opinion."

> "Mr. Justice Norris is determined to set the Hughly on fire. The last act of *zuburdusti* on his lordship's part was the bringing of a *salagram*, a stone idol, into court for identification. There have been very many cases both in the late Supreme Court and the present High Court of Calcutta regarding the custody of Hindu idols, but the presiding deity of a Hindu household had never before this the honour of being dragged into Court. Our Calcutta Daniel looked at the idol and said that it could not be a hundred years old. So Mr. Justice Norris is not only versed in Law and Medicine, but it also a connoisseur of Hindu idols. It is difficult to say what he is not. Whether the orthodox Hindus of Calcutta will tamely submit to their family idols being dragged into Court is a matter for them to decide, but it does seem to us that some public steps should be taken to put a quietus to the wild eccentricities of this young and raw Dispenser of Justice."

Surendra Nath's imprisonment called forth the first real political demonstration all over Bengal. He had already bcome the idol of the younger generation of his countrymen. His conviction and sentence was taken up by Young Bengal as an open challenge to their national honour and an attack on their love of freedom and patriotism. Crowded meetings were held not only in Calcutta but practically all over Bengal to express sympathy with him. Upon his release from prison Surendra Nath made an extensive tour in Bengal and Upper India collecting contributions to a permanent fund called the National Fund, which was to be devoted to the new political propaganda. The idea of this fund, so far as I remember, originated with Babu Tarapada Banerjee, who was at that time practising in the District Court at Krishnagar. He published an appeal for this fund in the columns of the "Bengalee," when Surendra Nath was still in jail. The amount collected came to about Rs. 20,000, and the subscribers at a meeting decided to make it over to the Indian Association of Calcutta for the promotion of political work.

The political movement in Bengal, started mainly through the inspiring propaganda of Surendra Nath and Ananda Mohan, had from the beginning an all-India outlook. The Indian Association worked for building up something like an Indian Parliament with its constituencies spread all over the continent. With this idea branches of the Indian Association, as already mentioned, were organised in every important town and city not only in Bengal but in Upper India from Allahabad to Amritsar. Surendra Nath's imprisonment helped forward this movement of Indian unity very considerably. It was, as Ananda Mohan wrote in the report of the Indian Association, a real blessing in disguise. "It has now been demonstrated", he said, "by the universal outburst of grief and indignation which the event called forth, that the people of the different Indian provinces have learnt to feel for one another, and that a common bond of unity and fellow-feeling is rapidly being established among them." The necessary sequence of this new national consciousness was the first National Conference which was held in Calcutta in 1883—December 28 to 30—in the Albert Hall. It was presided over, if my memory fails me not, by the Rev. Dr. K. M. Banerjee. So far as Bengal was concerned the two prominent political groups, one representing the landed aristocracy of the province, the British Indian Association, and the other representing the growing power of the educated middle class, the Indian Association, were united at this Conference. There were delegates not only from the different towns in Bengal but also from Upper India, about one hundred in all, and as Ananda Mohan remarked in course of his opening speech, "it was the first stage towards a National Parliament." The reform and expansion of the legislative councils as instruments of democratic self-government, the promotion of general and technical education, the separation of judicial from the executive functions in the administration of criminal justice, and the larger employment of Indians in the administration of their country,—these were the main demands put forward at this Conference. They were practically the same as found expression through the Indian National Congress that met in Bombay in 1885. I was present at this Conference, though rather too young to take any part in its deliberations.

The year 1884, as already noticed, was marked by a very strong wave of social reaction that passed not only over Calcutta but almost all over Bengal. In Calcutta the protagonists of this movement were Pandit Sashadhar Tarka-chudamani, who held many meetings in defence of popular Hindu ceremonialism and image worship and current Hindu social institutions. Pandit Sashadhar, however, did not follow the lines of the old exegeses and apologetics of Hinduism or the ancient Mimansakas and their later interpreters. But he adopted altogether a new line of apologetics. The old Mimansas worked upon the postulate of scriptural authority. The scriptures, and particularly the Vedas, were believed to be eternal. They were not the product of any person, they were *apaurusheya*. The old Mimansakas had tried so to interpret these terms and these claims that they might be reconciled with our ordinary reason. Their final conclusion was expressed in what may be called the Hindu doctrine of logos or logoi. Words, they declared, were of two kinds, namely, those that were composed of sounds and those that represented eternal ideas. The terms for these two kinds of words in Sanskrit were *dhvanyatmaka* and *sphotatmaka*. These *sphota savdas* meant exactly the same thing as the *ideas* or architypes or logoi of early Greek speculation. The Vedas to which were attributed eternal existence and supernatural scriptural authority were confined only to those parts of them that expressed or related to these *sphota savdas* or architypes, from which all creation evolved. Pandit Sashadhar Tarka-chudamani however did not follow the ancient Vedic exegeses and apologetics. He was concerned with the defence not of ancient Vedic religion but of current Pauranic rituals. Nor could an appeal to ancient scripture carry any weight with the generation with whom the Pandit had to deal in Bengal. His mission was among modern educated Bengalees. They had lost all faith in supernatural scriptures. Their mind was saturated with modern rationalism. They had commenced to think in the terms of 19th century scientific thought. Pandit Sashadhar Tarkachudamani therefore adopted a new line of interpretation seeking to reconcile ancient Hindu ritualism and mediaeval Hindu faith with modern science. The interpretation was as true or as false as that offered by the defenders of popular Christianity seeking to reconcile it with the advanced researches and discoveries of modern science. It was really neither honest faith nor correct science. But all the same it went down with large numbers of our countrymen who cared little for their faith and understood less of what they pretended to know of science. Sashadhar Tarkachudamani could not commend himself even to Hindu revivalists like Bankim Chandra, who refused to lend his approval to his propaganda.

This new revival movement had another powerful protagonist in Shree Krishna Prasanna Sen. He had the gift of oratory in a much larger measure than Sashadhar Tarkachudamani. He had the power to rouse popular sentiments by vulgar witticism and through playing upon words. One of his most popular presentations of the superiority of Hinduism was a pun on the words God in English representing the Supreme Being and *Nanda-Nandana* in Sanskrit and Bengalee, representing the Vaishnavic Deity Shree Krishna. "If you reversed the alphabets composing the word God you would find it converted into dog; if you reversed the letters *Nanda-Nandana* in this way you would find no change in it." This was a typical presentation of Shree Krishna Prasanna Sen. He was sentimental, vulgar and abusive, but this very sentimentality, vulgarity and abuse went down with a generation of half-educated Bengalees who had been wounded in their tenderest spots by the vulgarities of the Anglo-Indian politicals of the type of Branson and ignorant and unimaginative Christian propagandists.

Akshay Chandra Sarkar was perhaps the most powerful opponent of progressive social views represented by not only the Brahmo Samaj but even by such advanced Hindu social reformers as Pandit Iswar Chandra Vidyasagar. Babu Akshay Chandra delivered an address in defence of the disabilities imposed by Hinduism upon young widows in regard to re-marriage about the middle of 1884 before a large and distinguished audience. The meeting was held under the auspices of the Savitree Library. It was presided over, I think, by Dr. Gurudas Banerjee, who subsequently rose to the position of a puisne judge in our High Court and was knighted in recognition of his distinguished services. I was then Sub-Editor of the "Bengal Public Opinion." I had been relieved from the beginning of 1884 of the charge of Durga Mohan Babu's sons, who went to the new Civil Service classes opened by Dr. Aghore Nath Chattopadhyaya, who had been deported from Hyderabad (Nizam) a few months earlier, in consequence of some political intrigue, which is so common in our Native States, and had come and settled in Calcutta. I was present at this meeting and, though comparatively young and unknown, I did not hesitate to take up the challenge of the veteran Bengalee essayist. My speech in opposition to Babu Akshay Chandra Sarkar's attracted considerable notice not only at the meeting but also in the periodical press of that time. I reproduced a summary of it in our monthly, "Alochana." This was practically my first appearance before a large and distinguished Calcutta audience.

For some time, however, the Bengalee community of Calcutta, if not indeed of the whole of Bengal, was very considerably agitated over the controversy of this period between the representatives of Neo-Hinduism and the spokesmen of the Brahmo Samaj. Babu Nagendra Nath Chatterjee represented the Brahmo stand-point; while Pandit Sashadhar Tarka-chudamani and Shree Krishna Prasanna Sen represented the forces of Hindu religious revival and social reaction. Babu Nagendra Nath delivered a series of lectures in defence of the theology of the Brahmo Samaj and its social ideals. These were delivered to large audiences at one of the Calcutta Theatres, and were subsequently published in book-form under the title of "Dharma-Jijnasha." Babu Nagendra Nath was one of the most powerful Bengalee speakers of his day. Not an orator like Keshub Chunder Sen or Shivanath Shastri, Nagendra Nath however drew always crowded houses by the fascination of his wit and the incivisive logic of his discourses. His "Dharma-Jijnasha" or inquiry into religion is one of the best books of its kind not only in

Bengalee but perhaps even in English. It establishes the fundamentals of religion upon what the students of philosophy call the "logic of thought." Though it follows the essential lines of European theistic philosophy and theology of the last century, the presentation is certainly original. The fundamental issue in this controversy between the position of the Brahmo Samaj on the one side and that of the Neo-Hinduism of Sashadhar Tarkachudamni and Shree Krishna Prasanna Sen on the other, was regarding the nature of God. Is God with or without form?—"*Iswar sakara or nirakara*? Both sides accepted that God has no form. He is *nirakara* or without form. But can man in the present stage of his mental and spiritual evolution truly conceive of the formless God or worship Him as such? The whole issue was false. As regards the worship of the formless God, *Samkara Bhashya* or the commentary of Samkara on the Vedanta has an exhaustive examination of it. According to Samkara there are three ways of knowing the Absolute or Brahman. One is through direct cognition called *aparokshanubhuti* in Sanskrit. This is the only and real way to the realisation of Brahman. But few, very few indeed, are qualified to pursue this way, which requires absolute abstraction of the mind and understanding from all sense activities and consequently the cessation even of the ordinary processes of intellection. This highest and truest worship of Brahman is possible therefore in that beatific state which is known to Indian experience as *samadhi*. Those who have not acquired this state of beatitude cannot therefore worship God really "in spirit and in truth." The Samkara-

Vedanta, however, mentions two other forms of Divine worship. One is called *sampadopashana*, and the other *prateekopashana*. *Sampadopashana* means the contemplation of the Brahman through something that bears some analogy to Him. The worship of Brahman through the Sun belongs to this category. The Sun in revealing the world reveals itself. The Sun is therefore both self-revealing or *svaprakasha* and *world-revealing* or *jagatprakashaka*. If we concentrate our mind upon these two essential qualities of the Sun, and through such contemplation try to worship Brahman through the Sun-symbol, such worship is called worship through analogy or *sampadopashana*. This certainly has a place in what may be called the progressive realisation of Brahman "in spirit and in truth." But in the early eighties of the last century, our people had hardly any knowledge of the *Shareeraka Bhashya*, and neither Pandit Sashadhar nor Pandit Shree Krishna Prasanna seemed to have had any knowledge of these old Hindu exegetics. Their position was practically an agnostic position: Brahman is unknown and unknowable. In the present stage of our evolution, it is absolutely futile for us to pretend to know and worship Brahman. Our ancient seers and sages realised it and therefore they prescribed physical, psychophysical, mental and social or ethical disciplines for the purification of our mind and body. And this object, when attained, would qualify us for the worship of Brahman. Till then we must follow the way of the ancient seers and accept the disciplines prescribed by them. Current Hinduism consists only of these preliminary disciplines, and the pursuit of the popular rituals of the Hindu religion is the only law for ordinary men and women. Babu Nagendra Nath attacked this position of Neo-Hindu revivalists from the stand-point of the prevailing rationalism and the theistic theology of middle 19th century European thought. His defence of progresssive Brahmo thought therefore failed to seriously influence the forces of revival and reaction. It did not offer really any solution of the fundamental problem of theism, namely, the problem of the Personality of the Absolute. That came later, though not however fully, with the revival of the study of the Philosophy of the Absolute in the light of the realisations of Bengal Vaishnavism or the School of Shree Chaitanya Mahaprabhu.

CHAPTER XXIII.

THE TRIUMPH OF FATHER LOVE

In 1884 I was Sub-Editor of the "Bengal Public Opinion." My allowance was Rs. 70 a month. This was not sufficient to meet the requirements of a growing family. My eldest daughter was born in March 1883. In November 1885 my second daughter was born. All through 1884 I tried to make a little extra income by contributions to Bengalee papers. The "Bharat-Mihir" had transferred itself from Mymensingh to Calcutta about this time and it commenced to take regular contributions from me for which, on an average, I got from Rs. 20 to Rs. 25 a month. Even after the other Brahmo writers had cut off all connection with the "Bangabasee" I continued to write for it, for two reasons; one was that I was in need of money, and the other was that through the columns of this paper I could reach a much larger circle of readers than any other Bengalee weekly of those days. There was yet another reason why I did not give up the "Bangabasee", and that was this, namely, that I could not entirely fall in with the spirit of the "Sanjibanee", which seemed to me to be as dogmatic and hidebound in its own way as any organ of Hindu revival and social reaction. The "Bangabasee" accepted whatever I wrote, did not interfere in any way with the freest expression of my thoughts and opinions. But the "Sanjibanee" did not allow the same degree of freedom to those who were not on the editorial board. The editorial board of the

"Sanjibanee" consisted of Babu Krishna Kumar Mitra, Babu Heramba Chandra Maitra and Babu Kali Sankar Sukul, and I could never completely fall in with the Brahmo orthodoxy of these friends. And the "Bangabasee" paid me liberally according to the standard of those days, while the "Sanjibanee" paid nothing to its contributors, pleading poverty for this inability. Towards the fall of 1884 the "Bengal Public Opinion" practically ceased publication, being incorporated with Surendra Nath's "Bengalee", and I lost the greater portion of my income in consequence of it. From August 1884 onward I was struggling with my growing family and my decreasing income in Calcutta.

Two or three friends came to my help about this time. They were studying in the University. They came from my native district of Sylhet and they offered to come and live with me as paying guests. This was a great relief to my struggling finances. I had also a lady boarder with us at this time. She was a young Brahmin widow, who had been placed in the Brahmo Samaj by her brother-in-law with a view to give her some useful education and let her have a chance of getting herself re-married. She was brought to the Brahmo Samaj through the instrumentality of Babu Nagendra Nath Chatterjee, one of our missionaries, and his wife. Nagendra Babu was at that time resident Minister of the Konnagar Brahmo Samaj. This young widow belonged to Konnagar, and her people came into intimate contact with Nagendra Babu and his good wife. When this young widow was brought to the Brahmo Samaj, Babu Durga Mohan Das offered to pay for her board and lodging in some Brahmo family, and Nagendra Babu placed her with my family. She also was a paying guest of mine. I was then living in Ram Krishna Das's Lane. It was a fairly big house with an open compound on the south. This house stood next to the garden attached to the house of Pandit Iswar Chandra Vidyasagar in Brindaban Mallik's Lane. Babu Chandi Charan Banerjee, the biographer of Vidyasagar, shared this house with me.

In those days the Brahmo Samaj actively threw itself into the cause of social reform and particularly of widow re-marriage. Many a young Hindu widow found shelter in Brahmo families from where they subsequently got married. We also sometimes helped young Hindu widows to run away from their home and the protection of their families, and gave them shelter and education and, if possible, opportunities of re-marriage in the Brahmo Samaj.

About the middle of 1884 an application for help of this kind was received from a young and highly connected Kayastha widow of Konnagar. It came through the young lady from Konnagar who was at that time one of our boarders. My wife agreed to take her in if she was brought to the Brahmo Samaj. Arrangements were therefore made to help her to run away from her home. Babu Krishna Kumar Mitra and an elderly lady, Mrs. Umesh Chandra Bose, and myself (I forget if there were any others) went one morning by boat to Konnagar. According to previous arrangement this young lady came as usual for her daily Ganges bath to the *ghat* and got into our boat. We crossed the river immediately, and leaving our boat at the *ghat* in Panihaty drove with her to our house in Badur Bagan. There was no trouble on the way. Her people did not discover her flight in time to pursue us. Her elder brother came the next day and was directed to my house by Brahmo friends near our Prayer Hall. He saw his sister and pressed her to go back with him, but she refused. Going back disappointed this brother of hers returned after three or four hours with a number of rowdies with a view to intimidate me into refusing her protection in my house. This, of course, I could not do. In the course of a few minutes about a couple of hundred young men gathered in my compound and threatened to forcibly take the girl away from my house. I stood firm. And standing at the door leading to the inner appartments, I told them that if they wanted to take the girl by force, let them clearly understand it that they would have to do so by walking over my dead body, and there were my friends behind me who would not submit to any violence of this kind without breaking heads. , They were not prepared for this. Some of them declared that they would beat me with their shoes to submission. I went forward singly and advancing to the very centre of the threatening crowd I took off my own shoes and placed these at the hands of my opponents, saying, "Here are my shoes, if you dare, beat me into submission with these, why should you injure your own shoes for so small a thing." This took them aback. They came down from their threatening attitiude and said, "How can we assault a gentleman like you?" I said, "I may or may not be a gentleman, but by your conduct you have proved that you are not." Then somebody said, "Let us have the girl and we will go away." I replied, "No gentleman can hand over a helpless young woman to men of your character. If she will go with her brother, she is free to do so. But I will not allow her to be forcibly taken away from my home." At this time somebody asked her brother to go and bring her. He went up and came back saying that she refused to come with him. But the crowd urged him to say that we were keeping her by force. If she came down and told them herself that she would not come, they would go way. I refused also this offer, saying that no gentle-woman could come to a company like this, at which somebody suggested, "Let her then come to the window on the first floor, and tell us that she is here of her free will and choice." She did this. But the crowd first asked her brother if she was his sister. When he said, "yes", they asked him to say "no". But he could not refuse to identify her, and she in clear and loud voice declared that she would rather die than go back to her brother. This settled the matter. But the crowd still tried to create trouble. In the mean time, however, some one had sent intimation to the police, and it was whispered about that the police were coming in full force to disperse this unlawful assembly. At this the crowd melted away. This incident deserves record as one of many that occurred in those early days in connection with the social reform propaganda of the Brahmo Samaj. This young lady was connected with Babu Shib Chandra Dev and she was subsequently married to Babu Sitanath Datta, better known now as Pandit Sitanath Tattvabhusan.

About August 1885 my second daughter, a child of ten months, fell seriously ill. It was a case of suspected tuberculosis of the bowels. The doctors advised a change, but I had not the wherewithal to take her out of Calcutta. Babu Durga Mohan Das coming to know of it asked me to go and stay in his house in Camac Street, which would be something of a change from the crowded locality in Champatala, where I was then living. I gratefully accepted his offer. The change, slight though it was, did the little one great good. It was here in November 1885 that my first boy was born. After the usual period of confinement of my wife I was preparing to come back to my house in Panchanantala Lane (Bow Bazar). Just at this time my father sent me a verbal message through a young man from our village, then studying in Calcutta. When this young man on his way from home came to salute my father, he asked him, without mentioning my name, "where is he?" This young man said that I was in Calcutta. "What is he doing for his livelihood?" "Trying to eke out a pittance by contributing to the Press", was his reply. "Oh! Contributing to the Press! How much does he get?" "Not much, just enough to keep body and soul together", was the response. At this my father told him, "If you see him, tell him that my health is breaking down." This was all the message that he sent. When it reached me, I clearly saw that my father wanted to see me. For eight or nine years he had not sent me a word. Indeed, he had persistently refused even to read my letters. When after all these years he sent me word that he was not well, I saw in it that he was wanting me back. This was also the interpretation which Babu Durga Mohan Das put upon this message, and he insisted upon my immediately going to meet my father. But I had my difficulties. The first was how could I leave my wife just recently confined with her baby. The second was the wherewithal to pay for my passage. Babu Durga Mohan Das summarily rejected these objections, saying, "Your wife and children may very well remain with me, and you cannot refuse to let me advance to you the small sum that may be required to take you home." Thus I went to see my father in November 1885, after nearly nine years.

When I met my father he asked me to bring my family home, saying that his health was waning, and he was not able to look after what little property he had, and if I wanted to get anything out of these after he passed away, I must come home and take charge of these. I replied, I was willing to do so not in the hope of getting anything but only if he thought that it would be some relief to him. At this my father asked me to return immediately to Calcutta and come back home as soon as possible with my wife and children. And he paid for their passage, saying that after I had come home with them he would arrange for the settlement of my affairs in Calcutta. Here again Babu Durga Mohan Das, who had taken a fatherly interest in me ever since he came to know me, once more came to my help, by undertaking to pay all my debts in Calcutta, pending the redemption of my father's words to meet these himself. So towards Christmas 1885, I left Calcutta for home with my wife, two daughters and a boy, the youngest of our children, whose advent, had, perhaps more than any other thing, brought about this reconciliation between father and son.

My wife also had very materially prepared for this reconciliation. She came of a highly respectable Brahmin family. She had by her character and conduct won universal admiration and love before her marriage when she was living with Pandit Shivanath Shastri. She was not educated in the modern sense of the term. Of course, she was literate, but her literary culture was of the most meagre character. She hardly knew English. In fact, neither in her brother's home at Allahabad or elsewhere nor when she was brought to the Brahmo Samaj, did she go to any public school. All her education was only home education. But she proved in her mind and manners how a very high order of mental and moral development is not only possible but indeed, quite easy to acquire, through hereditary and domestic and social training, even without any literary education. This was really the case with my mother who was not at all literate, and her's was not a rare instance in those days. The same also was the case with my first wife, Nritya Kali. Her innate goodness and particularly her quiet strength of character, her spirit of service and natural dignity of bearing, compelled respect from all those who came in contact with her. My sister had met her in Calcutta only once and must have communicated to my father her impression of my wife. Other friends and relations had also met her and been profoundly impressed by her personality. All these had created a general pre-disposition in my father towards my wife. And it was very largely this good repute of my wife which must have slowly and silently worked upon my father to lead him to wish to receive me back and see his daughter-in-law and her family.

Thus it was that at the beginning of 1886, I found myself once more in my old home at Poil, sanctified by so many memories of my mother and my early life. In asking me to go back to it, my father made almost as large a sacrifice as any man could make under those circumstances. I had deliberately put myself out of caste. To Hindu orthodoxy of those days, I and my family were as much untouchables as Mahomedans. After asking me to come back home with my wife and children my father resolved to build a new home for himself, while the old family dwelling would be left to me and my family. Ours was not a *pucca* structure. Our homestead consisted of a number of bamboo and thatch houses. My father proposed to build a similar home for himself in the neighbourhood. It would not take long to build this home. Already orders had been put out for the necessary bamboos and thatch and other materials for it. But my father was extremely anxious that I should hasten back to him wth my wife and children and thus wrote to me repeatedly not to waste any time in taking train for our home to Poil. When, therefore, I arrived, the contemplated home for himself had not even commenced to build. My friend Dr. Sundari Mohan Das was at that time stationed at the headquarters of our Sub-Division, Habiganj, as the medical officer of the Local Board. Habiganj is about three miles from our home in Poil. On my way from Calcutta, I first got down at Habiganj, and leaving my family with Dr. Sundari Mohan Das, I arrived home by myself. My idea was to keep them there until the new homestead contemplated by my father was ready and he had removed there. But my father would not hear of it. On the other hand, he was aware of it that there might be social troubles if he lived in the same home with us. So my father temporarily secured part of a neighbour's house, where my step-mother would go every morning with one or two attendants, and cook the usual food for the whole family there; my father and other orthodox members of the family going there for their meals, while our food would be brought from there to the old home. This was certainly a great hardship on my step-mother and considerable inconvenience to others. But my father gladly accepted all this for my sake. A cousin of mine suggested to my father to consult the village elders on the matter and ask them why, in the face of the common practice of having Moslem servants in the house for agricultural operations, I should not live with him separately in the same homestead. My father replied that all through his long life he had never consulted any one in deciding what was right and proper for him to do, and simply because he was now in a difficulty, he was not prepared to break this life-long rule of his. He would rather suffer whatever inconvenience might be involved in the arrangements he had made regarding his meals pending the building of the new home. My cousin replied: "Why not build a home for Bipin, and in the meantime let him stay at Habiganj with

Dr. Das?" My father said: "I asked Bipin to come back to his own home, and not to a new home. I cannot change that now. So I must set up a new home and leave this home to him."

But he had not to do this. The day after my wife arrived at her new home, the home of the father of her own children, she fell ill of cholera, which was already paying its periodic visit to our village. For a full fortnight she lay hovering between life and death. At one time her life was despaired of. She lay in a complete comatose condition. Dr. Sundari Mohan Das was with her. I left him in charge, saying that he must do duty for doctor, minister and grave-digger himself. During these anxious days, my father's affection for his daughter-in-law seemed to grow almost hourly. This affection conquerred the rigid laws of Hindu orthodoxy. From early morning, and throughout the whole day and night, my father would sit by my wife, and personally nurse her. When the doctor prescribed meat soup, I suggested that pigeon soup might be provided for her. But my father said: "Why pigeon? I understand that doctors prefer chicken soup to pigeon soup for these patients, so give her chicken soup" Saying this he at once sent a Mahomedan peon in his service to fetch it from the Dak-Bungalow at Habiganj; and when it was brought, he personally poured out small doses of it and gave to his beloved daughter with his own hand. This was not a small thing for an old and orthodox Hindu of Bengal! When her life was despaired of my father naturally commenced to think of the end and how her dead body would be cremated. Throughout my wife's illness our house used to be crowded with kindly neighbours, Brahmins and Kayesthas and others. This morning there was a large company of Brahmins and other higher caste people in my father's *Nat-Mandir* (literally dancing hall) which was used during the *pujas* as a dancing hall and at other times as a common reception hall. And my father calling me to him said aloud: "We have to think of the end, also, however painful it may be. Do you think between yourself, Dr. Sundari Mohan and his bearer, you will be able to perform the final rites?" But without waiting for my reply, he said: "Not that it at all matters. We too may help you in this and then perform a little expiatory rite." And saying this, he asked the assembled Brahmins, "What do you, gentlemen, say? I see there can be no objection to it." At this the Brahmins, as a matter of course, said ditto to him. By the grace of the Lord that crisis was over in the course of the next twelve hours. And my wife gradually advanced towards convalescence.

Before, however, she was completely restored to health, my father caught the infection. Outwardly it was not at all a serious case. But he seemed to have somehow known that his end was near. Six months before, during the Durga Puja, when the family astrologer was making the images, my father one day incidentally told him that this was the last image which he would have to make for his house. A few days, about a fortnight, before we arrived home, he had invited our family priest to dinner and when he sat down to his meals my father remarked that this was the last meal that he would take in his house. The extreme impatience of my father to have me back with him also seemed to indicate that he had some kind of a premonition regarding his approaching end. Not that he was at all weak or ill. Though passed the psalmist's span of life, being seventy-three at this time, my father did not look his age and was as active as he had been at sixty. But when he had this somewhat mild attack of cholera he saw that this was his end. At dawn he had a first motion. A little later a Brahmin youngman was sent for. He was something of a singer. He was asked to sing the songs of Fakirchand, which had circulated far and wide all over Bengal in those days. Fakirchand's real name was Harinath Majumdar. Towards the close of his life he came to be known as Kangal Harinath. Most of these songs described the vanities of life, and called the mind to the hereafter. My step-mother came and told my wife of my father's illness. I at once went to see him, and found him sitting on his bed and listening to these songs. About an hour later I was called to him. He asked me to sit near him on his bed, and then commenced to ease his mind of the prolonged agonies through which he had passed during my absence from home. Owing to his marriage even my sister persecuted him. All these he suffered in silence, but to-day his heart burst out as if of all bounds, and communicated to me the great tragedy of his father-love. After this he gave me charge of his temporal affairs. Some people had placed their little savings with him and he named them one by one with the amount deposited with him by them, and asked me to see to it that they had every penny of this trust money returned to them after he had passed away. Having thus made over his charge he asked me to fetch his despatch box saying that in that box there was a will and he wanted me to tear it to pieces before his eyes. This was the will which he had made some years back in Sylhet disinheriting me. I brought the box, opened it with the key which my father placed in my hands; but somehow or other I could not find the will. He then asked me to send for the elders of the village, and asked the clerk, who was working in his office keeping accounts of his affairs, to bring a sheet of catridge paper and writing materials. When the village elders arrived, my father dictated a new will in their presence. By this will he left certain properties to my step-mother and sister, and I was mentioned as the executor of the will. At this some of the elders present asked, "What about Bipin?" My father replied, "All the residuary property naturally goes to him, as he is the legal heir, there is no need to mention him in the will. According to the Hindu law Bipin having disqualified himself from performing my *sradh* would not be to his inheritance from me. But all that was changed by the decision of the Privy Council in the case of the will of Prasanna Kumar Tagore." Saying this he signed the will and invited the elders present to put their signature as witnesses. When this was finished, my father gave an explanation to the elders of the community regarding his last decision concerning me. He said: "For ten years I did not see Bipin's face. By a previous will I disinherited him absolutely. All these years I would not allow him to come near me. But I am convinced that while he went his own way out of regard for what he believed to be his *dharma* he did not by practising one thing and professing another destroy my *dharma*. He is not a *haramzada*. All through my life I never drank a drop of water during the *ekadasee* fast by diving underneath the waves ; he also did not do it. He is not a *haramzada*. Besides I thought this also, that though there are people who would like to have whatever little property I may leave behind me, there is no one except Bipin, whatever may be his religious principles, who would after my death protect with all his life the honour of my wife and my daughter. This is why I have called him back."

These were practically his last words. After this he closed his eyes, and did not open them again during the next twenty-four hours. There was no sign of collapse common to cholera cases. There was no sign of comma either. Evidently having finished and closed finally his account on this side and having done with the vanities of life, it seemed my father entered into communion with his God. Next day at about noon he once opened his eyes and seeing both my step-mother and sister sitting by him he asked, "You are both here, who is looking after the diet of *Bauma*?" This was his last look upon the world, these the last words which his lips uttered concerning the affairs on this side of the grave. Twelve hours later on the break of day on the 12th of Magh, corresponding to the 23rd or 24th of January, 1886 my father's spirit flew out of its mortal abode, finding shelter, I doubt not, in the lap of his God.

With my father's death practically closed the days of my youth. As long as he was alive, near or far, rebel or reconciled, I was under his protection. With his death the burden of the world fell on my weak shoulders.

INDEX

SUBJECT.	PAGE.
"Abala Bandhab" ...	202
Abdul Latiff, Nawab ...	417
Acharya, Peary Mohan	360, 362
Ackroyd, Miss	380
Adi Brahmo Samaj	259, 262, 344, 361
Agasti, Surya Kumar ...	239
Ali, Mr. Justice Amir ...	417
"Alochana" ...	430, 431, 440
Amir Khan ...	269, 270
"Amrita Bazar Patrika"	157, 246, 271, 294
Anderson, Mr.	150
Annesty, Mr.	270
"Bamabodhinee" ...	431
"Banga-Darshan"	176, 226, 227, 228, 258, 301
Banga Mahila Vidyalaya	380, 391
"Bangabasee"	425, 431, 432, 433, 444, 445
Bannerjee, Bhairab Chandra	293, 361
Bannerjee, Chandi Charan	395, 396
Banerjee, Dr. Durga Charan	232
Banerjee, Captain Jitendra Nath	266, 267
Banerjee, Yogesh Chandra	224
Banerjee, Kali Charan	28, 29
Bannerjee, Dr. K. M.	226, 289, 291, 293, 436
Bannerjee, Dr. Gurudas	293, 439
Bannerjee, Hem Chandra	226, 228, 229, 252, 256
Banerjee, Indra Nath ...	432
Banerjee, Pandit Rajkrishna	209, 226
Banerjee, Mrs. Surendra Nath ...	149, 150
Banerjea, Surendra Nath,	149, 151, 152, 153, 155, 156, 157, 158, 159, 160, 203, 230, 232, 233, 234, 235, 238, 241, 242, 243, 244, 245, 246, 247, 248, 249, 251, 258, 267, 289, 311, 319, 320, 409, 433, 434, 435, 445
Bannerjee, Tarapada ...	435
Baroda, Gaikwad of	270, 271, 290
Basu, Amulya Charan ...	213
Basu, Bhupendra Nath ...	214
Basu, Durga Kumar	29, 34, 37, 177
Basu, Chandra Nath	226, 432
Bellet, Mr.	205, 206, 207, 208, 209, 223
"Bengalee"	346, 433, 434, 435, 445
Bengal Theatre	251, 253, 299, 300
"Bengal Public Opinion"	346, 423, 433, 434, 439, 445
Beveridge, Mr.	380
Bhajekar, Mr.	399
"Bharat Mihir"	280, 372, 373, 444
"Bharata-Samskaraka"	346, 431
Blavatsky, Madame ...	425
Bose, Ananda Mohan,	201, 202, 230, 232, 233, 249, 251, 258, 288, 289, 293, 340, 342, 343, 345, 348, 380, 422, 423, 435, 436
Bose, Bhai Amritalal	332, 386

SUBJECT.	PAGE.
Bose, Bipin Behari ...	396
Bose, Girish Chandra	240, 241, 361
Bose, Haranath	297
Bose, Jogendra Chandra ...	431
Bose, Lady Abala ...	403, 430
Bose, Manomohan ...	256
Bose, Mrs. Umesh Chandra	446
Bose, Nanda Krishna ...	239
Bose, Rajnarain	227, 242, 259, 260, 261, 262, 263, 264, 430
Bose, Sir Jagadish ...	403
Brahmo Samaj	137, 139, 227, 229, 233, 235, 236, 237, 241, 244, 251, 259, 268, 295, 296, 297, 298, 299, 301, 302, 303, 307, 310, 311, 314, 315, 316, 317, 319, 320, 322, 324, 326, 328, 336, 337, 338, 339, 344, 350, 360, 361, 362, 366, 371, 374, 377, 390, 395, 396, 424, 427, 429, 433, 451.
Brahmo Samaj of India	332, 333, 339, 341, 344, 345, 349, 361, 386
"Brahmo Public Opinion"	345, 421, 423
Branson, Mr. ...	410, 411
British Indian Association	436
Campbell, Sir George	54, 156, 157, 180, 203, 205, 230, 231, 264, 290, 347.
Chakravarty, Byomkesh	239, 240, 361
Chandravarkar, Mr. Justice	397, 399
Chatterjee, Bankim Chandra	176, 226, 227, 228, 244, 425, 426, 427, 429, 438
Chatterjee, Bhutnath ...	213
Chatterjee, Nagendra Nath	300, 344, 440, 443, 445
Chatterjee, Pankaj Kumar	214
Chatterjee, Taraprasad ...	226
Chaudhuri, Radhanath	370, 373, 385
Chaudhury, Raj Chandra	350, 365, 368, 370, 373, 381, 382
Chaudhuri, Tarakishore,	199, 204, 318, 320, 321, 322, 323
Chattopadhyaya, Dr. Aghore Nath ...	202, 439
City School	347, 348, 349
Chunder, Gonesh Chunder	293
Clarke, Dr. C. B.	187
"Dacca Prakash"	178
Das, Bipin Behari	375, 376, 377, 378, 379, 380
Das, Bhuban Mohan	345, 346, 422, 424
Das, Dr. Sundari Mohan,	137, 138, 178, 185, 186, 193, 197, 199, 200, 222, 298, 299, 301, 302, 303, 304, 318, 323, 341, 375, 384, 452, 453, 454, 455
Das, Durga Mohan	331, 340, 345, 346, 380, 391, 403, 404, 421, 422, 424, 439, 445, 449, 450
Das, Govinda Chandra ...	177
Das, Dr. Manomohan ...	192
Das, Mrs. C. R. Das ...	390
Das, Peary Mohan	304, 305, 372
Das, Sri Nath	253
Das, Upendra Nath ...	253
Dastidar, Haramani ...	67
Datta, Akshay Kumar	31, 175, 227
Datta, Dvijadas ...	240, 241
Datta, Haridas	300
Datta, Kalinath	346

SUBJECT.	PAGE.
Datta, Krishna Lal ...	213
Datta, Parvati Nath ...	214
Datta, Romesh Chandra	157, 409
Datta, Sashi Bhusan	201, 360, 361
Datta, Sita Nath, Tattva-bhusan	137, 322, 337, 338, 448
Datta, Shreenath	137, 201, 202, 332
Datta, Umesh Chandra ...	346, 347, 431
Deb, Kailash Chandra ...	152
Dev, Shib Chandra ...	448
Dev, Sir Radhakanta ...	292
Dhankar Bai ...	398, 399
Djemal ed Din	417
Duff, Dr. ...	28, 203, 213, 292, 293
Dutt, Bhaktivinode Kedar Nath	245
Dutt, Michael Madhusadan	228
Dutt, Jogesh Chandra ...	293
Dyson, Dr.	236
East India Company	231, 272, 292, 412
Eden, Mr. Ashley ...	281, 282, 283, 284, 285
"Education Gazette" ...	306
"Englishman" ...	281, 282
Fakirchand ...	456
Fayre, Col. ...	271
Ganguly, Dwarka Nath ...	202, 431, 432
Ghosh, Chunder Madhab ...	293
Ghosh, Gonesh Chandra ...	344
Ghosh, Jadumani	349, 350
Ghosh, Monohar ...	305
Ghosh, Lal Mohan ...	411
Ghosh, Nagendra Nath (N. N.)	421
Ghosh, Rash Behary	293, 321
Ghosh, Sishir Kumar ...	245
Goswami, Bijoy Krishna ...	166, 244, 344
Goswami, Krishna Kamal	83, 251
Gupta, Behari Lal ...	157, 408, 409
Gupta, Ganga Govinda	214, 215
Gupta, Sir Krishna Govinda	201, 214
Govindjee, Mr.	399
Guha, Anath Bandhu	280, 372
Halder, Baroda Nath ...	390
Halder, Sarada Nath ...	390
Halder, S. N.	390
Hand, Mr. ...	205, 208, 209
Harendra Krishna, Raja Bahadur	268
Hari Sabhas	428
Hari Mohan Babu ...	189
"Herald"	24
"Hindu Hitaishinee"	178, 285
Hindu Mela ...	259, 264, 266
"Hindoo Patriot"	252, 271, 397
Home, Gagan Chandra ...	318, 430, 431
Hume, A. O. ...	235, 418
Ilbert Bill	408, 410, 411, 414, 433
Ilbert, Sir C. P.	410
Indian Association	202, 239, 288, 289, 435, 436
"Indian Christian Herald"	29
"Indian Messenger"	345, 423
"Indian Mirror"	345
Indian National Congress	428, 436
Indian Social Reform Association	346
"Indu Prakash"	397
Iyer, Gopalswamy	387, 393
Kali, Dr. Chandra Sekhar	192

SUBJECT.	PAGE.
Kangal Harinath ...	... 456
Kar, Ramkrishna	... 5
Kathia Baba ...	... 321
"Kaumudee" ...	... 345
Khanna, Jagannath	... 293
Knight, Mrs. ...	... 176
Kripa ...	... 49, 163, 164
Lamb, Major ...	... 159
Long, Rev. Mr. ...	... 252
Lytton, Lord ...	265, 272, 274, 275, 288, 294, 371, 406, 407, 408
Lushington, Mr. ...	165, 166
Macdonald, Dr. K. S.	292, 293
Mackertich, Mr. ...	... 151
Maine, Sir Henry Sumner	333
Maitra, Heramba Chandra	214, 445
Majumdar, Harinath	... 456
Majoomdar, Rev. Pratap Chandra ...	... 339
Mazoomdar, Syedbakt	... 66
Mayo, Lord	... 269, 270, 271
Medical College Theatre	... 242
Mitra, Ananda Chandra	318, 319
Mitra, Dinabandhu	300, 309
Mitra, Krishna Kumar	... 338, 445, 446
Mitra, Nabagopal	259, 262, 263, 364, 265, 293
Mitra, Sarada Charan	... 251
Mitter, Kali Nath	... 293
Mookherjea, Sambhu Chandra	146
Montriou, Mr. ...	... 160
"Mookherjea's Magazine"	146
Mudaliar, Narayanaswamy	393, 394
Mudaliar, Rai Bahadur Arcot Narayanaswamy	385, 387, 388
Mudaliar, Singaravelu	... 405
Mukherjee, Bhudeb	227, 306
Mukherjee, Dr. Ganga Prasad	212
Mukherjee, Harish Chandra	252
Mukherjee, Jagadananda ...	253
Mukherjee, Justice Anukul Chandra ...	... 178
Mukherjee, Sir Ashutosh ...	212
Mukherjee, Rangalal ...	254
Mukhopadhyaya, Pandit Nilmani, ...	209, 223
Mullik, Kumudranjan ...	2
Mullik, Nitto Lal ...	293
Mullik, Probodh Chunder ...	293
Murari Chand College ...	385
Muspratt, Mr. ...	... 150
Nag, Iswar Chandra ...	174
Narayanee ...	... 5
National Conference ...	436
National Fund ...	... 435
"National" Mitra ...	264
"National Paper" ...	264
National Songs ...	... 254
National Theatre	251, 299
"Navajeevana"	426, 427, 429, 430
Nava-Vidhan ...	... 384
"New Dispensation" ...	237
"Navabibhakar" ...	... 293
Nayaratna, Pandit Ramgati	242
"New India" ...	... 399
Northbrook, Lord	156, 270, 271, 333
Norman, Chief Justice ...	270
Nritya Kalee (Mrs. B. C. Pal) ...	... 395, 396, 451
O'Kinealy, Mr.	159
Olcott, Col.	425
Pal, Hiranya ...	... 2
Pal, Kristodas ...	... 271
Pal, Dr. Navadwip Chandra	192
Pal, Ram Chandra ...	2
Palit, T.	... 293
Pan-Islamism ...	... 417

SUBJECT.	PAGE.
"Paridarshak"	373, 374, 382
Parker, Theodore ...	... 422
Parry, Mr. ...	... 206
Patriotic Fund ...	... 371
Piffard, Mr. ...	... 268
Posford, Mr. ...	... 150
"Prachar"	... 425, 429, 430
Prinsep, Mr. ...	... 158
Pryse, Rev. W. ...	... 27
Raghunathdas, Madhodas	397, 398
Rao, Madhusudhan	361, 362
Raja Gambhir Singh	... 70
Raghunathdas, Mrs. Madhodas ...	... 397, 398, 399
Ray, Kali Narayan	... 3
Ray, Raja Girish Chandra	385
Ray, Upadhyaya Gour Govinda	... 136
"Reis & Ryot" ...	... 146
Reynolds, Mr. ...	... 159
Ripon, Lord	406, 407, 408, 410, 411, 414, 415, 416, 417, 418, 419, 420, 422
Roy, Dr. Prasanna Kumar	201, 202
Roy, Govinda Chandra	... 255
Roy, Gouri Sankar	... 359
Roy, Jnanendra Lal	... 431
Roy, Kshirode Chandra	360, 361
Roy, Radhanath ...	361, 362
Roy, Raja Ram Mohan	... 136, 137, 292, 315, 341, 345, 428
Roy, Rajani Nath	201, 202, 389, 390, 391, 397
Roy, Sarat Chandra	... 318
Roy, Umapada ...	... 318
"Sadhana" ...	... 430
Sadharan Brahmo Samaj	322, 341, 342, 343, 344, 345, 346, 347, 348, 386, 402, 422, 430, 431.
"Sadharanee"	275, 276, 278, 293
"Samadarshee" ...	319, 423
"Samaj Darpan" ...	280, 282
"Sanjibanee"	432, 433, 444
Sarkar, Akshay Chandra	226, 251, 275, 426, 427, 430, 439, 440
Sircar, Peary Charan	31, 206, 208, 209, 210, 211, 213, 223
Sarma, Nabin Chandra	192, 196, 372
Sarma, Loknath ...	... 149
Sastri, Shivanath,	202, 268, 305, 306, 307, 308, 309, 310, 311, 312, 314, 315, 316, 317, 318, 322, 325, 329, 342, 343, 344, 347, 348, 386, 388, 393, 395, 396, 399, 401, 402, 423, 430, 431, 432, 439, 440, 451.
Sen, Ambica Charan	240, 241
Sen, Brojendra Nath	350, 365, 368, 370, 373, 430
Sen, Deenanath ...	... 24
Sen, Keshub Chunder	136, 137, 139, 202, 229, 233, 234, 235, 236, 237, 242, 244, 259, 262, 295, 296, 297, 298, 301, 307, 309, 310, 314, 315, 316, 322, 332, 333, 336, 337, 338, 339, 340, 342, 345, 346, 349, 360, 375, 384, 386, 390, 440.
Sen, Krishna Behari	297, 336
Sen, Kunja Behari	... 78
Sen, Mrs. Navakishore	176, 267
Sen, Nabakishore	24, 25, 26, 36, 42, 44, 55, 56, 167, 173, 176, 368, 369.
Sen, Paresh Nath	... 430
Sen, Priya Nath ...	... 24
Sen, Sree Krishna Prasanna	438, 439, 441, 442
Shastree, Pandit Srinivasa	378
Shaw, Mr. ...	... 51
Sher Ali ...	... 270

SUBJECT.	PAGE.
Shome, Jay Govinda	28, 29, 267, 268, 364
Shome, Nabin Chandra ...	137
Sircar, Dr. Bhuban Mohan	211
"Somprokas"	157, 271, 283, 293, 306
"Sreehatta Prakas"	304, 305, 372
Students' Association	230, 233, 238, 239, 242, 249
Sukul, Kali Sankar	318, 319, 320, 348, 445
Sukumaree	300
"Sulabh Samachar" ...	345
Sutcliffe, Mr.	204, 205, 207, 208, 209, 223
Sutherland, Mr.	150, 151, 152, 153, 158, 159
Sylhet Association ...	372
Sylhet Union ...	364, 365
Tagore, Dwijendra Nath	293, 430
Tagore, Jyotirindra Nath	265, 298
Tagore, Maharshi Devendra Nath	139, 227, 235, 236, 259, 265, 307, 336, 341, 344, 361
Tagore, Prasanna Kumar ...	457
Tagore, Rabindra Nath ...	430
Tagore, Satyendra Nath ...	157
Tarkachudamanee, Pandit Sashadhar	425, 426, 437, 438, 441, 442
Tarkalankar, Madan Mohan	31
Tattvabhusan, Seetanath	137,
Tattva-Bodhini ...	345
"Tattvabodhinee Patrika"	226, 227
Tattvabodhinee Sabha	307
"Tattva-Kaumudee"	345
Tawney, Mr. ...	205
Thakur, Sreepad Babaji	378, 379
Theosophical Society	402, 425
"Utkal Darpan" ...	359
Vernacular Press Act	275, 283, 288, 290, 293, 294
Vidyabhusan, Dwarkanath	306, 307
Vidyaratna, Pandit Ramkumar	344
Vidyasagar, Pandit Iswar Chandra	15, 31, 36, 175, 203, 209, 211, 227, 232, 238, 307, 395, 439, 446.
Vidyavageesh, Ram Chandra ...	227
Wahabis ...	269, 270, 290
Widow Remarriage Act ...	15
Wise, Mr.	3
Woodrow, Mr.	157
"Young Italy" ...	238